Crime in Verse

Crime in Verse

The Poetics of Murder in the Victorian Era

ELLEN L. O'BRIEN

THE OHIO STATE UNIVERSITY PRESS
COLUMBUS

Copyright © 2008 by The Ohio State University.
All rights reserved.

Library of Congress Cataloging-in-Publication Data
O'Brien, Ellen L., 1970–
Crime in verse : the poetics of murder in the Victorian era / Ellen L. O'Brien.
   p. cm.
Includes bibliographical references and index.
ISBN 978–0–8142–1085–7 (cloth : alk. paper)—ISBN 978–0–8142–9164–1 (CD-ROM) 1. English poetry—19th century—History and criticism. 2. Crime in literature. 3. Murder in literature. 4. Crime—Political aspects—Great Britain—History—19th century. 5. Poets, English—19th century—Political and social views. 6. Politics and literature—Great Britain—History—19th century. 7. Literature and society—Great Britain—History—19th century. 8. Law and literature—Great Britain—History—19th century. 9. Discourse analysis, Literary. I. Title.
PR595.C75O37 2008
821.'9093556—dc22
            2007052288

This book is available in the following editions:
Cloth (ISBN 978–0–8142–1085–7)
CD-ROM (ISBN 978–0–8142–9164–1)
Paper (ISBN: 978-0-8142-5742-5)
Chapter opening art:
Introduction: Detail, Useful Sunday Literature for the Masses, *Punch*, 1849, v 17, provided courtesy of The Ohio State University Cartoon Research Library
Chapter 1: Detail, figure 2, page 32
Chapter 2: Detail, figure 6, page 91
Chapter 3: Detail, figure 3, page 45
Epilogue: Detail, figure 7, page 99

Cover design by Laurence J. Nozik
Text design by Juliet Williams
Type set in Adobe Minion

For Linda and John

Contents

List of Illustrations
ix

Acknowledgments
xi

Introduction
1

Chapter 1
Murder, Execution, and the Criminal Classes
29

Chapter 2
The Murderous Subject and the Criminal Sublime
109

Chapter 3
"Household Law" and the Domestication of Murder
167

Epilogue
240

Notes
243

Works Cited
263

Index
277

Illustrations

Figure 1
Execution of John Gleeson Wilson.
31

Figure 2
The Last Moments and Confession of Wm. Sheward.
32

Figure 3
Particulars of the Life, Trial, Confession, and Execution of Courvoisier.
45

Figure 4
John Bull, Can You Wonder at Crime?
49

Figure 5
Verses on Daniel Good.
61

Figure 6
Lamentation of Samuel Wright.
91

Figure 7
Life, Trial, Sentence, and Execution of Catherine Wilson, for the Murder of Mrs. Soames.
99

ACKNOWLEDGMENTS

Many colleagues, mentors, and friends have contributed to this book—providing intellectual guidance, editorial comments, book loans, research tips, library access, database passwords, recommendation letters, skeptical remarks, encouraging words, computer repairs, comic relief, and good company. I am especially indebted to Florence Boos, Ann Brigham, Gina Buccola, Kristine Byron, Eleni Coundouriotis, Carrie Etter, Vincent Francone, Bonnie Gunzenhauser, Margaret Higonnet, Larry Howe, Rachael Lynch, Jean Marsden, Kashif Movania, Maureen O'Connor, Valerie Ritter, Anne Schwan, Katharine Capshaw Smith, Valerie Smith, Barbara Suess, Stuart Warner, Janet Wondra, and Jami Woy.

I am also grateful to the librarians and staff of many libraries: the Roosevelt University Library, the Harvard University Law Library, the British Library, the Newberry Library, the Library of the Health Sciences at the University of Illinois at Chicago, the Galter Health Science Library at Northwestern University, the Pritzker Legal Research Center at Northwestern University, the DePaul University Library, the Center for Research Libraries, the Cambridge University Library, and the St. Bride Printing Library.

The National Endowment for the Humanities supported my research with a Summer Stipend in 2004. I am grateful to Roosevelt University for two research leaves and two summer grants, and, in particular, I owe special thanks to Lynn Weiner, Dean of the College of Arts and Sciences, for her contributions to the several research trips and regular conference travel that shaped and sustained my work on this book.

I have benefited from the enthusiasm and expertise of the staff at The Ohio State University Press. I thank Heather Lee Miller for her early interest in the project and Sandy Crooms and Maggie Diehl for their sustained attention to and generous assistance with the manuscript. I would also like to thank the anonymous readers for their careful consideration and thoughtful advice.

Portions of chapter 1 first appeared as "'Every Man Who Is Hanged Leaves a Poem': Criminals and Poets in Victorian Street Ballads" in *Victorian Poetry* 39.2 (2001) and as "'The Most Beautiful Murder': The Transgressive Aesthetics of Murder in Victorian Street Ballads" in *Victorian Literature and Culture* 28.1 (2000). I am grateful to the editors and publishers of these journals for permission to revise and reprint that work here.

With her usual curiosity and generosity, Carolyn O'Brien has helped me to contemplate and consider murder as a subject of research for many years. For her genuine interest in all my ideas and endeavors, she receives my most special thanks and appreciation.

⊰ Introduction ⊱

> There is no essential incongruity between crime and culture.
> —Oscar Wilde, "Pen, Pencil and Poison"

THIS STUDY OF CRIME IN VERSE connects innovations in Victorian poetry to developments in the Victorian discourse of crime—a network of interrelated and often contradictory concepts informed by legal fictions, punitive mechanisms, medical theories, class conflicts, and gender codes.[1] Tracing dialectical links between criminal discourse and poetic representation, the study assembles multiple genres—the street ballad, the dramatic monologue, the verse novel, the verse drama—and examines the ways in which poets adopted and adapted particular verse forms in order to accommodate the evolving epistemologies of crime and to elaborate the poetics of murder. Because significant institutional and ideological changes throughout the Victorian period complicated and obscured the meanings of murder, *Crime in Verse* frames its textual analyses with investigations of the specific historical contexts in which these meanings were renegotiated. Generating moral ambiguities and cultural anxieties, shifting understandings of murder—as a material act, an abstract idea, and an aesthetic representation—created opportunities for poets to coordinate interests in formal innovation, generic experimentation, and political expression. Poetically productive and topically resonant, the theme of murder assisted poets, and can assist us, in reconceptualizing the literary achievements and cultural engagements of Victorian verse.

Historicizing murder, while carefully highlighting poetic form and genre, this project benefits from and responds to two ongoing critical projects in Victorian literary studies: the exploration of interdisciplinary and historicist approaches to literary representations of crime and, within the subfield of poetry studies, the development of interpretive methodologies that recognize poetry's political sensibilities. Predominantly, the novel, whether addressed in popular crime genres, such as Newgate, detective, and sensation fiction, or more broadly conceived in discussions of realist fiction, shapes our contemporary perspective of Victorian crime literature. Revealing the extent to which our studies of crime are bound up in understandings of genre, a scholarly concentration on the novel has generated a corresponding emphasis on the middle-class ideologies, interests, and fears of its authors and readers.

Following D. A. Miller's groundbreaking *The Novel and the Police* (1988), which proposed a "radical *entanglement* between the nature of the novel and the practice of the police" and connected the novel's "representational techniques" to cultural modes of "disciplinary power" (2), two decades of rigorous scholarship have refined our sense of the novel's literary accomplishments and political participation while acquainting us with the social arenas and professional fields of criminal discourse. Even a partial listing of the most recent work attests to the continuing productivity and increasing specialization of this approach: Ronald R. Thomas's *Detective Fiction and the Rise of Forensic Science* (1999) connects specific portrayals of criminal bodies, forensic technologies, and literary detectives to the emergence of an investigative science, the invention of a literary genre, and the renegotiation of cultural authority; Marlene Tromp's *The Private Rod: Marital Violence, Sensation and the Law in Victorian Britain* (2000) presents portraits of marital violence in middle-class sensation fiction as evidence of the genre's resistance to the high cultural conventions of literary realism and the conservatism of legal authority; Jonathan Grossman's *The Art of Alibi: English Law Courts and the Novel* (2002) emphasizes the "trial-oriented" (1) nature of Victorian culture and, isolating novels and trials as the "era's most prominent narrative paradigms" (2), reads juridical procedures and fictional texts as formal and logical analogues; Lisa Rodensky's *The Crime in Mind: Criminal Responsibility and the Victorian Novel* (2003) argues that the novel's third-person narrators and its "intensive exploration of the inner life" (7) granted readers access to the otherwise elusive interior of the criminal mind in ways that interrogated and affirmed legal definitions of criminal responsibility; and Lisa Surridge's *Bleak Houses: Marital Violence in Victorian Fiction* (2005) explores how the narrative and metanarrative operations of the domestic novel are "charged" (9) with the energies and anxieties of continuing wife-assault debates, which were staged in the courts, the legislature, and the newspaper.[2] Attentive to the narrative strategies of fiction, the political identities of the bourgeoisie, and the intricate correlations between textual details, genre codes, and legal developments, such studies have mapped important vantage points from which to survey the imbrications of literary genre and cultural discourse in representations of crime.

While novel scholars have been amassing and arranging texts in order to create assemblages of crime fictions that reveal patterns of political interest and literary inspiration, poetry scholars, also privileging middle-class literature, have tended to organize their work on crime poems around individual authors and texts. This tendency most likely reflects significant formal differences across genres of poetry, which render arguments for thematic cohesion and structural continuity less apparent. Foregoing the construction of comparative frameworks, analyses of verse representations of crime are largely focused in content and small in scope—and dispersed across decades of journal articles and book chapters. Even so, a loose constellation of poems could be said to define our view of poetry's criminal interests. In particular, dramatic monologues, which comprise a subfield of transgression studies in their own right, and verse novels, which reproduce the narrative scope of more popular crime fictions, have garnered the most attention. While key texts, especially Robert Browning's "Porphyria's Lover" (1836), "My Last Duchess" (1842), and *The Ring and the Book* (1868–69), seem to dominate discussions about the subject of murder and the evolution of genre, other poetic representations of crime have attracted attention as contemporary scholarly priorities renew interest in their authors and themes. A second-wave feminist revival of Elizabeth Barrett Browning's work, together with a corresponding focus on the gender, class, and racial politics of sexual violence, for example, has led to new work on the rape of Marian Erle in *Aurora Leigh* (1856) and the infanticide of the fugitive speaker in "The Runaway Slave at Pilgrim's Point" (1848). Similarly, Oscar Wilde's "The Ballad of Reading Gaol" (1898), long perceived as a less intellectually and aesthetically rigorous poem, has been revisited by scholars interested in biographical and sociological approaches to Wilde's experience as a prisoner, the poem's considerations of private and public forms of violence, and its relationship to late-Victorian prison reform.[3]

To a significant extent, *Crime in Verse* is marked by these same patterns. In collecting a range of murder poems, however, this study begins to locate thematic and generic continuities across seemingly disparate texts, and by incorporating minor poems, noncanonical poets, and street verses, which are typically overlooked in studies of Victorian poetry and crime writing, it also begins to reorganize the terms of our conversation. Inspired by the insights, strategies, and omissions of previous scholarship, this project maintains a double vision. Asking questions about Victorian representations of crime and scholarly presentations of Victorian poetry, it upholds a now well-established tradition of delineating the contours of genre and discourse in order to understand the textual strategies and political significance of crime writing in Victorian England. In extending that tradition beyond the realm of the novel, it also broadens our perspective on literary mediations of crime in terms of genre—and class. Insofar as they resonate across the generic divide of Victorian studies, the chapters that follow may nudge us toward a more trans-generic vision of Victorian literary crimes. In the meantime, however, each chapter remains invested in generic difference, privileging a poetry studies model attentive to the formal ingenuity and literary history of verse. Such an emphasis helps to foreground the dialectical and reciprocal processes of generic innovation and discourse formation, allowing us to consider how shifting epistemologies of murder influenced developments in poetic form and language—and how the tools of poetic form and language enabled poets to fashion topical critiques of Victorian England's evolving criminal discourses.

In performing this task, *Crime and Verse* does not catalogue the many poems about murder published in the Victorian period or attempt to locate a unitary poetics of murder crisscrossing disparate texts. Rather, with a restricted topic and a selective scope it offers detailed analyses of a relatively small subset of poems, carefully observing the political dimensions of genre and following the intricate arguments of specific poems. Positioning these poems with respect to a complex network of criminal discourses, it also references various nonliterary texts. Trial transcripts, parliamentary debates, legislative acts, newspaper reports, journal articles, medicolegal treatises, political pamphlets, critical reviews, and private correspondence are pressed into service to reveal the interlocking features of legal discourse, genre codes, and individual poems.

While the theme of murder supplies apt demonstrations of how relatively brief or highly condensed poems can embed multiple layers of cultural meanings and make pointed political arguments, it also accesses multiple questions of power—between killers and victims, between juries and defendants, between the state and its subjects. For this reason, the theme of murder also offers the practical advantage of class mobility. Of interest to Victorians of all classes for a variety of reasons, murder inspired verse representations for a variety of occasions and audiences. In bringing together the murder poems of anonymous street balladeers, recuperated minor poets, and established canonical poets, this book poses questions about our notions of Victorian poetry—as an art form defined by Victorian poets and critics and a field of study continuously reshaped by contemporary academics. The inclusion of working-class street verse, for example, invites us to explore the selection processes with which we demarcate the field of Victorian poetry. And juxtapositions of high and low, major and minor texts suggest more diverse paths of literary influence and alternate models of intertextuality, which, in turn, allow us to reassess the role of verse as a genre of literature and a mode of public or political speech in Victorian culture.

In negotiating the textual and contextual components of this agenda, *Crime in Verse* reconsiders the historical conditions of and cultural responses to murder in Victorian England. A topic of interest to writers of all genres and all periods, murder possesses a trans-historical and a trans-generic resonance and often seems a universally understood transgression and a well-worn literary trope. But a more specifically historicized examination of murder reveals its multiple and contested meanings. No singular notion of murder regulated the spectrum of commentaries on criminal matters ranging from apprehension and punishment to diagnosis and deterrence. And assessments of specific murders were inflected by unique combinations of circumstance and evidence and were openly debated in multiple public arenas ranging from the courtroom to the newspaper to the scaffold crowd. Entangled within the changing institutional mandates of legal codes, medical theories, and penal policies, the meanings of murder were also increasingly complicated by changing understandings and definitions of violence. Institutional and ideological reformulations of murder often met in distressing ways, leading to intense public scrutiny of crimes and punishments that enfolded politically contentious matters of class conflict (such as in the case of public execution) and gender inequality (such as in the case of wife-murder). In each of these contexts, determining the meanings of murder, the subjectivities of murderers, and the ethics of punishment became disconcertingly and frustratingly contingent.

As the chapters that follow demonstrate, these contingencies, together with their attendant anxieties and the starkly unambiguous consequences of murderous violence, allowed poets to manipulate the theme of murder for poetic innovation and political commentary. An emphasis on literary form may privilege the same kind of de-contextualized—and de-moralized—evaluations of criminal artistry advocated by Thomas de Quincey, who sought, however playfully, to evaluate murder as a "meritorious performance" (987) and to assign aesthetic value to particular crimes. But, because of the counterdiscursive ways in which poets often managed the theme of murder, a discussion of the more topical agendas and specific aesthetic practices involved in these texts further underscores murder's status as a diversely mediated act. Because murder has both a complex social history and a rich literary history, examining connections between modes of poetic expression and epistemologies of murder is accomplished most efficiently by linking textual minutiae and generic features to more local and specific cultural debates in which murder appears most politically contentious and poetically productive. Accordingly, while sustaining a focus on the strategic uses of poetic textuality, *Crime in Verse* subdivides its arguments about the poetics of murder into three separate chapters that explicitly align generic form and topical content.

The first chapter, "Murder, Execution, and the Criminal Classes," balances an analysis of the politically immediate content of murder and execution ballads with an overview of their evolution and reception. Imagining the voices of astonished witnesses and condemned murderers, these ballads, sold and sung in the streets, explored the shock of murder and the pathos of execution in ways that challenged class-based ideologies of crime and problematized hierarchies of poetic value. Constituting one of the most profitable branches of the broadside print industry, which flourished for most of the nineteenth century, crime ballads demonstrate a certain degree of generic cohesion, and thus despite significant shifts in classed definitions of criminality and adjustments to judicial applications of capital punishment, ballads written decades apart share fundamental rhetorical and structural characteristics. Yet, individual street ballads also register specific changes in criminal law, publicly aired attitudes towards particular crimes, and the micropolitics of individual murder trials and death sentences. While negotiating the mandates of genre, the tensions of class, and the unfolding histories of criminals, the broadside ballad industry developed and marketed the largest and most cohesive body of crime in verse. For these reasons, a careful study of the generic and discursive features of these texts assists us in accessing Victorian ideologies about those who commit crimes and those who write poems and expands our awareness of the cultural practices and social spaces of Victorian verse.

Chapter 2, "The Murderous Subject and the Criminal Sublime," moves from the working-class poetry of the street to the middle-class poetry of the drawing room—and from historically based fictions of crime and punishment to wholly imagined accounts of malice and madness. Pairing contextual references to psychological theories, criminal laws, and controversial trials with a discussion of dramatic poetry's capacity for sustaining irony and indeterminacy, this chapter explores the representation of murderous subjectivity in Browning's "Porphyria's Lover," "My Last Duchess," and "The Laboratory" (1844) and Dante Gabriel Rossetti's "A Last Confession" (1870). In these texts, Browning and Rossetti coordinate interests in the generic attributes of the dramatic monologue and the specialist language of mental science. Working together, the violent themes, formal structures, verbal complications, and metrical patterning of these poems produce commentaries on mid-century medicolegal theories, which challenged longstanding notions of criminal responsibility with exculpatory arguments about homicidal lunacy. Inviting—but frustrating—readerly attempts to determine the sanity or insanity of their violent speakers, these meticulously crafted monologues uphold the obscurity of murderous subjectivity, and in doing so, produce a topically resonant version of the sublime. Dramatic portraits of deviance, as many studies of the dramatic monologue have previously argued, influenced the themes and forms of Victorian poetry in important ways, but foregrounding the epistemological contingencies and political contentiousness of murder allows us to consider the mystified and mystifying murderous subjects of this hybrid form in terms of both poetic experimentation and cultural critique.

Examining accounts of domestic murder in the verse novel and the verse drama, chapter 3, "'Household Law' and the Domestication of Murder," also stresses connections between generic hybridity and the intertextual frameworks and political entanglements of criminal discourse. Browning's *The Ring and the Book* and two closet tragedies, Edward Robert Bulwer Lytton's *Clytemnestra* (1855) and Amy Levy's *Medea* (1884), place the problems of marital unhappiness and gender inequality on a trajectory of murderous consequence. Their domestic murder plots register substantial changes in the laws governing marriage and divorce and dramatize frustration with entrenched ideologies of patriarchal domesticity. Their murderous violations of hearth and home mark the increasing criminalization of domestic abuse and the implications of a new divorce court, which, opened in January 1858 and resembling a criminal court model, enforced England's newly revised matrimonial laws, established a public record of private conflict, and supported a print media culture of domestic scandal. As domesticity encountered criminal and matrimonial law, and as courts and newspapers broadcast the details, an explicitly adversarial and combative version of marriage gained currency.

Variously imagining murderers, motives, and victims, and written decades apart, these three dramatic poems produce strikingly similar commentaries on the failures of domestic idealism and discipline. As they use wife-murder, husband-murder, and child-murder to imagine the gendered aspects of murderous agency, they establish a range of intertextual references and metatextual meanings. Browning, mixing his "fancy" (I.679) with the "pure crude fact" (I.35) of the "square old yellow Book" (I.32), transcribes the documents of a seventeenth-century Roman murder trial and, in very explicit terms, submits the case to the judgment of his contemporary audience. Lytton and Levy, condensing high Greek tragedy into closet dramas, generate new psychological portraits of Clytemnestra and Medea and recast the deterministic powers of fate as the controlling forces of patriarchy. In reformatting and reforming old domestic crimes, each of these poets invokes a long history of domestic alienation in order to express the modern urgency of domestic reform.

As these brief chapter summaries suggest, historicizing murder while examining the components of poetic genre requires that strands of criminal discourse and varieties of poetic utterance be differentiated in order to speculate about how these modes of representation are intertwined. Nonetheless, a common system of cultural logic and aesthetic value unites the distinct agendas of each chapter and the specific meanings of each poem. The most succinct expression of this common logic forms the epigraph of this introduction. Wilde's claim that "[t]here is no essential incongruity between crime and culture" both alludes to and destabilizes the categories used to "other" criminals and abhor their crimes, particularly violent criminals and crimes. Insisting that crime and culture are congruous, Wilde suggests the uncanny and unsettling ways in which murderous violence might be considered not as a terrible social anomaly but as a profound cultural symptom.

Wilde's critique of incongruity appears in "Pen, Pencil and Poison" (1889), a witty and "brief memoir" of the famous nineteenth-century murderer, Thomas Griffiths Wainewright—a man who "followed many masters other than art, being not merely a poet and a painter, an art-critic, an antiquarian, and a writer of prose, an amateur of beautiful things and a dilettante of things delightful, but also a forger of no mean or ordinary capabilities and a subtle and secret poisoner almost without rival in this or any age" (993). As such, Wainewright represents a figure of high culture and, more generally, a member of British culture. Borrowing his title phrase from Swinburne, Wilde lists Wainewright's professional implements—pen, pencil, poison—and thereby aligns writing, drawing, and killing as modes of expression. In the biographical overview of Wainewright with which Wilde begins his essay, he makes this association more explicit, noting that, having mastered the arts of drawing and painting early in life, "[i]t was not till much later that he sought to find expression by pen or poison" (994). Sustaining this witty subtext throughout the essay, Wilde goes on to document Wainewright's "achievements in the sphere of poison" (995), multiple poisonings for financial gain, which resulted in the deaths of his uncle, his mother-in-law, and his sister-in-law, among others.

In arranging the details of Wainewright's life, Wilde strategically emphasizes—in order to deconstruct—the apparent signs of incongruity, documenting Wainewright's aesthetic sensibilities and social connections in order to address a collective misunderstanding of the relationship between crime and culture. A repeated reference to the fact that Wainewright was "susceptible to the spiritual influence of Wordsworth's poetry" (994) and "Charles Lamb's friend" (993), for example, allows Wilde to dismiss theories of crime and stereotypes of criminals while aligning this murderer's tastes, aspirations, and society with those of his readers. When claiming kinships of intellect and sensibility with notable and accomplished cultural elites, Wainewright proves most threatening to the reassuring binary logic of normalcy and deviance. In concluding his character study, Wilde openly challenges the opinion of the recent Wainewright biographer, W. Carew Hazlitt, who claimed that "his love of art and nature was a mere pretence and assumption" (1007), and he likewise critiques the habit of "others" to "den[y] to him all literary power" (1007):

> The fact of a man being a poisoner is nothing against his prose. The domestic virtues are not the true basis of art, though they may serve as an excellent

advertisement for second-rate artists.... That he had a sincere love of art and nature seems to me quite certain. There is no essential incongruity between crime and culture. We cannot re-write the whole of history for the purpose of gratifying our moral sense of what should be. (1007–8)

Wilde's assertions clearly configure an aestheticist argument, which separates the criteria for assessing art and judging morality, but they also challenge the apparent desire to protect the refinements of artistic creation from the vulgarities of criminal transgression. Because Wainewright signifies artistic sensibility, literary talent, class privilege, and murderous cunning, Wilde's pointed insistence on the sincerity of his "love of art and nature" is equally an insistence on recognizing the congruities of crime and culture.

In the case of Wainewright, Wilde suggests, applications of "moral sense" function as attempts to deny Wainewright-the-murderer legitimate membership in the culture and the class of which he was, in fact, a part. Attempts at scouring away this unwanted stain, with condemnations of his crimes or dismissals of his art, evince more fundamental cultural logics used to dispense with disturbing crimes—through acts of dissociation and defamiliarization. Wainewright's proximity to the centers of cultural power and the realms of artistic celebrity incites such acts: "he is just a little too modern to be treated in that fine spirit of disinterested curiosity to which we owe so many charming studies of the great criminals of the Italian Renaissance from the pens of Mr. John Addington Symonds, Miss A. Mary F. Robinson, Miss Vernon Lee, and other distinguished writers" (1008). Wainewright also approximates ordinary Britons in distressing ways: "But had the man worn a costume and spoken a language different from our own, had he lived in imperial Rome, or at the time of the Italian Renaissance, or in Spain in the seventeenth century, or in any land or any century but this century and this land, we would be quite able to arrive at a perfectly unprejudiced estimate of his position and value" (1008). Inconveniently modern and undeniably English, the murderous Wainewright presents an interpretive problem; he cannot be relegated to the realms of "disinterested curiosity" or "charming studies," and his cultural worth cannot be properly estimated or unanimously esteemed.

The rhetorical frameworks and spectacular punishments of nineteenth-century England, of course, systematically positioned the criminal at the margins of or beyond the borders of normative society by configuring crimes as the nearly exclusive domain of a delinquent class and by punishing crimes through official rituals of exclusion—incarceration, transportation, execution. Wilde uses Wainewright to scrutinize the moralizing tendencies of art criticism, admiring Wainewright not for his talents or character but for the mischief that he does to moral and criminal codes. With Wainewright as a case study, he can critique the political convenience of troping the criminal other, particularly when he records Wainewright's stubborn resistance to such othering techniques. Though Wainewright was never charged with the murders he was widely known to have committed, he was subject to such exclusionary acts when he was convicted of forgery and transported to Van Diemen's Land in 1837. His punishment, Wilde speculates, might also be plotted on an axis of crime and culture: "to a man of his culture," he explains, transportation was "a form of death" (1005). His social death imminent, Wainewright spent time in Newgate, where his cell became "a kind of fashionable lounge" visited by "[m]any men of letters," and where he proudly continued to "hold the position of a gentleman" (1006). "I occupy a cell with a bricklayer and a sweep," he reportedly exclaimed, "but they never offer me the broom!" (1006). Chronicling Wainewright's life, Wilde explains that, admitting no fall from the upper classes and no affinity with the putative criminal classes, the peerless Wainewright left England aboard a transportation ship among a group of convicts that he disdainfully characterized as "country bumpkins" (1006). Wainewright's description of his shipmates might appear an argument for the incongruity of culture and crime—he is the grand and snobbish exception to a rule separating ordinary gentlemen and common criminals. Yet, more characteristically, his comments serve a performative function: with them he stages his resistance to his literal and figurative cultural exile.

According to Wilde's concise little study, Wainewright employs this strategy repeatedly, placing and replacing himself at the center of culture and thus resisting the pressures of criminal law and social outrage. He connects, for example, the deviant motivations of criminal acts to the normative values of the marketplace when he interprets his forgeries for financial gain—and perhaps implicitly his murders for the same reason—in terms of capital speculation. To an insurance agent who visited Wainewright and announced, "crime was a bad speculation," Wainewright replied, "Some of your speculations succeed, some fail. Mine happen to have failed, yours happen to have succeeded. That is the only difference, sir, between my visitor and me" (1006). In this denial of difference, with which Wainewright willfully aligns himself with the centers of social power and the activities of the market economy, Wilde finds support for his contention that crime and culture correlate in significant ways. Imagining Wainewright's journey to Van Diemen's Land, Wilde supposes, "Crime in England is rarely the result of sin. It is nearly always the result of starvation. There was probably no one on board in whom he would have found a sympathetic listener, or even a psychologically interesting nature" (1006). Embedded in this reference to Wainewright's psychological alienation is a theory about the social foundations of criminal motive. Wilde suggests that, whereas most English crimes bespeak social conditions of poverty, starvation, and class oppression, the crimes of the well-fed, well-bred Wainewright, who committed forgeries and murders for capital gain, constitute a symptom of an acquisitive society or a sinister expression of its economic values. In this sense, the crimes of the greedy gentleman and the starving bumpkin simply represent two poles of the binary class model that defined nineteenth-century British culture.

A self-described "gentleman" among "bumpkins," a convicted forger among respectable businessmen, and a poisoner among poets—one "who might have poisoned Lord Tennyson, or Mr. Gladstone, or the Master of Balliol" (1008)— Wainewright, as Wilde represents him, functions as a symbol and symptom of nineteenth-century British culture. He exposes unsettling congruities between a singularly transgressive criminal and a collectively disciplinary culture. "[T]oo modern" to be regarded with disinterest, he activates anxieties about the presence of crime in modern metropolitan-industrial Britain and what many perceived as its appalling conditions of moral and social corruption. Such anxieties about an unprecedented national increase in crime and a marked degeneration of national character established crime as a central metaphor for modernity, and this metaphoric status helped to publicize the specialized discourses of social science, medicine, law, psychology, and, eventually, criminal anthropology that emerged to explain and deter crime. Everyone, it seemed, whether imagined or imagining oneself as a potential criminal or a potential victim, had a stake in this ongoing conversation. For this reason, representations of murder, with great semiotic efficiency, could address questions of institutional control and ideological conflict while conjuring the intertextual network of discourses used to define criminality, apprehend criminals, judge crimes, and measure punishments.

When crime and culture are reconnected, murderers are never entirely unfamiliar; they come to signify ominous expressions of common cultural values, and their actions appear transgressive variations on established cultural practices. Murder demands a public response (an explanation, a trial, a death penalty), but it also is a response. This discomfiting paradox informs the poetics of murder—and the political resonance of murder—explored in this book. Just as Wilde linked murder to other modes of expression, the poems under consideration in this study grant murders and murderers an expressive function. Operating as symbols and symptoms, murderers, however ethically abhorrent, psychologically grotesque, and socially marginalized, are always in some way addressing, contesting, or implicating the centers of culture—scrutinizing its institutions and enacting its ideologies—through acts of extreme violence.

The fundamental logic with which Wilde dismantles the presumption of incongruity in his analysis of Wainewright is given a more nuanced articulation and wider application in Peter Stallybrass and Allon White's influential study, *The Politics and Poetics of Transgression* (1986). Observing that "what is *socially* peripheral is so frequently *symbolically* central" (5), they define their sense of a "politics and poetics of transgression" with an examination of center-margin and high-low dynamics that establish "*symbolic* repertoires at borders, margins and edges" (20). With an emphasis on the "interrelating and dependent hierarchies of high and low" (2) and an insistence on their dialectical relations, they consider "how each extremity structures the other, depends upon and invades the other in certain historical moments, to carry political charge through aesthetic and moral polarities" (3–4). As they "[map] domains of transgression where place, body, group identity and subjectivity interconnect," they "illuminate the discursive sites where social classification and psychological processes are generated as conflictual complexes" (25). Stallybrass and White demonstrate the resonance of their theoretical claims by conceptualizing a variety of sites, "the human body, psychic forms, geographical space and the social formation" (2), but their terminologies and their Foucauldian interest in the "outsiders-who-make-the-insiders-insiders (the mad, the criminal, the sick, the unruly, the sexually transgressive)" (22) easily accommodate a more focused examination of murder, a discursive site and an extreme transgression, which registers and generates "conflictual complexes" at the intersection of social prohibitions and individual agency. Expressing and transgressing cultural norms and prohibitions, murders and murderers carry a political charge, as they expose the limits of and undermine confidence in social hierarchies and disciplinary authorities. Conjoining social and psychological conflicts, occupying the margins and hailing the centers of culture, murders evoke power struggles between the state and its subjects and troubling intimacies between perpetrators and victims, and they produce a corresponding and unsettling set of interpretive questions—about the identities of perpetrators and victims, about the circumstances of terrible violence, and about the efficacy of punishments.

In Victorian England, the attempt to reverse the disruptive effects of murder through the application of the death penalty offers one of the most conspicuous reifications of the margin-center logic of transgression. Scaffold theatrics positioned the hanging bodies of criminals at the center of an observing citizen-crowd in an effort to reinscribe state power on the bodies of the "outsiders-who-make-the-insiders-insiders." Yet, when carefully staged public executions produced a spectacle of death-dealing violence and sanctioned killing in the name of state, the reprehensible behavior of the margin met the righteous behavior of the center in profoundly contradictory ways. Particularly in controversial cases, the compounded and charged meanings of capital punishment raised questions about who occupies or what constitutes the stabilizing center and the transgressive margin of Victorian culture.

In the murder poems comprising this study, the problems of mapping margin and center and differentiating congruities and incongruities are reiterated in pointed representations of specific locales where socially prescribed and individually transgressive identities collide and conflict. While depictions of crime scenes, execution scaffolds, murderous psyches, and violated homes serve the purpose of institutional and ideological critique, the complexities of poetic voice, inflecting the psychologies and identities of their killers, further refine their portraits of "conflictual complexes." In imagining the social and psychological sites of murder, these poems delineate the social contours of transgression by exposing the anxieties and confusions that surrounded murder and by playing with the margin-center logics that structured and regulated epistemologies of crime. With these interpretive operations in mind, we can see more clearly the formal and thematic links between the politics and the poetics of murder.

Stallybrass and White's notion of politics and poetics, and their commentaries on the margins and centers of discourse formation, also signify with respect to the cultural status of poetry—both high and low—in the Victorian era. Just as the meanings of murder were shifting, so were the agendas and markets of verse, and for this reason, mapping intersections between poetic production and criminal discourse benefits from recent scholarship on intersections between verse forms and cultural politics. A specific interest in understanding the position of poetry and the concerns of poets in a post-Romantic, novel-oriented age has become an important part of contemporary scholarship on Victorian poetry and has yielded several important studies of the political and aesthetic life of Victorian poetics. In particular, Isobel Armstrong's *Victorian Poetry: Poetry, Poetics and Politics* (1993), Antony Harrison's *Victorian Poets and the Politics of Culture: Discourse and Ideology* (1998), and E. Warwick Slinn's *Victorian Poetry as Cultural Critique: The Politics of Performative Language* (2003) have produced comprehensive theoretical arguments and practical demonstrations of poetry's political interests by integrating the practices of formal analysis and cultural studies.

Armstrong's *Victorian Poetry* advocates a rereading and rehistoricizing of Victorian poetry in order to uncover Victorian poetry's "cultural project" (8) and its connection to "modern problems" (ix). At the outset of her book, Armstrong establishes a division between democratic and conservative approaches to poetry, which, borrowing an image from J. S. Mill, she describes as "two systems of concentric circles" (ix). Within these circles, Armstrong sees the experimentalism of Victorian poetry, and rescuing Victorian poetry from the neglect of twentieth-century criticism (a consequence of the Modernist projects of rejecting the immediate past and extolling aesthetic self-referentiality), she reexamines the modern sensibilities of the Victorians: "To see yourself as modern is actually to define the contemporary self-consciously and this is simultaneously an act which historicizes the modern" (3). Victorian "modernism," she notes, "as it emerges in its poetics, describes itself as belonging to a condition of crisis, which has emerged directly from economic and cultural change" (3). As a result of the "historicized consciousness" (6) of Victorian poetics, "[t]eleology is displaced by epistemology and politics because *relationships* and their representation become the contested area, between self and society, self and labour, self and nature, self and language and above all between self and the lover" (7). Armstrong later depicts this phenomenon as a "shift from ontology to epistemology" (16). Revisiting the split between the Victorians and the Moderns, Armstrong explains that whereas the Victorians "strive to give a content to these problems, political, sexual, epistemological, and to formulate a cultural critique, the moderns celebrate the elimination of content" (7). Because of these poetic proclivities and these critical silences, Armstrong contends, "[t]he task of a history of Victorian poetry is to restore the questions of politics, not least sexual politics, and the epistemology and language which belong to it" (7).

Laying a foundation for the recuperation of poetry's politics, Armstrong enumerates several sets of tensions that structure the linguistic and epistemological projects of Victorian poetry. She negotiates—or, in her words, "circumvent[s]"—the interpretive dilemma of political unconsciousness and intentionality with "a more generous understanding of the text as struggle. A text is endless struggle and contention, struggle with a changing project, struggle with the play of ambiguity and contradiction" (10). Doing so "gives equal weight to a text's stated project and the polysemic and possibly wayward meanings it generates" (10). This notion of struggle accommodates the burdens of poetry's unsettling (and self-consciously modern) content while offering a context for considering formal structures and verbal ambiguities. In the "underlying element of struggle in poetry of this period," she argues, we see "its engagement with a content, its political awareness" (11).

This sense of poetry's "aestheticised politics" and "politicised aesthetics" (8) allows Armstrong to elaborate her very influential notion of "double forms." Though inspired by the innovations of dramatic poetics, such doubling effects are not exclusively the prerogative of dramatic poetry and may be observed in "[o]ther devices, such as the framed narrative or the dream, dialogue or parody" (13). These features render the poem a feat of simultaneity in which the text functions both as "the *subject's* utterance" and "the *object* of analysis and critique" (12). As such, the "double poem" becomes a "deeply sceptical form" as it engages "an expressive model and an epistemological model simultaneously" (13):

> Epistemological and hermeneutic problems are built into its very form, for interpretation, and what the act of interpretation involves, are questioned in the very existence of the double model. It must expose relationships of power, for the epistemological reading will explore things of which the expressive reading is unaware and go beyond the experience of the lyric speaker. It is inveterately political not only because it opens up an exploration of the unsta-

ble entities of self and world and the simultaneous problems of representation and interpretation, but because it is founded on debate and contest. (13–14)

Presenting Victorian poems as "responsive" (15) rather than "symptomatic" (15), Armstrong replaces feminist and Marxist notions of a "political unconscious" with an active poetics that "dramatises relationships of power" (16) and leverages its historicized sensibilities for the "systematic exploration of ambiguity" (16) while insisting upon an "epistemological uneasiness in which subject and object, self and world, are no longer in lucid relation with one another but have to be perpetually redefined" (17). As these "double forms" encourage both "sceptical" and "affirmative" responses, they "compel a strenuous reading" (17).

Armstrong's rereadings of Victorian poetry have several important applications for examining the poetics of murder. Her fundamental points about the acts of self-historicization, the burdens of content, the struggles of the text, the problematization of epistemology, the dramatization of power relationships, and the objectification of interpretation help to clarify the "strenuous readings" developed by representations of murder. Subsequent chapters will bear out the particulars of those applications, but a brief reference to the epistemological (and meta-epistemological) dimensions of the poetics of murder is in order here. Viewed as a blight on a progressively civilizing and rapidly urbanizing culture, crime was repeatedly presented as a modern problem to be scrutinized and solved through modern means—whether it be the rationalization of criminal law, the transformative applications of penitentiary science, the policing of the "dangerous classes," the scientific methods of statistical societies, or the late-Victorian Darwinian approaches to criminal anthropology. As the fascination with civilization became an obsession with its corresponding failures, however, Victorians frequently claimed a responsibility to gather their intellectual and moral resources to control crime, while, at the same time, lamenting its unprecedented scale and frequency. Because such discussions of modern crime and punishment were concurrent with conversations about the modernization of poetry, the insights conveyed in Armstrong's critical lexicon offer a foundation for viewing the subject of murder as an example of vexed modern content. It allows us to investigate the stresses and struggles built into verbal representations of extreme violence as particularly poetic strategies and to examine how poems encode—through double forms—the epistemological disturbances that murderous violence engenders.

The rubric of strain and stress also corresponds to artistic debates about what it meant, in terms of form and content, to cultivate modern poetry. Barrett Browning, in the voice of her poetess, Aurora Leigh, famously characterized the modern age in violent terms: "this live, throbbing age, / That brawls, cheats, maddens, calculates, aspires" (V.203–4), she argued, possessed poetic value and energy, and for the poet to ignore this, she maintained, is "fatal" (V.210). The verbs that Barrett Browning selects to represent the activities of the Victorian age—"brawls," "cheats," "maddens," "calculates"—suggest the appeal of the more transgressive and destructive forces of modernity, the allure of criminal plots for establishing a socially relevant aesthetic, the range of the political responsibilities of the Victorian poet, and the kind of active principle observed by Armstrong. In this context, murder, though an age-old crime, offers a devastating and extreme example of the struggles of ordering a modern world, but it also curiously encompasses the fatalities of a poetry that ignores the violence of modernity. Barrett Browning, prefiguring Wilde's later comments on crime and culture—with their suspicion of "disinterested curiosity" and "charming studies"—argues that the poet who, investing in high cultural prestige, prefers to depict the violence of the literary or historical past, is poetically irresponsible, uninventive, and irrelevant: "To flinch from modern varnish, coat or flounce, / Cry out for togas and the picturesque, / Is fatal,—foolish too. King Arthur's self / Was commonplace to Lady Guenever, / And Camelot to minstrels seemed as flat / As Fleet Street to our poets" (V.208–13). An unflinching look at the unromantic and unchivalric violence of modern industrial culture, she maintains, will liberate the modern poet from the strictures of poetry's past, for modern themes will inspire formal innovation. "Never flinch" (V.215), she commands, and then instructs her readers to "[t]rust" that "the spirit" will "make the form" (V.224–25).

Considering relationships between the spirit of Victorian modernity and the form of Victorian poetry requires a closer examination of the most fundamental concepts of cultural studies criticism. In his book's introduction, also concerned with interdependent social and formal functions, Harrison distills Foucauldian notions of discourse formation and renovates Marxist concepts of ideology in order to uncover how poems act "as social and cultural artifacts of historical importance" and "display subtle if not covert attempts to seize describable categories of cultural power by transmitting ideology . . . under the guise of eliciting pleasure" (1). Concerned with "middle-class writers," and "a clearly established but nonetheless threatened" middle-class hegemony (2), Harrison explores their work as a "mode of cultural intervention" (1). Applying the insights of Terry Eagleton's *The Ideology of the Aesthetic* (1990), Harrison considers artworks as "eminently contradictory" (3) and "ideologies as multiple" (4) as he traces how poetry appropriates and challenges ideologies through the "living sensibilities of its subjects" (3). He also cites Trevor Purvis and Alan Hunt's definition of ideology, which, filtering Marxist understandings of ideology through Saussurian and Foucauldian articulations of discourse, allows us to "grasp the way in which language and other forms of social semiotics not merely convey social experience but also play some major part in constituting social subjects (the subjectivities and their associated identities), their relations, and the field in which they exist" (3).

Harrison's contention that "discursive practices can have ideological effects because they perpetually constitute and reposition the subjects engaged in them" (5) grants poetry's formal practices particularly political functions: "the highly developed formulaic and conventional aspects of poetry as a linguistic medium—its specialized verse forms, traditions of figuration, metrical structures, and so on, which carry with them certain experiential expectations—establish it as a remarkably useful example for understanding the ideological effects of discourse generally" (8). Drawing upon Purvis and Hunt, Harrison explains, "discourses operate as economies 'with their own intrinsic technology, tactics, [and] effects of power, which in turn they transmit'" (3). In this way, Harrison positions his readers to understand the intricacies and economies of verse forms as discursive technologies. Involved in numerous ideological conflicts, competitions, collaborations, and collisions, poems foster political meanings and perform "cultural work" (7) that "intervene[s] in discourse" and "accrue[s] power" (8).

With a similar interest in bridging formalist and cultural studies, Slinn's *Poetry as Cultural Critique* notes that literary studies have sidelined "the intensive use of language in poetry" and foregrounded "thematic approaches to the politics of social discourse" (1). In order "to understand fully the function of figurative language in cultural processes (of which poetry is the most sophisticated form)," he argues, "we need to restore attention to that language, no matter how specialized its use—without losing sight of its continuity with social and historical contexts" (1). Slinn "redress[es] the balance by analyzing poetic content and process in order to show how poetry may enact cultural critique through its self-conscious formalism, its foregrounding of just those language acts that many of the literary scholars most sympathetic to cultural critique have seemed least to take into account" (1). In articulating this critique, Slinn extrapolates from Robert Con Davis and Ronald Schliefer's *Criticism and Culture: The Role of Critique in Modern Literary Theory* (1991). He highlights their argument that critique need not be "applied exclusively to idealist discourses grounded in Reason" and cites their notion of "the study of literature as a form of cultural critique that examines the conditions and realization of discourse in its various groundings" (4). It is, in other words, an "*institutional* critique, which aims to discover the conditions and principles that govern existing institutions and cultural practices" (29). Slinn assembles a "range of contentious issues" to emphasize the scope of poetry's project of institutional critique: "slavery, sexual politics, prostitution, pornography, male liberalism, consciousness, individual agency, aestheticism, representation, liturgical language, belief, philosophical idealism" (6).

In establishing "continuity" between poetic form and historical context, Slinn dispenses with more conventional notions of poetry's liabilities: that poetry is "self-enclosed" because "highly organized" and "ideologically tainted" because "predominantly bourgeois" or that the lyric indeed embodies New Criticism's "transhistorical essentialism" (9–10). To overcome binary divisions between materiality and ideology, intrinsic and extrinsic frames of reference, and mimetic and passive models of literary production, he, like Armstrong and Harrison, postulates a poetic practice of discursive simultaneity:

> It is not a matter, in other words, of deciding whether the materiality of objects or the ideality of discourses provide the determining conditions for reality but of realizing—with both dialogism and textualism—that objects have no meaning outside a system of signification and that discourse performs no practice outside material existence. (23)

Slinn's sense of poetry's "performativity," a textual characteristic but also a literary theory, allows the critic "to attend to the material particularity of the poem, to its specifically textual as well as contextual requirements" (24). Slinn maintains that poetry "is homologous with performatives insofar as generically it privileges self-reference, flaunts elocutionary effects, reiterates conventions and formulae, creates its own meaning, and, above all, does something with words" (25). Via performativity, "poem as verbal act, poem as performance art, performatives as portrayed content—formalism performs a double function, both linking and distinguishing poetry from its contexts" (25). Therein lie the poem's capacity for and its mode of cultural critique: "poetry is more likely to expose, without necessarily subverting, enabling conditions" (29). As a poem simultaneously "reshapes" "reconstitutes" and "reiterates," it performs "a double action" (23).

Armstrong, Harrison, and Slinn each note that Victorian poetry, traditionally construed as an aesthetic domain less amenable to political engagement or less susceptible to topical distractions, has been marginalized in the cultural studies milieu of contemporary Victorian scholarship. Creating a repertoire of new critical methods and readings, their scholarship has helped to transform the interpretive questions and strategies shaping Victorian poetry studies. Significantly, as they seek to retell the story of Victorian poetry, they each theorize doubling as a formal practice and discursive function that allows the poem to participate in multiple arenas—to operate aesthetically because politically and vice versa. Whether conceptualized as a simultaneity rooted in performativity, a verbal technology rooted in discourse formation, or a double form rooted in epistemological contention, such awareness of the cultural and political interests of poetry provides an important foundation for examining the poetics of murder.

While each of these studies privileges middle-class poetry and emphasizes topical and political variety in order to demonstrate the ubiquity of the textual processes they theorize, their insights, which can also accommodate the poetry of the streets, provide multiple applications for a focused study of the poetics of murder. With poetry's formal qualities marked as political engagement rather than aesthetic retreat, for example, the expressivist impulses of the condemned subjects of last lamentations may be considered in the context of the criminal law that condemns them. Their layering of affective tropes and legal discourse can be viewed as skeptical readings of state authority and ambiguous readings of individual transgression while their oft-noted poetic inferiority can be viewed as performances of working-class challenges to cultural authority and artistic propriety. Or, the metrical subtleties with which Browning and Rossetti modulate the voices of their murderous speakers can reveal exercises in textual stress and epistemological frustration—their poems "compel a strenuous reading" by invoking and reproducing the cultural debates surrounding newfangled theories of criminal insanity in early and mid-Victorian England. Further, observing the function of poetic genres as discursive technologies assists in sorting out the ways in which the adversarial language of the divorce court and the generic hybridity of the verse novel and the verse drama allowed poets to invoke legal and literary history in order to create historicized critiques of matrimonial law and domestic ideology.

Such reassessments of Victorian poetics, and their applications for examining verse representations of murder, position this study on a broader terrain of historicist scholarship. In *Practicing New Historicism* (2000), Catherine Gallagher and Stephen Greenblatt write of a "methodological eclecticism" (4) that, among other things, consists in "tracking the social energies that circulate very broadly through a culture, flowing back and forth between margins and center, passing from zones designated as art to zones apparently indifferent or hostile to art, pressing up from below to transform the exalted spheres and down from on high to colonize the low" (13). The well-known New Historicist metaphor of circulation usefully links margin and center, high and low, in ways that are important for a study of murder and a study of poetry that seeks to revise assumptions about both. An emphasis on "circulation" encourages us to trace the movement of a theme—in this case, murder—but it also encourages the transgression of conventional and classed boundaries of poetic discourse. Social discourse ("hostile to art") but also "low" discourse to which art and criticism are often hostile find common cause in representations of crime, which was itself often dismissively considered a "low," vulgar, or sensational topic in Victorian culture. On another level, the notion of "social energies" that intrigues Gallagher and Greenblatt provides an apt term for describing the circulating social anxieties and cultural logics that determined and destabilized the meanings of murder.

But "social energies" also describes the interactive features of discourse and genre so important for explicating the poetics of murder. As Carolyn Williams has argued, "[t]he utility of the concept of genre for cultural study lies in its powerful fusion of historical and formal assumptions. For period study it is especially clear that the concept of genre enables a focus on synchronic relations while also depending upon the diachronic relations with antecedents of current practice" (519). Meanwhile, "discourse," she argues, "resolutely transgresses received genre categories, resolutely encompasses much more than literature, much more even than textual practices" (519), for "[t]he notion of a 'discourse' is produced by grouping texts and practices across generic boundaries" (519). Responding to Derrida's reflections in "The Law of Genre," Williams asks, "What is 'the law of genre' but the play of formalism and de-formation in sociocultural terms?" (520), and she asserts a program for cultural studies worth quoting in full:

> At this moment in literary and cultural studies, it might help to think of "discourse" and "genre" as a dialectical pair, one foregrounding synchronic study and the other foregrounding diachronic study; one emphasizing historical discontinuity and the other emphasizing historical continuity; one tending (potentially, but not necessarily) toward thematic and the other toward formalistic oversimplifications. But these relations are now fluid, recombinant, open to exchange. Perhaps *because* of the powerful work the concept of "discourse" has done in the last couple of decades of Victorian studies, now is a good time to rework the concept of "genre" as a fully cultural as well as a literary category. Cultural studies has shown us that literary studies do not corner the market on formal analysis; and it might well be that in the play of genres we can find one perfect place to study the way culture takes *form*. (520)

The idea of discourse and genre as a "dialectical pair," pulling in two directions while inspiring "recombinant" articulations and acts of "de-formation," offers valuable insight for exploring the ways in which poetry and murder operate in a "fusion of historical and formal assumptions," creating synchronic and diachronic chains of meaning and invoking the trans-generic and interdisciplinary pastiche of texts that characterized the criminal discourse of Victorian England.

In his recent discussion of the "inter-generic competition and cultural transformation" ("Novel Poetry" 493) marking the relationship between hegemonic realistic fiction and counterdiscursive poetic experiments, Dino Felluga considers the dynamics of genre in similar terms. Echoing the notion of social energies found in Gallagher and Greenblatt's discussion, he writes, "Genre should, I would suggest, be understood as an unstable field of energies affected as much by critical perception and debate as by specific structural features. In fact, I would go further: there is no such thing as a reference to a text that is not a performative ordering of that text's textuality, that does not in itself conform to and enact generic conventions" (495). Citing Ralph Cohen's point that genres and texts are marked by their "interrelationship with and differentiation from" other genres, Felluga describes this process as a "performative loop" of generic "identification" and "self-estrangement" (495). If we retain an appreciation for the counterdiscursive maneuvers of verse and the "performative loop" of textual meaning, but extend the scope of intergeneric identification and differentiation beyond a contest between novels and poems, we can use genre to conceptualize other textual and performative mediations of murder: the newspaper, the trial, the scaffold, the medicolegal treatise, the Greek tragedy, and the "old yellow Book," for example, all serve within a system of "fully cultural" genres and discourses, possess diachronic and synchronic markers, and encode varying degrees of identification, self-estrangement, and self-referentiality. From the lowly street ballad to the high Greek tragedy, we can see poets exploiting these multivalent qualities in their poetic representations of murder, which do not simply demonstrate the due course of heteroglossia, but rather suggest the measured participation of poets in the literary development of verse and in social responses to murder.

In acknowledging signs of participation, acts of intervention, and instances of differentiation, it is worth noting how poetic representations of murder, exploiting the performative features of verse, were poised to engage the dialectics of discourse and genre in ways that other textual forms were not. In the stories and testimonies of courtroom adversaries and witnesses, the social scientific and statistical data that quantified and charted a national crime epidemic, the biographical case studies that propounded etiologies for criminal lunacy, the newspaper reports that publicized shocking crimes and criminal trials, and the criminal acts, scandalous revelations, and detective plots of novels, murder was construed as a narrative event. At stake in the ceaseless activities of prosecuting, theorizing, documenting, legislating, pathologizing, punishing, publishing, and reading crime are the production and management of knowledge about crime and punishment. As these examples attest, it was most often by analyzing crimes as narrative constructs that Victorians attempted to comprehend murders and apprehend murderers. The fact that knowledge about crime and criminals was manufactured largely in narrative formats also helps to explain our contemporary focus on crime fiction; in the similarities between novels and other narrative forms—the trial, the newspaper report—we see obvious generic and discursive affinities.

Precisely because of the predominantly narrative contents and contexts of criminal discourse, poems, operating in the performative mode that Slinn identifies, could develop striking counterdiscursive representations of murder and murderers. Poems, of course, by no means exclude narrative formats: street ballads reproduced, often in order to contest, the narrative imperatives of criminal trials, and with *The Ring and the Book,* Browning, transposing novelistic polyphony into dramatic verse, creates an excessively mediated, virtually indecipherable web of transgressive plots, suspicious characters, and unreliable narrators. Relying upon narrative structures and reproducing narrative epistemologies, however, they nonetheless consistently expose and destabilize their foundations by manipulating the formal features of verse or the cultural status of poetry. Last lamentations overturn criminal stereotypes when they foreground the affective voice, the lyrical sensibilities, and the verse-writing inclinations of the condemned criminal, and *The Ring and the Book* further complicates the psychologies and claims of its narrators with verbal twitches and metrical irregularities. Taking up the tools of verse, poets responded variously to more prevalent representational modes generated in the realms of officialdom, the forum of the popular press, and the literary marketplace, but as they exploit textual resources unique to verse form—lyrical voices and dramatic personae, metrical stunts and verbal surprises—their poems generate suggestive frictions that alert us to the performative strategies and verbal technologies shaping the poetics of murder.

References to the chapters that comprise this study appear throughout this introduction, but a more substantial overview of the individual chapters helps to elucidate the structural logic of the book and demonstrate the relationships between the theme of murder, the genres of poetry, and the tools of criticism outlined here. Beginning the study of murder and poetry in the streets, chapter 1 reads working-class crime ballads as inscriptions of class politics and interrogations of state discipline. While high poetry grappled with a changing market of literary consumption that privileged the novel, the market for street poetry flourished and expanded during the first half of the nineteenth century. Street ballads circulated in the thousands among the working classes, often attracting the attention and scorn of the middle and upper classes. As the author of an article in the *National Review* explained, "there is still a very large section of the British public, though probably a decreasing one, which must and will have life put into doggerel verse for its special delectation" ("Street Ballads" 415). The disappearance of these ephemeral texts into Victorian trash bins and library collections have stalled the development of ballad exegesis. A selection of anthologies and archives has inspired a few studies, but, for the most part, ballads have attracted more documentary than analytical approaches. Within an atmosphere of recovery created by a developing field of print culture studies, a growing interest in working-class studies, and a new commitment to cultural studies approaches to poetry, this chapter questions longstanding assumptions about the transparency of this "bad" poetry and the cultural significance of translating life into "doggerel verse." In important ways, the apparent badness of street ballads establishes a central conceit of a street poetics that self-consciously flouts the standards of high poetry, and, in the case of murder and execution ballads, the judicial authority of high culture.

Drawing upon the resources of library collections as well as ballad anthologies, chapter 1 reappraises crime ballads by reconstructing their literary and historical contexts and challenging critical dismissals of them as vulgar, sensational, and morally unsophisticated. Their popularity demonstrates a pervasive and continuous mediation of crime in verse, but close readings of these texts reveal that their popularity also signals a well-developed and widely disseminated political sensibility informed by the working-class experience of poverty, policing, and punishment. Quite often, these occasional poems announcing murders and executions posed challenges to class-inflected ideologies of crime and invited reflections on the disciplinary power of the state. With their aestheticized renderings of crime and punishment, balladeers, sometimes tacitly and sometimes explicitly, constructed verse arguments that critiqued the disproportionate supervision of the working classes and protested the systematic discrimination of judicial practices.

Murder and execution ballads appeared in two main formats: third-person "astonishing disclosures," which alerted their audiences to the graphic details of crimes, and first-person "last lamentations," which informed the public of the tragic aspects of executions. Sometimes constituting portions of larger broadsides and sometimes circulating as lone poems, ballads alerted audiences to their perspective and voice through the use of title phrases that marked them as "accounts," "full particulars," and "disclosures" or "sorrowful lamentations" and "copies of affecting verses." The third-person ballad constructed the persona of the astonished witness, and the first-person ballad imagined the persona of the condemned criminal. Under close examination, the significance of these generic differences becomes strikingly apparent. Astonishing disclosures, for example, develop a political aesthetic in gruesome accounts of murders and descriptions of crime scenes. Deploying sublime images of violence, these graphic representations create highly condensed explorations of moral disorder. Their graphic detail—from exacting portrayals of the bloody remains of murder to imagined accounts of the frantic struggles of victims—simply overwhelms readymade ethical dichotomies and longstanding legal definitions. Emotionally and intellectually overwhelming, murder becomes a mode of expression, as Wilde suggested, and, as such, murder prompts acts of interpretation by astonished witnesses and ballad audiences seeking to address the moral and epistemological questions raised by outrageous crimes.

First-person lamentations, in contrast, were advertised by publishers as verse autobiographies. Outpourings of dreadful memories and terrifying fears, they were alleged to be written by condemned criminals in their cells on the eve of execution. With the persona of the criminal poet, these ballads destabilized ethical commonplaces and legal fictions by linking the sentimental poet and the violent murderer, thereby challenging a practice of capital punishment predicated upon the irremediable monstrosity of the condemned and the unimpeachable righteousness of the state. Slinn reminds us that "[f]ictive speech acts and real cultural practices are inseparable activities" (17), and he quotes Barbara Johnson's suggestive example: "If people are put to death by a verdict and not by a poem, it is not because the law is not a fiction" (17). A similar trope of mutual performativity operates in last lamentations in which balladeers pitted lyrical sensibilities against legal reasoning, thus suggesting that when a condemned criminal is exonerated in a street poem and not in a courtroom, it is not because the law is not a fiction. With their politically adept applications of poetic license, last lamentations frequently privileged the authenticity of the lyric over the artifice of the law, problematizing trial verdicts and sentences and establishing skeptical readings of murder trials and scaffold deaths.

Removing murder from the context of retributive justice, the poems discussed in chapter 2 exchange the problems of judicial review for those of medical diagnosis. As the idea of the criminal lunatic was continuously revised during the nineteenth century, interpretations of a murder's meaning, long predicated on legal procedures that pronounced judgments and meted out punishments by reading the details of the criminal act, were increasingly complicated by new theories of the criminal mind, which offered intricate definitions and expansive case histories to determine the responsibilities of and possible treatments for criminals. In differentiating and combining criminality and insanity, theories of homicidal lunacy and the extensive lists of symptoms that accompanied them synthesized Victorian moral values, legal codes, and mental sciences in disconcerting ways. Mental scientists expounded and applied their theories while attempting to establish the legitimacy of their knowledge and negotiate the conflicts between punishment and treatment. Meanwhile, their medicolegal analyses of specific cases, appearing in specialist texts, in courtroom testimonies, and in popular print, created rifts between theoretical abstraction and legal concreteness. In the charged environment of murder trials, the increasingly obscured boundary between sanity and insanity frustrated collective desires to define murder and punish killers and pitted the authority of medical experts against the fears of a concerned citizenry and the traditions of learned jurists.

The troubling distractions of complicated insanity defenses, "not guilty on the ground of insanity" verdicts, and new asylum treatments in cases of extreme violence and astonishing cruelty define the poetics of murder in Browning's "Porphyria's Lover," "My Last Duchess," and "The Laboratory" and Rossetti's

"A Last Confession." While Harrison emphasizes the notion that power circulates via discursive formations and that poems participate in this circulation via verbal and formal interventions, these dramatic poems suggest that anxiety circulates through these same discursive formations and that poets may exploit the curiosity and confusion surrounding these anxieties to simultaneously aestheticize and politicize murder. As they enforce tensions between psychological strands of medicolegal theory and commonsense traditions of criminal law, these dramatic representations of murderous subjects develop a criminal sublime, which upholds the fundamental obscurity of the murderer.

Demonstrating a shared interest in exploring criminal psychology and dramatic poetry, Browning and Rossetti prompt readers to consider the clinical or evidentiary meanings of their characters, and, situating their murderers outside the realm of judicial accountability, they withhold the comforts of moral resolution. Because they avoid normative scenarios of crime and punishment, their depictions of unapprehended killers allow them to imagine the states of consciousness and the problems of expression that characterize murderers—and that interest poets. With the careful modulation of voice, they establish the same conditions for epistemological doubt and ethical impasse that accompanied the medicolegal debates of the mid-Victorian period. Furthermore, in placing acts of murder and symptoms of madness in the context of sexual power and gendered violence, they generate a tension between the familiarity (literary or cultural) of violent sexual passions and the unfamiliarity of clinical medicolegal logic.

Balancing the discourses of sins and symptoms, Browning and Rossetti leave readers to question whether their speakers rehearse conventional stories of sexually charged violence or present medical specimens of a new diagnostic theory. In courting confusion, they aptly exemplify the kinds of doubling elaborated by Armstrong; they seize upon the strangeness of modern content and exploit the epistemological disturbances of a "double form" in order to develop an aesthetically playful but ethically serious mode of political critique, which enfolds questions about the codes of sexual power and the discipline of mental science. Compressing the voice of the murderous subject into a verbally dense transcript, each of these poems renders decisions on the matter of malice and madness impossible, and the persistence of indeterminacy sustains the aesthetic force of the criminal sublime.

Chapter 3 explores representations of domestic murder, which, repositioning center and margin, portray the home as a breeding ground for murderous intentions and actions. Aligning interests in generic hybridity and gender ideology, Browning's epic verse-novel, *The Ring and the Book,* and Lytton's and Levy's closet verse-tragedies, *Clytemnestra* and *Medea,* emphasize the social constructedness and historical contingencies of both gender and genre, in order to question the literary, legal, and ideological conventions and codes determining spousal relations. In imagining the devolution of domestic proprieties into criminal tendencies, these texts do not simply sensationalize the home, ruining cozy domestic interiors with bloody outbreaks of murderous violence. Rather, they embed outrageous acts of murder within complex portraits of premeditation and determination. Suggesting the psychological origins of violent agency, but explicitly tying them to domestic ideology and matrimonial law, they locate the origins of domestic murder in social institutions and cultural traditions. Whether hiding systematic abuse or fostering violent rebellion, these poems suggest, the private home is subject to the laws of a disciplinary state and the willfulness of outraged individuals. As such, it weakens and endangers—rather than strengthens and protects—its inhabitants.

The political arguments of these three poems become most apparent when viewed in light of mid-century marriage debates, which accompanied the renegotiation of matrimonial law and the public scrutiny of domestic violence. A wealth of contemporary scholarship has made us aware of the intricacies and contradictions of the middle-class separate spheres doctrine, which stressed the natural complementarity of empowered males and compromised females and mandated multiple strategies of paternalist protection and patriarchal discipline. Yet, while this optimistic vision of comfort and control circulated widely, Victorians also negotiated another model in which the home was populated not by angelic mothers and judicious fathers, but by self-interested legal adversaries negotiating the double binds of the state's disciplinary power and the husband's domestic authority. Deployed, like its idyllic counterpart, to discipline married couples and uphold gender hierarchies, this combative version of marital relations was given renewed public force in parliamentary debates about marriage reform and divorce law. With the establishment of a divorce court, which was modeled on the criminal court, and the incremental criminalization of certain forms of domestic abuse, the imperatives of an adversarial domesticity were frequently cited in the court and in the press. Stripping away the trappings of idealism and dismantling the façade of privacy, the very publicity of this model confronted Victorians with starkly pragmatic readings of the legal prohibitions and permissions of marriage contracts, while emphasizing the prerogatives of the state in sanctioning, enforcing, and dissolving marriages.

This distinctly combative version of marriage constitutes the primary frame of reference for understanding both the political resonance and the generic innovation of each of these domestic murder poems. With murder representing *in extremis* the more sinister aspects of a pragmatic adversarial script, Browning, Lytton, and Levy consider the kinds of spousal conflicts debated in parliament and publicized in divorce trials. Offering no sanctuary and affording no pleasure, domestic intimacy is characterized by the escalating pressures and accumulating resentments of everyday homelife—which culminate in extraordinarily violent methods of resistance and redress. In manipulating the domestic themes and narrative logics of already-plotted stories—of legal history, in the case of Browning's seventeenth-century Italian murders, and theatre history, in the case of Lytton's and Levy's ancient Greek crimes—these poets produced topically resonant metatextual commentaries on legal, literary, and cultural representation. Demonstrating how discourse and genre invoke synchronic and diachronic meanings, they forge intergeneric and intertextual links that enfold the disciplinary discourses of legal contracts and the melodramatic modes of public scandal. Implicating the long history of patriarchal power, and exchanging narratives of melodramatic villainy for narratives of institutional failure, they render a binary schema of innocence and guilt (central to divorce courts, criminal courts, and public opinion) inadequate and irrelevant while imagining the systematic pressures of public interests and private wrongs that mark and mar the domestic idyll.

In *The Ring and the Book*, for example, points of agreement in the monologues of the murderer, Guido, and his victim, Pompilia, establish arresting connections between divorce rights, husband rights, and murder rights. Providing rare moments of corroboration and consistency amidst a profusion of voices and a sprawling narrative, husband and wife (condemned murderer and dying victim) express strikingly similar interpretations of the domestic roots of their violent ends. As they both develop a cause-effect structure for their stories of marriage and murder, the unexpectedness of their coalescing voices establishes the interpretive authority of their critique and challenges the melodramatic codes shaping the public gossip and legal cases generated by their troubled marriage and their violent deaths. Working on the smaller scale afforded by closet drama and shielded from the censoring protocols of public performance, Lytton and Levy modernize the stories of high tragic murderesses by establishing congruities between the momentous agency of murderous violence and the everyday slights of gender inequality. They thus complicate traditional plots, which connected Clytemnestra's crimes to the deterministic forces of fate and Medea's crimes to a particularly feminine variety of vengeful monstrosity. Regretting their misguided investments in patriarchal fantasies of domesticity, Lytton's and Levy's murderers select killing as a response to the claustrophobia of domestic alienation. Dragging their private wrongs onto a public stage, their crimes force a reckoning with domestic ideology. Pessimistic and critical, these renovations of the epic poem and the tragic drama objectify the contemporary discourses of marriage law and genres of domestic scandal and ask their Victorian readers to confront and interrogate their own investments in domestic ideology and interpretations of household law.

As these chapters demonstrate, the theme of murder provided poets with a content and a context for establishing political arguments and reviewing poetic agendas. While the politics of murder allowed poets to scrutinize the practices and relations of power informing crimes and punishments, it also informed their exploration of the interactions between genres of discourse and forms of verse. Literary murders may present readers with ancient crimes or familiar plots, but when examined in their immediate cultural context, they offer very nuanced examples of the dialectical and historical interplay of genre and discourse. As they affiliate themselves with and differentiate themselves from other modes of understanding crimes and apprehending criminals in Victorian England, the murder poems explored in this study highlight the epistemological and interpretive dilemmas surrounding murders and murderers. Examining these tensions in a select number of texts, *Crime in Verse* offers a starting point for reimagining the intertextual and interdependent meanings of murder's political charge and literary resonance, and it allows us to glimpse more fully the social life and "cultural work" of Victorian verse.

CHAPTER 1

Murder, Execution, and the Criminal Classes

CIRCULATING IN PRINT and in song, the two central genres of the crime ballad trade, the third-person "astonishing disclosures" of bloody violence and the first-person "last lamentations" of condemned criminals, reported horrific murders and recorded terrible executions in ear-catching rhymes.[1] Marketed in oral performances by ballad singers, and often stamped with visually striking woodcut images or flanked by newsy prose reports, these songs of crime developed a remarkably public poetics, which, merging singsong rhythms, bloody excess, and sentimental rhetoric with case details and topical references, produced unexpectedly complex commentaries on the meanings of murderous transgression and capital punishment. When we remember that these verses were regularly sung and sold in Victorian streets and markets, the horizon of Victorian poetry and poetics broadens considerably.[2] And if we consider, as David Vincent does in *Literacy and Popular Culture* (1993), that they aided the advance of popular literacy—and that the "most striking characteristic of the first phase of the expansion of imaginative literature was the sheer volume and noise which accompanied it" (201)—we can begin to imagine the volume and noise of street balladry as a significant part of Victorian literature and culture.

The poetic and political significance of street balladry, however, has been lost within a long history of critical dismissals. Simply put, crime ballads suffer from bad reputations. On the one hand, they seem to embrace, with morbid enthusiasm, the abject and gory elements of murderous violence. In "Execution of John Gleeson Wilson" (1849) (figure 1), for example, meticulous sketches of terrible wounds (a jellied head and three-inch gashes) join stock phrases of gruesome excess ("weltering in their gore" and "blood did flow profusely") to produce a portrait of astonishing destruction. When ventriloquizing the voices of condemned murderers, on the other hand, last lamentations fascinated their audience with confessions of sin and professions of remorse. In "The Last Moments and Confession of Wm. Sheward" (1869) (figure 2), the killer remembers his outrageous wife-murder with sentimental regret: "I boiled her head, how sad to tell, / I was mad without a doubt, / I threw it in the different parts, / I placed it round about."

Responding to such representations of crime, many nineteenth-century critics cited the arraying of mutilated bodies as symptoms of working-class bloodlust and the sentimentalization of condemned murderers as inscriptions of working-class criminality. Yet, packaged in striking—and sometimes amusing—rhymes and accommodating the particulars of historical crimes, the verse-crimes of street literature frequently engaged stark appraisals of specific murder cases and confronted contentious issues in judicial and penal practices. At the very least, their public form and political content—and the image of Victorians singing "pools of blood as thick as mud, from all of them could trace" or "I boiled her head, how sad to tell, / I was mad without a doubt"—should inspire new questions about criminal representation in both poetic and political terms.

Yet, because applications of trite maxims, snippets of behavioral advice, and invocations of "feeling Christians" often accompanied such images of bleeding and weltering, murder ballads have more recently been labeled prim narratives of moral danger or simple-minded endorsements of state power. Critics have interpreted the confessing and regretting criminals of execution ballads as conventionally guilty subjects, affirming the terrible necessity of their public deaths and ratifying the retributive authority of the state. In this view, ballad recommendations of religious piety and personal restraint appear to betray the political interests and belie the social experiences of their working-class authors and audiences. Submitting to a ruthless law of genre, crime ballads as a whole become the inadequate and incongruous sum of their stock moral pieties and their stark bloody minutiae, and individual crime ballads are merely the indistinguishable products of a mechanized industry churning out unimaginative and inartistic reiterations of a strict melodramatic mandate. Caught between an uncompromising conservatism and an unabashed bloodlust, they are aesthetically and ethically suspect.

EXECUTION OF
JOHN GLEESON WILSON,

At Kirkdale Gaol, on Saturday, September 15th, 1849, the Murderer of Mrs. Hinrichson, her Two Children, and Female Servant.

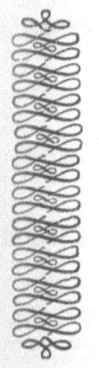  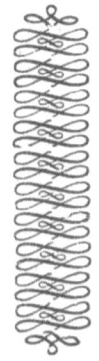

One of the most appalling murders which has for years startled and disgusted society took place on the morning of Wednesday, March 28th, 1849, at No. 20, Leveson Street, Liverpool, at mid-day. A miscreant in the most brutal manner murdered two unprotected women and two helpless children.

In due course Wilson was committed for trial, which took place before Mr Justice Patteson and a respectable jury, who, in less than five minutes, returned a verdict of GUILTY.

On Saturday morning, a few minutes before twelve o'clock, the iron gate leading to the drop was opened, and the prisoner appeared between two priests—the Rev. Mr Duggan and the Rev. Mr Marshall. A general feeling of horror seemed to pervade all present, which found expression in the most distant part of the assemblage by bursts of execration.

Calcraft, the London executioner, was unable to be present from illness, and the office was performed by Howard, from York, who was especially brought to Liverpool by the Under Sheriff. The priests read in English, the service of the Catholic Church for a departing soul until the bolt was drawn, and the wretched culprit was launched into eternity.

Thus terminated the life of one of the greatest criminals that ever disgraced the human family. Upwards of 100,000 persons were present, the railway company running cheap trains from all available parts.

THE LIVERPOOL TRAGEDIES.

Come all you feeling christians and listen unto me,
The like was not recorded in British history,
It's of three dreadful murders committed, I am told,
By one John Gleeson Wilson, for the sake of cursed gold.

On Wednesday the 28th, consternation did prevail,
In Leveson Street in Liverpool, where thousands did bewail,
The fate of this poor family, who we're left to deplore,   [more.
Snatched from a father's fond embraces, who ne'er will see them
This monster in human shape did go there to dwell,
And that he went for plunder to all it is known full well,
And when this callous villain saw their defenceless state,
He did resolve them all to kill and rob them of the plate.

His bloody work he did commence all in the open day,
By striking at the children while their mother was away,
The servant girl did interfere, said, "should not do so,"
Then with a poker in his hand he gave her a severe blow.

Numberless times he did her strike till she could no longer stand,
The blood did flow profusely from her wounds, and did him brand,
Then the eldest boy of five years old, in supplication said,
"Oh master, spare our precious lives, don't serve us like the maid."

This darling child of five years old he brutally did kill,
Regardless of its tender cries, its precious blood did spill,
The youngest child to the kitchen ran, to shun the awful knife,
This villain followed after and took its precious life.

The surgeon thus describes the scene presented to his view,
A more appalling case than this he says he never knew,
Four human beings on the floor all weltering in their gore,
The sight was sickening to behold on entering the door.

The mother's wounds three inches deep upon her head and face,
And pools of blood as thick as mud, from all of them could trace,
None could identify the boy, his head was like a jelly;
This tragedy is worse by far than Greenacre or Kelly.

To the hospital in this sad state they quickly were conveyed,
The mother with her infant dear, and faithful servant maid,
Thousands did besiege the gates, their fate for to enquire,
But in three days from incise wounds, both of them did expire.

'Twill cause the captain many a pang to know their awful doom,
His loving wife and children sent to an untimely tomb,   [save,
'Twill make his hair turn grey with grief, no skill their lives could
And he did go, borne down with woe, in sorrow to the grave.

But now he's taken for this deed, bound down in irons strong,
In Kirkdale Jail he now does lie, till his trial it comes on,
May God above receive the souls of those whom he has slain,
And may they all in heavenly bliss for ever with him reign.

J. Harkness, Printer, Preston.

Figure 1
Execution of John Gleeson Wilson. Courtesy The Newberry Library, Chicago.

The Last Moments and Confession
OF
WM. SHEWARD.

On Tuesday, April 20, the last dread sentence of the law was carried out in the case of Wm. Sheward convicted at the last Norwich Assizes for the murder of his wife. The culprit died without any very painful struggles. He showed a considerable amount of nerve, although he trembled a good deal at the drop, to which he had to be carried on account of his rheumatism. In the prisoner's confession he stated that he killed his wife in June, 1851, and that he afterwards mutilated the body. He placed the head in a saucepan, and put it on the fire to keep the stench away. He then broke it up, and distributed it about Thorpe. He then put the hands and feet in the same saucepan, in hopes they might boil away. Carried portions of the body away in a pail and threw them in different parts of the city. The long hair on my return from Thorpe, he cut with a pair of scissors in small pieces and they blew away as he walked. The blankets, where there was any blood he cut in small pieces, and distributed them about the city, and made off with anything that had the appearance of blood about them. The prisoner also stated that he never saw or knew his present wife until June 21, 1852, twelve months after the occurrence,—The confession was taken in the presence of a magistrate, and the governor and chaplain.

I am a sad and wretched man,
  Borne down in care and woe,
I am doomed to die for a murder done
  Near eighteen years ago;
A dreadful deed, as you may read,
  I long kept in my breast,
I'had no comfort day or night,
  Until I did confess.

With the dreadful knife I slew my wife,
  And her body round did throw,
Now I must die for a murder done,
  Near eighteen years ago.

I her body into pieces cut,
  And scattered it around,
Here and there, I scarce knew where,
  I placed it on the ground.
I now must die for that foul deed,
  And in a murderer's grave lie low,
I did her kill, her blood I spilled,
  Near eighteen years ago.

I boiled her head, how sad to tell,
  I was mad without a doubt,
I threw it in the different parts,
  I placed it round about;
Kept the secret eighteen years,
  Within my guilty breast,

And till the same I did divulge,
  I day nor night could rest.

For eighteen years, in grief and tears,
  I passed many a dreary night,
I had not one moment's happiness,
  Since I killed my own dear wife;
At length I did confess the deed,
  For which I now must die,
For a murder eighteen years ago—
  The which I don't deny.

There was letters sent from different parts,
  To say my wife did live,
To save me from the gallows,
  But none would they believe;
I could not from Justice flee,
  I do deserve my fate,
No pen can write, or tongue can tell,
  My sad and wretched fate.

My moments they do swiftly pass,
  I soon shall sleep below,
I done that dreadful awful deed,
  Near eighteen years ago;
I cut and mangled that poor soul,
  My heart was flinty steel,
Her limbs and body strewed about,
  In hedges, lanes, and fields.

H. Disley, Printer, 57, High street, St. Giles, London.—W,C.

Figure 2

The Last Moments and Confession of Wm. Sheward. Courtesy The Newberry Library, Chicago.

While an overemphasis on the poles of moral melodrama and vulgar gore has consistently diminished our confidence in the street ballad's capacity for textual complexity and political sophistication, notions about the laws of genre and the conditions of production join expectations about the nature of authorship to further diminish their social status. Commissioned by enterprising printers, penned by anonymous "hacks," and hawked in the streets by "the poorest of the poor" (O'Connell 168), street ballads flout our author-based and class-inflected definitions of literary creation. Lacking names and identities, ballad authors are chronically underestimated, and their verses, seeming to reflect the harried and impoverished existence of their authors, have rarely inspired careful literary analysis.[3] Further incriminated by their association with a presumably delinquent and illiterate class, ballads and balladeers, emanating from and entertaining the "dangerous classes," acquire a criminal taint.

This chapter seeks to extricate crime ballads from this limited conceptual paradigm by reviewing the analytical methods of ballad studies, the classed epistemologies of criminal discourse, and the cultural conditions of ballad production. Outlining interpretive strategies derived from the generic conventions of crime balladry and the topical details of individual songs, it presents careful readings of specific texts and historical contexts in order to demonstrate the street ballad's potential for poetic and political variety.[4] When contextualized and individuated, connections between the details of crime ballads and the details of historical crimes become more apparent, allowing us to reconsider the semiotic operations that underpin these ostensibly contradictory assemblages of moral didacticism, bloody abjection, sentimental lamentation, and spectacular death.

This approach also recognizes the usually unacknowledged distinction between first-person and third-person voices in ballad narratives, which organized criminal representations around the notions of astonished witnesses and lamenting criminals. Generalizing about the genre of "gallows literature," commentators have rarely distinguished the rhetorical significance and political relevance of these two distinct voices, but in many cases ballad writers leveraged these fundamental differences in poetic voice and narrative perspective for both generic development and political argument. Indeed, a glimpse at even a relative few of the hundreds and hundreds of crime ballads preserved in library collections reveals that the anonymous poets of the ballad industry regularly applied the poetic tools of their trade to influence the generic evolution of the crime ballad and to intervene in public discussions of criminal trials, laws, and theories.

For this reason, the generic regularity and formal simplicity of street verses can be read as a verbal technology, which, as Harrison explains—via Purvis and Hunt's idea of a "social semiotics" that "convey[s] social experience" while "constituting social subjects" (3)— performs "cultural work" (7). In this way, the lowly verses of the street, neither exploitative spectacles of gruesome misfortune nor smug recitations of moral law, generated a multiplicity of formal strategies, aesthetic meanings, and political engagements and disseminated them in the streets and amongst the crowds of Victorian England. Viewed in this context, the apparent vulgarity of their art—the sensationalism of their themes, the expediency of their rhymes, the simplicity of their rhythms—serves a performative function in Slinn's sense of the word: "both linking and distinguishing poetry from its contexts" (25), the ballad industry could pit its scrappy poetics of the street against the erudition of high literary culture and the authority of a disciplinary state.

Verse Crimes: "Atrocious Rhymes" and "Lawless Meters"

Discussions of street ballads, like discussions of criminality, are steeped in the ideology of class. When criminal representation and working-class authorship meet in the tradition of "gallows literature," the pressures of class ideology become strikingly apparent. Amidst ongoing Victorian conversations about urban streets and urban squalor, street balladry was seen as a particularly criminal poetics. For this reason the textual practices and the critical reception of street ballads must be understood with respect to Victorian economies and geographies of crime and class.

Though sometimes working at cross-purposes, the specialized rubrics of criminal discourse in nineteenth-century England often exploited the rhetorical convenience of an othered class while struggling to modernize and rationalize approaches to prevention and punishment. Across a range of projects—from establishing a police force and revising the criminal code to conducting statistical analyses and developing criminal anthropology—Victorians cited "the laboring classes," "the criminal classes," or the "dangerous classes" to organize vast amounts of data and reconcile competing theories. Reproducing this divisive epistemology of class, various print media consistently located the working classes in a cultural realm distinct from that of the middle and upper classes. The most striking and well-documented example of this logic is Henry Mayhew's influential *London Labour and the London Poor* (1861), in which, eagerly citing and applying the ethnological arguments of Dr. Andrew Smith, he categorizes London "street-folk" as a local variety of the "wandering tribes." With enthusiasm and precision, Mayhew explains to his readers that there are "two distinct and broadly marked races, viz., the wanderers and the settlers—the vagabond and the citizen—the nomadic and the civilized tribes" (1). Following this schema, he finds in the "vagabonds and outcasts" (2) of Victorian London the characteristics catalogued in Smith's work: overdeveloped jaws and cheekbones, underdeveloped heads, and a "different language" spoken "with the intent of concealing their designs and exploits" (2). Casting himself as a "traveller in the undiscovered country of the poor" (xv) and submitting his work to his civilized and settled citizen-readers, Mayhew promises an intimate "cyclopaedia of the industry, the want, and the vice" (xv) of the urban poor—a record of the their own stories told in their "own 'unvarnished' language" (xv). Interpreting his methodologies, contemporary scholars have underscored the ways in which Mayhew's expedition metaphors and ethnographic taxonomies reinforced the racial, geographical, and linguistic separation of the poor from other classes of English Victorians.[5] Underpinning this logic, as Simon Joyce indicates in his recent study of "literary geographies," is Mayhew's apparent preference for viewing "the London underclass as a distinctive social or cultural formation" rather than a "strictly determined economic class" (107).

The compatibility of and the tension between ethnographic and economic explanations for crime can be glimpsed in popular texts, judicial procedures, and legislative committees where a causal correlation between class status and criminal behavior became an axiomatic construct for addressing the collective experience of crime and its attendant anxieties. Joyce isolates the interpretive significance of the relationship between the forces of "capitalist accumulation" and the features of criminal character in this public discussion:

> [T]his is the key issue in midcentury debates about the etiology of crime, since there was a general agreement that its existence closely correlated with the quality of life in the slums: the question which followed was whether slum inhabitants themselves were to blame, or the social and economic conditions into which they were born and lived. (106)

Moreover, Joyce explains, the discourse of crime prevention stems from the "different answers to this question" which "helped to determine what combative schemes were developed and practiced, ranging from conservative calls for more police and slum clearance, through liberal reform measures aimed at improving environmental and social conditions, to Chartist or socialist platforms which saw those conditions as the by-product of political disenfranchisement and capitalist economics" (106–7). But, Joyce aptly notes, the difference between left and right strategies can be "difficult to maintain in practice" (247), and his overview of etiological theories and "combative schemes" highlights not only the ubiquity but also the contingency of the epistemology of class as it became entangled in and destabilized by shifting political alignments, competing ideological constructs, and evolving urban geographies. In the case of street ballads, seen to represent the geographically determined criminal tendencies of slumlife and the culturally debased economies of cheap print, the processes of entanglement and destabilization often played out in the context of specific murders and executions.

The appeal of establishing ethnographic and geographic, rather than economic, narratives of causation can be partly attributed to the popular and panic-inducing phraseology of "the dangerous classes" ("*les classes dangereuses*"), which, as David Philips explains, was coined in Paris in 1840 by H. A. Frégier and "was quickly turned into English and applied by some writers to the dangerous lower orders of Britain as well" (81). "The image of the 'dangerous classes,'" Philips explains, "united the threat to person and property of ordinary crime, with the wider threat posed to the whole society by a militant and possibly revolutionary working class" (81). At mid-century, as the demand for accurate and verifiable national crime statistics led to virtual inventories of these putative dangerous classes, questions arose concerning the effects of asymmetrical and inconsistent methods—across decades and regions—employed in collecting and interpreting the annual returns. While in 1810, when such data collection and analysis began, records suggested that "about one person in every seven was a pauper, a vagrant, or a criminal" (Radzinowicz 239), decades on, the measuring of crime rates was complicated by the redefining of criminal acts, and, as a result, "perception and practice were not completely synchronized" (Taylor 2). Nevertheless, as statistics were tabulated and published, vigilant Victorians began to carefully evaluate the meanings and interpret the warnings embedded in the numbers. In his review of a half-century of crime statistics, for example, Jelinger C. Symons analyzed the "fearful" social picture that recent statistics painted and warned Victorians to act immediately:

> Every country has its dangerous class. It consists not only of criminals, paupers and persons whose conduct is obnoxious to the interests of society, but of the proximate body of people who are within reach of its contagion, and continually swell its number. The magnitude of the dangerous class in England probably exceeds that of any European nation, and is largely increasing. However essential some political reforms may be, and others may become, any indirect remedies for an evil so urgent as this may well be postponed to the consideration of prompt, practical and direct means of attacking it. (1)

In Symons's desperate calls for an aggressive pragmatism—in order to prevent England's sinking deeper into criminality than any other European nation—we can glimpse the reactionary agendas and the reformist molds that shaped crime-class etiologies.

Operating within a similar rhetorical framework, the author of "Causes of the Increase in Crime" (1844), published in *Blackwood's*, explains that the working classes are criminal because they undergo a "demoralization among the vast crowd" in which "restraints of character, relationship, and vicinity are, in great measure, lost . . ." (7).⁶ Their numbers and associations render them criminal because "individual responsibility is lost among the multitudes" (13). In the next volume of *Blackwood's*, the journal presents a more overt Tory stance, accusing the Liberals of ignoring a profoundly disturbing increase in crime and seeking a misguided course of benevolent legal and prison reforms. Amidst metaphors of infectious contagion and rushing water, crime is presented as a problem of class uprising:

> Let us therefore no longer deceive ourselves, or attempt to deceive others. Crime is making extraordinary and unprecedented progress amongst us; it is advancing with a rapidity unparalleled in any other European state: if not arrested, it will come to render the country unbearable; and will terminate in multiplying to such an extent *"les classes dangereuses,"* as they have been denominated by the French, as, on the first serious political convulsion, may come to endanger the state. ("The Increase of Crime" 545)

In proclaiming the "extraordinary" and "unprecedented progress" of crime, such public conversations stirred anxieties about working-class organizing while essentially placing responsibility for overcrowding and urbanization on the poor. Government responses included legislating increased police surveillance in poor areas; developing and revising penitentiary and prison systems; enforcing and manipulating existing criminal laws, such as the Vagrancy Act of 1824, which defined and criminalized "idle and disorderly" acts of "rogues and vagabonds"; and designing and passing new crime bills, such as the 1869 Habitual Criminals Act, which accommodated the supervision, surveillance, and suspicion of former offenders and future offenders with inferences about "circumstance" and "character" (Wiener, *Reconstructing* 150). Meanwhile, assessments of class also informed strict common law notions of individual responsibility, applications of the Royal Prerogative of Mercy, and movements for the abolition of public execution.

While many discussions of working-class criminality imagined revolutionary upheaval and thus betrayed fundamental concerns about the accumulation of capital and the protection of property, reflections on murder also inspired wholesale indictments of the working classes. Sir Samuel Martin, a judge serving on the Capital Punishment Commission that oversaw parliamentary reconsideration of state execution in 1866, expressed the belief that murder is quite simply the exclusive domain of the lower classes:

> [F]or the purpose of forming a real judgment upon the efficacy of Capital Punishments you must have recourse to persons who are well acquainted with

the lower classes in this country, and . . . no man who is not is competent to give an opinion on the subject. It very seldom occurs that any person in the middle class of life is indicted for murder. (*Report of the Capital Punishment Commission* Q 245: 36)

With no acknowledgment of the class inequalities inherent in policing citizens and indicting criminals, Martin maintains that "real judgment" on the "efficacy of Capital Punishments" requires familiarity with working-class subjects, who constitute England's reserves of potential murderers. In order to benefit from the working-class citizenry's collective experience of and expertise in murder—and with the integrity of important parliamentary deliberations resting on their insights—the commission summoned policemen, figures "well acquainted with the lower classes," to describe and transcribe the working-class stance on murder and execution. Purporting to require access to their murderous voices and criminal psychologies, the commission hears the testimony of policemen-informants, who, having interpreted physiognomies and overheard conversations, serve as character witnesses for and behavioral experts on the entirety of Britain's working-class population. Although working-class Britons certainly performed police work, the commission's decision to restrict their interviews to policemen reified the characteristic silencing of the lower classes in a national conversation largely about them.

In *Apprehending the Criminal* (1992), Marie-Christine Leps presents an intertextual analysis of criminality in order to consider the "relation between the status of a discursive practice (as scientific, informative, or entertaining discourse), its mandate in the social production of knowledge, and the limits of its sayable" (3). Examining how criminology's "textual production of 'criminal man' as an object of scientific knowledge was entirely determined by intertextual ideological maxims on race, sex, class, and morality" (47), she notes its role in "serv[ing] to legitimate the broader development of social management policies for the supervision, discipline, and control of the 'lower orders' through better knowledge of deviance in all its forms" (132). The press, meanwhile, "worked to incite, entertain, and distract the public into recognition of hegemonic truths" (132). Emerging from these discursive practices, Leps contends, was a normative "consensual 'we,'" which, constituted "through its opposition to crime (economic, political, moral) and its perpetrators" (73), formed a "public united in its need for protection from criminal deviance" (132). While Leps's analytical conclusions highlight late-Victorian criminology in particular, her discussion of the construction of a consensual and concerned citizenry in opposition to a deviant and criminal class aptly characterizes the logic informing the theories and policies of earlier decades. Overlooking the generic strategies and political references of broadside ballads, Leps argues that "[s]uch measures were met with silence: working-class groups did not voice any systematic opposition, as no one could effectively side with criminals in social discourse" (132).

Insofar as genre can be construed as a system, the collective work of the crime ballads might be considered a fairly "systematic opposition" to circulating ideologies of criminality. In important ways, the class-inflected logics of criminal discourse, forged in the early-Victorian period, influenced the creation and the reception of crime ballads throughout the century. Responding to a hegemonic model that favored statistical prophecies of cultural doom, privileged the political anxieties of the propertied classes, and supported the prejudicial inclinations of the judiciary, ballads often adopted a counterdiscursive stance. In their locally contextualized and aesthetically stylized representations of crime, street ballads broached class politics, criminal theories, judicial procedures, and penal policies in explicit and concrete terms. With the trope of the astonished witness and the criminal poet, ballads narrowed the distance between the criminal other and the "consensual 'we.'" While often deconstructing institutional and ideological divisions between citizens and convicts, however, ballads also found ways to side against the state (and its binary logic) without simply siding with the criminal. Simultaneously advocating alternate readings of crimes, questioning already established punishments, and decrying the actions of murderers, ballads introduced uncomfortable ambiguities and uncertainties into the discourse of crime and punishment. In doing so, they articulated a political sensibility concerned with the vexed and overdetermined relationship to poverty, policing, and punishment that characterized the lives of working-class citizens. Cultivating an aesthetic of immediacy and particularity—with eyewitness accounts of crimes and lyrical autobiographies of murderers—ballads claimed a poetic form of political speech with which to contest the ideological foundations of judicial and penal systems.

While class operated as a heuristic for explaining crime, it also suggested associations between bad behavior and bad poetry. Given the widespread insistence on the inherent deviance of the working classes, it is not surprising that street ballads about murder and execution, entangled within this network of presumptions about class and criminality, were often deemed accomplices to crime or that ballad singers, whose songs were believed to foster immorality and to glorify transgression, were suppressed by the police (Radzinowicz 275). Confident that the slums produced criminals, not poets, critics envisioned causal links between ballad depravity and ballad production in London's economically depressed Seven Dials district, where ballad printers operated and where "order [was] maintained by an extra force of policemen, and the first symptoms of riot [were] summarily suppressed" (Smith, *The Little World* 252). Even a somewhat sympathetic article in *The National Review* remains wary of the neighborhoods that curious parties must traverse in order to locate a ballad singer. Disgusted by the abundance of debris and filth, the author proves mindful of the artistic void that will inevitably greet intrepid ballad scouts (and interested periodical readers) seeking out "some unspeakable ditty" sung in a "brazen twang" (398): "They will scarcely find a gleam of poetic power to repay them for weltering in whole seas of slip-slop" ("Street Ballads" 399). Punning, perhaps, on the gory "weltering" so common in ballad crime scenes, this author maintains that these intriguing but disappointing curiosities are both socially polluted and poetically debased.

Like their working-class authors and audiences, these slum-dwelling ballads are demoralized and disempowered, criminalized and ghettoized, silenced and suppressed. Marked by the class hierarchies of urban geography, they appear tainted by the vulgar technologies of mass-production. In them, the voices of the murderous poor flowed forth in badly composed songs, creating a flood of cheap commodities, defying respectable mores, and threatening public safety. Such frightful ideas about working-class production and consumption of ballads have contributed not only to scholarly dismissals of their aesthetic sophistication but also to widespread suspicion of their criminal tendencies. Appearing in late-Victorian England as the ballad trade waned, several classed ethnographies of the ballad trade paired aesthetic degeneration and moral debasement. John Ashton, who collected ballads as records of "social manners and customs" in *Modern Street Ballads* (1888) and lamented their late-nineteenth-century decline, nevertheless disputed their artistic value: "taking them as a whole, we must fain confess that art as applied to these Ballads was at its very lowest. Their literary merit is not great—but what can you expect for half-a-crown?" (Ashton vii–viii). Similarly, an article in *The Quarterly Review*, noting that "the metres employed" are "lawless" ("The Poetry of Seven Dials" 385), explains, "though they teach little or no history, they show, at least, what kind of Poetry finds the most favourable reception and the readiest sale among our lowest classes" (404).

When Francis J. Child, England's dedicated collector of folk ballads, documented the "ancient national poetry" of the rural folk (366), he vigorously differentiated England's traditional rural populace from its modern urban masses: "The vulgar ballads of our day, the 'broadsides' which were printed in such huge numbers in England . . . belong to a different genus; they are products of a low kind of *art,* and most of them are, from a literary point of view, thoroughly despicable and worthless" (367). Child's references to such "huge numbers" and "a different genus" suggest a hierarchical taxonomy of literary culture, in which ballads, by virtue of their accessibility and their modernity, occupy the realm of the "low," the "despicable," and the "worthless." Fully invested in the cooptation and authority of rural peasant voices, the pastoral romance of national culture cannot abide or acknowledge the cultural evolution or literary innovation of a working-class population in an industrialized state. Degraded by urban locales and signifying modern corruption, they defile a national culture and sully an antique past.

With similar concerns, Sabine Baring-Gould, the collector responsible for preserving the British Library's massive broadside collection, launched one of the most comprehensive assaults on the literary character of the street ballad. In an essay entitled "Broadside Ballads," Baring-Gould criticizes, and virtually criminalizes, street ballad authors for favoring "the story of murder" and elevating the "vulgar assassin" to heroic status, and he explicitly blames street ballads for the sad demise of the "old romantic" ballads (190). Exhibiting a flagrant disdain for national tradition and an "overweening" (212) faith in their own poetic powers, he explains, street balladeers audaciously penned their own unsavory verses while opportunistically purloining random lines from rural ballads when inspiration failed them. Instead of collecting and preserving the pastoral songs of the country folk, acts which would have popularized the ancient rural ballads and edified modern urban readers, "these pot-poets loafed about in the low London public-houses, where it was only by rarest chance that a country man, fresh from the fields, and woods, and downs, with his memory laden with the fragrance of the rustic music, was to be found" (213).

Languishing in "public-houses" and possessing "neither taste, nor ear, nor genius," they "poured forth floods of atrocious rhymes, and of utter balderdash, as was required as an occasion offered, and as they stood in need of half-crowns" (213).[7] With "half-crowns" as their muses, these drunken bards alternately cannibalized ancient texts and spewed poetic filth. Aggravating these acts of gross literary indecency are their sinister affiliations with the morally unregenerate and economically opportunistic broadside print industry, which indiscriminately printed "the vile stuff composed by the half-tipsy, wholly-stupid band" (213) and, disseminating degenerate poetry throughout the streets and marketplaces of the nation, "did much to corrupt the taste of the peasant" (213). In Baring-Gould's formulation, the positively criminal street-ballad writers, mired in urban sleaze, become "vulgar assassin[s]" guilty of the foulest of literary crimes. With "atrocious rhymes" and "vile stuff" as their weapons, they have driven ancient rural balladry, the literary essence of the nation, to an ignominious extinction.

Baring-Gould's accusations—in which aesthetic ineptitude and criminal aptitude as well as bad taste and bad manners come to define the murderous verses of the urban poor—participate in a larger aesthetic argument that demarcates the domains of artistic achievement and criminal sensibility along class lines. In an odd yoking of elderly women and the newspaper-reading masses (perhaps connected by a perceived lack of education or taste), Thomas de Quincey, the enthusiastic advocate of murder as fine art, dismisses the possibility of interpretive sophistication when the masses read about murder. In "On Murder Considered as One of the Fine Arts" (1827), he writes, "As to old women, and the mob of newspaper readers, they are pleased with anything, provided it is bloody enough. But the mind of sensibility requires something more" (1008). De Quincey, interested in establishing a set of refined and structured aesthetic "principles of murder"—"not with a view to regulate your practice, but your judgment" (1008)—sees a lack of representational purpose and intellectual complexity in catalogues of bloody detail and gory imagery. In this formulation, the cognitive shortcomings of an unrefined mob and a populist aesthetic defined by quantities of blood combine to debase the aesthetics of murder. Along similar lines, in *The Picture of Dorian Gray* (1891), Wilde's Lord Henry Wotton articulates late-Victorian aestheticism in classed terms when he confidently explains to Dorian that he is simply incapable of murder because "[c]rime belongs exclusively to the lower orders." He adds, "I don't blame them in the smallest degree. I should fancy that crime was to them what art is to us, simply a method of procuring extraordinary sensations" (252). Within this statement about the procurement of "[e]xtraordinary sensations" lies an aesthetic distinction between the sensationalist excess of criminal acts and the intellectual restraint of aestheticist arts.

Coded in various formats and cited with impressive frequency—by both historical figures and fictional characters with both playful irony and sincere gravity—these ideas about practice and judgment, sensibility and vulgarity, crime and culture, insist that the theme of murder presents a representational obstacle for the working-class imagination. Each of these literary theories of murder exhibits a characteristic reluctance on the part of the middle and upper classes to ascribe textual power to the lower classes, and, demarcating the realm of high literary culture, they also reflect a pervasive investment in the notion of their cultural illiteracy. Collapsing working-class subjects into an indistinguishable mass, adamantly denying them the ability to aestheticize crime, and liberally bestowing their ability to commit crimes, they uphold the criminality of the working classes while overlooking any artistic or political sensibility in criminal matters. Because crime substitutes for art, it would seem, the "lower orders" stand capable of committing murders but incapable of representing them.

Retheorizing the "poetic power," aesthetic sensibility, and cultural work of crime ballads—the most popular, profitable, and accessible genre of Victorian crime writing—requires consideration of these persistent stereotypes that shaped the content and the context of street literature. For with their representations of astonishment and lamentation, balladeers issued a substantial working-class reply to the nightmare of a dangerous and murderous mass. In "unvarnished" language and with a "brazen twang," they challenged the totalizing categories of social scientific epistemologies, the ethical integrity of the criminal code, and the aesthetic and political discourses of the "consensual 'we.'"

"Wondering at Crime": Moral Pretexts and Criminal Politics

Confident of crime balladry's ethnographic import, an article in *The National Review* presented it to a middle-class readership as "one of those windows through which we may get a glimpse at that very large body of our fellow-citizens of whom we know so little" ("Street Ballads" 399). When peering through this window, however, its author advocates reading practices that simplify ballad ethics and depoliticize ballad contents. Distinguishing crime ballads from "political ballads," which explicitly cite government legislation or specific statesmen, the essay examines a few murder ballads merely to exhibit their uniformity: "the whole of the last dying speeches and confessions, trials and sentences, from whatever part of the country they come, run in the same form of quaint and circumstantial detail: appeals to Heaven, to young men, to young women, to Christians in general, and moral reflections" (405). Adding that "[w]e have seldom met with one of a different character" (405), the author strips these songs of poetic distinction, textual variety, and political intentionality while overestimating the significance and misrepresenting the consistency of moralistic frameworks.

While many Victorian critics expressed disdain for the criminal reputations and murderous intentions of crime ballads, contemporary critics have established a strong tradition of dismissing crime balladry on the grounds that it is poetically, politically, and morally conservative. Influenced by a critical legacy of ethnographic and historical analysis and limited by fixed definitions of political speech and textual complexity, contemporary studies have emphasized the language of didacticism and the limitations of genre. These commentaries, surprisingly consistent, almost always imagine a comparative narrative history in which ballads serve as foils to more successful and significant political protests or literary projects.[8]

Accusations of conservatism have not gone wholly uncontested. Douglas Jerrold, for example, blamed the moral mandates of an increasingly conservative mainstream culture for the broadside ballad's decline: "[t]he public ear has become dainty, fastidious, hypocritical; hence, the Ballad-Singer languishes and dies" (qtd. in Hindley, *History* xxxviii). More recently, acknowledging the threat of censorship, Richard Altick has suggestively articulated the dilemma of ballad morality as an imposition "from above" rather than an initiative "from below." The moral frame, he argues, was often simply "a device employed by the printer's hireling lyricists to fend off the persistent complaints of the pious that crime literature of the streets was morally poisonous" (49). Such reflections on the precise causes and effects of ballad moralizing remind us of the street ballad's dynamic public presence, and they suggest that, in foregrounding aphorisms and overemphasizing uniformity, we overlook other important features of the genre.

Remedying the problem of critical literacy in the study of street ballads is most easily accomplished by examining ballads. For in them we see that murder ballads join other surviving broadsides of various genres to reveal a consistently and explicitly class-conscious approach to criminal representation, and even brief examples sufficiently demonstrate their aesthetic diversity and ethical nuance. Moral advice, for example, often appeared in precepts that were either marginal to or overwhelmed by the act of murder, and where tangential or inverted, such advisories subverted or obscured conventional moral authority. At a time when emotional, psychological, and medical causes for crime were being considered, while common law rigorously resisted mitigation, traditional explanations continued to serve—often with ironic implications.

In many ballads, for example, Satan, bearing the burden of some, if not all, criminal responsibility, introduces legal and ethical complications. "He was by Satan led" and "he with Satan did connive" frequently explained sin, absolved guilt, or sensationalized crimes. In the "Copy of Verses" printed or "Particulars of the Life, Trial, Confession, and Execution of Courvoisier" (1840) (figure 3), when the condemned aristocrat-killer cries out, "the fiend exulting stood before me / For he had worked my overthrow," he disrupts the unitary nature of criminal responsibility. Moreover, interpreting his crime with a Christian mythos, this ballad criminal intimates the political versatility and ethical ambiguity of Christian discourse in which practices of retribution conflict with notions of forgiveness. In "Going to See a Man Hanged" (1840), Thackeray records the experience of witnessing Courvoisier's hanging and reminds his readers that the ostensibly simple identity of Christian England is, in fact, politically complex. In a sharply ironic depiction of this Christian nation, he explains, "government, a Christian government, gives us a feast every now and then: it agrees, that is to say, a majority in the two houses agrees, that for certain crimes it is necessary that a man should be hanged by the neck" (157). In a similar way, in "The Life, Trial, Sentence, and Execution of S. Adams for the Murder of His Sister-in-Law, Martha Page" (1859), the condemned speaker challenges distinctions between himself and his audience using a Christian notion of original sin: "Do not condemn before you listen, / None is without their crimes on earth; / None without some stain upon him, / We are all sinners from our birth." Whether constituting allusions to committed abolitionists or acknowledging an audience of fellow sinners, the "feeling Christians" so often hailed in street ballads, and so often decried by critics as evidence of political conservatism, evoke the moral complexities of apprehending and punishing criminals.

Further demonstrating the ways in which crime balladry created opportunities for interpretive license, "Miles Weatherhill, the Young Weaver, and his

Figure 3
Particulars of the Life, Trial, Confession, and Execution of Courvoisier. Dying Speeches Portfolio 271: Hollis no. 8094160. Courtesy of Special Collections Department, Harvard Law School Library.

Sweetheart, Sarah Bell" (1868) challenges expected moral linkages between criminal acts and crime prevention. The lesson attached to Weatherhill's slaying of Jane Smith, who interfered with his courtship of the young Sarah Bell, is not, "Thou shalt not kill," but rather, "Where true love is planted, there let it dwell." Targeting potential meddlers rather than potential rogues, the ballad proposes an unexpected schema of causation and remedy. If romantic chaperoning and sexual propriety incite lethal passions, and if didacticism should address the cause and not the effect, then the nurturing of "true love" offers a particularly pleasant solution to the national problem of crime.

We might similarly consider the subversive meanings made possible by the subtleties of poetic form and literary language. For example, in another Courvoisier ballad, "Trial, Sentence, Confession, and Execution of F. B. Courvoisier for the Murder of Lord Wm. Russell" (1840), moral outrage is subjected to the humorous effects of alliterative flourishes when his murderous actions are diagnosed as a problem of "pilfering passions." Not merely accidents of mass production or hasty composition, such moments of suggestive irony and irreverent humor suggest the awareness of authors and audiences of their verbal and political impact. Attentive to the interplay of genre and discourse, we can read such moments of poetic play and criminolegal wit in the context of Victorian laws, trials, and punishments in which they circulated.

With more overt references to historical context, which generated institutional critiques on a larger scale, ballads often redirected moral judgments away from the crimes and punishments of individual criminals and toward structural analyses of social inequalities. The song of the "Dreadful Murder at Eriswell," for example, sidelines the condemnation of two poachers who murdered a groundskeeper, preferring instead to argue for the repeal of "those cursed Game Laws," which "has been the cause, / Of many a life's blood to be shed." With such ethical surprises and political allusions, balladeers, enjoying the interpretive liberties conferred by poetic license, privileged topical assessments of the crimes they documented. Linking social inequalities to criminal activities, they defamiliarized the moral conventions of criminal discourse and unraveled the didactic threads of a centuries-old genre. In these cases, ballads implicitly or explicitly absolved individuals of criminal responsibility while providing contexts that indicted social hierarchies. Representing crimes and punishments in both ethically playful and politically sobering ways, these maneuvers invited readers to reconsider the implications of particular crimes as well as more general theories of criminality.

In some cases, specific crimes provided opportunities to overturn expedient divisions between the dangerous masses and the respectable classes. For example, "Murder of A Wife at Ashburnham, Near Hastings," highlights a scene of inverted class relations when a group of "servants" and "labourers," acting as policing authorities, hunt Jeremiah Stubberfield, the son of an "aged, wealthy sire" who has fled after murdering his wife:

> They did pursue the murderer,
> They in numbers went along,
> Searched the hedges and the ditches,
> Dragged the river and the ponds;

Traveling "in numbers" (the stereotypical working-class mob), these upstanding laborers defy ordinary moral hierarchies when they take extraordinary measures to apprehend a wealthy, propertied, and hitherto respectable wife-killer. The crime's political force takes shape in the image of household servants and farm laborers "pursu[ing] the murderer"—their fugitive master and landlord—across the countryside.

Similarly, references to the physical and emotional pain of capital punishment, the judicial context of all murder and execution ballads, created troubling juxtapositions of disgust for perpetrators of outrageous violence, empathy for their unsuspecting victims, and sympathy for condemned criminals. "The Execution of Five Pirates" (1864), for example, emphasizes the contradictory responses elicited by execution: "And though they were not fit to live, / We pity to them on the gallows, / Englishmen could not deny." The pairing of ethical disgust and undeniable pity, which reconnects marginalized criminals to mainstream sentiments, is so common in crime balladry that we must consider it a central trope. When the processes of abhorring the crime and abhorring the punishment are conjoined, ballads express the irresolvable moral dilemma of capital punishment, which answers one killing with another.

Reiterating this dilemma, ballads often realign margin and center in ways that recall Stallybrass and White's definition of transgression. In tracing relations between social margins and symbolic centers, Stallybrass and White adopt Barbara Babcock's definition of "symbolic inversion." Babcock writes, "'Symbolic inversion' may be broadly defined as any act of expressive behavior which inverts, contradicts, abrogates, or in some fashion presents an alternative to commonly held cultural codes, values and norms be they linguistic, literary or artistic, religious, social and political" (qtd. in Stallybrass and White 17). In the aforementioned examples, from Satan manipulating murderers to poor laborers hunting wealthy wife-killers to bad pirates inspiring sympathy pangs, ballad writers deploy the rhetorical power of inverted meanings. Even in these brief excerpts, we can see how balladeers politicized as they publicized scandalous crimes and spectacular punishments. Rather than simply applying the discourses of conventional moral authority, ballad writers often explored the classed politics and the collective experience of crime and punishment with nuanced narrative details and allegorized symbolic inversions. Diminishing the significance of conventional moralistic framing devices, the inclusion of digressive and unexpected references to mitigating factors, ethical conflicts, and class tensions opened up the street ballad genre to poetic and political variety.

As balladeers exploited the poetic and political opportunities of historical crimes, they often exposed the internal contradictions and institutional interests of criminal policies. In "John Bull, Can You Wonder At Crime?" (figure 4) the narrator criticizes the privileged classes of the nation, with their "riches in heaps stowed away, / Mouldy with age and mildew," for willfully mystifying the rising crime rate while impoverishing (and endangering) the working classes. Apostrophizing John Bull, and continuing with an ironically charged "sir," the speaker suggests the economic roots of crime by noting discrepancies between England's scenes of abject poverty and the hoarded wealth of the nation and its wondering elite: "Your gold to yourself you confine, / Where a little would make a great change, sir, / In our terrible increase of crime." Describing temptation and desperation, the ballad contrasts the harassment and imprisonment of earnest, hard-working, "poor Costermongers" with the relative impunity of "grinning," pick-pocketing "rogue[s]." Meanwhile, "poor needle girls," who are "[t]rying their best to exist," the ballad explains, inevitably resort to sexual labor: "Can you wonder at their prostitution, / When blood-sucking forms barely give / Enough to ward off destitution." The narrator then admonishes "Mr. Bull," asking him to acknowledge the modest aspirations and vulnerable sensibilities of these impoverished girls, as they function "[w]ith feelings as keen and as tender, / As your proud city ladies, remember." Having gentrified criminality with an indictment of the parasitic pastimes of the nation's wealthy, the violent effects of capital accumulation, and the predatory varieties of roguish privilege, the narrator critiques, in an authoritative and commonsensical tone, the lingering perplexity of the nation: "And still you keep wondering at crime."

"John Bull, Can You Wonder at Crime" sketches an England in which the rarefied discourse of criminal theory and the policing mechanisms of the state justify the continued arrogance and privilege of an elite class, which masks its investments in the continuation of poverty with an anxious rhetoric about the "increase in crime." Exasperated by this situation, which is presented in this ballad as a calculated performance, the narrator commands, "Go and listen to the great pangs of hunger / And never more wonder at crime." The narrator also prescribes a remedy for both the disingenuous bewilderment of the nation and the debilitating suffering of the poor: "[j]ust visit the dens of the poor" and "scatter your hoarded up gold." Demanding a redistribution of wealth and an end to mystification, the ballad narrator inverts the relationship between expertise and common sense and removes moral authority from the propertied classes and places it at the criminalized margins.

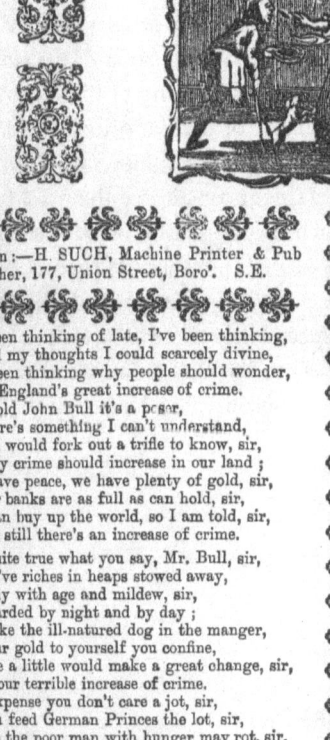

JOHN BULL, CAN YOU WONDER AT CRIME?

London:—H. SUCH, Machine Printer & Publisher, 177, Union Street, Boro'. S.E.

I've been thinking of late, I've been thinking,
  And my thoughts I could scarcely divine,
I've been thinking why people should wonder,
  At England's great increase of crime.
Cries old John Bull it's a poser,
  There's something I can't understand,
And I would fork out a trifle to know, sir,
  Why crime should increase in our land;
We have peace, we have plenty of gold, sir,
  Our banks are as full as can hold, sir,
We can buy up the world, so I am told, sir,
  Yet still there's an increase of crime.

It's quite true what you say, Mr. Bull, sir,
  We've riches in heaps stowed away,
Mouldy with age and mildew, sir,
  Guarded by night and by day;
But like the ill-natured dog in the manger,
  Your gold to yourself you confine,
Where a little would make a great change, sir,
  In our terrible increase of crime.
For expense you don't care a jot, sir,
  You feed German Princes the lot, sir,
While the poor man with hunger may rot, sir,
  Mr. Bull, can you wonder at crime.

Can you wonder at crime any longer,
  When you see the police on their beat
Preventing the poor Costermongers
  From earning their bread in the street;
While the rogue on the stool stands grinning,
  At the broad open face of the day,
Your pocket he will pick for a shilling,
  And the law cannot touch him he'll say:
He defies all the police divisions,
  He laughs with contempt and derision,
While you send the poor Coster to prison,
  Mr. Bull, can you wonder at crime.

I am sure you will own, Mr. Bull, sir.
  Temptation is hard to resist!
Look at our poor needle girls, sir,
  Trying their best to exist;
Can you wonder at their prostitution,
  When blood-sucking forms barely give
Enough to ward off destitution,
  A girl tho' she's poor she must live.
The poor needle girl, God defend her,
  With feelings as keen and as tender,
As your proud city ladies, remember,
  Mr. Bull, can you wonder at crime.

Can you wonder at crime when you see
  Rich lords with a star on their breast,
At marriage time laughing with glee,
  A disgrace to their title and crest;
While rogues like those are protected,
  They will laugh at the strength of our law,
Mr. Bull, it must be expected,
  That crime will increase more and more.
Don't it fill you with dire consternation?
  It's a shame and a great degradation,
To let such as these rule our nation,
  And still you keep wondering at crime.

Just think when you're drinking your wine, sir,
  How the poor of old England are fed,
While you with your rich friends can dine, sir,
  It's a godsend for them to get bread.
Just visit the dens of the poor, sir,
  Such a sight you will rarely behold,
The fever dens go and explore, sir,
  And scatter your hoarded up gold;
For a little would soon break asunder
  The chain that the poor suffer under,
Go and listen to the great pangs of hunger
  And never more wonder at crime.

Figure 4
John Bull, Can You Wonder at Crime? © British Library Board. All Rights Reserved.

With a similar attention to the politics of crime and class, ballads about the metropolitan police, which constituted a ballad genre in their own right, problematized the deployment of a centralized police force and the recruitment of policemen from the working classes. These ballads frequently questioned the methods of distinguishing between the state and the people and scrutinized the practices of delineating power and its subjects. Proclaiming that "in the country all around, / The people do severely frown," "Complaints Against the New Police" considers the financing of the new police force and documents the activities of a petitioning underclass. Their political organizing offsets the silencing tactics of an overzealous police state in which public speech constitutes provocation and justifies incarceration: "And if a word to them you say, / They'll drag you off without delay / Unto the Station-House." The persona of the upwardly mobile policeman also appears in many ballads. "I'm One of the New Police," for example, highlights the performance quality of the uniform: "My gloves of white, my coat of blue, / My dignity increase" (qtd. in Hindley, *Life* 207).

A long-running joke about police harassment constituted the most popular ballad characterization of the police, which began in 1829 with Peel's Metropolitan Police Act but which Hindley traces well into the Victorian era. In this comical scenario, policemen are presented as gluttonous mutton thieves who attempt to capitalize on the illusion of respectability and the access to authority (and mutton) secured by their uniforms. "The New Policeman, and the Somers Town Butcher" confronts the policeman and deconstructs his props:

> Hollo! New Police,
> Who in blue coats strut on,
> Your fame you won't increase
> By stealing joints of mutton.
> Who would e'er suppose,
> In such handsome rigging,
> Spick and span new clothes,
> Men would go a prigging? (qtd. in Hindley 203)

With the anxious topic of crime depicted as a question of "prigging" and the mechanisms of state supervision reduced to "handsome rigging," the ballad parodies cultural anxieties about increasing crime and mocks the disciplinary power of the police.

In ballad scenarios of poetic justice, mutton-thieving policemen often suffer a humiliating comeuppance at the hands of an unsympathetic judicial bureaucracy. In "The Lamentation in Newgate of the Police-Man, Who Boned the Mutton," the sentencing judge invokes the criminal stereotypes that code the desperation of urban poverty as the dissipation of a criminal class. As he narrates his "downfall," the lamenting policeman receives a judgment commonly passed on the poor in English courts:

"We are certain, Mr. Jones,
You intended for to take away
Both mutton, meat and bones.
You did not steal the meat for want
To pay you was not willing
When you stole the meat, you had
In your pocket fifteen shillings."

Effecting a symbolic inversion and subversion of official power, this narrative logic is crucial to the ballad's comedic and political content. In establishing his criminal intent, negating the existence of "want," asserting his disdain for honesty, ruling that he simply was not "willing" to pay, and concluding that he "must in confinement dwell," the court demotes the policeman to the criminal classes. Replete with parodic reversals and comical self-references—from the exaggerated lamenting of the former policeman ("O the mutton! / That fatal bit of mutton!") to the contrived villainous testimony of the "cruel greasy Butcher"—this ballad manipulates the metonymic significance of the police in order to analyze the social effects of law enforcement and judicial practices. Applied to the police rather than the criminal, and mutton-thieving rather than murder, these lamentation tropes exemplify the self-parodic and self-reflexive engagements of the genre.[9]

The ethical and interpretive dilemmas surrounding murder, of course, offered balladeers more shocking subject matter and inspired more complex representational strategies. When deploying murder for the purpose of cultural critique, ballads often broached their political arguments more forcefully and more gravely. Of murder's symbolic function, Foucault writes, "Murder establishes the ambiguity of the lawful and the unlawful" (*Rivière* 206). This ambiguity arises because "murder posits the relation between power and the people, stripped down to its essentials: the command to kill, the prohibition against killing; to be killed, to be executed; voluntary sacrifice, punishment inflicted; memory, oblivion. Murder prowls the confines of the law, on one side or the other, above or below it; it frequents power, sometimes against and sometimes with it" (206). A shorthand for dissecting the power relations that determined lawfulness and unlawfulness, murder effectively fragmented *and* condensed the circulating ideologies of crime and class. If murder "prowls" the borders of the lawful and the unlawful, it is not surprising that the class which was understood to exist at that same limit might buy and sell songs that scrutinized those explanations.

Contemplating the criminal broadside's popularity, Foucault reads its marketplace success as a fantasy of criminal resistance: "if these true stories of everyday history were received so avidly, if they formed part of the basic reading of the lower classes, it was because people found in them not only memories, but also precedents; the interest of 'curiosity' is also a political interest" (*Discipline and Punish* 68). Yet, in perceiving ballad popularity as a mark of criminal potential—and crime ballads as accomplices to or inspirations for crime—Foucault links, with stereotyping fascination, ballad reading and criminal activity. With respect to English street ballads in particular, "curiosity" and "political interest" intersect quite differently; the popularity of the crime ballads does not signify merely a fascination with blood or outlaws but, more, a critique of power. Because the law mandated death for murder and because most convicted murderers were working-class, the unlawful circumstances of particular crimes and the lawful deaths of the scaffold were of particular importance. And while murder exposed the relationships of power between the criminal and the state in the most explicit terms, it also accessed more intimate manifestations of power between murderers and their victims. For this reason, the often overwhelmingly graphic representations of specific crimes and the intricately politicized rendering of specific executions can be seen as attempts to claim interpretive authority.

An interest in mediating authority also informed the ways in which ballads constituted their audiences. For example, although many crime ballads constructed their audience as a collection of morally edified innocents, an equally significant number acknowledged an audience of murder tale aficionados schooled in the astonishing violence of individual criminals and state policies. The verses in the "Life, Trial, Character, Confession, and Execution of Stephen Forward" (1866), for instance, construct readers as crime history enthusiasts: "Of all the crimes we ever heard, of all the crimes we read, / Sure none on earth did ever know, a more sad dreadful deed." The narrator of the "Lamentation of J. Mapp" (1867) places Mapp's crime within a comparative framework: "Such a dreadful murder, as you may see, / Which we may compare to the Alton tragedy." Similarly, "The Liverpool Tragedies," printed on the broadsheet "Execution of John Gleeson Wilson," registers the crime's magnitude by citing notorious murderers, such as James Greenacre, whose ballads sold well into the millions in 1837. And "Lamentation of H. Lingley" (1867) references the notorious James Bloomfield Rush, whose execution ballad sold two and a half million copies in 1849. Lingley, the ballad informs us, will die "[o]n the very tree where Rush met his fate" and will lie "[b]y the side of Rush in a murderer's grave."

Such name-dropping implies a readership interested in historical crimes and executions and steeped in the knowledge of violent death, but it also reveals that ballad writers exploited anxieties about the pervasiveness of crime and invoked the prevailing crime-obsessed spirit of the age. The narrator of the "Lamentation of J. Mapp" reports:

> How sad and dreadful it is to state,
> The horrid murders that have been of late;
> In every quarter both far and near,
> Such atrocious deeds before this no one did hear.

These intertextual and historicist references ask readers to assess individual crimes against a backdrop of cultural history and to consider their national significance. Offering rough sketches of unprecedented "horrid murders" and "atrocious deeds," this comparativist mode undoubtedly served to heighten the marketplace appeal of ballads, but it also underscored the textual history of the ballads and the cultural literacy of their audience.

In each of these ballad techniques—ethical ambivalence, symbolic inversion, legal intervention, historical contextualization—we can see efforts to renegotiate moral equations and conduct political analyses. Their aesthetic innovation, political interests, and poetic variety remind us that crime balladeers continually renegotiated the relationships between generic conventions and historical events. As they selected content and shifted emphasis to create fictionalized representations of actual crimes, they produced meaningful tensions between the details of historical cases and the details of ballad crimes. In these tensions, we can glimpse the political charge of ballad poetics. With arguments about the criminal tendencies and moral primness of crime ballads delineated and dismantled, the remainder of this chapter explores the specific representational strategies of astonishing disclosures and last lamentations and considers the relationships between poetic crimes and historical criminals.

The Aesthetics of Astonishment: Acts of Murder and Scenes of Crime

Narrated from the point of view of an astonished witness, third-person astonishing disclosures proclaimed the news of crime to a shocked and saddened citizenry, and deploying their rubric of astonishment and disclosure, they parsed the complex meanings of murder. Rarely depicted as isolated instances of appalling deviance, murders appeared in these texts as socially entangled mishaps and wholly collective tragedies worthy of close scrutiny and sustained reflection. In privileging astonishment, they differentiated moral and aesthetic responses to crime. Their notorious "full particulars" of gruesome killings and blood-soaked crime scenes constructed a political aesthetic of murder rooted in the signifying power of murderous agency and hapless victimization.

Assessing the aesthetic dimensions of murder, Joel Black writes, "Our reactions to ... fictional representations of murder may range from horror to admiration, but whatever shock we experience will consist of aesthetic astonishment rather than of moral outrage" (9). This distinction between "moral outrage" and "aesthetic astonishment" sheds light on the repeated ballad promise of astonishing disclosures that would "make the blood run cold." As stylized violence proliferates in these songs of murder, aesthetic astonishment overtakes moral outrage as the genre's epistemological mode.

As legend has it, James Catnach, the publisher credited with bringing the crime ballad to new literary heights and unprecedented sales in the first half of the nineteenth century, extolled the textual power of "the most beautiful murder" (Mayhew 302) and thereby established a market value in which aesthetic criteria, not ethical dichotomies, informed the contemplation of "barbarous deeds" (Hindley, *Life* 361). The preference for contemplation over judgment also informed the advertising slogans used by ballad singers to peddle their scenes of murderous violence in the streets. Accordingly, "those connected with murder-patter" (Mayhew 302) conceived of their economic opportunities in aesthetic terms: "There's nothing beats a stunning good murder, after all" (223).[10] Recalling his own peripatetic investigations into the ballad trade while researching his *History of the Catnach Press* in August 1869, Charles Hindley explains that, even as a respectable scholar conducting research, he reacted not to the promise of a morality tale, but to the promise of gruesome detail:

> [O]ur ears voluntarily 'pricked up,' on hearing the old familiar sounds of a 'street, or running patterer' with the stereotyped sentences of 'Horrible.'—'Dreadful.'—'Remarkable letters founds on his person.'—'Cut down by a labouring man.'—'Quite dead.'—'Well-known in the town.'—'Hanging.'—'Coroner's Inquest.'—'Verdict.'—'Full particulars,'—'Most determined suicide.'—'Brutal conduct.'—&c., &c., *Only a ha'penny—Only a ha'penny!* (*History* x)

Conducting his study during the decline of the ballad trade, Hindley records his nostalgia for "old familiar sounds," but, in isolating the resonant "stereotyped sentences," he also documents the aesthetic project of the crime ballad marketplace. Framed in such energetic and exclamatory language, the components of "the most beautiful murder" privilege the poetics of astonishment and diminish the force of didacticism.

With their emphasis on violent agency ("most determined"), passionate excess ("brutal conduct"), and gory minutiae ("full particulars"), these songs required audiences to confront and consider the contingent and contentious meanings of murderous violence. The narrative strength of bloody descriptions and the iterative force of brutality contribute to what Martha Vicinus has described in general terms as the crime broadside's ability to "provide forms and language for understanding the daily violence of one's own life" and to "provid[e] readers with a means of interpreting and managing violence" (*Industrial Muse* 16). Astonishing disclosures in particular managed the theme of murder by forcing questions about the particular causes, the collective effects, and the social consequences of extreme violence.

Through the voice of an anonymous narrator, third-person ballads enumerate the full particulars of murders by elaborating on details gleaned from official sources. Such reconstructions embed the multiple perspectives of criminals, eyewitnesses, neighbors, policemen, and judges. Submitting details for our interpretation, ballad murders often involve planning stages, explanatory letters, and murderer-victim dialogues, which punctuate, disrupt, or incite violence, and they frequently dramatize fragments of official discourse, such as coroner reports or signed confessions, excerpts of which might be supplied in prose sections of the broadsides on which they appear. Recasting official information, ballads elaborate any idiosyncrasies that might serve the needs of aesthetic effect or political suggestion.

The interplay of historical record and fictional elaboration extends to ballad crime scenes, the remains of murderous force discovered by authorities and documented by ballad narrators. Offering meticulous renderings of the grotesque arrangement or bloody disposal of bodies, crime scenes fulfill the promise of astonishment and disclosure with scenes of stylized gore. It is thus via the poetics of astonishment that "full and energetic" representations of murder produce both riveting aesthetic scenes and complex ethical situations. The business of ballad writing mandated this aestheticized treatment of murder by attempting to supply the artistic flair overlooked by the historical criminal who, as Mayhew's informer reports, had no "regard for the interest of art and literature" (225).

In this strange collaboration, the murderer and the balladeer create grotesque bodily texts that develop the aesthetically overpowering and culturally resonant anatomy of a murder. Not simply a sensational or disinterested aesthetic, "the stunning good murder" voiced concerns about the social origins of murderous transgression and the cultural conditions of astonishing victimization. Exploring the social complexity of appalling violence, they demand interpretation—not outrage. In explicitly framing this terrible aesthetic in stunning or astonishing narratives, street ballads popularized an aesthetic of the sublime. In *A Philosophical Enquiry into the Origin of Our Ideas of the Sublime and Beautiful* (1757), Edmund Burke argues that astonishment constitutes the "effect of the sublime in its highest degree" (101), and his reflections on bodily pain and hideous objects assist in sorting out the strategies with which the murder ballad scrutinized the baffling conflicts between individual agency and social prohibition that surrounded murder and execution.

The affective force of astonishment also created opportunities for ethical impact, and, although critics have often aligned ballads with melodramatic forms in order to underscore their textual incompetence, more recent articulations of melodramatic forms are instructive in exploring the ethical complexities of ballad poetics. Peter Brooks's "rehabilitation" (xi) of melodrama in *The Melodramatic Imagination* (1976), for example, defines melodrama as a "mode of excess" that deploys the "aesthetics of astonishment" in order to engage moral conflicts. Explaining that melodrama enacts rhetoric of "overstatement and overemphasis" (36), which forces a confrontation with an evil that "astonishes" and "disarms" (34), Brooks concludes, "melodramatic rhetoric, and the whole expressive enterprise of the genre, represents a victory over repression" (41). Forcefully depicting that which has been subject to "censorships, accommodations, tonings-down" in other literary forms, melodrama "achieves plenitude of meaning" (41).

While ballads frequently privilege tragic plots or sublime aesthetics over melodramatic structures—and likewise astonishment over outrage—Brooks's "rehabilitation" of melodrama usefully acknowledges the signifying complexities inherent in the ostensibly reductive exhortations and clichéd hyperboles that frequently operated in melodramatic texts—and in street ballads. Viewing street ballads in a similarly rehabilitative mode, we can see that, like stage melodramas, they developed a confrontational aesthetics of astonishment and achieved a "plenitude of meaning" that produced an epistemology of ambivalence, differentiation, and critique. With a plenitude of violence in particular, they fostered new levels of astonishment as they configured collective distress, and, in unsettling aphoristic equations of innocence and guilt, ballads rendered murders as reflections of, rather than deviations from, mainstream Victorian culture.

Revising and challenging Brooks's psychologized schema, Elaine Hadley's *Melodramatic Tactics* (1995) envisions the "melodramatic mode" as an embodiment of a "polemical" and "reactionary rejoinder to social change" (3). It is a textual project, which, through "a productive friction" or "a creative disjunction," challenges cultural shifts within the market system of nineteenth-century capitalist production with a "resistant energy" that "emerges from what Jonathan Dollimore calls 'the inevitable incompleteness and surplus of control itself'" (10). Hadley briefly catalogues the stock features of this mode: "its familial narratives of dispersal and reunion, its emphatically visual renderings of bodily torture and criminal conduct, its atmospheric menace and providential plotting, its expressions of highly charged emotion, and its tendency to personify absolutes like good and evil" (3). Hadley's list of melodramatic features lends insight into the causes and effects of ballad innovations, which deploy similar "melodramatic tactics" to explore the social dynamics of control. Their "emphatically visual renderings of bodily torture and criminal conduct" challenged the axioms of crime and class, and, applied to specific crimes, they also staged shocked and saddened reactions to crimes in order to demonstrate the collectively shared experience of criminality and victimization. Hadley's assertion that the melodramatic mode "exerted an impact on the production of cultural meaning" in spite of its existence as a "less autonomous" (10) discursive practice has useful applications for a revision of ballad hermeneutics. Such a definition of textual power accounts for multiple layers of crime ballad signification, from the conventional features of melodramatic emplotment, to the polemical qualities of "less autonomous" literature, to the culturally reactive force behind the melodramatic mode.

Applying these critical insights, we can see the processes of what Hadley labels "productive friction" in ballad representations of murderous acts and crime scenes. With them, murder ballads frequently introduced troubling details that highlighted the intimate complexities of violent circumstances and insinuated the epistemological shortcomings of legal fictions and judicial reasoning. While these astonishing disclosures explored obscure sequences of causes and effects and intentions and actions, they also addressed the painful consequences of collective reckoning. The bloody particulars of murderous violence suggested that, both literally and figuratively, murder is messy, and where De Quincey perceives bloodlust, ballad writers sensed, to borrow John Kucich's phrase, "the political use of moral *disorder*" (2).

Offering a particularly vivid and gory example of the ballad aesthetic of astonishment is the ballad of "The Liverpool Tragedies," which was printed on the broadside "Execution of John Gleeson Wilson" (1849). This ballad engages the political uses of moral disorder by reconstructing Wilson's murders of Mrs. Heinrichsen, her two children, and a female servant "for the sake of cursed gold." Detailing these "dreadful murders" for "feeling christians," the ballad invents snippets of dialogue to undertake the task of explication:

> His bloody work he did commence all in the open day,
> By striking at the children while their mother was away,
> The servant girl did interfere, said, "should not do so,"
> Then with a poker in his hand he gave her a severe blow.
>
> Numberless times he did her strike till she could no longer stand,
> The blood did flow profusely from her wounds, and did him brand,
> Then the eldest boy of five years old, in supplication said,
> "Oh master, spare our precious lives, don't serve us like the maid."
>
> This darling child of five years old he brutally did kill,
> Regardless of its tender cries, its precious blood did spill,
> The youngest child to the kitchen ran, to shun the awful knife,
> This villain followed after and took its precious life.

In the "open day" a killer, with clearly inscribed motive and clearly expressed intent, commences his "bloody work" and destroys a household as his victims appeal to sympathy and attempt to escape. Garrett Stewart, who maintains that literary Victorians tended to die "vocally," argues that deathbed conversations could "inscribe the indecipherable" (13). Like these more benign and less violent deathbed conversations, street ballad dialogues between murderers and victims allowed murder narratives to articulate the indecipherable nature of violent death and to accommodate the audience's expectations of disclosure.

The desperate final words of the servant girl ("should not do so") and the "tender cries" of the five-year-old "darling child" attempt to check the forces of disorder. With their meager pleas for the preservation of their "precious lives" and "precious blood," the ballad highlights Wilson's merciless intentions and avaricious motives. Readers are asked to contemplate the intensity and intentionality of his violent actions, for "[r]egardless" of moral arguments and "supplication," Wilson, wielding a "poker" and an "awful knife" and "striking at the children while the mother was away," destroys their lives with "severe blow[s]." These murdered ballad-children embody uncorrupted innocence, but, in this contest between meek supplication and violent renunciation, they also signify ethical frailties and moral failures. Their invocations of mercy cannot check Wilson's violence, and, unsuccessful in inspiring restraint and escaping Wilson's weapons, the children emphasize the utter failure of the lawful, which, the ballad suggests, even collective witnessing and state-sanctioned punishment cannot fully restore.

While the broadside's prose report portrays the murder victims in terms of conventionally gendered notions of vulnerability ("two unprotected women and two helpless children"), the ballad broadens the notion of victimization to include witnesses and survivors. The grief-stricken father, whose "hair [will] turn grey with grief," mournfully acknowledges that "[n]o skill their lives could save," and the citizens of Liverpool form a suffering collectivity, which laments the "fate of this poor family." Just as, in the aftermath of the quadruple murder, "[t]housands did besiege the gates" of the hospital to ascertain the fate of the victims, "thousands did bewail" the victims' sad ends. As the traumatized members of the community gather together, we are told, "consternation did prevail." Broadening the scope of the crime's impact even further, the ballad also interprets it in terms of national history. Noting that "[t]he like was not recorded in British history," it dramatizes the inadequacies of moral authority and the pain of a national "tragedy."

Just as the murder dialogue, consisting of verbal supplication and violent dismissals, stages the inefficacy of moral law, the crime scene reiterates this sad failure in the brutalized bodies of the victims. In "The Liverpool Tragedies," the surgeon reads the crime scene in terms of both bodily abjection and social tragedy:

> The surgeon thus describes the scene presented to his view,
> A more appalling case than this he says he never knew,
> Four human beings on the floor all weltering in their gore,
> The sight was sickening to behold on entering the door.

The surgeon's claim that he "never knew" a "more appalling case" and that the sight was "sickening to behold" attests to the unprecedented and, therefore, astonishing nature of the case. Here, the corpses "weltering in their gore" confront and overwhelm the surgeon, and the reader, with the "appalling" effects of murderous violence. The ballad then produces the precise details of the "sickening" scene:

> The mother's wounds three inches deep upon her head and face,
> And pools of blood as thick as mud, from all of them could trace,
> None could identify the boy, his head was like a jelly;
> This tragedy is worse by far than Greenacre or Kelly.

With abject similes ("blood as thick as mud" and a head "like a jelly"), clinical details ("wounds three inches deep"), and the overall image of four bloodied and disfigured "human beings," the ballad uses a melodramatic "mode of excess" to produce astonishment. This excess is reinforced by accentual stresses on the most grotesque elements: "pools," "blood," "thick," "mud." While critics consistently note the visual impact of ballad gore, the aural impact produced by metrical arrangements, and, in these particular instances, sheer monosyllabic force, also contribute to the poetics of astonishment.

In this way, ballads could use the bodies of victims to reject simple understandings of moral order and violent disorder. The interpretive process of reading the bodies of the victims is repeatedly invoked in the ballad trade. In a broadside printed by the infamous Catnach, under a woodcut entitled "The Arrest of the Prisoner," a caption connecting murderous speech and violated corpse appears: "For murder, though it have no tongue, will speak with a most miraculous organ" (qtd. in Hindley, *History* 274). The heteroglossic layers of these lines from *Hamlet* invite more than a moral warning about clues and capture.[11] The phrase turns an investigative notion into an aesthetic one by suggesting the communicative value of the corpse, which utters a miraculous speech in a miraculous form—literally in the "organs" of the murdered. In the context of ballad crimes, such grotesque utterances cannot be easily absorbed by a disciplinary ideology or deflected by a didactic morality. In "The Liverpool Tragedies," the "sickening" vision of four mutilated corpses signifies stark and brutal truths. As spectacles of violent disorder, they inform their audience that something is rotten in England, and eliciting astonishment and "consternation," rather than outrage and panic, they propose grim reflections on crime as a shared social affliction.

"The Liverpool Tragedies" links outrageous violence to the temptations of "cursed gold," but more often, ballads, reflecting the historical realities of violent crime, reported the murders of acquaintances and family members. In these songs, ballad authors, exposing the cultural contours of "conflictual complexes," often forged more explicit connections between transgressive behavior and social prohibitions. Finding congruities and continuities between criminal acts, cultural practices, and social pressures, they disputed essentialist class-based ideas of criminality, intervened in legal debates about mitigation, and interrogated the principles of capital justice. "Verses on Daniel Good" (1842) (figure 5), for example, reports the execution of Daniel Good, a gentleman's coachman, convicted of the "barbarous and cruel" murder of Jane Jones, who "kept a mangle in South street." The impending "recital" of his "wild deeds," the narrator assures us, "[is] enough to turn your blood cold."

Good's crime intrigued and disgusted the public because he murdered, dismembered, and burned his victim, who by most accounts was said to be living as his common-law wife and was often referred to in broadsides and newspaper reports as "Mrs. Good." Situating Good in a "gallery of evil men" (*Men* 140), Martin Wiener explains that as models of civilized, rationalized, modernized, middle-class manhood developed, masculine aggression in general—and extreme violence in particular—was most often associated with a reprobate and outmoded form of working-class masculinity. As a result, instances of impassioned male violence, from the mild to the extreme, attracted increasing public scorn.

Articulating such scorn, the judge at Good's trial summed up his horrific crime as a murderous manifestation of his habitual sexual indulgence: "There is no doubt that it is the owing to the indulgence of your inclinations for one woman after another, that being tired of the unhappy deceased, and feeling that you could not enjoy to its fullest extent the fresh attachment you had formed, that you resolved upon destroying the unhappy woman who was the former object of your affection" (*Times*, 16 May 1842, 6).[12] While in many ways, of course, Victorian gender ideologies accommodated and condoned erasures of feminine subjectivity and masculine prerogatives for "fresh attachment[s]," the combination of Good's working-class masculinity and his apparently murderous philandering suggested a menacing figure who perfectly embodied criminal alterity—in its classed and gendered forms.

VERSES ON DANIEL GOOD,

Who was executed this morning May, '42, for the Murder of Jane Jones

Of all the wild deeds upon murder's black list,
Sure none is so barbarous and cruel as this,
Which in these few lines unto you I'll unfold,
The recital's enough to turn your blood cold.

In the great town of London near Manchester square,
Jane Jones kept a mangle in South street we hear,
A gentleman's coachman oft visiting came,
A cold-blooded monster, Dan Good was his name.

As a single man under her he made love,
And in course of time she pregnant did prove,
Then with false pretences he took her from home,
To murder his victim and the babe in her womb.

To his master's stables in Putney Park Lane,
They went, but she never returned again,
Prepare for your end then the monster did cry,
You time it is come for this night you must die.

Then with a sharp hatchet her head did cleave,
She begged for mercy but none he would give,
Have mercy dear Daniel my wretched life spare,
For the sake of your own child which you know I bear.

No mercy, he cried, then repeated the blow,
Alive from this stable you never shall go,
Neither you nor your brat shall e'er trouble me more,
Then lifeless his victim he struck to the floor.

And when she was dead this sad deed to hide,
The limbs from her body he straight did divide,
Her bowels ript open and dripping with gore,
The child from the womb this black monster he tore.

He made a large fire in the harness room,
Her head, arms, and legs in the fire did consume,
But e'er his intentions were fulfilled quite,
This dark deed by Providence was brought to light.

To a pawn-shop the coachman he did go one day,
A boy said some trowsers he did take away,
A policeman followed unto Putney Lane,
The coachman and trowsers to bring back again.

When in searching the stable the body he spied,
Without head, legs, or arms, and ript open beside,
Then a cry of murder he quickly did raise,
And the coachman was taken within a few days.

And when he was tried, most shocking to state,
The evidence proved what I now relate,
That Daniel Good murdered his victim Jones,
Then cut up and burnt her flesh and bones.

He soon was found guilty and sentenced to die,
The death of a murderer on the gallows high,
The blood of the murder'd must not cry vain,
An we hope that his like we shall ne'er see again.

J. Harkness, Printer, Preston.

Figure 5
Verses on Daniel Good. Courtesy The Newberry Library, Chicago.

Such casual links between murderous motive and sexual rakeism established the crime as a grotesquely disproportionate application of force. Compounding these meanings was the gruesome fact that Good attempted to dismember the body of his victim and burn her remains in the stable of his employer. And further complicating the meanings of this astonishing brutality was the speculation about his victim's pregnancy at trial. Although the consulting trial doctors could not "speak with certainty" on the matter, they speculated that Jones was pregnant, and press coverage of the trial frequently concentrated on the death of the unborn child in order to make the case for Good's barbarity (*Times,* 14 May 1842, 8).

Given this context, we can see that when this particular broadside ballad labels Good a "cold-blooded monster," it upholds a well-established consensus. But the ballad also undercuts these more common readings in important ways. In a realignment of motive, it challenges popular belief in the motivating force of a "fresh attachment" by presenting the murderer lashing out at the responsibilities of paternity. In contextualizing Good's crime in these (unfortunately) familiar terms, the ballad connects his crime to the socially constituted pressures of paternal responsibility rather than to the sexual pleasures of a fickle working-class rogue.

Quite unequivocally the ballad confirms the pregnancy and claims that the illegitimate child inspires Good's resolve "[t]o murder his victim and the babe in her womb." The doubly murderous intent is then depicted in a dialogue between killer and victim and in the mutilation of her body, an act that confronts the socially inscribed meaning of one transgression in terms of another:

> Then with a sharp hatchet her head did cleave,
> She begged for mercy but none he would give,
> Have mercy dear Daniel my wretched life spare,
> For the sake of your own child which you know I bear.

In imagining the content of Jones's appeals, the ballad deploys a common ballad trope of contrasting willful force and enfeebled resistance in carefully arranged murder dialogues that bespeak a disturbing intimacy. After Jones invokes moral obligations to "mercy," her "wretched life," and Good's "own child" and accusingly establishes his knowledge of the child—"which you know I bear"—Good verbally and physically rejects them:

> No mercy, he cried, then repeated the blow,
> Alive from this stable you never shall go,
> Neither you nor your brat shall e'er trouble me more,
> Then lifeless his victim he struck to the floor.

In her desperate appeals to the imperatives of paternity, Jones cites moral obligations, but according to the narrative logic of this ballad, such invocations only serve to incite his violence and inspire his categorical rejection of her pleas with a resounding "no mercy." Because this dialogue of moral bargaining also builds upon public discussions of Good's motives and Jones's potential pregnancy, Jones's references to his "own child" and Good's merciless renunciation of parental responsibility complicate judicial interpretations of his case. Ridding himself of a "brat" and "trouble," Good clearly defines links between intentions and actions.

In the subsequent hiding of his crime, Good reinscribes his stated intentions on the bodies of his victims, a number that the ballad decisively doubles. Rendering Jones's pregnancy a medical certainty, the ballad depicts a gruesome disemboweling and affirms the existence of a distinctly formed unborn child. With great symbolic weight, Good separates mother and child, thereby portraying a visual image of Good's sexual sins and Jones's fallen status:

> And when she was dead this sad deed to hide,
> The limbs from her body he straight did divide,
> Her bowels ript open and dripping with gore,
> The child from the womb this black monster he tore.

As stock phrases ("dripping with gore") join significant topical references, the ballad interprets his crime. The astounding force of his attempt "to hide" this "sad deed" resonates in vividly descriptive verbs: "ript," "divide," "tore." In this way, the details of the crime again encode both his murderous agency and his precise motivation.

After the murder, we are told, "He made a large fire in the harness room, / Her head, arms, and legs in the fire did consume." The disposal of the burned and mutilated body, catalogued as separate parts, establishes the astonishing crime scene, which is discovered by a policeman, who, looking for a pair of trousers that Good has stolen, interrupts Good's act of incineration. As ordinary policework intrudes upon extraordinary violence—as the search for a stolen pair of trousers becomes the discovery of a brutal murder—aesthetic astonishment is secured in the gaze of the unsuspecting witness: "When in searching the stable the body he spied, / Without head, legs, or arms, and ript open beside." And though the ballad has already twice dwelled on the dismemberment of Jones, it repeats the "shocking" details once more in an account of Good's trial:

> And when he was tried, most shocking to state,
> The evidence proved what I now relate,

That Daniel Good murdered his victim Jones,
Then cut up and burnt her flesh and bones.

With stresses on violent actions—"cut" and "burnt"—and abject parts—"flesh" and "bones"—the ballad fulfills the mandates of astonishment. Significantly, although the crime is "most shocking to state," "Verses on Daniel Good" insists upon a triple "recital" of Good's horrific violence. Details of the murder, the crime scene, and the trial enable a persistent return to the terrible murder that defines the crime ballad's poetic power and the audience's political curiosity.

In refusing to equivocate about the origins of motive, the nature of responsibility, or the existence of the child—in confidently asserting what "evidence proved"—this particular narrative of Daniel Good insistently explains personal motives with respect to sexual and gender codes, and it thereby undercuts other circulating narratives highlighting his inexplicable monstrosity. The vulnerability of Jane Jones, a mangle keeper, arises from the intersection of her class disadvantages, her ambiguous common-law status, and her illegitimate pregnancy. She occupies a position fully outside the normative codes of sexual propriety, and she pays the exorbitant cost of sexual transgression even as—or precisely when—she attempts to appeal to domestic obligations and paternal responsibility. In the ballad, these codes clearly shape Good's motive, which he unequivocally proclaims, despite the fact that the historical Good denied his sexual sins and his criminal guilt publicly throughout his trial and after. As the *Times* reported, Good "solemnly declare[d]" at every interview, "I never touched the body of the woman, alive or dead! so help me god!" (23 May 1842, 6). His continued insistence on his innocence, the *Times* explains, disrupted the seamless application of capital punishment: Good's "obstinacy of denial . . . if truthful, involved terrible ideas of judicial murder" and, "if false, involved hardly less terrible impressions of frightful, impenetrable obduracy of impenitence" (23 May 1842, 6).

In marked contrast, operating with an agenda of (astonishing) disclosure and (full) particularity, the ballad's certainties complicate the ethics of guilt in a way that the historical Good's repeated claims to total innocence could not. The ballad's preference for a clearly defined motive, the rejection of paternal responsibility, and its confirmation of Jones's sexual impropriety, which other reports obscured with references to "Mrs. Good," forces readers to confront a vision of villainy and victimization in terms of sexual politics. Further underscoring this agenda is the fact that, while other ballads addressed subgroups of Victorian culture (e.g., "listen all ye virgins fair"), this ballad addresses no one in particular. It thereby privileges the "productive friction" of astonishing violence over a pat recommendation of normative sexuality. The implied method of crime prevention in this ballad scenario is not religion and education, as the

Times earnestly advocated for this "fatal fruit" of "rank soil" who "never had in his youth any religious instruction" and was "awfully utterly ignorant" (23 May 1842, 6). Sidestepping clichéd moral instruction, "Verses on Daniel Good" insists upon a "recital" of the crime's astonishing gore in order to suggest congruities between culturally defined hierarchies of sexual power and the tragically violent dynamics of sexual intimacy.

In a similar mediation of familiar and unfamiliar violence, "Cruel and Inhuman Murder of a Little Boy by his Father" (1866) connects the unlawful hanging of a child to the lawful practice of execution. In the late 1860s, with execution theatrics and abolitionist arguments on the national political agenda, the notion of a father hanging his little boy underneath the city in a dark cellar and then hanging for the crime high above the crowd on a public stage easily accommodated the methods of symbolic inversion so common in crime ballads. Accordingly, in condemning the inhumanity and cruelty of an extrajudicial hanging of a boy by his father, the ballad questions the manner in which a paternalistic state disposes of its outcast criminals.

In its prose report, this broadside emphasizes the obvious analogy between cruel murderer and cruel executioner: "the cruel father tied [the boy's] hands behind, and had literally enacted the part of executioner of his own child, holding its legs, and forcing down its body to complete the strangulation of the poor boy." In generating such detailed imagery the broadside exploits the audience's familiarity with scaffold practices. As Thackeray noted, execution audiences witnessed the stark demystification of the "drop into eternity": "those who have paid for good places may see the hands of the government agent, Jack Ketch, coming up from his black hole, and seizing the prisoner's legs, and pulling them, until he is quite dead—strangled" (157). The broadside's execution analogy—with its emphatic imagery of hands-on killing—is thus doubly significant. It underscores the murderous intentions of a reprehensible child-killer, but, recalling familiar images of public execution, it insinuates the murderous inclinations (and inspirations) of the state.

This parallelism between criminal and state violence serves the poetics of astonishment at work in the ballad; for, while the state presumably executes guilty criminals, John Richard Jefferys executes an innocent child. In problematizing the categories of guilt and innocence, the ballad registers contempt for "a wretch named Jefferys," a "sad, a base, and cruel villain," who murders his own child in the Seven Dials district, a locale that is noted four times in the ballad. The Seven Dials district, of course, formed the center of ballad publication, and, thus, his crime astonishes the very community that reproduces his crime in verse:

> His little boy named Richard Arthur,
> By the wretched father, we are told,

> Was cruelly and basely murdered,—
> The child was only seven years old;
> The villain took him to a cellar,
> Resolved his offspring to destroy,
> Tied his little hands behind him,
> And hanged the pretty smiling boy.

Like other ballads, this ballad highlights the failure of innocence in contrasting images of murderer and victim. Rather than adhering to stock conceptions of villainy, its suggestive allusions to the details of the historical case imbue its melodramatic mode with "productive friction." Contextual details about the child's seventeen-week residency at his grandmother's house and Jefferys's three-year estrangement from the child's mother, which also circulated in press accounts of the crime, focus attention on the pressures of a defunct family romance. Accordingly, we are informed that Jefferys, enacting a "[v]engeance," was "[d]etermin'd for to take his life" and that he "demand[ed] him" and "clandestinely took him away" because "he determined / Was his little boy to slay." Acknowledging these circumstances, the ballad uses familial relations to comprehend Jefferys's murderous intentions and constitutes its audience as a collective of "kindest fathers," "tender mothers," "sisters, too, and brothers."

The murder is then rendered in striking detail. In the account of the hanging, the ballad abandons the previous hearsay mode ("we are told"), dispenses with hesitation ("can scarce reveal") and supplies startling eyewitness detail:

> Then he to the cellar took him,—
> His heart was harder far than steel,
> The wicked, base, inhuman monster,
> His actions no one can reveal.
> His only child, to hold beside him,
> With rope he bound his little hands,
> When behind his back he placed them,
> He in the cellar did him hang.

In spite of the claim that "[h]is actions no one can reveal," the narrator provides a concrete set of images, which are apparently gleaned from the familiar procedures of hanging. Though the ballad insists on Jefferys's "steel" cruelty, and later claims that "hanging is too good for such a villain," it also tempers this condemnatory posture by asserting that "[w]e all have got our cares and trials / And unto fate are compelled to yield." Perhaps an allusion to stories that his wife had left him for another man (*Times*, 13 September 1866, 9), which were discussed in the press and at Jefferys's trial, this platitude also suggests that "cruel monstrosity" can be sung as a matter of "fate."

Whether intimating that the roles of murderer and victim are fated or that Jefferys might have yielded more gently to his "cares and trials," the ethical ambiguities and private circumstances alluded to in the ballad effectively reinforce or recenter the poem's scaffold imagery. The privatization of scaffold violence—its application in domestic disputes—elides the practices of state-sanctioned hanging and "cruel and inhuman murder." In this way, the murder's eerie recasting of a "proper" hanging, in which the execution of personified innocence is carried out by a guilty patriarch, offers an ironic symbolic inversion. It implies, of course, that the very means by which social order was to be maintained and by which violent criminality was to be suppressed actually inspires crimes and fosters violence. The uneasy parallel between Jefferys's disturbing transgression, hidden in a cellar beneath the city, and the state's spectacular hangings, elevated on public stages, disorients the poles of margin and center, the hierarchies of high and low, and the binaries of criminals and citizens. In this context, relations between transgression and retribution lose their explanatory power and their ethical clarity.

Cases of infanticide signified quite differently when mothers murdered their children. Yet, even in maternal infanticide cases, the poetics of astonishment and the judicial treatment of murder often intersected in unexpected ways. As psychological theories and legal understandings of infanticide evolved, insanity defenses for infanticidal—particularly neonaticidal—mothers gained increasing interpretive power, and ballads registered these legal changes and grappled with their ethical implications. As Lionel Rose affirms, in infant-murder cases, the "likelihood of a conviction for murder was negligible" and, after 1849, no women hanged for killing their newborn infants (77). When a rare murder conviction occurred, "the Home Secretary invariably reprieved mothers who killed their own infants under twelve months" although "the ordeal of formal sentence to death still had to be endured in court" (76).

In spite of fairly consistent legal trends, representations of infanticide varied from sympathy to condemnation, and from pathos to outrage, and, as Christine Krueger argues, while mental science offered frank testimony on uncontrollable impulses, affective and sentimental frameworks "were still swaying judges and juries in the 1850s" (275). In her study of Victorian discourses on child-murder, Josephine McDonagh asserts that medicalizing infanticide and pathologizing women confirmed gendered prejudices about female mental weaknesses, secured the careers of medical men, and rhetorically diminished the necessity of repairing related social problems (125). Moreover, she explains, in the "phantom of public opinion" that constituted Britain's child-murder "epidemic" (126), notions of Englishness or Britishness—riddled with assumptions about barbarity and civilization—were granted more explanatory relevance than individual hardships, family influences, and compounded oppressions (127).[13]

As mental science offered clinical solutions of cure and containment—while national(ist) anxieties dulled reformist sensibilities and contextual insights—ballad infanticides, functioning neither as instances of national degeneration nor as symptoms of medical pathologies, resisted totalizing narratives by highlighting the astonishing and specific details of individual cases. And while ballads often responded sympathetically to circumstantial mitigation and physiological indicators of insanity and, thus, reflected the court's increasing leniency, the spectacle of maternal violence continued to figure prominently. "Copy of Verses on the Murder of Two Children, By Their Mother, On Battersea Bridge" (1846), for example, examines the case of Eliza Clark, who threw her three young children into the Thames and was attempting to jump into the river herself when bystanders stepped in and detained her (*Times*, 18 May 1846, 9). Two of her children drowned, and one survived. At trial, witnesses recounted instances of her motherly devotion and noted the perils of her domestic life, which was shaped by the stress of working-class poverty and the abuse of her alcoholic husband, a journeyman painter. The jury found her not guilty on the ground of insanity.

This particular ballad, printed soon after the crime's commission and, therefore, not privy to the facts of the case or the trial verdict, announces the astonishing crime for public speculation. Neglecting any mention of Clark's own attempt at self-murder, the ballad emphasizes the drowning of her children. An affront to parenting, her crime is unprecedented in "history's annals," and the opening lines proclaim, "Oh! list ye tender parents," thereby submitting the case to sensitive and sensible parents for scrutiny and judgment. The ballad forcefully pits Clark's guilty criminal intent against the children's sweet innocence: "Her three sweet little infants / She did intend to slay." Such conventional diminutive phrasings—"three sweet little infants," "three pretty smiling babes," "pretty smiling boy"—are maintained throughout the text and uphold the astonishing contrast between unsuspecting innocence and calculating malice. Clark's violation of maternal ideals inspires exclamatory pathos: "A mother, oh! how sad to tell." The chorus of the song underscores the notion of her destructive agency, expresses the distress of documenting her crime and, thus, ensures the reiteration of sadness and regret: "She threw her babes, how sad to name, / Into the fatal river Thames."

Placed beyond comprehension, Clark's motivations and intentions are ambiguous, but a reference to her "wicked deed" implicates the inscrutability of her conduct rather than the possibility of mental sickness: "Whatever could her mind possess. / Such a wicked deed to do, / There is no one can imagine. / The neighborhood all through." The unintelligibility of her deeds defies the collective imagination as she is subjected to the local standards of the "neighborhood." Yet, while the ballad introduces the issues of psychological disorder and domestic abuse that surfaced in Clark's case, it also undercuts them with the dismissive assessments of local gossip and thereby looks skeptically at mitigating circumstances and criminal lunacy:

> She said her husband her ill-used,
> Which did affect her mind,
> But such by neighbors is denied,
> For he to her proved kind.

Here, the ballad records the social dynamics of psychological testimony. As Hilary Marland has argued, the observations of neighbors and other lay-witnesses often influenced outcomes in infanticide trials, which in many cases "did not depend upon the evidence of a forensic expert or medical man experienced in treating insanity, but on the opinion of a surgeon or general practitioner and a collection of witnesses—neighbors, friends and passers-by—all of whom found it appropriate to comment on the woman's state of mind and felt equipped to testify to the existence of insanity" (181). Positioning Clark's mental state beyond imagination and discrediting her claims of domestic abuse through the citation of neighborhood testimony, the ballad insinuates that Clark was a premeditating killer and a self-interested liar. Such narrative choices document the inconsistencies of insanity defenses and the disadvantages of abused wives in the arena of public opinion. Circulating in 1846, amidst contentious legal reconsiderations of domestic violence and medicolegal debates about insanity, Clark's ballad reflects the profound difficulties of interpreting child-murder while, at the same time, retaining a primary interest in astonishing spectacle.

A concern with the aesthetics of astonishment, of course, addresses the generic conventions of murder ballads, but it may also reflect the ballad's timing with respect to the case. With limited press details to draw from and with the criminal case in progress, it carefully highlights the painful experience of witnessing such a public crime. It devotes an entire stanza, for example, to enumerating the children's ages and describing their reactions as they are flung into the Thames:

> The first was only ten months old
> She in the river threw.
> The second but two years and a half,
> How sad, but yet how true;
> The third a pretty smiling boy,
> As I do now unfold,
> Thrown by the mother in the Thames,
> And he was five years old.

By cataloging each of her murderous actions, the ballad dramatizes the terror of observing the destruction of innocence. The Thames, the "fatal river," becomes both the weapon and the crime scene, and a subsequent stanza reports the tense rescue of the five-year-old, who, taken out in "an exhausted, wretched, / Sad and dreadful state" was saved "[f]rom a sad and watery grave." The reclamation of the second child's body and the total disappearance of the infant, who "far down the fatal stream / Was carried right away," prioritize the suffering of the children over the desperation of the mother, whose psychological struggles remain unaddressed and whose suicidal efforts remain unacknowledged.

These eyewitness details also stress the pain of the London citizenry, which suffers intensely when apprehending and contemplating the spectacle. In doling out sympathy to both victims and witnesses, the ballad rather explicitly addresses the poetics of astonishment that characterizes third-person crime ballads. The figure of a single witness, functioning as a readerly surrogate, is inscribed in the poem: "Upon the bridge at Battersea / A person did her see, / Commit this sad and horrid deed, / This dreadful tragedy." And as the recovery of the children's bodies ensued, the ballad records the community's response:

> Each side the river with folks was lined,
> Who when the tale did hear,
> Did cause each heart to beat.
> And every eye to shed a tear.

In the beating hearts and teary eyes of witnessing "folks," this "dreadful tragedy" configures the crime as a source of collective pain visible in "every eye." The affective power of an astonishing crime defines the shared experience of murder.

The final stanza returns to the figure of the murderous mother. A prisoner awaiting trial, she occupies a liminal position. "[C]onfined / Within a prison dark," the ballad explains, the "cruel woman" confronts her own terror and terribleness: "Her dreadful deeds must surely strike / A terror to her heart." The ballad then summarizes the consequences at stake in her case:

> Investigations will take place,
> And that most speedily
> And if 'tis proved she is not mad,
> Then she will punished be.

Abstaining from a pronouncement or judgment, the ballad adopts a tentative stance. In its final two lines, however, the ballad acknowledges the legal contest between criminal insanity and capital punishment that affects her case. As in numerous other ballads, Clark's murders present the astonishing spectacle of moral failure, but also the potential presence of madness. In highlighting sustaining ethical ambivalence and legal uncertainty, the ballad redirects attention away from legal judgment or moral outrage and toward the spectacle of murdered children and the experience of collective pain.

Also attempting to grapple with the social implications of murderous mothers, "The Esher Tragedy" (1854) depicts Mary Ann Brough's murders of her six children. The cultural connotations of her motherhood and infanticide are reinforced by the twice-mentioned fact that she once "nursed the blooming prince of Wales." This revelation resonates on many levels, suggesting, for example, the precarious safety, criminal affiliations, or potential contamination of the royal family.[14] Although Brough's crime fully accommodated the sensationalizing tropes of criminal contagion and moral degeneration, the speaker of "The Esher Tragedy" emphasizes the pathetic dimensions of her crime with the narrator's pleas for "feeling christians" to "give attention" and "sympathize with me" during the "tale of sorrow." This tragic frame is complemented by a prose report that reproduces text from Brough's voluntary statement. Entitled "Confession of the Murderess," the report details her decision to "go down and get a knife and cut [her] throat" after her children repeatedly wake her with requests for "barley water" late into the night. She notes, "I was bad all day; I wanted to see Mr. Izod, and waited all day. I wanted him to give me some medicine." In representing this shift from suicidal to homicidal intentions, the broadside underscores the mitigating presence of insanity and emplots Brough's case as a personal, psychological tragedy.

In Victorian commentaries on her case, Brough's tale shifted between medicolegal tragedy and sexual melodrama. Brough's crimes became an important case study in medicolegal debates, and, because of the testimony of leading mental scientists, she was eventually acquitted on the grounds of insanity and committed to Bethlem. In *Trial by Medicine* (1981), Roger Smith notes that Brough's case riveted public attention not only because of the extent of her crimes and her former position as wet-nurse to the prince, but also because it assembled questions about insanity, adultery, and revenge. The press reported that just before the murders, Brough's husband had confronted her with an accusation of adultery. As Smith argues, her case "had all the elements of a Victorian morality play" (158):

> Many special legal elements and medico-legal problems came together at the trial of Mary Ann Brough. It was equally plausible to reconstruct her life in terms of depravity or of disease. The crime was child murder, with evidence of weakness following her last confinement. But her crime was also a vengeful act against her husband. Medical evidence played an important role in her defence, and though the jury found insanity, both lay and medical critics

considered it an "escape." Her case is the most striking example of the constraints on meaning in Victorian discourses.[15] (*Trial* 157)

Taking these easily sensationalized details of scandalous adultery and intimate revenge into account, we can see the extent to which the ballad sidelines them. Appearing early in the case and announcing the murder as event, "The Esher Tragedy" foregoes the widely publicized drama of marital infidelity and, instead of proposing a conventionally moralistic melodrama, favors a narrative of tragic mental illness.

The text embeds official information in a summary of the tragic facts, "[w]hich causes each kind heart to bleed": "'Twas with a sharp and fatal razor, / She committed this foul deed, / And one by one she cut their throats." Conventional murder dialogues accommodate the recurrent ballad theme of moral frailty and enfeebled innocence. Her son, Henry, "cried aloud with eyes of pity, / 'Mother, dear, don't murder me.'" And though behaving "like a demon fierce and wild," she responds to her victim's entreaties with an unsettling blend of motherly affection and pathetic resignation: "'My dear,' said she, 'it must be done.'" The juxtaposition of endearing appellations, methodical throat-cutting, and frenzied activity establishes the representational excess and friction fundamental to the poetics of astonishment. Together, such details achieve a "plenitude of meaning," which cannot be reduced to a set of moral conventions or a theory of criminal malice. The murders, established as inevitable, are perpetrated with the "sharp and fatal razor":

> From bed to bed, and to each chamber,
> This wretched woman she did go,
> While all around her own dear children,
> Streams of crimson blood did flow.

The shift to trochees in the final line of this stanza underscore the importance of ballad gore—crimson streams of blood overflow the well-defined boundaries of moral outrage and force aesthetic astonishment. Throughout this account, the baffled narrator explicitly voices such questions of astonishment: "What on earth could urge it on" and "Oh! what must be the woman's motive." These questions also enfold the ever present issues of crime prevention and criminal responsibility: "Did she think she'd done amiss, / Or did she think of death and judgment / To perpetrate a deed like this?" These overwrought questions direct audiences toward the difficult and painful ambiguities involved in contemplating extreme violence.

In constructing the crime scene, the ballad renders a tableau of perverted domesticity, as the image of slumbering children transforms into a "surprising" scene of murdered children with ear-to-ear throat wounds:

The dreadful sight was most surprising,
To behold these children dear,
How their cruel hearted mother,
Cut their throats from ear to ear.

Having presented these details, the ballad imagines Brough in "a prison's gloomy cell, / Where midnight dreams to her will whisper / And her deeds of blood will tell." Haunted by the "phantoms of her six dear children" and subject to "midnight dreams," Brough experiences a fully psychologized tragedy. Somewhat sympathetically tracing Brough's case from murder to crime scene to memory, the ballad forces uncomfortable linkages between suicide and homicide, motherhood and infanticide, control and desperation, sanity and insanity.[16]

More than a decade later, a broadside entitled "Barbarous Murder of a Child by a Schoolmistress" (1869) listed the ballad of Emma Pitt, who, "in such a barbarous manner killed / Her tender infant child." Highlighting the alienation and vulnerability of the fallen woman, the historical circumstances of Pitt's case reveal a debilitating social context in which the dangers of sexual transgression, the terror of postpartum madness, and the strictures of respectability establish the conditions for a murderous breakdown. The *Times* reported Pitt, aged twenty-four, to be a "young woman of most respectable connexions" and a "mistress of the national school" who birthed her child alone and in secret. The judicial interpretation of her case hinged upon the mutilated state of the infant's body, which bore the signs of excessive, "barbarous" force. In particular, the infant's severed tongue and bruised body introduced a debate about whether or not the infant's injuries were sustained before death but while the child had a "separate existence" (*Times*, 26 July 1869, 11). The presiding judge summarized the essential legal question: "Was the child an inhabitant of this world, having an existence independent of the mother, and was its life extinguished by the act of the mother?" (*Times*, 26 July 1869, 11). Ultimately, Pitt was found not guilty of murder but guilty of concealing the birth, and she was sentenced to two years' imprisonment with hard labor.[17]

The astonished narrator of this particular ballad intones moral conventions, faulting Pitt, a schoolmistress "[w]ell known for miles around," for setting a "sad example" for her students. The narrator also apostrophizes an audience of concerned mothers, asking them to contemplate, in conventional ballad terms, an unprecedented horror that "we seldom find" in the "annals of history." The words of the chorus reiterate this horror, intimating the distressing incongruity of a child-murdering schoolmistress: "This Emma Pitt was a schoolmistress, / Her child she killed we see, / Oh mothers, did you ever hear, / Of such barbarity." Contemplating this "murderess"—"the author / Of this dreadful tragedy"—the narrator reassures readers on matters of justice, "When before a Judge and Jury, / This monster soon must stand; / And if she is found guilty, / She her deserts will get." But collectively the ballad verses destabilize such moral confidence when considering the death penalty. Lamenting, "if she is found guilty, / How sad will be her case," the narrator explains, "If she has a woman's feelings, / She surely will go wild." Though Pitt's "barbarous murder" requires a public response, execution is not unqualifiedly condoned, and acknowledgments of sympathetic concern for her solitary suffering and her "womanly feeling" diminish her imputed barbarity.

Offering a startling version of the speaking body, the historical particulars of Pitt's crime fuel the poetics of astonishment. Accordingly, the ballad fixates on the removal of the child's tongue from its mouth:

> With a large flint stone she beat its head
> When such cruelty she'd done,
> From the tender roof of the infant's mouth
> She cut away it's tongue;
> Sad and wicked, cruel wretch,
> Hard was her flinty heart,
> The infant's tongue from the body was
> Wrapped in another part.

In fusing her weapon and her psyche—a "flint stone" and a "flinty heart"—the ballad enforces the notion that she is simultaneously, and contradictorily, "sad and wicked."

The crime scene also focuses on the displaced tongue of the victim: "The murderess placed in a drawer, / And it there, alas! was found." In using the severed tongue as a central image and symbol, the ballad considers the origins and condition of Pitt's murderous psychology. The tongue's removal, with symbolic resonance, suggests a desperate need to conceal and silence the child. The coroner's statement, which is quoted in the broadside's prose report, asserts that "the child was born alive and murdered by someone," and this chronology and the violent intensity of Pitt's actions suggest the possibility of postpartum derangement. The gruesome silencing depicted in the ballad, however, confers a communicative power upon the severed tongue. A "most miraculous organ" of speech, wrapped and hidden in a drawer, the tongue forces aesthetic memory: "And mother's, miles round Wimborne, / Will remember Emma Pitt." Laden with implications about her sexual vulnerability and her mental derangement, the traumatic image of the child's tongue constitutes the interpretive crux of the legal case, and in the ballad directed specifically at mothers, disturbs the memory of "the barbarous Emma Pitt."

As a comparison of the ballads of Jefferys, Clark, Brough, and Pitt suggests, the ballad trade did not subscribe to uniform or stock responses to infanticide—

or any other crimes. Rather, they examined a spectrum of conflicting forces in their stylized representations of lethal force, and they exploited significant case-specific circumstances to nuance the meanings of murders. Finding unsettling congruities between criminal acts and social pressures, they developed suggestive mediations of the familiar and the unfamiliar. In "Shocking Murder of A Wife and Six Children" (1869), the ballad writer explores the all-too-familiar problem of urban poverty by conjoining expressions of astonishment and tropes of sentimentality to represent the murder-suicide deaths of an entire family.

According to the *Times,* the father, Walter Duggan, a thirty-nine-year-old silversmith, who had recently been dismissed from work because he suffered from consumption, sent a letter to the police stating, "Your attendance will be required at the above house early this morning" (1 July 1869, 10).[18] The contents of the home and the testimony of witnesses uncovered a tale of tragic misfortune, and letters between Duggan and his brother documented a psychologically debilitating cycle of poverty and disease. At the inquest, the coroner summed up the unsettling revelation of this case: "It was deplorable to find people so despondent and distressed that they should be led to commit such fearful crimes in the very heart of the metropolis" (*Times,* 1 July 1869, 10). Ideologically and geographically central, this domestic tragedy unsettles the middle-class newspaper readership that witnesses this social failure occurring on a "street occupied by a 'respectable class of artisans and their families'" (29 June 1869, 11). The Duggan case not only intimated the precariousness of respectable family life in London, but it also problematized the attribution of crimes to the "dangerous classes" and their displacement into urban slums. The verdict at the inquest stated, "Walter James Duggan and Emma Duggan murdered their children and afterwards destroyed themselves while in an unsound state of mind" (*Times,* 1 July 1869, 10).

In imagining the fatalistic resolve of the patriarch, the ballad highlights the confessional letter sent by Walter James Duggin—father, murderer, suicide—to the authorities:

To the police he did a letter send,
That he was about this life to end,
And that he had poisoned, he did declare
His wife, and his six children dear.

As the letter replaces the characteristic shocking moments of discovery in murder ballads, Duggin's actions appear less the sensational expression of an impassioned killer than the pitiful communication of a poor unemployed worker, whose eviction, the broadside notes, was scheduled for twelve o'clock the day the bodies were discovered. Presented in these terms, the deaths embody a desperate response to escalating poverty. Privileging this reading, the ballad explicates, with mournful irony, the crime as a fulfillment of a paternal obligation to protect and provide: "Lest they should want, that fatal day, / His wife and children he did slay."

The crime scene, accordingly, depicts death as a form of protection from poverty: "They found him stretched upon the bed, / His troubles o'er—was cold and dead." This unlawful "shocking sight" affords no weltering gore but rather, the fatal tableau of a Victorian family tragedy which "[c]aused in many an eye a tear." The social conditions apparent in the arranged bodies signify impoverished and beleaguered domesticity:

> They found upon another bed,
> The ill-fated mother, she was dead,
> While two pretty children we are told,
> In her outstretched arms she did enfold,

As a family of abject corpses displays the affections and attitudes of ideal domesticity, the ballad, deploying the common strategy of symbolic inversion, asks us to read the everyday conditions of poverty in astonishing images. The decomposition of the loving family establishes a grotesque juxtaposition of excess and order with which the ballad indicts political indifference to poverty and the deterministic forces of economic struggles. Uninterested in ethical questions of agency or legal analyses of murder and suicide, the narrative of the "ill-fated" family confronts the marginalization and silencing of the diseased and disenfranchised in the center of London.

As Judith Walkowitz has written of the Jack the Ripper murders:

> If, traditionally, the "classical" body has signified the "health" of the larger social body—of a closed, homogenous, regulated social order—then the mounting array of "grotesque," mutilated corpses in this case represented the exact inverse: a visceral analogue to the epistemological incoherence and political disorientation threatening the body politic during the "autumn of terror." (*City* 198)

Although Walkowitz speaks here about a very particular set of bodies at a very particular time and although she clarifies how such "visceral analogue[s]" easily served reactionary panic mongering, her explanation of the semiotic power of "mutilated corpses" aptly articulates the political charge of the violated bodies of third-person murder ballads. They offer collective testimony about the epistemological challenges and legal questions—the incoherence and disorientation—created by eruptions of murderous violence.

It is thus in their insistence on graphic violence and bodily gore that murder ballads developed a poetics of critique with which to imagine congruities between crime and culture. With their revelations of astonishment and their attention to particulars, they complicated epistemologies of crime and representations of murder, developing a genre of occasional poetry that encouraged public reflection and political skepticism while expressing collective anxieties, regrets, and fears. In presenting murder as an interpretive and interpretable act, and cultivating the political curiosity of their readers, ballads constructed murders and crime scenes as sites where "social classification and psychological processes are generated as conflictual complexes." Addressing precarious lives and fragile moralities, they reveal the capacity of verse forms to constitute public discourse and foster political debate.

On the Gallows High and in a Murderer's Grave: Last Lamentations and the Criminal Poet

While third-person murder ballads highlighted the social contexts and consequences of astonishing crimes, first-person ballads focused on condemned murderers and their relationship to capital punishment. Cast as "last lamentations" or "copies of affecting verses," these ballads were marketed as the overflow of powerful feeling on the eve of death, and, supplying condemned criminals with expressive sensibilities and lyrical voices, they established the persona of the criminal poet and the trope of public lamentation. Inspiring one Victorian commentator to quip, "every man who is hanged leaves a poem" (*Literature of the Streets* 73), the confessional verses and wistful voices of these poet-murderers imagined the psychologies of violent agency and the traumas of public execution.

Central to the political context of lamentation poetics is the fact that this fictional affective voice enabled the condemned criminal to seize speech at the moment of official silencing by the state. Of their French counterparts, Foucault has argued that last lamentations posit the "lyrical position of the murderous subject," and they "[mark] the place—fictitious, of course—of a subject who both speaks and is murderous" (*Rivière* 208). Imagining this "lyrical position" and highlighting the occasion that gained their voices a hearing, lamentation ballads emulated stage tragedies, procuring pity and inspiring fear as dispirited criminals were "launched into eternity." In this way, criminal poets and their occasional poems examined matters of legal representation and political speech, which Foucault casts as "a subterranean battle ... around two rights, perhaps less heterogeneous than they seem at first sight—the right to kill and be killed and the right to speak and narrate" (207).

In Victorian England, this contest of speech rights and murder rights included the state's rights to disciplinary silencing. As the merits and methods of the death penalty were studied by the Royal Commission on Capital Punishment in the 1860s, Sir Samuel Martin confidently explained its awe-inspiring effects: "a sentence of death has a most serious effect upon all the people in court; you have perfect silence, as perfect as can be, all the people seem very much interested in it, and the sentence does carry a very strong impression upon the persons present" (*Report of the Capital Punishment Commission* Q 246: 37). The versifying criminals and singing crowds of the lamentation trade disrupted the silencing mechanisms of capital punishment through the elaboration of poetic voice and the encouragement of public noise. Generating arresting connections between the historical criminal, the ballad criminal, and the ballad consumer, singing consumers might reproduce the "I" of the ballads and thus perform the identity of the murderer: "It is the song of crime; it is intended to travel from singer to singer; everyone is presumed able to sing it as his own crime, by a lyrical fiction" (Foucault, *Rivière* 207–8). Public and performative, this criminal voice suggestively undermined distinctions between the condemned criminal other and what Leps terms the "consensual 'we.'" Though the principle of scaffold deterrence was founded on the premise that an ignorant and impressionable working-class crowd would feel disgust for the criminal and respect for the state, the gruesome and violent nature of the hanging invariably elicited sympathy for criminals and disgust for the state. Working-class Britons in particular were familiar with the violence and suffering of scaffold deaths, and, accordingly, their execution ballads addressed scaffold suffering, giving voice, at this public silencing, to the violence witnessed by spectators.

Exploring the political contentions of "perfect silence" and eternal silencing, execution ballads, and their generic features, reflect the evolution of nineteenth-century criminal law. While the steel-frame printing press and the business savvy of urban printers stimulated the broadside trade early in the nineteenth century, specific alterations in English criminal law shaped the development of the criminal poet later in the century. As an article in the *Quarterly Review* explained to its Victorian readership, "The 'Dying Speech and Confession Ballad,' strictly so called, is said to have been unknown in the trade until the year 1820, when a change in the law prolonged the term of existence between the trial and death of the criminal" ("The Poetry of Seven Dials" 399). Mayhew reports, "'Before that,' I was told, 'there wasn't no time for a Lamentation; sentence o' Friday, and scragging o' Monday. So we had only Life, Trial, and Execution'" (283). While legal changes allowed more time for ballad composition, the continued reductions in capital crimes decreased the number of executions, and after 1837, executions for an offense other than murder became rare.[19] Early nineteenth-century balladeers often accommodated multiple executions with "lamentations and prison groans," which catalogued the names—and sometimes listed brief biographies—of several criminals to be executed while reserving fully drawn character studies for the most notorious criminals.[20] In contrast, Victorian ballad writers responded to a restricted capital code, a decrease in the number of hangings, and an almost total cessation of multiple hangings by developing the well-defined persona of the single murderous subject that came to define the genre. Exploiting these legal changes, ballad writers and publishers maintained the profitable relationship between execution and broadsheets.

The poetic and political opportunities created by the newly individuated scaffold subject also contributed to the last lamentation's concern with trial procedures and defensive testimony. Altering the nature of legal representation, the Prisoners' Counsel Act of 1836 allowed defense counsel to address the jury on behalf of prisoners in capital trials while restricting prisoners from giving evidence in their own defense when such counsel was retained.[21] Arguing that Victorian novelists investigated the contest between the passionate speech of criminals and the rational rhetoric of learned counsel engendered by the Prisoner's Counsel Act, Jan-Melissa Schramm notes that Charles Dickens's "fear that the professional rhetoric of the law displaces personal narrative was most pronounced when he dwelt upon the plight of the prisoner condemned to death" (111). "His creativity," she adds, "was activated by a profound interest in the ways in which punishment excluded men from the wider community of stories; he was interested in the ultimate obliteration of evidence" (111). Inserting their affective verses into the "wider community of stories" surrounding condemnation and execution, last lamentations reflect a similar concern. Indeed, if any one consistency exists among the hundreds and hundreds of last lamentations circulating in the Victorian era, it is that they privileged the personal testimonies of the hooded and bound criminals on the scaffold. Entering a charged legal arena, they assigned emotionally intimate and psychologically complex identities to criminals just as the state demanded death by public hanging and the anonymity of an unmarked grave.

In restoring voices to silenced figures, many ballad writers exploited the contested quality of criminal speech by mimicking official confessions and simulating legal testimonies. In these instances, as criminal poets narrated their crimes, ballads effectively reopened criminal cases and reassessed legal defenses. Casting doubts on established guilty verdicts and death sentences, they not only complicated notions of criminal alterity, but also questioned the integrity of the judicial system. When criminals proclaimed murderous guilt and criminal responsibility at the same time, their speech established them as monumental transgressors and victims of state violence, positions that secured their status as tragic authors. In contrast, when they acknowledged violent acts but not malicious intents, they challenged murder charges and capital punishments. Whether rebutting intentionality or proclaiming responsibility, their expressions of mental stress and emotional pain effected symbolic reversals of criminality that were founded on reformulations of guilt rather than on pleas of innocence. Adding personal narratives and verse soliloquies to the visual spectacle of execution, lamentations favored representations of psychological complexity and emotional vulnerability that problematized legal fictions and punitive codes.

Although their anonymity has aided their fall into literary obscurity, in their original context, it was authorial anonymity that authorized the lyrical fiction of the criminal poet.[22] Stitching together the case details, genre codes, and legal terms—and imagining the violent death of the author—last lamentations resemble Roland Barthes' authorless text, which he describes as "a tissue of quotations drawn from the innumerable centres of culture" (146) to be "disentangled," not "deciphered" (147), by readers. Along these lines, they foster the new kinds of interpretive questions that Foucault associates with the authorless text and an authorless analytic. Displacing the "tiresome repetitions" of the "author-function," "[n]ew questions will be heard":

> "What are the modes of existence of this discourse?"
> "Where does it come from; how is it circulated; who controls it?"
> "What placements are determined for possible subjects?"
> "Who can fulfill these diverse functions of the subject?"
> Behind all these questions we would hear little more than the murmur of indifference:
> "What matter who's speaking?" ("What is An Author?" 138)

With attention to modes of contestation, citation, and circulation—as well as the constitution and determination of subjectivities—we can begin to understand the poetic performance of authorship and the political meanings of the criminal poet.

At the most fundamental level, the murderer's identity as a sentimental poet placed between murder and execution offers a striking inversion of murderous guilt. If "every man who is hanged leaves a poem," then every condemned murderer is a reflective poet whose own self-judgments, challenging judicial authority and legal reasoning, disrupt the edifying power of their public deaths. In "Trial and Sentence of George Britten" (1867), when Britten laments, "I have been the cruel author, / Of the cruel Woolverton tragedy," his words express the condition of the criminal poet.[23] An author of tragic violence and an actor in a violent tragedy, the lamenting and dying murderer alerts audiences to the profound moral difficulties of assessing crimes and measuring punishments.

In organizing this critical perspective, balladeers arranged strands of personal narrative, legal commentary, and social critique around the two events that conferred criminal identity, the murder and the execution. Because the criminal poet is born "between two deaths—murder and execution" (Foucault, *Rivière* 208), the violent actions of murderers retained aesthetic significance even as ballads attempted to explore the violent nature of execution. In fact, because graphic violence forced the coincidence of poetic sensibility and violent agency, ballad authors often used gruesome details to generate interpretive ironies and conflicts. The sentencing judge in "Life, Trial, Confession, and Execution of Martin Brown" (1868) remarks, "So sad a crime, and so revolting," and such descriptions of murder as both tragically "sad" and morally or aesthetically "revolting" dismantled distinctions between ordinary citizens and extraordinary criminals.

This combination of the sad and the revolting forms the framework for "The Last Moments and Confession of Wm. Sheward" (1869), which highlights the psychological struggles encountered by Sheward, who embodies the dramatically opposed identities of the criminal poet. Mediated by Sheward's voice of grave sadness, the ballad records his wife-murder in 1851 and his confession and condemnation eighteen years later. The lamentation appears on a broadside that includes a report of the gruesome details of an apparently official confession:

He placed the head in a saucepan, and put it on the fire to keep the stench away. He then broke it up, and distributed it about Thorpe. He then put the hands and feet in the same saucepan, in hopes they might boil away. Carried portions of the body away in a pail and threw them in different parts of the city. The long hair on my [*sic*] return from Thorpe, he cut with a pair of scissors in small pieces and they blew away as he walked.

The song that follows sets these details within the larger narrative frame of a "sad and wretched man, / Borne down in care and woe." In emphasizing the personal tragedy of Sheward and elaborating the burdens of "care and woe," the ballad decenters the narration of violence and highlights the psychology of guilt. The details within the ballad, therefore, though shocking, are relatively muted and impressionistic compared to the graphic precision of the prose report. Sheward recalls, "I her body into pieces cut," but his recollections of the disposal of the body, so graphically depicted in prose, remain less clear in verse: "[I] scattered it around, / Here and there, I scarce knew where, / I placed it on the ground." Responding to the needs of rhyme, the vague language here also intimates the peculiar circumstances of his confession to an eighteen-year-old crime.

When reporting the more gruesome aspects of his crime, Sheward is consistently concerned with the tragic nature of his narrative and the sadness of expressing his actions: "I boiled her head, how sad to tell, / I was mad without a doubt." His reference to madness further dissociates him from his violence, which, the ballad repeatedly asserts, occurred eighteen years before his own violent death. Presented in this way, Sheward's lament emerges from a confrontation with his contradictory selves: the past and the present, the violent and the sentimental, the criminal and the poet. The last lines of the ballad reiterate this grotesque combination of revolting violence and pathetic language:

> I cut and mangled that poor soul,
> My heart was flinty steel,
> Her limbs and body strewed about,
> In hedges, lanes, and fields.

This passage further underscores a contrast between two Shewards—the one who presently regards his wife as a "poor soul" and the one who eighteen years ago "cut and mangled" her and "strewed" her fragments in "hedges, lanes, and fields." This juxtaposition of two selves develops the pitiable persona of the criminal poet who can simultaneously recall his own "heart" of "flinty steel" and express affection or sympathy for his victim, a "poor soul."

For the most part, Sheward's ballad produces a murderous subject preoccupied with portraying his intense emotional experience of an eighteen-year-old crime. Although the secret murder and gory dismemberment of a wife easily accommodates sensationalism, the ballad as a whole sidelines the crime and foregrounds the criminal. Explorations of psychological struggle are privileged over examinations of legal guilt, which Sheward repeatedly and unequivocally acknowledges: "I done that dreadful awful deed / Near eighteen years ago." In a repetitive cycle, Sheward's crime narrative is interrupted by reflections on the burden of guilt, the anxiety of discovery, and the compulsion to speak. This cycle implies that the conflict between silence and speech has "borne" Sheward "down in care and woe":

> Kept the secret eighteen years,
> Within my guilty breast,
> And till the same I did divulge,
> I day nor night could rest.

With a restless need to "divulge" a "secret" lodged in his "guilty breast," Sheward locates psychological guilt in a tension between anxious silence and confessional speech. He explains, "I'had no comfort day or night, / Until I did confess." His wish to communicate, however, confronts the representational limitations of his unusual plight: "No pen can write, or tongue can tell, / My sad and wretched fate."

This reference to the limitations of "pen" and "tongue" also alludes to the eighteen-year delay between his secret crime and his public condemnation. Reinforcing the epistemological difficulties and ethical dilemmas of defining murderous subjects and condemning them to death, his psychological confusion and emotional turmoil disarm moral outrage:

> For eighteen years, in grief and tears,
> I passed many a dreary night,
> I had not one moment's happiness,
> Since I killed my own dear wife;
> At length I did confess the deed,
> For which I now must die,
> For a murder eighteen years ago—
> The which I don't deny.

While highlighting an obligation to express his "grief and tears," this passage also suggests that shame and remorse—not state protections or judicial resources—discipline and punish the criminal. Sheward passed as a law-abiding family man, while "God's all seeing eye" or "the eye of Justice," powers that function in some ballad narratives, failed to apprehend his crimes. Rather than demonstrating that criminals are always subdued by society, Sheward's ballad imagines criminals subduing and punishing themselves.

In covering Sheward's unusual case the *Times* also highlighted the unsettling gap between confessional truth and evidentiary truth and noted the difficulty of prosecuting in 1869 a crime that allegedly occurred in 1851. Detailing the "strangeness of the story," the *Times* reports that when Sheward confessed his crime and asked to be taken into custody, a skeptical police force only reluctantly complied after some preliminary fact-checking (1 April 1869, 9). Adding to the peculiarity of Sheward's case, the newspaper reports that once taken into custody, "the man had revoked his confession and affirmed his innocence of that crime, so that it was on a plea of 'Not Guilty' that the trial actually proceeded" (1 April 1869, 9). Although circumstantial evidence eventually corroborated Sheward's confession to the court's satisfaction, his defense counsel maintained that Sheward "had revealed nothing in his confession which might not have been collected from the facts already known to the public" (1 April 1869, 9). At trial the jury had to "decide between his acknowledgement and his recantation" (1 April 1869, 9).

The *Times* eventually came to agree with the state's action in this case, but Sheward's street ballad fixates on the peculiarities of the case. In imparting an obsessive quality to Sheward's need to confess his crime, the ballad insinuates that criminal speeches and confessional narratives—speech acts rather than criminal acts—define relations between crimes and punishments. Continuing to highlight the slippage between truth and testimony the ballad rather mischievously exploits the ironies of the state's reversal. Initially hesitating to charge

Sheward, the state now insists upon his death. The limitations of judgment are embellished by references to letters of protest, which not only proclaim his innocence but also deny the crime:

> There was letters sent from different parts,
> To say my wife did live,
> To save me from the gallows,
> But none would they believe;

Arriving from "different parts," these letters imply widespread support for Sheward and challenge the authenticity of his official confession. With these epistolary protests and their implausible claims, the ballad raises questions about the methods of naming, judging, and punishing criminals. If execution constitutes a response to crime narratives, not criminal acts, and if criminals subdue and punish themselves, then judicial procedures and capital punishments lose their authority.

Just as "The Last Moments and Confession of Wm. Sheward" reconfigures Sheward's particularly shocking acts of murder and dismemberment as a tale of care and woe, "Lamentation & Execution of James Longhurst" (1867) frames Longhurst's "cruel murder" of seven-year-old Jane Sax—for which he "was doomed to die" at "Horsemonger lane on the scaffold high"—within a narrative of a "wretched youth." The historical Longhurst was tried and hanged for murder, but newspaper reports also attest to the fact that the murder followed a rape, and euphemistic references to the "terrible outrages [his victim] had suffered" appeared in newspaper reports (*Times*, 27 March 1867, 11). Accordingly, in his lamentation, Longhurst explains that first he "shamefully did her illtreat" and reports, "Then coward-like I drew my knife, / To rob this helpless child of life." Longhurst recalls the murder in graphic detail: "I stabbed her in the throat—her blood did pour,— / Then left her welt'ring in her gore." Continuing with the scene of discovery, he narrates a shocking attempt to conceal his crime:

> She cried for help, did poor little Jane,
> David Ensor to her assistance came;
> Whilst I, a guilty wretch did stand,
> And licked her blood from off my hand.

From the confession that he "did her illtreat" to the acknowledgment that he "stabbed her" to the claim that he "licked the blood from off [his] hand," the ballad chronicles his descent into increasingly horrific behavior—from rapist to murderer to cannibal—and thus accommodates ballad conventions of grotesque violence.

In spite of Longhurst's multiple affronts to ethical sensibilities and his devastating violation of fundamental taboos, this ballad, embodying the political interests of lamentation poetics, forces the coincidence of violence and sensibility—tempering Longhurst's outrageous conduct with multiple references to his remorse for the crime, his sympathy for his victim, and his terrified anticipation of his impending execution. Helping to sustain the sympathetic tones of his ballad voice, the broadsheet documents in its prose section the "Terrible Scene in the Prison with the Culprit" and highlights his remarkable display of "contrition" since his condemnation. The report relays the "frightful scene" of a "wretched youth" struggling against the certainty of his own violent death: "The moment the culprit saw Calcraft, the executioner, approach him with the straps to pinion his arms, he started back with an aspect of terror depicted on his countenance, and began to struggle violently with the turnkeys." The report also speculates about the nature of Longhurst's resistance: "The prisoner's conduct seemed to be actuated by an uncontrollable horror of the executioner and the apparatus of death." This vision of the terrible punishments of the state and the intense suffering of the condemned is supported by the historical Longhurst's youthful appearance. He was described in the press as "short in stature and very boy-looking," and before her death, his victim reportedly identified him with the words, "That boy did it" (*Times*, 27 March 1867, 11).

In this context, the lamentation develops a fictional voice to reinforce the pathos of the historical Longhurst. Denouncing his crimes, the ballad Longhurst acknowledges his guilty agency and his shameful remorse: "James Longhurst, it is my name, / I've brought myself to grief and shame." Highlighting her innocence, his references to his victim as "poor little Jane" and a "helpless child" also underscore his regret. Having claimed his identity as condemned criminal, he also casts himself and his death in a family tragedy:

> My tender parents came to visit me,
> My heart was breaking their grief to see,
> Tears from their eyes did in torrents fall,
> While for mercy to my God did call.

Tearful parents and merciful prayers domesticate Longhurst, as he responds to the emotional pain of his grief-stricken family. He explains, "I hope that none will them upbraid, / While I am in my silent grave," and like so many execution ballads, his song thus acknowledges the consequences of death penalties on the families of condemned criminals.

Essentially imparting a plea for mercy, such details conjure the historical context in which the jury that found Longhurst "guilty" recommended mercy on the grounds that that his crime did not seem premeditated (*Times*, 27 March

1867, 11). The ballad's, and the jury's, interest in mercy reflects the ongoing conflicts between the state and its citizens when interpreting capital crimes and assigning capital punishments. Such conflicts consistently establish the foundation for last lamentation voices, which depict the contest between the irrevocable decrees of condemnatory judgment and the ethical ambiguities in allocating mercy. The instability of interpretation is also underscored in Longhurst's apostrophe to "[g]ood people," whom he asks to "draw near" and listen to "[his] sad history," from which, he surmises, they "will a warning take." The particular instruction of this warning, however, remains wholly unspecified. While critical assumptions about the lamentation ballad's habitual capitulation to state authority might lead us to find a simple advisory against bad behavior, the various strands of Longhurst's "sad history" also register a more emphatically critical commentary on state retribution.

Casting the criminal as a beloved son facing "the apparatus of death" and the "silent grave," the ballad constructs a personal tragedy, but the narration of his movement through the criminal justice system increases the scale—and significance—of his experience: "Then I was taken for this cruel deed, / And sent for trial, as you may read; / At Kingston assizes, tried and cast." In the courtroom scene of his sentencing, the ballad explicitly represents the language of law and punishment:

> The Judge said, James Longhurst, you are guilty found,
> You will go from here to London town
> And there you'll die a death of shame,
> And meet your fate at Horsemonger lane.

This account of Longhurst's sentencing, with its stresses on "die," "death," and "shame," exposes the performative qualities of state authority, which fixes his criminal identity with the words "guilty" and condemns him to a "death of shame" using the deterministic rhetoric of "fate." Yet, at the same time, the ballad's many empathic tones diminish the truth-claims of this judicial posture. In contrast to the imperious and anonymous judge, the personalized and conflicted criminal poet appears straightforward and sincere, conveying the most truthful—because the most precisely rendered and emotionally fraught—account of capital punishment. In a curious realignment of political authority, the sentimental speech and emotional authenticity of the condemned criminal awaiting the "silent grave" suggests that the social rupture created by Longhurst's terrible crimes will not be repaired with the execution of a "boy."

The tensions of speech and silence generate for Longhurst the same problems of communication that afflicted Sheward. Seeking to convey the suffering of the condemned criminal, Longhurst requires language unavailable in official discourses about criminal guilt and retributive justice:

While I lay in my prison cell,
My state of mind no tongue can tell;
I could not rest by day or night,
Poor Jane was always in my sight.

In this fashion, the ballad situates the essence of murderous guilt—and the consciousness of the criminal poet—somewhere between painful memories of violent agency and grim anticipations of violent death. Accordingly, Longhurst's mournful and haunted attempt at articulation arises out of a confrontation with the "silent grave" and an obligation to "recall the past." As the desire to speak and the difficulty of expression shape the experience of eternal silencing, the justifications for capital punishment are challenged by a troubled "state of mind" which both requires and defies communication.

In yoking the violent criminal and the sentimental poet, blurring a presumed line between deviant criminals and normal citizens, Sheward and Longhurst invite reexaminations of their crimes and punishments. In consistently spotlighting the condemned criminals of scaffold dramas, rather than highlighting the hapless victims of terrible crimes, lamentation ballads do not simply dismiss victims, who often haunt their killers or elicit their sympathy, but they do redirect attention to the definitions of criminal responsibility and the practices of execution that shaped the marketplace where ballads were sold and, of course, determined the immediate political context in which they were read. In their reevaluations of crimes and condemnations, lamentation ballads sometimes placed graphic imagery aside and concentrated instead on the legal language of criminal trials. As J. F. Stephen noted, "A crime being an act punished by the law as voluntary, intentional, and malicious, and the act being admitted, or proved, the only way in which criminality can be disproved is by rebutting the ordinary presumptions of will, intention, or malice. If either of these presumptions is rebutted, crime is disproved" (*General View* 86). Seizing upon these important distinctions, and undercutting legal fictions with lyrical fictions, balladeers often entangled murders in impressionistic memories of inexplicable impulses in ways that challenged guilty verdicts and death sentences.

In the "Execution of F. Hinson" (1869), for example, Frederick Hinson details his murder of the "false-hearted" adulteress, Maria Death. Tinkering with the legalities of the historical Hinson's case, the ballad rehabilitates his murderous character by failing to acknowledge sexual improprieties shaping his conduct. Hinson's victim was his cohabitating mistress, not his legal wife (who lived elsewhere), yet, as the *Times* reported, in spite of the taint of adultery and illegitimacy Hinson "laboured under the hallucination that he was justified in taking the life of the woman under the belief that she had proved unfaithful to him, and that, though not in law his wife, he regarded her as such in all respects." The report also adds, "It may also be remembered that he has two young children, one by his wife, who is still living, and the other by the murdered woman" (13 December 1869, 6).

Perhaps because of its legal and ideological liabilities, this lamentation ballad avoids Hinson's domestic scandal completely. Hailing an audience of "[y]oung men and maidens" as well as "[y]ou married and you single all," Hinson instructs his audience to "list to my sad lamentation" and to "pity, pity my downfall." Although Hinson specifically warns "young men" against the passions that lead to crime and punishment—"Your passions curb, 'ere 'tis too late"—his narrative privileges moral justifications and legal defenses rather than cautionary tales and behavioral advice.

Hinson mystifies the circumstances of his crime by piecing together a crude psychology of impassioned jealousy, and he questions the murder charge by situating the crime in the context of his victim's adultery: "When I found she was false-hearted, / Jealousy filled my mind, 'tis true." Building a case for adulterous provocation, Hinson connects his jealousy to his desire to maintain both marriage and family: "I grieved from her for to be parted, / For I loved her, and our offspring too." With the mad passions of jealousy, the legal mitigations of adultery, and the ideological force of domesticity invoked to explicate and expiate his crime, Hinson also intimates that he was mentally absent—rather than willfully present—at the time of the murder. Effectively disavowing legal responsibility, he proclaims, "Recall the dead I never can, / I saw her fall, and gazed in sadness, / A guilty and heartbroken man." Unlike other ballad criminals who confess to stabbing, ripping, mangling, and boiling, Hinson admits only that he "saw" and "gazed" and thereafter became "a guilty and heartbroken man." Hinson further diminishes culpability by describing his victim's provocative behavior. When he finds her "[i]n company with that treacherous man," he explains, "One kindly word from her would saved her / And stay'd alas my murderous hand." Maria Death, however, "braved [his] anger" and provoked his "murderous hand."

With murderousness attributed to his "hand" and his victim cast as an unrepentant adulteress, Hinson's ballad revisits the prerogatives of enraged and wronged husbands, which informed Hinson's defense at trial where, pleading "temporary insanity," he requested a reduced charge of manslaughter on the basis of provocation (*Times*, 13 December 1869, 6). As Wiener has explained, while provocation as a mitigating factor in wife-murder had less and less impact on judges as the nineteenth century wore on, it continued to sway juries and influence public opinion (*Men* 199). At the same time, "[k]illings on the basis of sexual unfaithfulness," characterized by familiar circumstances and the use of weapons, "presented a unique and stark situation for the criminal justice system: a confrontation between the worst provocation and the clearest intent to kill" (204). This gap between judicial and public opinion helps to explain the defensive strategies of this particular lamentation ballad, which counteracts the historical Hinson's known impropriety with the ballad Hinson's projected righteousness. The ballad rather explicitly alludes to this rift between the judiciary and the public when Hinson claims to be "condemned by some, [but] by many pitied."

Amidst the contradictions and ironies of criminal and matrimonial law that influenced Hinson's case, the notion that Hinson was done in by impropriety—not murder—informed public commentary on his case:

> When Frederick Hinson went to the Newgate gallows in 1869 for killing his apparently unfaithful common-law wife, the author of a printed circular asking for his reprieve acknowledged, while decrying, this distinction: "Had Hinson been married to the woman he murdered, thousands of people would have commiserated with him, and have considered him partially justified. It is, therefore, a morbid caprice to say he ought to be hanged because he was not married to the woman. He considered her his wife, she had children by him, and it appears that he had used her well." (Wiener, *Men* 207)

Resurrecting the failed defensive strategies invoked at trial and infusing his reflections with affective tones, the ballad similarly negotiates a culture of consent for wife-murder in order to question the legal and moral grounds of his execution. More interested in the classed injustices of capital punishment than the gendered injustices of marriage law, this ballad, like many others, contests the murder conviction and the capital sentence by upholding the domestic privileges of men. The ballad Hinson, a legitimate and proper patriarch, claims the rights to violence unavailable to his improper historical counterpart.

Accordingly, as the condemned Hinson awaits execution in his prison cell, he is victimized by memories of his crime and haunted by the apparition of his victim:

> My days are spent in lamentation,
> My sleepless nights were spent in prayer,
> My mind was filled with agitation,
> For Maria's shade was always there.

Engaged in "lamentation" and "prayer," Hinson becomes a family man of deep religious faith whose ignominious death contrasts his respectable life:

> At Wood Green I was respected,
> With all around in peace did dwell,
> Now broken-hearted and dejected,
> I pine within a gloomy cell.

His piousness is also underscored as he links justice to an anticipated meeting with "[his] offended God." Wondering to himself, "How can I meet my heavenly father, / Or dare to him for mercy cry," and hoping, "the Lord [will] have mercy on my soul," Hinson characterizes his ballad as a "dying prayer" and admonishes his audience, "My dying prayer do not be scorning."

Rehabilitating Hinson in this way, the ballad redefines his crime—he loved Maria and wanted her to stay—and his execution—his "poor darling orphans" will be left behind. Wholly invested in domestic propriety, callously thwarted by an adulterous "wife," and mercilessly condemned by a home-wrecking state, Hinson is rescued from the criminal margin and restored to the ideological center where he performs the roles of moral teacher, loving father, devoted Christian, peaceful neighbor, and pitied victim. In this instance, the reflective criminal poet rather pointedly dismantles legal arguments and exploits gender inequalities to protest a state execution.

Also intervening in judicial procedures is the "Lamentation of Samuel Wright" (1864) (figure 6), which aggressively challenges the legal language of intent in Wright's case. In doing so, the ballad fully relies on the notorious facts of his condemnation and execution, which many Victorians of all classes publicly denounced as a case of judicial murder. A London bricklayer, Wright was executed in 1864 for killing his "mistress," and, as the *Times* reported, Wright had no defense counsel and pleaded "Guilty" at trial. After rejecting the *prosecutor's* suggestion to the court that Wright obtain access to legal counsel and reconsider his plea, the judge sentenced Wright to death a mere three days after the crime was committed. Wright was then executed less than a month after his sentencing, despite a fully articulated public outcry. The speed with which Wright's case moved through the criminal justice system was often cited as a fundamental injustice in his case, and the circumstances of his trial and execution featured prominently in abolitionist arguments and the deliberations of the Capital Punishment Commission.

In his reflections on the abolitionist movement in Victorian England, Alfred Dymond cites Wright's case as tragic consequence of a flawed system of capital punishment:

> But the year 1864 was marked by events that hastened affairs to a crisis. The execution of Samuel Wright, in the teeth of public opinion, for an offence that would probably be denominated murder in no other civilized country, without even the form of a trial, or the slightest means of defence, upon the *ipse dixit* of a judge whose sage opinion was founded upon *ex parte* depositions taken before the police magistrate, and after every class of the people had in turn prayed that his life might be spared—this case brought home to men's minds the conviction that not in the humane professions of the law's

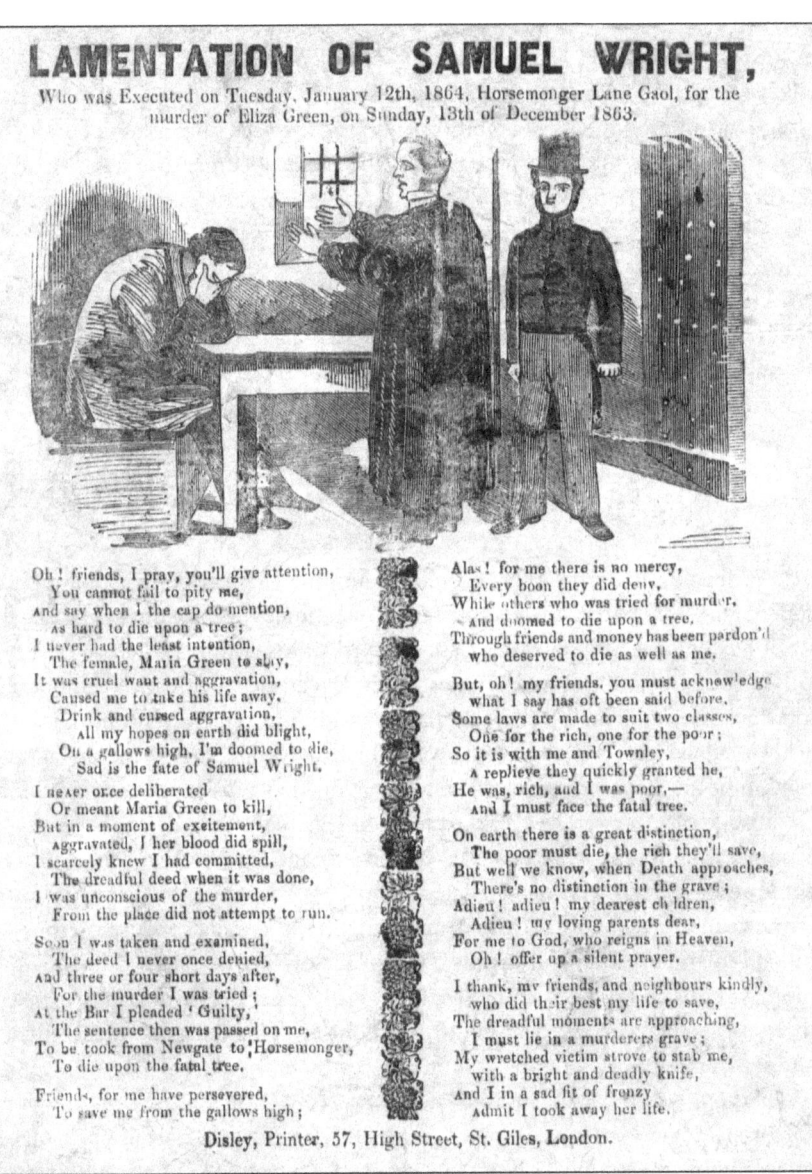

Figure 6
Lamentation of Samuel Wright. Trials Broadside 205: Hollis no. 6909725. Courtesy of Special Collections Department, Harvard Law School Library.

administrators, but in a radical alteration of the law itself, was alone to be found safety from judicial error. (295)

Upon Wright's conviction, working-class citizens, as well as members of the judiciary and proponents of abolition, mobilized to save him. Many Londoners boycotted his execution in protest, and, as the *Times* documented, as the scaffold was erected for Wright, a handbill condemning the execution circulated through the crowd:

> A Solemn Protest against the Execution of Wright—Men and women of London, abstain from witnessing this sad spectacle of injustice. Let Calcraft and Co. do their work this time with none but the eye of Heaven to look upon their crime. Let all window shutters be up and window blinds be down for an hour on Tuesday morning in Southwark. Englishmen, shall Wright be hung? If so, there is one law for the rich, and another for the poor. (*Times*, 13 January 1864, 12)

Acknowledging these protests and referencing the charged political context of capital punishment debates, "Lamentation of Samuel Wright" contests the legality of his sentence and reiterates class critiques of his criminal case.

As the circulating handbill attests, "the spectacle of injustice" embodied interlocking problems of class oppression and legal representation. A widely acknowledged procedural travesty, one which necessitated the "radical alteration of the law itself," Wright's trial also functioned as a disturbing counterpoint to murder cases in which access to learned legal counsel and applications of criminal insanity theories conspired to allow financially privileged and socially empowered killers to "escape" justice. As Wright was going to his death for a crime that was arguably a case of manslaughter, the audaciously unremorseful and unapologetically misogynist George Victor Townley, responsible for the more heinous and premeditated murder of his fiancée, who had recently broken their engagement, received respite three months after his trial and sentencing and was removed to an insane asylum for treatment.[24]

Though controversial insanity defenses were by no means unfamiliar to Victorians in 1864, the uncanny timing of the two cases attracted particularly intense public scorn. On 11 January 1864, just as the Home Office was rejecting Wright's final petition for mercy and upholding his hasty conviction and sentencing, Townley was being transferred from Derby Gaol to St. George's-in-the-Field's Criminal Lunatic Asylum in London (*Times*, 12 January 1864, 9). In light of the Townley reprieve, Wright's case symbolized the extreme vulnerability of the working classes within a biased and inconsistent criminal justice system, and among the taunts from the crowd at Wright's execution were: "Shame," "Judicial murder," and "Where's Townley?" (*Times,* 13 January 1864, 12).

Explicitly concerned with the Wright-Townley scandal, "Lamentation of Samuel Wright" dispenses with conventional moral frames entirely and opens with the criminal poet exclaiming, "Oh! friends," and insisting, "You cannot fail to pity me." Contrasting the disingenuous and unscrupulous qualities of Townley's "escape," the speaker signals his own integrity and honesty with a frank and direct proclamation of his involvement in the death of Maria Green. He then goes on to carefully scrutinize criminal responsibility and construct a legal defense, which interrogates definitions of murder and methods of sentencing. In this fashion, the street ballad grants Wright the opportunity to testify at length on his own behalf using legal language that the ill-informed and unrepresented historical Wright was seemingly unaware of and incapable of articulating at his hasty trial "three or four short days after" the crime. Wright, with his right to speak restored, denies intent in wholly unambiguous statements: "I never had the least intention, / The female, Maria Green to slay." He also dismisses premeditation: "I never once deliberated / Or meant Maria Green to kill." The crime, he explains, occurred in "a moment of excitement":

> Aggravated, I her blood did spill,
> I scarcely knew I had committed,
> The dreadful deed when it was done,
> I was unconscious of the murder,
> From the place did not attempt to run.

In refuting the murder conviction, Wright cites the forces of "drink and cursed aggravation" and euphemistically professes that he "her blood did spill." While Wright clearly denies malice aforethought, he consistently acknowledges his actions—even those taken in court: "At the Bar, I pleaded, 'Guilty.'" This statement, of course, reflects the actual plea of the historical Wright, but, in the context of the Townley case, its reiteration here also contributes to the ballad's emphatic representation of Wright's personal integrity. Fraught with meaning, his plainspoken plea also alludes to the historical Wright's initial ignorance of legal distinctions between murder and manslaughter and reminds readers that his death hinges on his political disenfranchisement, not his murderous guilt. That he killed Maria Green is not in question, but the ballad's rehearsal of this defense echoes and addresses public calls for a judicial review of his case.

The defensive posture assumed in this ballad is reinforced with an allusion to dedicated protesters—a network of friends and the working-class community—intervening on his behalf. Proclaiming, "Friends, for me have persevered, / To save me from the gallows high," Wright acknowledges the inadequacy of their pleas in a summary of the class injustices of his case:

> Alas! For me there is no mercy,
> Every boon they did deny,
> While others who was tried for murder,
> And doomed to die upon the tree,
> Through friends and money have been pardon'd
> Who deserved to die as well as me.

In this comparative study of judicial procedures, the "boon" of money and the doom of poverty indict the effects of class privileges on the criminal justice system. With the claim that Townley "deserved to die as well as me," Wright does not simply contest capital punishment but rather cites the bias of class that informs all judicial procedures. Gatrell has argued that execution ballads of the 1860s were politically "safe" because Parliament was scrutinizing capital punishment and "abolitionism was in fashion" (Gatrell 164). Yet, as Wright's ballad demonstrates, the case-specific analyses and the dynamics of poetic voice allowed balladeers to extend their commentaries beyond the rhetorical fashions of abolitionism and enfold life-and-death questions about class stratification and, in this particular case, the moral and legal economies of criminal psychology.

In fact, Wright interprets the verdict in his case wholly in terms of class conflict without any apparent concern for abolition as a political agenda:

> But, oh! my friends, you must acknowledge
> What I say has oft been said before,
> Some laws are made to suit two classes,
> One for the rich, one for the poor;
> So it is with me and Townley,
> A reprieve they quickly granted he,
> He was, rich, and I was poor,—
> And I must face the fatal tree.

Apostrophizing his "friends," Wright articulates the social necessity of his death ("I must face the fatal tree") in terms of "rich" and "poor." And, as this criminal poet articulates what "has oft been said before," his personal tragedy, which he characterizes as the case of "me and Townley," points to the vulnerability of the working classes in the criminal justice system: "On earth there is a great distinction, / *The poor must die*, the rich they'll save" (emphasis added). Ordained by laws "made to suit two classes," Wright's death on a "gallows high" and his disappearance into a "murderers grave" are depicted as wholly overdetermined. The necessity of his death even disturbs the leveling force of "the grave." Although Wright announces, "But well we know, when Death approaches, / There's no distinction in the grave," in the political context of his execution and Townley's institutionalization, this maxim only serves to reinforce the material disadvantages of class hastening Wright to an unmarked murderer's grave.

His delivery of emotionally wrought "adieus" to his "dearest children" and his "loving parents dear" and his thanks to his friends and neighbors who "did their best [his] life to save" heighten this effect. But the ballad's last four lines revert to legal discourse, as Wright concludes with the self-defense plea that informed public protests on his behalf. "My wretched victim strove to stab me, / With a bright and deadly knife," he explains, and this introduction of a "bright and deadly knife" into the ballad further complicates the relationship between the condemned killer and the murder victim by displacing the language of intent onto the victim ("strove to stab me") and the imagery of sensational violence onto her weapon ("bright and deadly knife"). The final two lines encapsulate the persona of this criminal poet: "And I in a sad fit of frenzy, / Admit I took away her life." With this earnest and emotional voice, simultaneously bidding farewell and articulating mitigation, the ballad again sharply distinguishes between manslaughter and murder and pits the desperate expressions of sorrow against the looming condition of silence.

While Wright's ballad documents a particular instance of widespread public sympathy for a condemned criminal at a time when abolition was "in fashion," other ballads demonstrate that the trope of the criminal poet also produced critical readings of class conflict and criminal justice against the grain of mainstream public opinion. In 1840, when Francis B. Courvoisier, a valet and a Swiss national, murdered his aristocratic English employer, Lord William Russell, his crime dramatized very specific early-Victorian anxieties about class. Accommodating conventional stereotypes of a deviant and dangerous class, the class politics of his crime, the public stature of his victim, and the newspaper coverage of his trial mobilized elite Victorians, and his public hanging brought members of the aristocracy and the literati—including Thackeray and Dickens—into the scaffold crowd. Inciting public paranoia and outrage, Courvoisier's crime and punishment were consistently narrated in terms of working-class threats to the property and persons of the upper classes. With Victorian England's upper-class citizens playing the curious and horrified potential victims of working-class violence, the cultural scripts generated to explain his case sparked what Richard Altick has termed a "Victorian servant-neurosis" (220). Documenting the symptoms of this upper-class pathology, he cites diarist Charles Greville who explained that the Courvoisier case "frightened all London out of its wits": "Visionary servants and air-drawn razors or carving-knives dance before everybody's imagination and half the world go to sleep expecting to have their throats cut before morning" (220–21).

Motivated by the immense popularity of Courvoisier's case, ballad publishers printed an array of broadsheets containing assessments of his crime and copies of his affecting verses. Though divergent in detail and emphasis, these ballads consistently highlighted the same motive for the killing: Lord Russell discovered Courvoisier's thefts and terminated his employment, so Courvoisier resolved to murder him.[25] Establishing causal links between property crimes and violent crimes, of course, easily confirmed prejudices about a criminally oriented underclass. Yet, the lyrical voice and narrative perspective of the criminal poet also confused that logic. The "Copy of Verses" printed in "Particulars of the Life, Trial, Confession, and Execution of Courvoisier," for example, in addressing the classed tensions of Courvoisier's crimes, renders the evolution from robbing to killing as a condition of master and servant relations—not from the perspective of the nervous propertied classes but, rather, from the perspective of a compromised and delinquent employee.

Invoking commonplace explanations for Courvoisier's motivation and condemnation, the ballad describes the murder of Lord Russell as the actions of a servant being discharged without recommendation. Reflecting a precise circumstantial motive, it sidesteps the more common panic-inducing scenarios of a "frightened" London subject to revolutionary uprisings. A self-reflective criminal poet, Courvoisier acknowledges his misdeeds and regrets his errors in judgment, but he links them to the more local conditions of Russell's household and the idiosyncrasies of his own character in ways that temper paranoid or neurotic readings of his crimes. Courvoisier laments, "I valet was unto Lord Russell / Who lived in Norfolk Street, Park Lane, / Where I might have lived a life of comfort / But for one thing which gives me pain." In mournful retrospect, elaborating the "one thing which gives [him] pain," Courvoisier contemplates his folly and hubris in expecting that daily pilfering would not be noticed or that servants would not be monitored:

> I day by day my master plundered,
> And did the property conceal,
> Thinking I should not be suspected
> And no one could the tale reveal;

He explains that Lord Russell, upon discovering Courvoisier's theft, "threatened that he would discharge me, / From his service the next day." "It was then," this ballad version of Courvoisier states with absolute precision, "I formed the horrid plan, / For to commit the awful crime." Far from denying malicious forethought or criminal intent, he affixes the moment of murderous inspiration and explicates his "horrid plan" as a response to the threat of a "discharge." Reiterating this notion, Courvoisier explains that, amidst the wealth and comfort of Russell's home, he made his murderous decision on "the fifth of May" at the precise moment when "my master ... threatened to discharge me." And, operating in a confessional mode, unlike the historical Courvoisier who acknowledged his guilt but demanded to be "defend[ed] to the utmost" by counsel (Cairns 130), the ballad Courvoisier infuses his recollections with the affective tones of lamentation poetics while intimating the difficult circumstances of the servant class.[26]

In contextualizing Russell's murder in this way, and in reconstructing the notorious character of the historical Courvoisier, the ballad refuses to reproduce simple causal links between crime and class. While arguments about the dangerous classes typically imagined working-class crime in generalist and reductive formulae of urban "demoralization" or collective rebellion, the criminal poet, redirecting attention toward the particular anxieties of a particular servant on a particular day, casts his violence not as a collective assault on aristocratic privilege but as the bad decision of a discharged servant. As in many ballads, Courvoisier's verses also provide gory recollections of the murder: when "all was hushed in sleep," he explains, "I armed me with a fatal knife, / And sought the chamber of my master, / Determined for to take his life." And, in a moment of graphic reportage, the ballad forces the coincidence of sensitive poet and murderous agent: "His throat I severed in an instant," he explains, and "from the wound life's blood did flow." In this striking symbolic inversion of power relations, such details connect issues of agency and premeditation to the theme of Courvoisier's desperation.

In this "instant," which occurred in his "master's chamber" where "in peace Lord William [was] sleeping," however, a more famous and more menacing murderous agent appears. Just as Courvoisier "severed" the throat and the "blood did flow," he explains, "The fiend exulting stood before me / For he had worked my overthrow." If only for a moment, the appearance of the "fiend" shifts the ethical terms of the narrative, muddling criminal responsibility and displacing agency. Fulfilling the codes of lamentation poetics, this symbolic imagery is also joined by emotional reflections. Courvoisier remembers his murderous actions with regret, and he frames his narrative, after all, with a dreadful awareness that he is "doomed to die a death of shame." He then addresses his futile attempts to conceal his guilt:

> In my innocence I still persisted,
> But God ordained it otherwise,
> A British jury found me guilty,
> And I am to answer with my life.

Subject to the powers of three inexorable forces, an overthrow by "the fiend," the ordination of "God," and the verdict of "a British jury," Courvoisier, a multiply disadvantaged servant and foreigner, must confront his overdetermined scaffold fate: "blood for blood will be required, / And I must the dread forfeit pay." While the historical Courvoisier manifested the nightmare of a revolutionary criminal class and his execution encapsulated the disciplinary authority of a "consensual 'we'" (who attended in the tens of thousands), the ballad's application of lamentation poetics interferes in both constructions. A throat-severing murderer, an anxious thieving servant, and a condemned criminal poet, this particular version of Courvoisier fragments readings of the historical Courvoisier's crimes, the nature of his character, and the necessity of his public death.

If songs about crime offered ballad writers opportunities to contest charges, convictions, and sentences, songs about execution afforded the possibility of interrogating the spectacle of public hanging. The verses printed on the broadsheet entitled "Life, Trial, Sentence, and Execution of Catherine Wilson, for the Murder of Mrs. Soames" (1862) (figure 7) foreground the subjective experience of the criminal in the condemned cell and at the scaffold. Between twenty and thirty thousand spectators attended the execution of Catherine Wilson, who, in 1862, was the first woman to be hanged at the Old Bailey in fourteen years (*Times*, 21 October 1862, 5). Public interest in her case was also increased by the eerie signs of calculating intent apparent in murder by poisoning, the crime for which she was convicted, and in the possibility of many more poisonings, which she was assumed to have committed but for which she was never tried.

Judith Knelman explains that because Wilson "posed as a nurse," her "perversion of medical assistance" made her seem especially "diabolical" (72). As an alleged serial poisoner, "who supported herself by killing off acquaintances for their money and possessions" (72), she inspired "not one application to the Home Secretary for remission of her sentence, not even from the Society for the Abolition of Capital Punishment" (73). Because "through wholesale poisoning she managed to uphold her position reasonably well in middle-class London society" (72), Wilson presumed to outwardly mimic but secretly undermine the tenants of bourgeois respectability. The notion of an aggressive murderess opportunistically using her role as caretaker and cunningly exploiting the cover of femininity constituted aggravating factors in the eyes of the court, the press, and the public.

Negotiating these contentious issues, the ballad emphasizes the public spectacle of femininity and feminizes the psychological traumas of condemnation. Unlike many ballads, this one identifies a tune to which this crime ballad can be sung: "Ave Maria." And with this ambitious musical allusion, it constructs a distinctly feminine criminal poet—or poetess—who reflects on the irrevocable sentence of death and her fate as a convicted poisoner. Anxieties about her "last night on earth" and her imminent public death, rather than recollections of her crime, convey her murderous subjectivity and establish her affective persona. In contrast, her ominous crimes, multiple poisonings, occupy a single stanza:

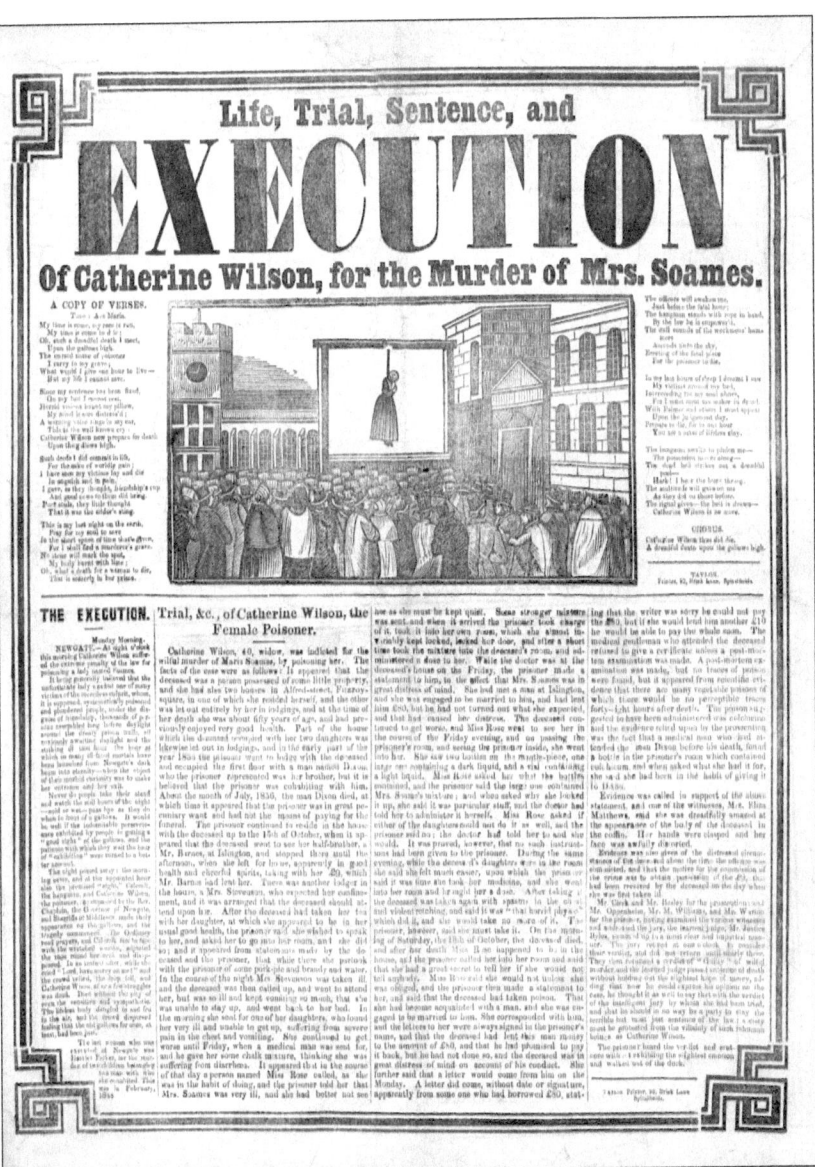

Figure 7
Life, Trial, Sentence, and Execution of Catherine Wilson, for the Murder of Mrs. Soames. Trials Broadside 233: Hollis no. 8120856. Courtesy of Special Collections Department, Harvard Law School Library.

> Such deeds I did commit in life,
> For the sake of worldly gain;
> I have seen my victims lay and die,
> In anguish and in pain.
> I gave, as they thought, friendship's cup
> And good news to them did bring.
> Poor souls, they little thought,
> That it was the adder's sting.

Taking responsibility and outlining motivation, Wilson elaborates the sinister guises (the "friendship's cup" and "good news") and financial motives ("worldly gain") of her crimes—the details that generated disgust for Wilson and support for her execution.

Having revealed her murderous duplicity and her base materialism and arranged her victims into a collective of "poor souls," Wilson focuses solely on the projected scenes of her hanging and its tragic qualities, which are underscored by the rare spectacle of a condemned woman: "Oh what a death for a woman to die, / That is scarcely in her prime." With the assertion that she is "scarcely in her prime," the ballad alludes to newspaper reflections on Wilson's sexual appeal. The *Times* reported that Wilson was rumored to be a "good-looking woman," who was "well dressed on her trial," and speculated that the execution crowd "went to see, not a triumph of justice and an object of indignation, but something more hideous and revolting even than ordinary executions" (22 October 1862, 6). Continuing this analysis of the convict and the crowd, the *Times* asserts:

> Such was the respectable and prepossessing person who was to walk out of a window in the Old Bailey with her hands pinioned behind her, ascend a scaffold, be tired with a cap, noosed, and let go like a dog whose transgressions have provoked this requital, or who is no longer worth his keep. A woman dangling in mid air in broad daylight, in a London street, and over the heads of an immense rabble of low men and low women, is certainly a most disgusting sight. (22 October 1862, 6)

The severe criticism of Wilson's trial and execution in the *Times* serves as a striking example of the classed and gendered semiotics of public execution. It is not only the hanging of a woman that so distresses this writer, but also the fact that a well-comported, "good-looking," "respectable and prepossessing," figure will be "noosed, and let go" in front of and "over the heads of" representatives of the low and criminal classes.

Just as the historical Wilson's gender and class complicated the spectacle of her execution, it informs the ballad's approach to her lyrical voice. Exploiting and objectifying feminine passivity and sentiment, this ballad uses the affective power of a woman's lament to intimate the perversity of state killing. Highlighting her lack of agency, Wilson announces, "What would I give one hour to live— / But my life I cannot save" and reports, "A warning voice rings in my ear," calling, "Catherine Wilson now prepare for death / Upon the gallows high." Breaking from the lamentation trope of criminals haunted by their victims, this ballad criminal is instead haunted by a vision of her own impending victimization:

> Since my sentence has been fixed,
> On my bed I cannot rest,
> Horrid visions haunt my pillow,
> My mind is sore distressed.

Wilson's victims, in contrast, are presented as sympathetic witnesses whom she envisions "around [her] bed, / Interceeding for [her] soul above." With some irony, then, her victims, but not the state acting on their behalf or the public supporting her execution, apprehend the tragic weight of her circumstances and assist in the reclamation of her soul.

Also included in these "horrid visions" is Wilson's abject and anonymous decay in the "murderer's grave." She reflects, "No stone will mark the spot, / My body burnt with lime." Wilson's self-directed terror is then interrupted by the internalized disciplinary voice of the state proclaiming, "Prepare to die, for in one hour, / You are a mass of lifeless clay." Such blunt and abject articulations of her humiliating death—the "mass of lifeless clay" and the "body burnt with lime"—serve to underscore the violent consequences of execution.

Wilson's ballad fully exploits the illusion of the criminal poet hastily and desperately penning verses as execution day breaks, for Wilson continues to express her sorrows even as the "hangman stands with rope in hand." Recording the erection of the scaffold, she exposes the *mise-en-scène* of public hanging and highlights the integral set piece that transforms judicial killing into social justice:

> The dull sounds of the workmen's hammers
> Ascend unto the sky,
> Erecting of the fatal place
> For the prisoner to die.

These details attribute a calculating intent and mechanized agency to the state, for with them Wilson establishes the scaffold as a stage, the "fatal place" where "the prisoner" plays a role in a traditional and tragic political drama. As she writes her own tragedy, she exposes the performative, disciplinary function of her scaffold death, and her speech personalizes the spectacle of her public suffering. With a dirge-like pace and tone, she describes the procession:

> The hangman awaits to pinion me—
> The procession moves along—
> The dead bell strikes out a dreadful peel—
> Hark! I hear the busy throng,
> The multitude will gaze on me
> As they did on those before.

The ballad's review of the "dreadful peel" of bells, the sounds of the "busy throng," and the "gaze" of the "multitude" implies the routine and ritualistic history of this punitive drama and the role that Wilson, like "those before," will play in this terrifying spectacle of justice.

At the ballad's conclusion, Wilson projects the moment of her death: "The signal given—the bolt is drawn— / Catherine Wilson is no more." The cessation of her life and her speech is further realized in the chorus: "Catherine Wilson thus did die, / A dreadful death upon the gallows high." Formally and forcefully encoding the theme of interrupted speech, the ballad contrasts the impersonal and performative authority of state punishment with the intimate and authentic expression of criminal lamentation, and with the refrain of the chorus, it explicitly depicts the tragic conclusion implied in all execution ballads—the violent death and the eternal silence of the criminal poet.

Reproducing, in order to interrogate, the contests of speech and silence involved in judicial procedures, last lamentations restored the voice of the condemned criminal to the proceedings that ritualized and celebrated his or her violent death. As they restored and often rehabilitated the personal identities of murderers, they presented criminals as psychological subjects rather than spectacular objects. Their strategies of political resistance are rooted in the publicity of execution and the performativity of verse. The memorable speech of the criminal poet—exploiting the idea of authenticity associated with constructions of lyrical expression—disrupted the semiotic operations of and moral arguments for capital punishment. And complicating the public deaths of historical criminals, they blurred divisions between the "consensual 'we'" and the criminal other and established congruities between criminal acts and cultural circumstances.

"I Shall Be Read By My Peers": A Poetry of Critique

While the enormous sales of murder and execution ballads alert us to their popular appeal, more precise readings of individual ballads reveal their remarkably innovative approach to murder—one that reconstituted working-class audiences as critical, rather than criminal, subjects. The qualities that contributed most to crime balladry's public stature and cultural significance—their circulation in large quantities, their noisy presence in the streets, their availability in cheap print, their political immediacy, their anonymous authorship, their working-class audience—have fostered a long tradition of scholarly neglect. But contemporary theoretical frameworks, which have privileged questions of genre and discourse and examined the influences of literary markets and print media, enable us to reconsider their contributions to Victorian culture. "Genre" and "discourse," of course, have been fundamental to studies of crime in the novel, but as these terms increasingly inform analyses of poetry, particularly in terms of cultural circulation and political participation, they foster new understandings of crime balladry's fundamental generic tropes (criminal acts, crime scenes, and criminal poets) and formal qualities (simple rhythms and crude rhymes) with respect to legal and literary representation.

While providing new foundations for ballad exegesis, these theories of discourse and genre also encourage reconstructions of the field of Victorian poetry in ways that allow us to reconsider the literary legacy of the crime ballad. In particular, Williams's description of genre "as a fully cultural as well as a literary category" and her interest in genre and discourse as a "dialectical pair" recombining and deforming thematic and formal codes of representation illuminate the ways in which individual crime ballads (as technology, as performance) responded to the class ideologies and disciplinary institutions informing criminal discourse. This concept of dialectical pairing allows us to read Victorian poetry as a network of shared and contested formal techniques, generic conventions, aesthetic tropes, and verbal technologies—just as we read criminal discourse as a network of shared and contested institutional mandates, political interests, epistemological modes, and specialist terminologies.

Reviewing recent work in and suggesting future priorities for the field of Victorian poetry studies, Armstrong considers a network of poetry in similar terms:

> If we take seriously the idea of networks, of intertext, of multiple inter-relations and connections, if we take seriously the notion of poetry as technology,

then we will not understand the cultural work of the poets or the poetics and formal experiment of different groups by remaining with the "minor," the "marginalized," for that is to reinforce the categories we mean to challenge. ... The whole point of a network or a field is the different ways of cutting or crossing it, ways that we constitute ourselves. ... Landon–Tennyson, Chartist poetry–Browning, Michael Field–Wilde, street ballads–Swinburne's ballads, sensation novel–sensation poem–sensation journalism, railways–the poetics of railway time, these are just a few ways of constituting networks. ("The Victorian Poetry Party" 25)[27]

New pairings of high and low or marginal and central texts—and recognition of their formal, thematic, and discursive affiliations—produces a vision of Victorian poetry as an open system of intertextual exchange less beholden to hierarchies of literary form and social class.

In imagining new constellations of texts, we can begin to look at how poets themselves invoked textual networks in their own stylistic appropriations and textual allusions. For example, the tale of Robert Browning quoting from "a ghastly [ballad] stanza" on James Thurtell's murder of William Weare ("His throat was cut from ear to ear / His brains they battered in") signifies, perhaps, not a passing sensational interest or an insignificant biographical tidbit, but a curiosity about and a recognition of the multiple realms of verse (Paul 338). Similarly, Browning's reference to crime balladry in *The Ring and the Book,* in which Guido fears the poetic power of "portraiture in white and black / Of dead Pompilia gracing a ballad-sheet" (XI.1827–28), forms a part of the verse novel's self-reflexive representations of legal and literary intertextuality.[28]

Offering a much more comprehensive example of poetic networks, Wilde's "The Ballad of Reading Gaol" pairs aesthetic images and political arguments in ways that suggest a strategic identification with the public poetics of the "criminal" classes. To be sure, the ballad form was in no way the exclusive domain of street poetry. A nineteenth-century revival of the literary ballad, a Romantic tradition of lyrical balladry, and a popular tradition of political balladry, developed by Chartists and Irish nationalists among others, all inform the literary context of Wilde's poem. Signifying its more immediate political context and content, however, are the striking resemblances between the language and logic of "The Ballad of Reading Gaol" and the language and logic of execution ballads. In one of his lectures on poetry's modes of redress, Seamus Heaney usefully acknowledges the poem's broadside genealogy: "Obviously, in one way, there is something entirely conventional about the subject of murder and retribution, the setting of gaol yard and gaol cell, the cast of warder and hangman and chaplain, the dreadful props of gallows and quicklimed grave—all of these things belong in the tradition of the broadside ballad" (Heaney, "Speranza in Reading"

92).²⁹ Yet, in addition to the most obvious features of "subject," "setting," "cast," and "props," the structural foundations of the poem's critique—the elaboration of lyrical criminal subjects (the narrative "I" and the "wistful" killer), the invocation of the tragic and the sublime (emotional terror and bodily pain), the scrutiny of speech and silence as disciplinary technologies, and the correlation of individual suffering and collective guilt—recall the conceptual terrain of the broadside ballad.

Highlighting the plight of the condemned criminal, the poem's dedication registers an intent to memorialize Charles Thomas Wooldridge ("C. T. W."), but Wilde, like anonymous balladeers before him, also uses the emotional appeal and the life-and-death urgency of a particular capital case to construct a more wide-ranging critique of the institutions and ideologies supporting all aspects of "Man's grim Justice" (3.187). Aligning himself with the condemned murderer— "A prison wall was round us born, / Two outcast men were we" (2.73–74)—the speaker establishes two criminal personae with which to circulate through the prison grounds and record the procedures of incarceration and execution. References to "a hangman close at hand" (3.84), a "little heap of burning lime" (4.59), and the anonymous "dishonoured grave" (4.128) evoke the imagery of the street ballad and the obsessive concerns of the criminal poet.

Granting access to the interior of the prison and the minds of the prisoners, Wilde elaborates the psychological traumas of punishment—stony hearts and spectral visitations—in ways that further these associations. Casting prison life as a repetitive course of pathos and fear, the speaker proclaims, "Alas! it is a fearful thing / To feel another's guilt!" (3.91 92), and recalls execution day as a distressing combination of the routine and the sublime: "And Horror stalked before each man, / And Terror crept behind" (4.47–48). At the end of the ballad, having reviewed the grotesque images of a quicklimed corpse lying in a "pit of shame" (6.2), the speaker remarks, "And there, till Christ call forth the dead, / In silence let him lie" (6.7–8), thus exposing the conflicts between the mandates of Christian ethics and the measures of capital punishment. Mediating the full particulars of prison life through the affective tones of the speaker, and developing ironic links between individual and institutional acts of violence, the poem uses the authenticity of the suffering criminal to diminish the ethical authority of the state.

While "The Ballad of Reading Gaol" does not rely solely on the manipulation or citation of the generic codes of crime balladry, it does similarly exploit the political immediacy of its themes in order to manage its polemical and emotional content. Within the more sensational story of a murder and execution lie important reflections on prisoners who have not killed and will not be killed but who are subject nonetheless to the silencing and humiliating procedures that Wilde condemns. In this respect, Wilde's ballad exhibits a pointed engagement with the late-Victorian discourse of prison reform. Penning his ballad just after his own release from prison in 1897, he inserts himself into parliamentary and public debates surrounding the 1895 Gladstone Report on prison reform that preceded the 1898 Prisons Act. As Seán McConville notes in *English Local Prisons: 1860–1900* (1995), the pressing problem of penal reform initially suffered from neglect in the periodical and newspaper presses, but Wilde, via letters to the *Daily Chronicle* and the publication of "The Ballad of Reading Gaol," helped to publicize the contentious issues of inadequate diet, unproductive labor, and enforced silence as well as the "ill-treatment in prison of children and the weak-minded" (708).

At the same time, Wilde's ballad registers a late-Victorian disillusionment with the centralization of prison management and a growing distaste for the uniform treatment of all prisoners, which became increasingly problematic with the growth (and acknowledgment) of a more heterogeneous prison population. Lumping together "shrewd professional burglars, prostitutes, drunken brawlers, juvenile delinquents, weak-minded vagrants, respectable clerks who had succumbed to temptation and pilfered the cash register, misdemeanants who could not pay fines, and so on" (Wiener, *Reconstructing* 367–68)—and, we might add, a celebrity author for acts of "gross indecency"—late-Victorian prisons finally forced difficult questions about regulating prison culture.

In *Crime and Criminals* (1910), R. F. Quinton offers an account of the reassessment process that finally began, in 1894, "after sixteen years experience of prison centralization" (190), when Home Secretary Asquith finally assembled a committee, to conduct a "strict investigation and overhaul" of "the whole prison system," its "administrative machinery," and the "conditions under which prisoners are confined" (192–93). Asquith's committee recommended abolishing unproductive labor, improving the classification system, developing penal reformatories for young prisoners, establishing special sentences for "habitual criminals," designating training prisons for officers, and including medical representatives on the Prisons Board (Quinton 193). With such changes, the committee noted, "the system should be made more elastic, more capable of being adapted to the special cases of individual prisoners" (193).

The particularities of this reformist agenda, especially a concern with the identity and integrity of individual prisoners, structure the speaker's many observations of prison culture—informing both the critical arguments and the lyric tones of his critique. Arguing that "every prison that men build / Is built with bricks of shame" (5.15–16), Wilde highlights tensions between the sensibility of the criminal subject and the suffering of the criminal body. "And by all forgot, we rot and rot, / With soul and body marred" (5.65–66), the narrator explains, and the conditions of mental and physical decay constitute a spiritual death, which parallels the gruesome physical death of the executed prisoner. An "open grave" (3.60) awaits the condemned man, and a "numbered tomb"

(3.72) houses the speaker. The poem's attention to the physical space of prison life, like the street ballad's attention to the structures and stagecraft of scaffold death, exposes the performative technologies of state discipline. Subject to the monotony of unproductive labor—"We turn the crank, or tear the rope, / Each in his separate Hell" (5.57–58)—prisoners succumb to the dehumanizing effects of psychological alienation. Regimented exercises render prisoners a "herd of brutes" (4.50) watched over by "strutt[ing]" (4.49) warders in "uniforms spick and span" (4.51)—descendants, perhaps, of the new police of ballad infamy who were said to "strut" in "spick and span" uniforms while stealing mutton. Intensifying the brutishness of the prisoners, this well-supervised routine is contrasted with the degrading, but no less supervised, neglect of sanitation: "Each narrow cell in which we dwell / Is a foul and dark latrine" (5.37–38). Similarly, a diet of "brackish water" (5.43), which "[c]reeps with a loathsome slime" (5.44), is served with portions of "bitter bread" (5.45), carefully weighed in scales but full of "chalk and lime" (5.46).

As these images of abjection and alienation address concerns about the rights and wrongs of individual prisoners, they also contribute to a more broadly conceived indictment of the collective guilt of a disciplinary culture whose "shame" forms each brick of its prison walls and whose indifference sanctions the wrongs catalogued by Wilde. In emphasizing the privatized sufferings of prisoners, and thus sidelining the publicized crimes of criminals, the poem privileges the notion of social shame over the notion of individual guilt—an argument that appears most conspicuously in the reiterated line, "Each man kills the thing he loves," as well as the accompanying qualification, "Yet each man does not die" (1.54). For this reason, perhaps, Wilde's speaker claims indecision on the matter of "whether Laws be right / Or whether Laws be wrong" (5.1–2). The terms "right" and "wrong" are simply too reductive to accommodate the excesses of a sinning and punishing society or the belatedness of prison reforms.

A schema of ethical and epistemological paradox, which insists upon establishing congruities between criminals and citizens, is unique neither to Wilde's crime ballad nor to the street ballad. But considered together, their verbal, generic, and discursive parallels reflect shared political and critical postures. While its historical context explains the poem's manipulation of the theme of murder and the discourse of crime, the multiple implications of genre are best understood via notions of poetic performativity. Because poetic performativity, as Slinn argues, involves self-conscious engagements with literary form and political content, "both linking and distinguishing poetry from its contexts," Wilde's late-career turn to crime balladry stages an affiliation with a working-class genre and its audience.

Exchanging the stance of the dandy for the persona of the ex-convict, Wilde imagined his audience as a criminal class and himself as a criminal poet. In a letter to Robert Ross, Wilde recommended that his ballad be published in

Reynold's Magazine because it "circulates among the lower orders, and the criminal classes, and so ensures me my right audience for sympathy" (*Letters* 661). Making the same case to Reginald Turner, he explained that it constitutes "an organ that appeals directly to the criminal classes, so my audience is gathered together for me" (662), and to Leonard Smithers, he explained that it "circulates widely amongst the criminal classes, to which I now belong, so I shall be read by my peers" (663). His concerns about audience, peers, and sympathy suggest the poem's role in refashioning his public persona, reconstituting his professional relationship to literary culture, and fulfilling his personal and political commitment to penal reform upon his release from prison, a task that required him to negotiate markets for publication, genres of literature, and modes of "propaganda" (*Letters* 661)—which, he explained, characterizes the content of the poem after the lines, "For his mourners will be outcast men, / And outcasts always mourn" (4.137–38). Precisely because Wilde's ballad was not relegated to the streets and because it also exceeds the length and scope of the typical street ballad, Wilde's mingling of high and low literary styles can be read in terms of Felluga's "performative loop" of "identification" and "self-estrangement," which he defines via Cohen's notion of genre as an "interrelationship with and a differentiation from" other forms and texts (495).

Insofar as Wilde's ballad has often been viewed as a strange break with his literary past or a symptom of his altered post-prison consciousness, the generic and discursive associations of the ballad form—including its affiliation with the criminal classes—offer a way to reconsider "The Ballad of Reading Gaol" as another example of Wilde's textual appropriations, performative aesthetics, and thematic interests. In her examination of the sexual economies and aesthetic theories influencing Wilde's work, Regenia Gagnier reads Wilde's ballad as a "solemn" version of Wilde's formerly "light" expressions of paradox with which he interrogated the "politics of inside/outside social relations" (145). A similar interest in the politics of exclusion and inclusion inform the meanings of the ballad genre, the performance of criminality that Wilde implies, and the poem's status as a mode of institutional critique.

Applying Armstrong's image (via Mill) of Victorian poetry as a "system of concentric circles," we can imagine these circles not only as domains of democratic and conservative ideologies but also as domains of institutional and aesthetic discourses, of high and low genres, and of classes of authors and audiences. In tracing the poetic and political uses of murder across systems of overlapping circles and intertextual networks, we can reconnect Wilde's ballad, and street ballads, to the generic and discursive practices that they reproduced and interrogated. It is, thus, perhaps unexpectedly, not only through examinations of literary or sociopolitical themes, such as the theme of murder, but also through considerations of generic form that we can reassess the role of the working classes and the place of print culture in Victorian poetry studies.

Chapter 2

The Murderous Subject and the Criminal Sublime

IN MARCH 1843, following the jury's acquittal of the infamous Daniel M'Naghten, the *Times* printed the following lines "On a Late Acquittal" by Thomas Campbell:[1]

Ye people of England! exult and be glad,
For ye're now at the will of the merciless mad.
Why say ye that but three authorities reign—
Crown, Commons, Lords?—You omit the insane!
They're a privileg'd class, whom no statute controls,
And their murderous charter exists in their souls.
Do they wish to spill blood—they have only to play
A few pranks—get asylum'd a month and a day—
Then heigh! to escape from the mad-doctor's keys,
And to pistol or stab whomsoever they please.

Now, the dog has a human-like wit—in creation.
He resembles most nearly our own generation:
Then if madmen for murder escape with impunity,
Why deny a poor dog the same noble immunity!
So, if a dog or man bite you, beware being nettled,
For crime is no crime—when the mind is unsettled.

With their brisk tetrameter and straining anapests, these satirical verses capture the collective frustration of Victorians who, observing murder trials and scrutinizing insanity defenses, feared the disappearance of legal consequences for insane criminals "whom no statute controls." While legal terminology had long addressed mental states as fundamental elements of crime, the elaboration and application of counterintuitive concepts of criminal lunacy in the 1830s and 1840s challenged traditional notions of madness and malice and provoked concerns about new forms of legal "immunity" and "impunity." At M'Naghten's trial the mandate of judging his crime according to the features of the act succumbed, at the request of defense counsel, to a process of applying theories of the mind.[2] Examined through the lens of a newfangled science, his conduct—his fatal shooting of Edward Drummond, private secretary to Prime Minister Robert Peel, and his expressed intention to attack Peel in order to elude murderous Tories—confounded legal practices of regulation and redress.[3] Informed by competing interpretive frameworks and sensationalized by the role of political figures and parties in his violent actions and expressed intentions, his acquittal appeared to secure the "murderous charter" of a "privileg'd" criminal class and to threaten England with an ascendancy of the "merciless mad," who baffled legal reasoning and flouted judicial authority.

As "On A Late Acquittal" suggests, the legal and the symbolic meanings of M'Naghten's case highlighted concerns about the power of the state to interpret criminals and punish crimes. Immediately after the trial such concerns inspired a government inquiry into the judicial status of insanity pleas, which resulted in the articulation of the "M'Naghten Rules."[4] The particulars of M'Naghten's case—the pathologizing of his character and the decriminalization of his conduct—also participated in a broader cultural renegotiation of responses to insanity. Several converging early-Victorian projects, the centralization of a national asylum system, the professionalization of mental science, and the publication of new mental science theories, as well as the increased use of insanity defenses at murder trials, confused already difficult distinctions between madness and malice and character and conduct.[5] Changes in the diagnosis and treatment of insanity, which began in the late eighteenth century, combined with the early-Victorian revision of the criminal code and abolitionist scrutiny of capital punishment to complicate the meanings of murder. And as medical theories began to disrupt fundamental but troubled legal fictions, an obligation to ascertain and enforce responsibility continued to nag the collective conscience.[6] Disturbing the boundary between the normative citizen and the criminal other—and the alignment of "Crown, Commons, Lords"—the resulting confusion and conflict placed the discourses and the methods of interpretive power under intense scrutiny and inspired public bouts of sober reflection and sensational alarm.

Responding to the highly publicized interpretive crisis surrounding

M'Naghten's acquittal, an editorial in the *Times* requested clarification of the psychological theories invoked at his trial. Noting that the *Times* had respectfully withheld comment or question while the trial unfolded, the author, "in a spirit of humble and honest earnestness, of hesitating and admiring uncertainty, and of almost painful dubitation, ask[s] those learned and philosophic gentlemen to define, for the edification of common-place people like ourselves, where sanity ends and madness begins; and what are the outward and palpable signs of the one or the other?" (6 March 1843, 4). Continuing in this mock-obsequious tone, the editorial upholds a division between the values of "common-place" people and mental scientists while asking specific questions about the medical testimony in M'Naghten's case, which, the writer reports, included a diagnosis of "homicidal monomania" and a "conviction that the prisoner had laboured under a *morbid delusion* of which this murder was the climax" (6 March 1843, 4). In the interests of self-preservation and public safety, the author explains, "simple folks" require an "accurate and general description" of monomania so that persons may take precautions against a "monomaniacal pistol or a climacteric stiletto" (6 March 1843, 4). In spite of any intellectual merits or practical applications, however, the medical theories in question offer this writer no sense of justice. Agreeing that murderous monomania might be "highly curious . . . in a medical point of view," the author concludes, "it is but poor consolation to reflect that a fellow man has been prematurely cut off from the duties and enjoyments of a well-spent life by the unsuspected blow of an assassin who 'laboured under a morbid delusion, of which murder was the climax'" (6 March 1843, 4). The finality and fatality of murder, a transgression posing ontological and ethical as well as legal and psychological questions, renders the notion that "crime is no crime—when the mind is unsettled" wholly unsettled and unsettling.

With their agitated and sardonic tones, these two texts document the anxiety and the rhetoric that characterized Victorian conversations about mental science and criminal responsibility, especially in cases of murder. Struggling to comprehend shifting epistemologies while desiring straightforward notions of criminal guilt or accessible diagnostic definitions of insanity, a "nettled" public requested descriptions and symptoms with which they could decode criminal behavior or recognize mental debility. The question of where sanity ends and madness begins, and a corresponding search for a stable boundary that might resonate with fundamental and familiar ethical sensibilities, was frequently linked to fears about the demise of common sense within the legal system. In the *Juryman's Guide* (1845), Sir George Stephen charts a devolution of sound moral and legal judgment: "Our fathers and grandfathers troubled their heads but little with such subtleties in criminal proceedings; if their practice was less remarkable for its humanity, it certainly was more distinguished by good sense than our own" (485). As collective "good sense" gave way to medical specialization, the juror's task of determining consciousness of right or wrong during a crime's commission became increasingly difficult. Sensitive to the severity of capital punishment, mental scientists publicly doubted the average juror's qualifications for rendering verdicts in murder cases: "To the solving of this difficulty, our juries are, as at present constituted, totally unfit. Respectable men, but ignorant alike of the constitution of the human mind in health and of its varied symptoms in disease, it is strange they have ventured, and been so long suffered, and that too when the life of a human being hangs in the scale, to decide this important question" ("Criminal Insanity" 39). The marginalization of "unfit" jurors symbolized the predicament of all citizens and institutions seeking to assess moral character, define criminal conduct, and convict indicted criminals. Entangled in early-Victorian debates about capital punishment, murder further complicated these problems as jurists and doctors competed for the right to sentence and execute or to diagnose and treat convicted murderers. Amidst this struggle for interpretive and disciplinary power, the authority of "common-place" citizens, commonsense ethics, and common law traditions seemed imperiled—subject to the whims of mental scientists or the "will of the merciless mad."

The conflict between good sense and new science was fueled not only by the sensational appeal of murder but also by the publicity of insanity. Despite the reputation of mental science as a highly specialized and fundamentally impractical form of knowledge, Victorians were consistently exposed to and engaged with its ongoing developments. Public lectures, political pressure groups, and a series of legislation advanced the cause of a humane national asylum system that could assist in negotiating criminal punishments and medical interventions.[7] And just as the government was seeking to rationalize and institutionalize its responses to insanity, a flurry of comparative statistics warned that the conditions of modern life were effecting a dramatic increase in England's rates of insanity.[8] Keeping laypersons conversant with the subject, a flourishing print culture granted access to theories of madness in a variety of formats. Joining satirical verses and skeptical editorials (and broadside ballads) were newspaper transcripts of criminal trials, book reviews of mental science theories, psychology articles in mainstream periodicals, and monographs targeting a generalist readership. In 1843, the *Times* reviewed, with recommendation, Dr. Forbes Winslow's *Plea of Insanity, in Criminal Cases*, noting that "[i]t is his object to establish, that the capability of distinguishing right and wrong, which is the admitted legal test of responsibility in criminal cases, is most fallacious in its character" and to make a case for a "disease ... seated in the moral affections or propensities" rather than in "ideas" (4 March 1843, 3). This favorable review, appearing as Winslow's medical testimony at the M'Naghten trial was coming under public scrutiny in the aftermath of his acquittal, afforded the public some perspective on the case. While the press provided opportunities to browse and peruse, the "learned gentlemen" of mental science attempted to translate, disseminate, and legitimize their work, and, fostering medicolegal literacy, they sometimes addressed the general public directly. J. C. Prichard's *On the Different Forms of Insanity, in Relation to Jurisprudence* (1842), for example, condensed the major points of his groundbreaking and specialized *Treatise on Insanity* (1835) in order to establish a resource for ordinary citizens subject to mental illnesses and legal interventions.

As the combined effects of trial publicity, institutional reform, and moral panic created a marketplace for the circulation of medicolegal theories and secured their place in the public imagination, their potential for metacommentary on aspects of character and acts of interpretation inspired literary innovations. Exploring how narrators access and mediate subjectivity in order to assess character and conduct, scholarship on the novel has made particularly productive connections between developments in literary form and cultural scripts of selfhood. Tracing Brontë's examination of "the problems associated with the decipherment of external form" and "the issues of individual responsibility and control" (56), Sally Shuttleworth's *Charlotte Brontë and Victorian Psychology* (1996) documents the rhetoric of Victorian psychology used by first-person narrators to selectively interpret "act and impulse" according to contrasting versions of the self as a "unified, self-determining agent" or a "fragmented site of conflicting forces" (56). Also attuned to narrative strategies and, of course, particularly relevant to this study, Rodensky's *The Crime in Mind* analyzes fictional representations of legal predicaments. Because "[d]etermining whether or not a defendant had committed a crime meant (and means) judging an external and an internal element" (3), Rodensky argues, the novel's "power to represent the interior life of its characters" (7) allowed writers to address public concerns about ascertaining a crime's internal element and assessing a criminal's legal responsibility.

Whether first-person or third-person, the narrators of Victorian novels created vantage points from which to explore diagnostic gazing and disciplinary surveillance, as Shuttleworth concludes, or narrative omniscience and subjective transparency, as Rodensky demonstrates. Interacting with the languages of mental science and the dilemmas of criminal law, in order to consider correlations between external and internal manifestations of the self, Victorian novelists deployed a multifaceted notion of character as a literary trope, a psychological concept, and a legal construct. Exploiting the transgeneric and interdisciplinary meanings of genre and discourse (Williams's "dialectical pair"), novelists imagined the "interior life" and psychological foundations of their fictional characters while engaging the cultural resonances of the word "character"—a mechanism of self-government, a collection of behaviors, a force of the will, a subject of the law.

Similarly attentive to dialectical relationships between discourse and genre and textual mediations of intentions and actions, this chapter examines the dramatic monologues of four murderers whose speech unsettles distinctions between willful agency and uncontrollable impulse and thus reproduces the same interpretative tensions that defined medicolegal debates. The four murderers in question, the speakers of Robert Browning's "Porphyria's Lover" (1836), "My Last Duchess" (1842), and "The Laboratory" (1844) and Dante Gabriel Rossetti's "A Last Confession" (1870), complicate fundamental questions of character and conduct by combining dismaying accounts of murder and bewildering eccentricities of speech. Entangling speech acts and criminal acts, these dramatic poems deny or destabilize the kinds of perspective that narrative fiction often imagined or affirmed, and in doing so they align the interpretive difficulties of dramatic poetics and criminal politics.

Exploring modes of poetry and epistemologies of murder, these monologues exemplify Slinn's definition of poetic performativity—the "double function" of poetry's formalism, simultaneously "linking and distinguishing poetry from its contexts" and thereby revealing a "continuity" between verse forms and historical contexts (25). The dramatic monologue's "lyrical-dramatic-narrative hybrid[ity]" in particular allows Browning and Rossetti to reproduce the struggles of legal judgment and medical diagnosis (Slinn, "Dramatic Monologue" 80). Speaking of Browning's early monologues, Slinn explains, "Through absorbing all three views (expressive, dramatic, fictive), Browning makes possible the politics of the dramatic monologue. The expressive subject becomes a matter of psychological process, objective drama becomes a matter of public representations, and poetic fiction becomes a matter of cultural construction and discursive practices" ("Dramatic Monologue" 90). Such an awareness of the genre's performative hybridity—which recognizes a dynamic interaction between the literary significance of lyrical, dramatic, and narrative representational modes and the cultural meanings of psychological processes, public representations, and discursive practices—provides a way to examine the intertwined political and aesthetic effects of these murder poems. With their now familiar assortments of strange scenes, sinister murders, and grotesque characters—a cottage assignation, a lover-murderer, a companion-corpse; an art tour, an arrogant aristocrat, a curtained wife-portrait, an unsuspecting envoy; a toxic laboratory, an angry courtesan, a mercenary chemist; a deathbed confession, a dying revolutionary, an attending priest, a ghastly hallucination—these poems exploit such poetic and cultural resonances. Inflected by unusual arrangements of character and circumstance, their crimes and their speech are also informed by expressive idiosyncrasies and metrical oddities. The controlled iambs, tidy couplets, and contorted dactyls of Browning's poems and the verbal excess and narrative circularity of Rossetti's monologue serve to complicate their murderous subjects and exacerbate the difficulties of interpretation.

As they shade understandings of character and conduct, the imbrications of dramatic scene, narrative fragments, and lyrical voice operate, in Harrison's terms, as discursive technologies producing "ideological effects" and doing "cultural work." Contrasting the novel's explorations of surveillance and transparency, these poems, lacking narrator-intermediaries and limiting readerly perspective, cultivate obstruction and obscurity. Expressing their selves and their crimes, their murderous speakers signal unmediated and unregulated access. Yet, their dense monologues elaborate and conflate the signs of malice and the symptoms of madness, compelling readers—lay alienists, amateur jurists, poetry enthusiasts—to oscillate between definitions of insanity and criminality. As Smith argues, discussions of criminal insanity involved "the substitution of alternative languages to describe a single crime" and required people to shift between mental science and criminal law ("Boundary" 371). At the same time, more general ethical sympathies and "a basic tension between the power of the individual and the power of the collective" also formed a context for evaluative disagreement ("Boundary" 376). The tensions created by "alternative languages" and discursive struggles allowed dramatic poets to develop the psychological and the political intrigues of their murderous speakers. Here, Stallybrass and White's "conflictual complexes," derived from tensions between "social classification and psychological processes" and between social prohibitions and individual agency, are configured by poets, enacted by murderer-speakers, and experienced by readers as a struggle for interpretive power.

Exercises in poetic complexity and epistemological frustration, these monologues generate aesthetic effects from the interpretive controversies that informed the context of their composition and publication, and while their dramatic scenarios accommodate historical explanations, they do more than locate psychological conditions in social histories. Just as medical theories defamiliarized legal fictions and ethical commonplaces, the medicolegal ambiguities of these poems defamiliarize the more familiar literary tropes and cultural ideologies informing their themes of sexual violence, class privilege, courtly corruption, and revolutionary fervor. Exploring historically contingent or sanctioned violence while engaging medical explanations of causation and consequence, their insistence on the obscurity of murderous subjectivity allows them to place the violent acts of their speakers within the familiar contexts of sexual conflicts and gender hierarchies *and* to locate them within an epistemological contest between volitional agency and diseased determinism.[9] Blending explanatory frameworks of the past and present—historicizing, criminalizing, pathologizing—the poems use their murderous speakers to engage contemporary anxieties about murder's cultural congruities and incongruities and explore social sites of institutional control and ideological conflict.

Such an emphasis on the contingent status of the murderous subject supports a reconsideration of the more general historical relationship between psychological theories and dramatic poetics, which has been well documented in Ekbert Faas's *Retreat into the Mind* (1988). Noting that the 1830s ushered in the dramatic experiments of Browning and Tennyson and psychological theories that blurred distinctions between mental soundness and mental disorder, Faas argues that mental science and dramatic poetry, both privileging examinations of character over evaluations of conduct, were deeply intertwined Victorian phenomena.[10] As the destabilizing of the individual subject and the lyric poem found common ground in new articulations of mental science, dramatic poems were drawn into the national conversation on insanity when mental science journals offered clinical analyses of dramatic monologues and mainstream periodicals printed suggestive juxtapositions of poetic and psychological texts (46). Because mental scientists sometimes cited dramatic poems to demonstrate their theories, Faas explains, monologues "were thought of as objective, case-history-like studies" (14), for "what such scientific studies described in the abstract, a poem might often render far more plausibly, perhaps even more accurately, in concrete" (174).

Without diminishing the significance of these observations about the coincident paths of poetry and psychology, it is worth reconsidering the case study approach which Faas attributes to Victorian readers and pursues in his study, for it implies a passive model of literary production and, in these instances, separates the theme of criminal lunacy from the particularities of poetic device. Neither case studies nor legal testimonies, the speech of verbally complex and psychologically obscure murderers poses unsettling questions about plausibility and accuracy. Fracturing the speech of the expressive criminal and prolonging the struggles of interpretation, Browning and Rossetti construct a poetics of indeterminacy so that, rather than concretely embodying the abstractions of mental science, the unknowable killer embodies an aesthetic of the sublime rooted in questions of subjectivity and what Burke, describing the book of Job, articulates as the "terrible uncertainty of the thing described" (106). The sublime always involves "some modification of power" (107), and a writer's use of a "judicious obscurity" (103) can reproduce the causes and elicit the *affects* of sublimity. Burke's examples—a fear of death, a sense of danger, perceptual difficulty, emotional distress, and bodily pain—are remarkably apt for articulating the inexplicable force of or considering poetic representations of murderous agency, whether emanating from a maddening disease or a malicious will. Judiciously obscure, the sublime criminal developed in these poems pits the desire for moral discernment against the anxiety of epistemological doubt and the possibility of medical diagnosis against the certainty of terrible disgust. Politically and poetically skeptical and mischievous, rather than satirical and polemical, these monologues, to borrow Armstrong's phrase, "compel a strenuous reading" of the medicolegal theories, criminal codes, and collective fears complicating murder in Victorian culture.

"Enveloped in Obscurity": Madness, Badness, and Mental Science

In order to consider the poetics of the criminal sublime—and the complex interactions between the formal strategies, generic structures, and medicolegal discourse with which Browning and Rossetti manipulate the theme of murder—it is important to note that conversations about criminal lunacy pivoted around a desire for and the denial of a distinction between willful agency and pathological determinism.[11] As Smith argues, the simplest distinction that "corresponds to common Victorian usage" was that medical explanations were "determinist" and legal explanations were "voluntarist" (*Trial* 10–11). Beginning in the 1830s, however, reformulations of madness challenged this distinction, generating interpretive battles between modern theories and legal, ethical, and medical traditions and inspiring public reflections on the discourses and methods used to apprehend criminals.

In 1835, Prichard published his *Treatise on Insanity and Other Disorders Affecting the Mind*, in which he presented the typology of criminal madness that remained the standard for the next twenty years. Dedicating his treatise to French psychologist, J. E. D. Esquirol, whose research constitutes the majority of Prichard's source materials, Prichard imported prominent continental theories of criminal insanity into English discourse.[12] Early in his *Treatise* Prichard explains that the work grew out of his earlier essay on insanity in the *Cyclopaedia of Practical Medicine* (1833), a project that convinced him of England's need to modernize its approach to mental pathology. The *Treatise* refines and expands Prichard's original encyclopedia essay, offering a schema, already established in continental psychology, of two principal manifestations of insanity: an intellectually based insanity, which disrupts reasoning faculties to varying degrees, and an emotionally based insanity, termed "moral insanity," which leaves reasoning processes unaffected.[13] Emphasizing a fundamental difference between intellectual and moral insanity and dismissing the need for extensive subcategories, Prichard argues that madness appears in two forms:

> [It is] a chronic disease, manifested by deviations from the healthy and natural state of the mind, such deviations consisting either in a *moral perversion*, or a disorder of the feelings, affections, and habits of the individual, or in *intellectual derangement*, which last is sometimes partial, namely, in *monomania*, affecting the understanding only in particular trains of thought; or general, and accompanied with excitement, namely, in *mania*, or *raving madness*; or, lastly, confounding or destroying the connections or associations of ideas, and producing a state of *incoherence*. (*Treatise* 7)

In advocating this succinct but comprehensive typology, within which all varieties of madness could be placed, Prichard sought to simplify and advance society's understanding of madness, but because his definitions (with the possible exception of raving madness) challenged ethical commonplaces and voluntarist-determinist distinctions, they caused instead a "profound sensation in the legal and psychological world" (Tuke, *Prichard and Symonds* 1).

For moral insanity, Prichard provides the following definition: "madness consisting in a morbid perversion of the natural feelings, affections, inclinations, temper, habits, moral dispositions, and natural impulses, without any remarkable disorder or defect of the intellect or knowing and reasoning faculties, and particularly without any insane illusion or hallucination" (*Treatise* 6). It is a "form of mental derangement in which the intellectual faculties appear to have sustained little or no injury" but in which "the moral and active principles of the mind are strangely perverted and depraved, the power of self-government is lost or greatly impaired; and the individual is found to be incapable, not of talking or reasoning upon any subject proposed to him; for this he will often do with great shrewdness and volubility, but of conducting himself with decency and propriety in the business of life" (*Treatise* 4). As Ann Colley observes, the disorder, "almost too 'Victorian' to be true," pathologizes failures of "self-government," "decency," and "propriety" (15). In elaborating on this condition in its murderous form, Prichard explains, "M. Esquirol has repeatedly declared his conviction that there exists a species of homicidal madness, in which '*no disorder of intellect can be discovered*'; the murderer is driven, as it were, by an irresistible power" (*Treatise* 388). By definition the morally insane person violated fundamental ethical principles, but when manifesting itself as homicidal lunacy, moral insanity exceeded the limits of plausibility. Overtaking one's moral capacity while leaving the intellect intact, the disease linked an uncanny psychology, a monumental transgression, and an ill-defined "irresistible power" in ways that often seemed too un-Victorian to be true.

In popularizing the term "moral insanity," Prichard sought to establish a paradigm-shifting psychological concept that would parallel the diagnostic achievement of "monomania," a term that Esquirol substituted for "melancholy" in 1820. In coverage of criminal lunacy, in popular and specialist texts alike, "moral insanity" shared the limelight with "monomania," the predominant form of intellectual madness, which affected only "particular strains of thought." Naming and defining temporary and localized manifestations of mental breakdown, theories of moral insanity and monomania claimed that intermittent or even singular episodes of madness could be spliced with moments of clarity and rationality of varying duration and degree. In affirming the possibility of singular manifestations and unanticipated eruptions of madness (the "monomaniac pistol" or the "climacteric stiletto") these classifications of madness supported a spatial model of the mind in which specific faculties or regions of the mind succumbed to madness while others remained unaffected.

Such definitions of insanity further complicated the already vexed problem of ascertaining *mens rea*—of assessing relationships between the internal features of character and the external features of conduct. Partial insanity all but eliminated boundaries between the sane and the insane, and as Smith explains, criminal law could not accommodate such a radically compartmentalized subject: "Medical and non-medical writers referred to 'partial insanity' as a legally problematic area. This term could mean either insanity coming and going (with lucid intervals or sane periods) or insanity limited to certain mental faculties. Given that responsibility was a unitary concept, it was a severe problem to determine the responsibility of the partially insane" (*Trial* 37). As Prichard himself acknowledged, the notion of moral insanity, a state in which reason and madness coexist, deviated from English cultural and legal assumptions about insanity and irresponsibility:

> I must first observe that no such disorder has been recognized in the English courts of judicature, or even admitted by medical writers in England. In general, it has been laid down that insanity consists in, and is co-extensive with, mental illusion. English writers admit only that form of insanity which the Germans term *wahnsinn;* they know nothing of moral insanity either as requiring control in the exercise of civil rights, or as destroying or lessening culpability in criminal ones. (*Treatise* 380)

Making note of this gap between medical and legal discourses, Prichard cites jurists whose rulings illustrate that insanity had traditionally denoted a delusional and hallucinatory subject in English law. As a result, he explains, it is "very difficult to maintain a plea on the ground of insanity in this country, with a view to the removing of culpabilities in a criminal accusation" (382). Relying on interrogation and testimony in scrutinizing mental states, the law saw mental competence when morally insane criminals displayed sensibility, logic, and "great ingenuity in giving reasons for the eccentricities of their conduct" (*Treatise* 14). As Smith argues, Prichard "recognised two of the key medico-legal problems which the notion of moral insanity created: the possibility that cognitive disorder was not necessarily present in insanity, and that insanity and eccentricity were continuous" (*Trial* 38). Similarly challenging conventional ideas of insanity and eccentricity, theories of monomania located insanity in "one subject" or "one train of ideas" (*Treatise* 6) and thus asked juries to parse the thoughts of criminals and to determine incompetence in a person who reasoned well on all subjects except for the very actions under scrutiny at trial.

Witnessing the trials, acquittals, convictions, or sentences of the criminal justice system, an often incredulous public construed these theories of partial insanity as overly intellectualized and contrived conveniences for defense counsel—especially when the accused did not inspire sympathy or identification, the threat of hanging implied a motive for launching an implausible medical defense, or, as in the Townley case, an insanity plea signaled class privilege.[14] Exploiting such skepticism, it was not unusual for jurists to deflect the challenge that mental science posed to juridical procedures in a language of plainspoken common sense. Discussing the problem of jurors and the probability of insanity, James Fitzjames Stephen described the plea argument for moral insanity as "generally speaking, at least as consistent with the theory that he was a great fool and a great rogue, as with the theory that he was the subject of a special disease, the existence of which is doubtful" (*General View* 96). Stephen's archetypes ("great fool" and "great rogue") undermine the specialist discourse of mental science, which, advocating for a "special disease" and espousing professional interests, claim an interpretive power that thwart the interests of commonplace citizens and common law traditions. Alert to juridical predicaments and public relations, mental scientists frequently sought to address public skepticism and legal dilemmas directly. Challenging the law's interpretive practices, an article in the *Journal of Psychological Medicine and Mental Pathology* argued that the imperatives of courtroom theatrics and the processes of the human mind are simply incompatible: "Our courts of justice, whether civil or criminal, demand that the evidence shall on all occasions, be clear, conclusive, and indisputable. But, unhappily, the human mind, when affected by disease, cannot in every case have its morbid features unveiled in open court" ("The Plea of Insanity" 184). While these comments critique the differences between the mechanisms of the mind and the court, in alluding to "morbid features" that cannot be "unveiled," they also point to the central problem of psychological obscurity.

As charges of implausibility, if not absurdity, were lobbed at mental scientists from the realms of common sense, the admission of obscurity became a recurring theme in mental science texts. Sorting rogues from lunatics in his efforts to legitimize moral insanity, Prichard admits that the "precise limitation of insanity and eccentricity is very difficult to discover" (*Treatise* 383) but provides a list of characteristics "to lessen the ambiguity" (397) in murder cases. Quoting Esquirol, Prichard notes that periods of homicidal lunacy are often "preceded by other striking peculiarities of action" or "a total change of character" and that homicidal lunatics "have attempted suicide," have "expressed a wish for death," and have sometimes "begged to be executed as criminals" (397). He also adds that their "acts are without motive" and "in opposition to the known influences of all human motives" (398). After the crime, he explains, the criminal lunatic "seeks no escape or flight; delivers himself up to justice; acknowledges the crime laid to his charge; describes the state of mind which led to its perpetration: or he remains stupefied and overcome by a horrible consciousness of having been the agent in an atrocious deed" (398). Another crucial distinction between the criminal and the lunatic lies in the processes of premeditation: "The murderer has generally accomplices in vice and crime: there are assignable inducements which led to its commission, motives of self-interest, of revenge, displaying wickedness premeditated. Premeditated are in some instances the acts of the madman; but his premeditation is peculiar and characteristic" (398). Catalogued and inventoried, these signs and symptoms nonetheless fragmented unitary concepts of selfhood and responsibility. Asking Victorians to believe that two mental states, long considered mutually exclusive, might coexist with disastrous and horrifying results, these elaborate illnesses required close readings of eccentricities, peculiarities, and behaviors preceding and following a crime—but not of the terrible crime itself.

Most importantly, such interpretive methods conflicted with conventional concepts of the will. Central to coding agency and determinism and considering criminal responsibility and criminal lunacy, the will inhabited legal phrasing ("willful murder") and informed psychological theories, and the idea of partial insanity was bewildering in part because the will, like responsibility, had long been a unitary—albeit multipurpose—concept. As the locus of character, the will was a site of self-regulation, and as the force of conduct, it was a subject of judicial discipline. "Individual wills," Smith argues, "were facts to Victorians" (*Trial* 73), and the embodied wills of ordinary citizens or extraordinary criminals seemed more real than the speculative abstractions of mental science. Stephen, highlighting the will's tangible qualities, presents it as a series of physical reactions:

> The man wishes in that peculiar way which is called willing, and thereupon the different members of his body go through certain motions. The muscles of the calves and thighs raise the trunk; the head and the hands assume a certain position; the shoulders are thrown back; the head is erected; the tongue, the mouth, the throat, and the cheeks, all do their parts in saying what the mind has thought of saying, resolved to say, intended to say, and now says. What the nature of this crisis is, how such a wish differs generically from other wishes, why it instantly fulfils itself, are questions which have never been answered; but about the fact there can be no doubt. Every human creature attaches to the words 'to will,' or their equivalents, as vivid a meaning as every man with eyes attaches to the words 'to see.'" (*General View* 77)

Though linked to "crisis," the verb "to will" appears as an extension of wishing and desiring, and, resonating as clearly as the verb "to see," it constitutes an empirically "vivid" form of agency.

In various formats and contexts beyond the realm of medicolegal debates, the will figured prominently—in popular ideas of self-help, self-control, and self-reliance, in philosophical formulations of cognition and consciousness, and in theological interpretations of human and divine purpose. Often described as an empirical reality, the will also inspired acts of faith in preventive measures and asylum treatments stressing moral management and attempting cures. Veida Skultans argues that "[f]aith in man's powers of emotional self-discipline and control created a different outlook towards the possibility of a complete cure of nervous disabilities" (*English Madness* 56) and informed an optimistic strain in asylum practices: "Foremost among moral causes are lack of moderation and excesses of all kinds. Given this aetiology of insanity, moral factors are seen as forces against insanity. Habit, perseverance, the will and character may each constitute such a counteracting force" (*Madness and Morals* 2–3).

The paradoxical corollary to this self-disciplinary schema appeared in formulations of the will that suggested individuals might be responsible for their own mental illnesses. In *The Victorian Will* (1989), John R. Reed explains that both material and moral schema for explaining insanity "were concerned with the large question of responsibility and stressed discipline as a safeguard against madness. In doing so, [the] advocates of improved self-government assumed some power in the self, ordinarily defined one way or another as will, that could oversee that process of self-government" (133). Eager to uphold the notion of responsible self-regulation, John Barlow's *On Man's Power over Himself to Prevent or Control Insanity* (1843) defines "mental derangement" as a breakdown of the will. Arguing that "the difference between sanity and insanity consists in the degree of self-control exercised" (45), Barlow finds records of individual failure in alarmist reports on recent increases in insanity cases: "of these cases it is calculated that less than three hundred in one thousand are the result of disease, or of unavoidable circumstances, thus leaving above seven hundred resulting from bodily excess or mental misgovernment" (49). With a similar interest in moral causes and effects, William Carpenter, in *Principles of Mental Physiology, with their Applications to the Training and Discipline of the Mind, and the Study of its Morbid Conditions* (1874), compares monomania to "intoxication by Hachisch" (672) and argues that strict applications of the will at the onset of morbid tendencies can contravene full-scale mental disorder: "many a man has been saved from an attack of Insanity, by the resolute determination of his Will *not* to yield to his morbid tendencies" (673). Because of such links between moral willing and mental failing, individuals are always at least "remotely responsible" for their psychological health, their mental disease, and their transgressive actions (672). Written thirty years apart, these statements demonstrate the lingering interpretive power and ideological work of the will in medical, legal, and moral discourses.

While mental scientists inserted ideas about pathology into discussions of crime, the role of the will in considering legal and moral questions of character and conduct created a circular logic that implicitly, if not explicitly, reinstated voluntarist notions of responsibility and thereby cast distinctions between criminality and lunacy into further obscurity. When asylums and advocates of moral management used responsibility to structure medical treatments for the insane, for example, they too suggested that the criminal lunatic was always at least a tad guilty. Discussing Samuel Tuke's Retreat at York, which established the precedent for moral management when it was founded in 1792, Foucault labels the asylum a "Quaker world" where routines of labor and the cultivation of self-conscious moral guilt combined to restrain inmates (*Madness* 247). The result, he argues, was the "marking out and glorifying [of] a region of simple responsibility where any manifestation of madness will be linked to punishment" (246). Because the inmate is asked to "feel morally responsible for everything within him that may disturb morality and society" (246), Tuke's asylum "organized [guilt] for the madman as a consciousness of himself" (247) and thus "substituted for the free terror of madness the stifling anguish of responsibility" (247).

Prichard also advocated "moral discipline" and "personal controul" as potential treatments for insanity (*Treatise* 297). Revealing the contrasting interests of theory and practice, however, his typologies, particularly his understanding of moral insanity, challenged the optimistic principles of management and organization that underwrote the projects of asylum reform and the professionalization of mental science. His treatise characterizes the prognosis for moral insanity as "more unfavourable than in other forms of mental derangement" (25) and admits, "it must be confessed that this subject [of moral insanity] is as yet enveloped in obscurity" (114). This obscurity persisted (indeed increased), and writing almost ten years later in the *Plea of Insanity, in Criminal Cases,* his colleague, Dr. Winslow, echoed this sentiment. Asking, "Can we safely draw the line of demarcation between vice and moral disease? Where does one commence and the other terminate?" (60–61), he promises only unsatisfactory answers, for the "subject is necessarily involved in many obscurities" (61). Such claims about obscurity also informed practical arguments about policy and reform. In *An Inquiry Concerning the Indications of Insanity* (1830), Dr. John Conolly's persuasive argument for the reform of asylums and the revision of the criminal code is accompanied by the striking claim that medical men "have sought for, and imagined, a strong and definable boundary between sanity and insanity, which has not only been imaginary, and arbitrarily placed," but "considered a justification" for "unnecessary and afflicting measures" (295–96). While in the interests of reform, such insistence on the obscure and imagined features of mental science intentionally troubled the practices of traditional legal, moral, and medical institutions, they also generated broader epistemological questions about the nature of interpretation.

As they produced and encountered interpretive obstacles and frustrations, medicolegal debates about criminality continued to inspire contests between lay and specialist heuristics. In the 1860s, Dr. Henry Maudsley, the foremost mental scientist of the late-Victorian period, retrieved old commonplaces in order to explain to his readers that "[i]t is not possible to draw a distinct line of demarcation between insanity and crime, either when we have to deal with them socially as events or when we investigate their causation in a scientific spirit. There are criminals who are more mad than bad, insane persons who are more bad than mad" (*Pathology of Mind* 82). Appearing with almost comical absurdity in an ambitious work attempting to link the material and immaterial aspects of the mind and "to integrate psychology, reflex physiology, and psychiatry into a single synthetic whole" (Bynum 240), this phrasing is historically instructive. Marking criminal insanity in vague degrees along a mad-bad continuum, Maudsley's claim, and his plainspoken lexicon, underscore the lingering difficulties in distinguishing between criminality and insanity whether for social or scientific purposes.[15]

Medicolegal debates attracted the attention of a range of Victorians—criminals, advocates, journalists, poets, scientists, jurists, citizens—eager to imagine boundaries between madness and badness or to insist upon the impossibility of the task. Sustained for decades, the discursive ironies, circular logics, and cultural anxieties characterizing these interpretive struggles inform Browning's and Rossetti's dramatic explorations of murderers, which not only offer representations of strange killers but also integrate textual and cultural matters of interpretation. The stubborn obscurity of the murderous subject constitutes the poetic and the political appeal of the criminal sublime, and the persistence of that obscurity foregrounds problems of interpretation in medicolegal contexts and poetic texts.

Moral Insanity and Malicious Intent in Robert Browning's "Porphyria's Lover"

A "judicious obscurity" defines one of Browning's earliest dramatic experiments, "Porphyria's Lover," a poem that mixes old themes of sexual violence with new formulations of homicidal lunacy. The entanglement of sexual malice and homicidal madness develops a tension between competing epistemologies: the speaker's thoughts and actions are congruous with gendered and classed manifestations of power, but they also engage incongruities between traditional concepts of badness and emergent theories of madness. Failing to lessen the ambiguities of the text, an inventory of signs and symptoms merely produces a collection of points and counterpoints that alternately provoke and obstruct attempts to understand this dramatic character in moral, medical, and literary terms. Informing these interpretive struggles, the speaker's candid account and artful rhetoric, the reader's exegetical agendas and inconclusive inventories, and even the God who "has not said a word" evoke the questions of interpretive authority and the experiences of epistemological frustration surrounding the murderous subject.

These interpretive struggles also inform critical attempts to sort out the poem's psychological and sexual content and contextualize its generic form. For two reasons in particular the poem has been viewed as a case study of homicidal lunacy: because, accompanied by its poetic twin "Johannes Agricola in Meditation," it appeared under the heading "Madhouse Cells" in printings between 1842 and 1863 and because its two primary antecedent texts, John Wilson's "Extracts from Gosschen's Diary" (1818) and Brian Procter's "Marcian Colonna" (1820), explicitly depict homicidal lovers and episodes of madness.[16] The paratextual marker "Madhouse Cells," of course, encourages a diagnosis of lunacy.[17] Faas attributes confessionals, madhouses, and prison cells to the pressures of the marketplace: "By and large, reviewers tolerated the portrayal of mental perversion only as long as it was done the way in which an alienist would diagnose a morally insane delinquent so as to have him hospitalized for further observation and treatment" (185). Linking publishing strategies and generic qualities, he notes that "[l]ike Victorian asylums, dramatic monologues in this sense are a means of sequestration, particularly of their authors' own morbidities. Wherever they deal with mental aberrations, they are 'madhouse cells' like 'Porphyria's Lover' and 'Johannes Agricola in Meditation'" (185). Added, perhaps, to orient readers by contextualizing the speakers of both poems, the heading might also constitute an allusion to anxieties about murderers and madmen during a decade in which asylum treatments and criminal codes were under scrutiny and in flux.

In what remains the most comprehensive examination of Browning's negotiation of psychological discourse and poetic genre, Michael Mason describes the poem as an "extraordinary" and "sophisticated" representation of "alien states of mind" (265) which constitutes the "bedrock" (253) of Browning's innovations in dramatic poetry. Distinguishing itself from its sources, which suggest moral insanity but have difficulties with "their pictures of relatively cool, reflective homicidal lunacy" (258) and "fall back on the stock notion of lunacy as mania marked by delusions" (265) to solve the dilemma of motivation, "Porphyria's Lover" sustains the dispassionate voice of the speaker who might even be construed as "an anti-lunatic, an illustration of how an act conventionally referable to insanity might be the act of a rational being" (257). For Mason, its "analysis of homicidal lunacy" blends Browning's "theory of psychological consistency and contemporary ideas of rational lunacy" (264). Finding the coherence of character amidst the contingency of circumstance, the poem suggests that "[t]he distinction between the 'circumstances' of loving and murdering is dispelled when both are seen as the same 'primitive colour' of the soul's spectrum" (254). The logical continuities of "alien impulses" and "familiar and accepted impulses" (254) create a "strange but plausible" (255) mental state and a "surprisingly sympathetic" (254) figure, which reflects the humanizing effects and reformist agendas of new psychological theories.

In considering how the poem manages insanity as a theme and a theory, a greater emphasis on the obscurity of this dramatic character and the controversy of homicidal lunacy restores the poem's more skeptical ironies—which inform the conjoined agendas of generic development and cultural engagement. Rather than containing a madman or affirming mental science, Browning draws both the contours of moral insanity and the lineaments of criminal malice, and, thus, while the poem signals an interest in examining insanity as a mental disease, it demonstrates an equally strong interest in exploring murder as a criminal act and sexual power as a violent motive. Seeking to negotiate the poem's sexual and psychological content, scholars have tended to see gendered violence and homicidal lunacy as incompatible themes requiring one to choose between a sexually charged (and class-inflected) motive or a psychologically diseased impulse. The relationships between these themes are difficult to disentangle, but a focus on epistemological struggle allows us to reconsider their interrelatedness as poetic strategies of cultural critique.

In creating a speaker who slips between two baffling identities, Browning highlights the fundamental irreconcilability of abstracted medical theories and commonsense readings of male sexual passions. Assessing several of Browning's homicidal lovers and husbands, Daniel Karlin, using the phrase "sexual hatred," locates these passions in a tension between masculine entitlements and sexual desires, and he sees this particular murder as an attempt on the part of the murderer, a sullen working-class cottage-dweller, "to achieve the desired balance of power in his relationship" (214) with his victim, who dutifully prefers his company to a "gay feast" but also disloyally prioritizes "vainer ties" over sexual commitment. Informing Karlin's reluctance to think of this poem as "about" insanity, this emphasis also leads to his glossing of the paradoxes of character and conduct. He notes, "[h]e may be mad, but he hasn't lost his mind" (212), and concludes that his actions constitute "an insanely logical act of redress" (214). Also interested in the dynamics of sexual power, Armstrong examines the speaker's violent objectification of the feminine in terms of a cultural "pathology of sexual feeling" ("Browning" 288). If we understand this poem to be about articulating and examining the paradoxes of medicolegal debates, the simultaneity of madness and badness—and the comparable interpretive value of and competition between an entrenched gender-class system and a new mental science—become central to the poem's meaning, for they constitute fundamental tensions and epistemological resources in a cultural debate over the meanings and motivations of murder.

The distinction between the impassioned heat of sexual jealousy and the reasoning cool of moral insanity, for example, was a central feature in early-Victorian reconfigurations of homicidal lunacy. Criminal cool defines the morally insane subject, who, without frenzy or fever, transcribes criminal impulses into rational statements. Prichard quotes French psychologist M. Broussais, following Pinel, who describes moral insanity as a "chronic and apyretic" disease, which often includes "a delight in destroying" and "an impulse unreasonable . . . to inflict suffering upon the friends whom he tenderly loves, and to put them to death" (*Treatise* 113). This "delight in destroying" resonates with the aesthetic enjoyment of Porphyria's lover as he adores her propped, dead body and constructs an apparently reasoned explanation for his actions. Broussais labels the illness "extremely obstinate" and notes its potential to "conceal itself under the appearances of calm, of joy, of benevolence, until the lunatic finds the opportunity of executing his horrible project" (113). Such attributes apply to Browning's infamous speaker, who stages the passive and sulking reception that draws Porphyria to her death, and then, with an uncanny equanimity, narrates the incident in well-measured iambs.

But the speaker, we discover, maintains his blasé posture and produces his dispassionate account in the presence of a murdered corpse, which, embodying a dead silence, inflects the meanings of his speech and troubles interpretations of his violence. In her essay "Browning's Corpses," Carol T. Christ notes that Browning "frequently stages poems in the presence of a corpse" (393). "These poems," she explains, "reflect importantly upon his understanding of writing poetry," for "he sees the dead body as the object that can constitute its own representation" (393). Complicating the diagnostic process is the abject body, which, Kristeva agrees, is fundamentally disruptive: "from its place of banishment, the abject does not cease challenging its master" (2). Because it speaks for itself, the mere presence of the murdered corpse undermines the speaker's narrative authority. While an actual medical examination or legal interview would take place away from the corpse and thus prioritize the speech of the murderer, here the victim's abject presence, the corpse's self-constituting meaning, upstages the speaker and challenges the detachment required for clinical diagnosis.

Juxtaposing a traumatic murder and a theoretical madness, this impossible fictional scenario starkly represents a fundamental tension of medico-legal debate—the conflicts between condemning or pathologizing murder. When summing up the implications of moral insanity in his *Treatise,* Prichard remarks:

> On the whole it seems fully manifest that there is a form of insanity, existing independently of any lesion of the intellectual powers, in which, connected in some instances with evident constitutional disorder, in others with affections of the nervous system excited according to the well-known laws of the

criminal economy, a sudden and often irresistible impulse is experienced to commit *acts which under a sane condition of mind would be accounted atrocious crimes*. . . . It must be allowed that instances may and do occur in which the discrimination would be difficult between manifestations of insanity and acts of a criminal nature, and that this difficulty would be increased by the admission of a form of insanity free from hallucination or illusion. (397, emphasis added)

While Prichard's methodology includes a suspension of judgment, Browning's side-by-side positioning of murderer and victim forces readers to imagine the possibility of moral insanity while confronting the certainty of an atrocious crime and considering the "well-known laws of the criminal economy." In this way, "Porphyria's Lover" produces the epistemological stress and moral unease that mental scientists sought to contain with lists of symptoms and categories of illness.

Bringing together the themes of desire, disgust, and diagnosis, Porphyria's corpse also highlights the verbal ironies that became fundamental to dramatic poetry. Christ proposes that "[i]n Browning's poetry in particular, the animation of corpses is closely connected to his conception of the dramatic impulse and to the form of the dramatic monologue" (394). In "Porphyria's Lover" this connection is suggested when the speaker's rhetoric animates Porphyria's corpse: "[Browning] portrays this attempt as a macabre project on the part of the living to use corpses to support their own fictional construction of reality" (393). His descriptions of Porphyria's dead body simultaneously illuminate aspects of his psyche and reinforce Porphyria's status as a corpse. He enthusiastically explains that "her cheek once more / Blushed bright beneath my burning kiss" (47–48) but then subtly, and perhaps inadvertently, reveals the more grim reality: "this time *my* shoulder bore / Her head, which droops upon it still" (50–51). In the contest between lively blushing and deathly drooping, the significance of deathly drooping wins out—with ironic effects.

Likewise, the bizarre metonymy of the following passage introduces a revealing manipulation of the "will"—the contentious keyword of criminal law and moral management. In this instance, the speaker transfers his own will to his victim, or, more pointedly, to his victim's "head":

The smiling rosy little head!
So glad it has its utmost will,
That all it scorned at once is fled,
And I, its love, am gained instead, (52–55)

The enthusiastic attribution of consciousness to a lifeless "smiling rosy little head," coupled with the dehumanizing declaration that "it" is finally enjoying "its utmost will" and that "its love" is "gained" again, conjoins the atrocious crime and the obscure murderer. These jarring ascriptions of agency constitute a rhetorical tic, the same one that leads him to assign destructive intentions to the "sullen wind" (2) that "tore the elm-tops down for spite" (3) and "did its worst to vex the lake" (4). The scattering of passions and wills also informs the poem's strange final tableau. Announcing, "And thus *we* sit together now, / And all night long *we* have not stirred,— / And yet God has not said a word!" (58–59, emphasis added), the speaker implies that the two lovers are acting in concert, a claim attributable to moral insanity but also verbal irony. And punctuated with an exclamation point, this declaration of impunity also suggests a sinister satisfaction with his homicidal work and thus introduces another irreconcilable piece of evidence.

Such instances suggest that the speaker might be struggling for interpretive power, not with an "irresistible power." But while the concept of moral insanity offered a term with which to define the disturbing calm that some criminals demonstrated, mental scientists claimed that the disease was also marked by a loss of control: "The morbid and irregular excitement of the active propensities, and the total want of self-controul, which are so conspicuous in moral insanity, display themselves in various ways" (Prichard, "Insanity" 829). This paradox informs the poem's instability. Prichard explains that morally insane subjects "often display great ingenuity in giving reasons for the eccentricities of their conduct, and in accounting for and justifying the state of moral feeling under which they appear to exist" (*Treatise* 14). Such verbal ingenuity applies to the speaker's account of his crime:

> That moment she was mine,—mine, fair,
> Perfectly pure and good: I found
> A thing to do, and all her hair
> In one long yellow string I wound
> Three times her little throat around,
> And strangled her. (36–41)

While his claim that he "found / A thing to do" acknowledges murderous agency in somewhat oblique terms, his strikingly frank and precise admission that he "strangled her" suggests the calm of the morally insane criminal. Just as the speaker unflinchingly details his crime, however, metrical irregularities, such as the iteration of stresses in "mine,—mine, fair," register the possessive intensity of the speaker and disrupt the mad cool of the poem's well-regulated cadences.

As the murderous subject oscillates between control and chaos, the text begins to implicate the intellect, which was believed to operate independently from moral-emotional manifestations of lunacy. The speaker's seemingly delusional animations of the corpse, his confident protest, "No pain felt she— / I am quite sure she felt no pain" (41–42), and his disturbingly calm case for murder indicate moral insanity. But other features of the poem imply a more malicious "macabre project" and introduce the sinister possibility that a coherent and controlling will informs his speech and actions—or that this possessive lover simply "wishes in that particular way which is called willing" (Stephen, *General View* 77). Several of these ambiguities emerge from the genre's hybrid characteristics. As the speaker imparts a narrative structure to the events shaping his all-night vigil, contradictions between its narrative, expressive, and dramatic meanings generate frictions between genre and discourse.

As early as the opening stanzas, theories of moral insanity and ideas of criminal premeditation are combined. The speaker, telling the story of his violent agency, begins by contrasting his careworn passivity with Porphyria's careless activity. He begins an account of his crime and its circumstances with references to his performance as a brooding lover who waits for Porphyria to arrive amidst a storm to which he "listen[s] with heart fit to break" (5). In contrast, upon her arrival, Porphyria "shut[s] the cold out and the storm" (7), builds a fire, and initiates sexual intimacy. When "last, she sate down by my side / And called me" (14–15), the speaker explains, he maintains a purposeful and indignant silence, which leads her to approach him sexually and submissively:

> When no voice replied,
> She put my arm about her waist,
> And made her smooth white shoulder bare,
> And all her yellow hair displaced,
> And, stooping, made my cheek lie there. (15–19)

As Porphyria unwittingly places herself in the position of murder victim, uncovering the fetishized "smooth white" skin and letting down the "yellow hair" that he will transform into a murder weapon—as emotional manipulation becomes physical destruction—the speaker's nuanced account implies a performance of emotional instability and a manipulation of sexual power.

As the poem progresses, Browning continues to assemble symptoms of disease and evidence of malice. Throughout the poem, the lover marks moments of decision and acts of manipulation. His silence entices Porphyria into a vulnerable state and elicits the very words that establish motive and opportunity. She sits, he recalls, "Murmuring how she loved me" (21) but explaining that she is

> Too weak, for all her heart's endeavour,
> To set its struggling passion free
> From pride, and vainer ties dissever,
> And give herself to me for ever. (22–25)

At this point where the secrecy of their transgressive affair is affirmed, the idea that "passion sometimes would prevail" (26) informs his anger and increases Porphyria's danger. The speaker uses Porphyria's murmurings of love, her refusal to "give herself to [him] for ever," and her "weak" submission to "vainer ties" to interpret his own violence. Reading these important lines as an "interpretation of Porphyria's actions," Karlin considers the poem as a "struggle in the speaker's mind between two judgments of Porphyria: one that she is weak and selfish, the other that she is strong and devoted" (209). But they are equally an interpretation of his own actions—a reading or misreading of his crime as the freeing of a "struggling passion." Along these lines, he rather selectively misrecognizes her words as a declaration of complete devotion:

> ... at last I knew
> Porphyria worshipped me: surprise
> Made my heart swell, and still it grew
> While I debated what to do. (32–35)

Perhaps more than any other, this brief passage compresses the unsettling difficulties of diagnosis. The character's presumptions about Porphyria's worshipful sentiments, his use of the word "surprise," and his swelling heart suggest the category of moral insanity as a disease that arises out of emotional excess and irresistible impulse. The character's internal debate, however, reproduces the problems inherent in separating responsible criminals from irresponsible lunatics. That the speaker "debated," and that he recollects a process of debating, insinuates intellectual clarity and willful agency.

Compounding these medicolegal meanings, Browning gives his speaker an ironic edge, which creates even more startling contrasts between the slyly performative and the insanely frank. When he claims, "she guessed not how / Her darling, one wish would be heard" (56–57), the speaker reveals a smug awareness of his own interpretive license in deciding that Porphyria might welcome her own murder as an appropriate relief from the burdens of pride and vanity. Even if a reader were to ascribe every other utterance in the poem to symptoms of moral insanity, this passage poses problems, for with these words the speaker acknowledges a calculated interest in the advantages of interpretation. To a significant extent, this interpretive tension pivots around questions of intention. Prichard explains that morally insane acts are "not the result of fancied provocation" or "the revenge of supposed injury, but [of] an immediate impulse arising spontaneously in the mind, which is diseased only in its moral constitution" (*Treatise* 112). But the lover's motive, of course, can be construed precisely as a vengeful response to a "supposed injury" arising from Porphyria's commitment to "vainer ties" and, if arising from a partial rejection, the murder seems less a consequence of partial insanity than of "sexual hatred." Defying more commonsense attitudes about violent passions, the placement of this character in the category of moral insanity or in a madhouse cell courts medicolegal controversies about murderous charters and murderers' impunity, which, of course, the speaker boldly claims for himself at the end of the poem.

As chilling examples of the kinds of linguistic betrayal central to the dramatic monologue, the speaker's interpretive gestures present readers with a medicolegal dilemma. Offering no psychological revelations or interpretive advantage, they generate a dramatic irony that foregrounds the "substitution of alternative languages" and increases the frictions between epistemological frameworks. It is thus in the courting of controversy and confusion that the thematic strands and generic innovations of the poem come together. Readers consider the terrible familiarity of a sexual violence congruous with patriarchal power and the theoretical possibility of a mental disease incongruous with common sense. As generic design and discursive tension conspire to obscure murderous subjectivity, the only certainty of the poem is the murdered woman. The relationship between this obscurity and this certainty generates the ambiguities that inform the poem's cultural critique: the murderer expresses a "pathology of sexual feeling" which afflicts lovers and lyrics while the violent manifestation of moral insanity provokes unsettled and unsettling questions about character and conduct. Confronted with a shocking instance of transgressive conduct but offered only a partially contextualized rendering of character, the reader can document and denounce the conduct, but criminal character and murderous agency remain inexplicable.

The obscurity of Porphyria's lover produces an eerie effect, which suggests that Browning is less interested in launching a full critique of mental science than he is in distilling specific poetic effects from a collective frustration with violent crimes and medicolegal dilemmas. Commenting on the features of the genre, Christ has identified the discovery of the (speaking) subject as the aesthetic pleasure of the dramatic monologue: "The form allows a wide range in its application of irony, permitting the poet to create grotesque characters whose distortions we delight in discovering (like the speaker of "My Last Duchess") and characters whose blindness is shown to be our own" ("Introduction" 5–6). Although such distortions lay the foundation for the dramatic monologue's notorious grotesqueries, "Porphyria's Lover" distinguishes itself by thwarting discovery and delight. Subjecting the politics of crime to an aesthetic of the sublime, Browning's early foray into dramatic poetry uses the imaginary speech of an imaginary murderer to scrutinize an imaginary boundary between madness and badness.

As an exercise in "judicious obscurity," the poem demonstrates Burke's point that "[i]t is one thing to make an idea clear, and another to make it *affecting* to the imagination" (103): "And I think there are reasons in nature why the obscure idea, when properly conveyed, should be more affecting than the clear. It is our ignorance of things that causes all our admiration, and chiefly excites our passions" (105). As the murderer, amidst the sciences and laws that attempt to explain him, remains sublimely inexplicable, "ignorance" becomes a problem of discourse. Murder has always been terrible, but when the discourses that societies use to apprehend murderers conflict, plunging them into deeper obscurity or elevating them to a position of impunity, obscurity accumulates political and poetic force. It is this force that animates "Porphyria's Lover."

"Single-Eyed Insanity" and Aristocratic Vanity in Browning's "My Last Duchess"

Browning's poetry continued to explore the obscurity of the murderer in the 1840s as public controversy over criminal lunacy intensified. While "Porphyria's Lover" generates poetic speech and aesthetic effects from the materials of moral insanity, two monologues of the 1840s, "My Last Duchess" and "The Laboratory," explore its intellectual counterparts, monomania and mania. After outlining his theory of moral insanity in the *Treatise,* Prichard sketches these two variations of intellectual insanity in the following terms:

1. *Monomania,* or partial insanity, in which the understanding is partially disordered or under the influence of some particular illusion, referring to one subject, and involving one train of ideas, while the intellectual powers appear, when exercised on other subjects, to be in a great measure unimpaired.
2. *Mania,* or raving madness, in which the understanding is generally deranged; the reasoning faculty, if not lost, is confused and disturbed in its exercise; the mind is in a state of morbid excitement, and the individual talks absurdly on every subject to which his thoughts are momentarily directed. (6)

The specific symptoms of these two illnesses—the singular fixation of monomania and the impulsive vigor of mania—accommodate suggestive configurations of dramatic, lyrical, and narrative modes. In both "My Last Duchess" and "The Laboratory" notions of homicidal lunacy as a struggle between excess and control are embedded in speech patterns and formal structures.

Integrating interlocutors (the envoy and the chemist) into the poems' dramatic scenes, however, Browning also engages notions of criminal plotting. Speaking to subordinates, the duke and the courtesan delineate the practical motives and tangible benefits of their murders, and their self-serving arguments and presumptions of impunity trouble distinctions between malice and madness. Because of the remarkable similarities between these medical typologies and Browning's poems—and because of the historical timing of their composition and publication—they too merit closer attention as exercises in "judicious obscurity." While joined together by their careful depictions of dramatic circumstances, their explicit references to historical context, and their well-crafted allusions to intellectual insanity, these poems develop the obscurity of the murderous subject in different ways and thus merit separate discussions.

A general inventory of symptoms inspires one to diagnose the Duke of Ferrara with a severe case of monomania, and in contemporary criticism, unquestioningly categorizing the Duke in these terms has become fairly commonplace if not axiomatic. However, in the 1840s, as we have seen, monomania, invoked at trial but satirized by skeptics and scorned by jurists, was a contentious theory and a controversial diagnosis. Revisiting the symptoms of monomania helps to clarify the poem's specific allusions to the disease, but it also helps to demonstrate how the occasion of his speech and the gist of his argument offer equally significant indications of the Duke's malicious intent. Rather than clarifying things, the historicization of his character and his conduct exacerbates problems of interpretation by producing a tension between two fundamental modern perspectives: a disdain for outmoded and corrupt aristocracies (and an increasing disdain for wife abuse and domestic violence) and a frustration with newfangled and obscure medical theories.[18] Whether exhibiting a peculiarly aristocratic and misogynistic form of badness or a distinctly intellectual and partial form of madness, the Duke belongs to a "privileg'd class whom no statute controls." Exploiting this coincidence of immunity and impunity, the poem cleverly entangles cultural anxieties about interpretive authority and disciplinary power.

As a concentrated and localized form of insanity, monomania required clinical close reading in order to be detected and treated and, thus, the poem's alignment of medical diagnosis and poetic exegesis serves the theme of murder and madness particularly well. In his *Treatise,* Prichard explains that the individual suffering from monomania appears calm but that upon close inspection "it will be found that his mind is in many respects in a different condition from that of perfect health" (28). Described as "single-eyed insanity" or "self-concentration on a criminal object," monomania was linked to localized malfunctions within the regulatory systems of the will and the intellect (Stephen, *Juryman's Guide* 156). In cases of monomania, Prichard explained, "[t]he will seems in fault or defective as much as or more than the power [of reasoning]" (*Treatise* 120), and as a "partial derangement of the understanding," it "is characterised by some particular illusion or erroneous conviction impressed upon the understanding, and giving rise to a partial aberration of judgment. The individual affected is rendered incapable of thinking correctly on subjects connected with the particular illusion, while in other respects he betrays no palpable disorder of mind" (26).

Like other forms of insanity, however, monomania was also linked to concerns about intellectual and behavioral excesses, particularly an "[e]xcess of self-love," which was considered an "ingredient in every modification of monomania" (*Treatise* 33). The monomaniac "fancies himself a king, the pope, a favourite of heaven" (33), and the monomaniacal illusion is "always some notion as to the powers, property, dignity, or destination of the individual affected, which is engrafted upon his habitual state of desire or aversion, passion and feeling" (34). As such, monomania, Stephen argued, could be prevented by a judicious regime of self-government and a calculated avoidance of self-indulgence in all things: "Men who habitually practise self-control, not merely over their acts, but over their inclinations, are never betrayed into such excesses; but those who allow thought to ramble at pleasure into excess, give reigns to the passion, till it becomes uncontrollable, and sets consequence at defiance; this, in the slang of science, is called monomania; or in simple English, lunacy on a single subject" (*Juryman's Guide* 156). Amidst these Victorian arguments about the regulation of "acts" and "inclinations" and the risks of excessive self-love and freely reigning passions, Browning's Renaissance Duke—whose ancient class privileges and immense self-regard underwrite self-indulgence and wife-murder—seems to embody a perfect clinical specimen of monomania.

Helping to secure the theme of lunacy on a single subject, the poem's title, "My Last Duchess," which was changed from its original title, "Italy," in 1849, privileges the Duke's monomaniacal expression and perspective. Supporting the implications of this reiterated phrase, the Duke's monomaniacal symptoms emerge most clearly when viewing and describing the painting of his last Duchess. He exhibits signs of "single-eyed" madness as he levels his possessive gaze (and directs his interlocutor's gaze) at the lifelike portrait of the Duchess: "That's my last Duchess painted on the wall, / Looking as if she were alive" (1–2). And when, in an ostensible tribute to the artist's skill, the Duke proclaims, "I call / That piece a wonder, now" (2–3), the lively image of the capitally punished "last Duchess" produces an unsettling chain of speculation. Attempting to establish his interpretive control over the painting, he establishes a pretense for explicating "the depth and passion of its earnest glance" (8), his particular obsession, by informing his listener that "never read / Strangers like you that pictured countenance, / . . . / But to myself they turned / . . . / And seemed as they would ask me, if they durst, / How such a glance came there" (6–12). Within this claim that everyone who sees the painting questions the glance lies a contrived parenthetical reference to his complete control over the painting—"(since none puts by / The curtain I have drawn for you, but I)" (9–10). As his interests in control of the painting and displays of his power chart the course of his apparently monomaniacal logic, the Duke betrays both a single-eyed focus on a single object and an excessive regard for his own interpretive authority.

With his disorders of the mind artfully preserved in and demonstrably aggravated by the painting, however, the Duke's acts of interpretation are fraught with difficulties. Explaining "[h]ow such a glance came there" (12), he postulates and repostulates the origins of the insubordinate "spot of joy" (21), the very thing that "disgusts" (38) him. His multiple conjectures—that "Frà Pandolph chanced to say 'Her mantle laps / Over my Lady's wrist too much,' or 'Paint / Must never hope to reproduce the faint / Half-flush that dies along her throat'" (16–19) and that the Duchess interpreted such flattery as "courtesy" (20) and "cause enough / For calling up that spot of joy" (20–21)—reveal the circularity of his thinking. In a remarkably single-eyed reading of the painting, he betrays an agitated and exaggerated focus on the "glance," the "spot," and the "[h]alf-flush." Having commissioned, and now displaying and explicating the painting, he reproduces and reencounters the disgust for a "heart . . . too soon made glad" (22). Still cycling through this monomaniacal loop, at the end of the poem, before turning his attention to marital bargaining and to Neptune "[t]aming a sea-horse" (55), the Duke repeats the idea with which the poem begins, "There she stands / As if alive" (46–47)—a double-edged affirmation of his fixation and her death.

These densely and intricately layered verbal symptoms generate important tensions within the poem. As he shifts from displaying his painting to critiquing his Duchess, the Duke highlights two sets of acts and inclinations, which assemble and fragment the elements of the poem's dramatic scene and the speaker's essential character. The Duke, attempting to combine an art tour (as object lesson) and a marriage negotiation (as financial transaction), functions as a willfully murderous husband performing rhetorically strategic maneuvers. But, reacting (or overreacting) to the image of the painted and murdered Duchess and reasoning spuriously on the meanings of blushes, glances, and smiles, he malfunctions in ways that signal the presence of an expressive and excessive monomaniac. As the obscurity of the murderous subject arises from these tensions between rhetorical performance and expressive dysfunction, the poem offers a particularly striking example of the double functions of poetic form by sustaining the interpretive possibilities of two competing frames of reference. A "deeply sceptical" double poem in Armstrong's sense of the word, the poem becomes "an expressive model and an epistemological model simultaneously" (*Victorian Poetry* 13) and thereby situates itself within a mid-century context of medicolegal debate.

The poem's rigid formal structure also contributes to this tension. Its regulated and rhyming couplets have been read as an assertion of authorial presence or evidence of the speaker's calculating interests, but in creating a tension between poetic voice and poetic form, the couplets engage medicolegal strategies of interpretation.[19] Placing the symptoms of unregulated excess against a backdrop of well-maintained order, the meticulous symmetry and economy of the couplets highlight the asymmetry and excess of an intellectual disease—they supply the ordered form over which the Duke's enjambed lines and contorted sentences spill. Combining the use of the rhymed couplet with a "syntax that enjambs more lines than it stops," Tucker argues, the poem "bears witness to a conflict between conventional form and informing spirit" (*Browning's Beginning* 177). Situated within the context of medicolegal debates, this conflict addresses very specific questions about assessing the external form of murderous conduct and the internal "informing spirit" of the murderous subject.

Such distinctions become increasingly troubled as the poem forges links between the Duke's desire to control interpretations of his painting and his desire to control interpretations of his crime. In what appears to be a self-conscious rhetorical maneuver, which acknowledges the historical context in which the murder of a wife was lawful in cases of a wife's adultery, the Duke makes a charge of adultery by finding willful slights and betrayals in her blushes and smiles. In demonstrating the husband rights of *honoris causa*, the intentionally murderous but apparently monomaniacal Duke hovers between Renaissance and Victorian understandings of murder. Conjoining the immunity of insanity pleas and the impunity of aristocratic privilege in this way, the poem reproduces the epistemological and ethical discomfort surrounding medicolegal reconfigurations of agency.

A desire to condemn the Duke as a bad aristocrat is thus consistently undercut with his resemblances to a mad monomaniac. As the Duke makes his provocation argument, the anxious suppositions that constitute his case against the Duchess suggest the influence of "misanthropical monomania," a "very frequent form of the disease" in which the lunatic "fancies himself the object of hatred and persecution, of secret machinations, of plots of all descriptions, sees enemies in his dearest friends, suspects poison in his food, and imagines that injuries of every kind are perpetrated or at least designed against him" (Prichard, *Treatise* 33). He explains his injuries by ascribing unrestrained and unregulated excess to his wife: she "liked whate'er / She looked on; and her looks went everywhere" (23–24). Further accommodating an argument for disease, the Duke's brief catalogue of the Duchess's domestic insubordination merely includes her enthusiastic responses to "[t]he dropping of the daylight in the West, / The bough of cherries some officious fool / Broke in the orchard for her, the white mule / She rode with round the terrace" (26–29). With this list, which finds evidence of adultery and provocation for murder in a sunset, a bough of cherries, and a white mule (the "officious fool" remains grammatically subordinated), and the Duke's indignant exclamation, "Sir, 'twas all one!" (25), Browning stretches the Duke's critique to the point of absurdity. In not being the single object of her smiles, he finds himself persecuted—cuckolded—by an odd assortment of tempters who are hardly the usual suspects in criminal conversation suits and wife-murder cases. Continuing with this line of thinking, the Duke describes her behavior as a discourteous, if not contemptuous, act of under-ranking:

> . . . She thanked men,—good! but thanked
> Somehow—I know not how—as if she ranked
> My gift of a nine-hundred-years-old name
> With anybody's gift. (31–34)

Finding "plots" and "machinations" in his wife's smiles and courtesies, the Duke suggests the intellectually and misanthropically disordered murderous subject who "fancies" and "imagines" injuries "of every kind."

And yet, just as Browning develops these psychological pathologies, the monologue shifts from an elaboration of perceived betrayals to a discussion of disciplinary domestic management. In these lines, which escalate from matters of discipline to methods of punishment, the Duke not only establishes the signs of willful agency and malicious intent, but also expresses a record of tactical and analytical thought on those very matters. Having disingenuously asked, "Who'd stoop to blame / This sort of trifling?" (34–35), the Duke develops a self-reflexive commentary on the power of rhetoric and the force of the will as he reflects on the dilemma of "lesson[ing]" without "stooping":

> . . . Even had you skill
> In speech—(which I have not)—could make your will
> Quite clear to such an one, and say, "Just this
> Or that in you disgust me; here you miss,
> Or there exceed the mark"—and if she let
> Herself be lessoned so, nor plainly set
> Her wits to yours, forsooth, and made excuse,
> —E'en then would be some stooping; and I chuse
> Never to stoop. (35–43)

With these reflections on his tenuous verbal skills and her potential verbal retorts, the Duke reveals that the problem of words and wills is not simply a matter of his "skill / In speech" but one of the will and "wits" of the Duchess. Added to his existing list of her offenses—smiles, looks, blushes—this allusion to her "wits" affirms that what "disgusts" him is the fact that she embodies agency. This agency—her capacity for "excuse" and other forms of defiance—informs the preference for murderous "commands" that he reveals a few lines later. He thus suggests that the expression and authorizing of his will is best accomplished not with a lesson but with a murder. Connecting his will to her death—and suggesting that murder is a mode of expression and instruction—these lines challenge applications of mental science theories of monomania, which replace assessments of criminal responsibility and moral agency with clinical and detached observations about intellectual disorder and mental strain.

Further complicating efforts to define and reconcile the internal and external elements of his crime is the fact that the discussion of the will is punctuated with expressions of rhetorical self-consciousness, which further entangle the signs of aristocratic reserve and monomaniacal symptoms. Returning readers to the tensions between rhetorical and expressive speech, the Duke's self-interruptions, "how shall I say," "I know not how," and "(which I have not)," suggest a kind of mental duress. Attentive to this relationship, Tucker explains:

> Browning never created a more patently skillful speaker, and it is a measure of the Duke's conversational skill that his critics have generally dismissed the hesitant gesture repeated in these lines as an item from his rhetorical stock of commonplaces. But when a skilled rhetorician reaches three times in the space of fifteen lines for the same commonplace, especially for this one, the commonplace is no longer common but an expression of a private struggle. (*Browning's Beginning* 178)

Already apparent in the poem's many contrasts between order and disorder, this struggle is also registered in the Duke's brief reference to his interlocutor at the end of the poem. Attempting to depart the Duke's company, the envoy elicits the Duke's exclamation, "Nay, we'll go / Together down, sir!" (53–54), and this attempt registers, within the poem, the difficulties and discomforts of apprehending this murderous subject, who, rather than displaying his powers, has betrayed his strange pathologies. Compensating, perhaps overcompensating, for his loss of control, the Duke's closing exclamation about and identification with his prized Neptune sculpture—a "rarity / . . . cast in bronze for me!" (55–56)—appears as an attempt to regain his equilibrium. Moving his gaze from the vivid painting to the bronze sculpture, he attempts to reassert the authority that was lost in his encounter with the painted and murdered Duchess.

And yet, situated between the Duke's discourse on lessoning wives and the envoy's gesture of departure is the poem's carefully crafted representation of murder. Encrypted in three short statements, this representation fully privileges the internal elements of murderous intention over the external element of murderous action: "This grew; I gave commands; / Then all smiles stopped together" (45–46). The synecdochic "all smiles stopped" recalls the Duke's monomaniacal fixation. But, the strict verbal economy of this confession, ominously rendered in perfectly communicative gaps, and its curious separation of intention and action highlights the speaker as an aristocrat who commissions both works of art and acts of murder. Not the physical agent of the crime, he is quite simply *mens rea* laid bare. In underscoring a hierarchical system of "commands" and services, the Duke's statements adhere to medicolegal visions of the archetypal murderer with his "accomplices in vice and crime," "assignable inducements," "motives of self-interest," and "wickedness pre-meditated." In spite of the poem's many compelling signs of intellectual disorder, then, the monologue upholds a strikingly literal representation of criminal responsibility.

In doing so, the poem also references "the well-known laws of the criminal economy." Prichard explained that murderers "seldom shed more blood than is necessary for the attainment of their object" (*On the Different Forms* 127) while lunatics act "without motive" and "in opposition to the known influences of all human motives" (*Treatise* 398). The Duke, dwelling on the possibility of a large dowry, courtesy of the Count's "known munificence" (49), pursues the interests and objects of the murderer. Prefacing his remarks on dowry, the Duke states, "I repeat" (48), thereby marking a conscious and consistent interest in a large dowry and a new wife. Promising to restore, even perhaps increase, the value of his "nine hundred years old name" (33), his expectations about wifely behavior and his demands upon the Count's "munificence" render the murder itself a readable expression of aristocratic malice.

Collapsing a single-eyed art tour and a scheming marital negotiation into one scene and one monologue, Browning entangles the attributes of dramatic poetics, the terms of medical diagnosis, and the signs of criminal guilt. In tinkering with theories of monomania, Browning casts a skeptical eye at the minuscule distinctions necessary to detect insanity and affirm malice. As "My Last Duchess" explores the problem of distinguishing between a criminally self-interested motive and an insanely excessive self-love, it generates another inconclusive inventory of madness and badness. Among his Victorian readership, the political resonance of this critical gesture and its attendant interpretive frustrations could only be increased by the Duke's excessive indulgence in and stark expressions of aristocratic entitlement and male privilege. For these aspects of his apparent impunity, however subtly, enfold the frequently classed contexts of insanity defenses and the gendered dynamics of violence. And, more generally, amidst the middle-class ascendancy of the reading public and the cultural descendancy of the aristocratic ruling class, a bad aristocrat with a mad obsession produces a particularly politically charged version of the criminal sublime.

The Extravagance of Mania and the Economy of Murder in Browning's "The Laboratory"

Although "The Laboratory," which first appeared in *Hood's Magazine* in 1844, has received less attention from contemporary scholars than its aforementioned counterparts, it performs "cultural work" very similar to that of "Porphyria's Lover" and "My Last Duchess." Set in the *ancien régime,* this dramatic monologue records the voice of an embittered courtesan undertaking preparations for the murder of her romantic rival. As she prattles and exults, the chemist-interlocutor silently distills arsenic for her fully articulated murderous purposes. In presenting a character in the plotting stages of a murder, "The Laboratory" imagines the expression of intent and the experience of malice in explicit terms. In the 1840s, in spite of the fact that the M'Naghten Rules had recently codified the notion of "knowledge of right and wrong at the time of the crime," these internal elements of crime remained central issues about which mental scientists, criminal courts, and the general public disagreed. At trial, the rules continued to be inconsistently evaluated and applied, and the reconstruction of these mental states involved vexed readings of medical interviews, courtroom testimony, and cross-examination. In "The Laboratory" Browning approaches the question of mental states by retaining an unsettling obscurity as the speaker fluctuates between manic disarray and rational premeditation. While the business transaction between the courtesan and the chemist records malice aforethought and the poison suggests measured calculation, the speaker's verbal style and energy bespeaks intellectual chaos.

In both manner and content, the speech of the courtesan-poisoner signifies the *intellectual* disorder that Prichard associated with mania. She represents a murderous mania so erratic and so frenetic that "The Laboratory" seems to mock the criminal cool associated with moral insanity and depicted in "Porphyria's Lover." As Prichard speculates, mania is moral insanity's intellectual antithesis, but it also distinguishes itself from the more somber intellectual madness of monomania: "[t]he phenomena of mania in its ordinary form are very distinguishable from those of monomania. The aspect, the voice, the gestures of the lunatic in the active state of maniacal derangement, form a contrast with the retired and morose habits of the sullen monomaniac" ("Insanity" 834). A more extroverted disease, mania, a "general disturbance" of the intellect, counts among its symptoms the transformation of the subject's speech patterns: the manic subject "utters rapid and confused sentences in a hurried and impetuous manner" (834).

The symptoms of energy and vigor, disorder and speed, impetuosity and verbosity, underscore the disease's links to willfulness in action. When manifesting itself as "exaltation," Prichard explains, mania generates a violent and active will (*Treatise* 9). The manic person generally exists in a state of "raving madness" in which "the mind is perpetually in a state of confusion and disturbance, which affects all the intellectual faculties, and interferes with their exercise even for the shortest period" (71). Mania also differs from monomania in that the derangement does not involve a circumscribed set of ideas; it infects completely, and, thus, "the patient talks with vehemence, or raves on every subject which for the moment occupies his attention" (72). Playing upon the idea of disordered subjectivity, "The Laboratory" constructs a peculiar vision of premeditation.

Replete with striking sound effects, the poem's twelve quatrains of mostly end-stopped rhyming couplets establish a sense of manic speed and energy. The couplets do more than quicken the pace, however, for like "My Last Duchess," "The Laboratory" contrasts structural order and mental disorder. Though predominately anapestic tetrameter, the pace is disrupted by rhythmic accidentals throughout, and each line's metrical oddities jar against the perfect couplets, creating a confusing incongruity. The impact of these metrical idiosyncrasies gains strength from the poem's syntax. The speaker shifts erratically between sets of commands, questions, and exclamations, which are generously punctuated with question marks, dashes, and exclamation points. Within each sentence, phrases strung together with commas compress a multitude of thoughts and impulses into each of the well-crafted quatrains. The resulting sense of confusion feeds the poetics of indeterminacy, as one wonders whether to privilege the poem's perfectly end-stopped sentences and phrases as evidence of rational order or to emphasize the speaker's verbal density and strained metrical arrangements as symptoms of manic disorder.

The poem's verbal profusions and unusual metrics garnered attention upon its publication in *Dramatic Romances and Lyrics* in 1845, when critics commented on the rhythm of the first lines of the poem, which thrust unsuspecting readers into the erratic consciousness of a plotting killer:

> Now that I, tying thy glass mask tightly,
> May gaze thro' these faint smokes curling whitely,
> As thou pliest thy trade in this devil's-smithy—
> Which is the poison to poison her, prithee? (1–4)

Tennyson called the opening line a "very difficult mouthful" (qtd. in Woolford and Karlin, *Poems* 219), and Elizabeth Barrett Browning criticized the poem's "perplexed" rhythm and "clogged," "forced" expression (qtd. in Woolford and Karlin 221–22). In a letter to Robert Browning, she explained:

> And the Laboratory is as hideous as you meant to make it:—only I object a little to your tendency . . which is almost a habit . . & is very observable in this poem I think, . . of making lines difficult for the reader to read . . see the opening lines of this poem. Not that music is required everywhere, nor in *them* certainly, but that the uncertainty of rhythm throws the reader's mind off the *rail*. . & interrupts his progress with you and your influence with him. (*Letters*, ed. Kintner 131)

With hurried anapests and laborious dactyls, Browning manipulates the difficulties of reading in order to characterize the anxious, plotting murderer. The wayward and impulsive rhythms of the monologue form the objective correlative of the homicidal lunatic's psychology. As she eagerly anticipates her crime, the speaker's troubled language operates as a readable symptom while, of course, enabling Browning's lively prosodic experimentation.

While concerned with the aural signification of lunacy, Browning also exploits the generic opportunities of dramatic poetics by sketching the sinister dramatic setting emphasized in the title. A laboratory, of course, symbolizes intellectual concentration rather than mental derangement, and this laboratory, a well-described "devil's-smithy," constitutes the transgressive margin where the murderous plot takes shape. Inspired by this grotesque scene, Rossetti's first watercolor, using distorted perspective and dark colors, places the figures in a laboratory filled with distillation equipment, poisonous concoctions, and scattered books. Amidst such symbols of terrible intent, the speaker and the chemist examine the jewels with which she will pay for the poison that "does it all" (36). In the poem, Browning focuses on the toxicity of the poison and marks the laboratory as a dangerous place where the speaker and the chemist must wear masks to prevent exposure to fumes and dust. At times, the speaker's carelessness is contrasted with the chemist's apparent cautiousness. She says, "Is it done? Take my mask off! Nay, be not morose" (41), and then imagines that her revenge, because of its singularity of purpose, grants her immunity from toxins—and remorse: "If it hurts her, beside, can it ever hurt me?" (44). Upon leaving, however, as she revels in her destructive power, the speaker takes a precautionary measure: "But brush this dust off me, lest horror there springs" (48).

This scene in a laboratory creates a clear portrait of premeditation. The vengeful murderer procures her deadly weapon, observes the distillation, revels in the process, and praises the scientific precision of the fatal poison. She marvels at the aesthetic intrigue of the pastes and powders, the gum and the "gold oozings" (14) and the "soft phial, the exquisite blue, / Sure to taste sweetly" (15–16). She commends the concentrated and easily disguised power that poison represents:

> Had I but all of them, thee and thy treasures—
> What a wild crowd of invisible pleasures—
> To carry pure death in an ear-ring, a casket,
> A signet, a fan-mount, a filigree-basket! (17–20)

The speaker even incorporates the poison's aesthetic attributes into her murderous plot; condensed, portable, discrete, and, perhaps, sweet, it will lure her victim to her death. Criticizing the "too grim" (25) color of the chemist's mixture, she exclaims, "Let it brighten her drink, let her turn it and stir, / And try it and taste, ere she fix and prefer!" (27–28). In marked contrast, the speaker then hopes that her victim's dying body will record the violent and vengeful nature of the crime, thereby conveying a message to the lover who will witness her death: "Let death be felt and the proof remain: / Brand, burn up, bite into its grace— / He is sure to remember her dying face!" (38–40). In this way, murder will serve an expressive purpose.

In elaborating this character, Browning draws upon popular notions of poisoners whose methods revealed dispassionate intention and calculated premeditation. The speaker prefers poison because: "[i]t kills her, and this prevents seeing it close" (42). Poisoning, of course, was also frequently perceived as a particularly feminine crime. Browning underscores the gendered aspects of his character and her conduct when the speaker self-consciously alludes to her status as a woman who kills as she boasts that she ignores the prescribed role of a rejected woman: "they believe my tears flow / While they laugh—laugh at me—at me fled to the drear / Empty church, to pray God in, for them!—I am here" (6–8). With these last words—"I am here"—the speaker unequivocally proclaims her transgressive agency and murderous pride.

Undoubtedly, Victorian stereotypes of the *ancien régime* also contribute to this poem's representation of criminal guilt. Suggesting a gendered economy of courtly crime, arising from social and sexual corruption, the speaker's jostled commentary conveys a conventional motive of sexual jealousy:

> For only last night, as they whispered, I brought
> My own eyes to bear on her so, that I thought
> Could I keep them one half minute fixed, she would fall
> Shrivelled; she fell not; yet this does it all! (34–37)

The trochaic weight of "Shrivelled" intensifies the speaker's destructive anger, and the speaker's initial attempts at shriveling her rival with the application of a sustained gaze suggest an impractical foolishness if not a manic delusion. Regardless, however, the escalation from staring to poisoning highlights her violent, criminal resolve. At the end of the poem, Browning again indicates corruption and excess when the speaker offers a most improper sexual payment to her chemist-accomplice as she leaves to "dance at the king's" (48): "Now, take all my jewels, gorge gold to your fill, / You may kiss me, old man, on my mouth if you will!" (45–46). This offer constitutes a symbolically apt exchange: the courtesan offers sexual and material compensation for the murderous powers with which she hopes to regain the sexual and material benefits of courtly favor. As Browning sketches a criminal motivation derived from courtly culture, he configures her transgression, perhaps paradoxically, as a reasoned and strategic attempt at social survival in a corrupt system.

And yet, amidst all of the signs of criminal malice, symptoms of madness continue to accumulate. Against the backdrop of poisonous chemicals, the speaker carefully observes the preparation and boldly issues commands: "Grind away, moisten and mash up thy paste, / Pound at thy powder,—am I not in haste?" (9–10). Such exclamations, indicative of both passion and calculation, simultaneously point to mania and to reason. As we have already seen, Prichard deems the homicidal lunatic a singular actor while the murderous criminal employs "accomplices in vice and crime" and acts upon "assignable inducements" and "motives of self-interest, of revenge" while "displaying wickedness pre-meditated" (*Treatise* 398). At the most fundamental level, the monologue underscores criminal collaboration: the chemist silently perfects the poison while the speaker volubly plots her crime. Even though the speaker marvels at the power concentrated in a minute form, she doubts the poison's efficacy in destroying her victim's large body:

What a drop! She's not little—no minion like me;
That's why she ensnared him: this never will free
The soul from those strong, great eyes:—say, 'no!'
To that pulse's magnificent come-and-go. (29–32)

Her concern that her rival's size, which constitutes her ensnaring attractiveness, might also immure her to the carefully distilled poison underscores the social and material interests informing her murderous plans—the sexual competition at court and the importance of masculine favor. But it also explains the speaker's references to the economy of her crime and the exorbitant costs of murder. "The delicate droplet," she notes, is gained at the expense of "[her] whole fortune's fee!" (43).

This economy of crime recalls the "criminal economy" with which Prichard differentiates "[t]he insane homicide," who "often kills a number of victims at a time, slaughtering all within his reach," and the murderer, who "seldom shed[s] more blood than is necessary for the attainment of [his] object" (*Treatise* 127). The speaker of "The Laboratory," awed by the power of poison, considers the potential for killing more rivals and imagines increasing the swath of her murderous spree:

Soon, at the kings, but a mere lozenge to give,
And Pauline should have just thirty minutes to live!
But to light a pastille, and Elise, with her head,
And her breast, and her arms, and her hands, should drop dead! (21–24)

In imagining the growth of her destructive realm and the death of her rival in a blazon of the sexualized attributes against which she competes, the courtesan expresses a dream of an efficient but unchecked power in a way that conforms to Victorian notions of manic impulse.

After much waiting, rehearsing, and anticipating, the speaker concludes with a payment and a departure. At the end of the poem, the chemist and the reader witness a murderer, poison in hand and motive intact, setting out to commit a fully premeditated crime. The speaker's departing statements adhere to the poem's overall pattern of juxtaposing manic energy and malicious intent. But even here, "The Laboratory" exemplifies poetry's potential to develop the contentions of legal and medical discourse by embedding alternative meanings in verbal style and dramatic form. The speaker's ebullient manner and excessive payment combine with her self-possessed murderous intent to blur the boundaries between criminality and insanity. Her symbolic resonance emerges from the conflation of two stereotypes: the sexually corrupt courtesan and the morally deviant poisoner. Planning a crime congruous with the sexual politics of courtly culture and incongruous with the cold persona of the female poisoner, she, too, enforces the obscurity of the murderous subject.

Taken collectively, "Porphyria's Lover," "My Last Duchess," and "The Laboratory" demonstrate Browning's use of the dramatic monologue to conjoin irreconcilable subject positions by jumbling murderous content and mad form, and vice versa. As a result, decisions on matters of character are impeded. In exploring the Derridean deferrals of meaning that characterize Browning's texts, Tucker explains:

> Browning's moral doctrine of incompleteness finds a clear aesthetic analogue in his poetics. From the formal effects of its largest structures to the minutiae of its verbal style, Browning's is an art of disclosure, an art that resists its own finalities. He typically prolongs the curious action of his longer poems and his plays through strategies that defer and thus continually anticipate what another author might make the narrative or dramatic climax. . . . [I]t is essential to an understanding of Browning's dramatic irony to see irony as a way of composing a question for the reader's benefit without resolving it. (*Browning's Beginning* 5)

In these three poems, Browning's approaches to questioning, anticipating, and deferring serve to invoke and interrogate the discourses of law and medicine as they intersect with and diverge from the discourses of gender and class. Confronted with voices of violent killers, readers attempt—and indeed are invited to attempt—to locate that speaker discursively while the text resists interpretation.

Though the sublime aesthetic effects of this obscurity and "disclosure" constitute poetic achievements in their own right, they also implicate the uncomfortable limitations of a medicolegal discourse "involved in many obscurities" and challenging commonsense ethics. These epistemological tensions complicated social responses to the problem of crime *and* frustrated the public's desire for a coherent discourse and settled law with which to categorize and contain unruly subjects. In this sense, these monologues can be understood with respect to Slinn's arguments about speech act theory and Victorian poetry's project of critique, which arises from poetry's deliberately formalist engagement with cultural discourse. Slinn explains that the poems surveyed in his study address important Victorian cultural issues but makes the distinction that "[t]he poems do not resolve these issues but expose their complexities": "These poems show how deliberately conceived performative language may focus central cultural issues in an era, since, while determinedly tied to the terms of specific speech acts, their themes encompass several of the significant debates in mid-nineteenth-century England" (6). In a similar way, Browning's interest in cultivating the complexity and obscurity of murderous subjects establishes the formal and cultural significance of these three texts, which align, in order to explore, poetic and political acts of interpretation.

"Guilty But Insane": Frenzy and Agency in Dante Gabriel Rossetti's "A Last Confession"

Lacking the strict verbal economy of Browning's dramatic monologues, Rossetti's "A Last Confession" has been viewed as a slightly inferior and derivative Browningesque specimen of the form. In this poem, a wounded Italian revolutionary confesses to a Catholic priest as he lies on his deathbed. His confession recounts his lustful and murderous desire for a young woman whom he raised from youth—after finding her abandoned by her parents, who "left her to God's chance, / To man's or to the Church's charity" (87–88) rather than watch her starve during a famine. The blank-verse poem consists of five hundred and fifty-eight lines, fifty of which are a "rude" and "ill rhymed" (278) Italian folk song into which the speaker lapses during the course of his confession. Set in Austria-occupied Italy and narrated by a patriotic outlaw, the poem partially emplots the Italian struggle against occupation. The poem's historical context, Rossetti's self-proclaimed pride in its Italian subject, and its original composition between the revolutionary days of 1848 and the fall of the republic in 1849 have directed critical analyses toward political allegory.[20]

A focus on political allegory, however, cannot fully address Rossetti's use of a sexually motivated crime to center the monologue—nor can it fully account for the text's aesthetic interests in Pre-Raphaelitism and Art Catholicism.[21] Although there are arguably several aesthetic and thematic projects embedded in the poem, the problem of murderous subjectivity, which informs the speaker's consistent swaying between expressions of madness and malice, centers the political references and aesthetic features of the poem. Significantly, the trauma that terrifies the speaker and compels his speech is not his revolutionary activity, of which he remains proud, but his murder of a young woman, the former foundling child whom he raises and then murders when, in her adolescence, she assumes her independence and resists his possessive eroticism. In fact, his revolutionary political activities and his aestheticized sexual passions—as he represents them in his confessional narrative—always pivot around his terrible identity as a killer, and his character is defined by his narration of murderous intent, wrought, he explains, when "[h]er eyes looked on me from an emptied heart / When most my heart was full of her" (455–56).

Because Rossetti's politics have sidelined critical discussions of the poem's links to medical debates, a reconnection of text and context is needed. With the exception of Faas, modern critics have not explicitly linked "A Last Confession" to theories of mental science. Yet, even Buchanan's famously insensitive critique in "The Fleshly School of Poetry: Mr. D. G. Rossetti" (1871) documents the Victorian sensitivity to the intricacies of transgressive subjectivity. While Buchanan's comments primarily focus on the "naughtiness" (337), "nastiness" (338), and "fleshly feeling" (339) in Rossetti's *Poems,* in comparing Rossetti's visual and verbal arts, he also expresses a discomfort with the preponderance of mental disorder: "There is the same thinness and transparency of design, the same combination of the simple and the grotesque, the same *morbid deviation from healthy forms of life,* the same sense of weary, wasting, yet exquisite sensuality; nothing virile, nothing tender, *nothing completely sane*" (emphasis added, 336–37).[22] Buchanan's reaction underscores the cultural anxieties and aesthetic agendas surrounding sanity and insanity, and it alerts us to Rossetti's manipulation of that elusive boundary.

In many ways, it seems, "A Last Confession" generates a poetics of "nothing completely sane." A focus on the speaker's mental states and the problems of mental norms and aberrations reveals how fully Rossetti's poem engages the central difficulties of medicolegal debate—the discernment of mental defect and the enforcement of criminal responsibility. Although the poem's somewhat un-Browningesque metrical regularity and narrative expanse have deflected attention away from its careful manipulation of the dramatic monologue form, Rossetti fully exploits the genre's integration of dramatic setting, lyrical voice, and narrative structure to obscure the nature of the speaker's murderous subjectivity. The confessional setting, allegorizing judicial authority, introduces the polarities of criminal lunacy and criminal law into the poem. With questions of salvation and damnation looming, the monologue pivots around the declaration and denial of responsibility. The speaker, recalling his sexual past and securing his spiritual future, must explicate his crimes and his sins, as well as his *self*. In exploring the relationships between self and sin, character and conduct, Rossetti turns to elements of lyrical stylization, which allow the speaker to alternately embody madness and badness. While the speaker constructs, in a confessional mode, a moral history of his own character, problems of will and responsibility, control and excess, character and circumstance, emerge. The poem's narrative expanse allows Rossetti to enfold the testimony of a criminal and the mental history of a lunatic, and the modulation of poetic voice enables him to inflect mad symptoms with criminal motivations. By pairing moments of frenzied disorder with instances of rhetorical spin, Rossetti generates the same kind of sublime obscurity that we see in Browning's monologues.[23]

As we have seen, in contending with new theories of criminal madness, Victorians often longed for a clear mark of distinction between the criminal and the lunatic—something completely sane or insane. The ethical and legal difficulties created by monomania and moral insanity inspired some mental scientists to reinstate frenzy and delusion as requisites of criminal insanity—distinctions that many jurists had demanded all along. In 1848 an article in the *Journal of Psychological Medicine and Mental Pathology* proclaimed, "We think the opinion that there is a sudden frenzy, an instantaneous eclipse of reason at the moment of the act, is preferable to, and more in consonance with moral science, than the hypothesis of medical jurists, who hold that the monomania, whether it be homicidal, suicidal, or incendiary, &c., may terminate in the execution of the deed, *without frenzy* or disorder of the intellect" ("Homicidal Insanity" 331). These gestures towards frenzy sought to resurrect common sense and to offer certainty in legal and medical matters: "Besides, in our opinion, a disorder of the reason will always be more easily appreciated and verified by the common sense of mankind than a perversion of the will joined to an effective lesion without frenzy in the act, which no one, after all, is able peremptorily to prove . . ." (331). In sum, the author explains, "We reject that species [of homicidal insanity] which is said to be without frenzy in the act" (333).

Because Rossetti's Italian patriot exists in emotional extremities and because he locates his crime in the "whirling brain's eclipse" (536), "A Last Confession" seems to respond directly to a growing nostalgia for frenzied madness. The speaker consistently exhibits signs of manic disorientation. Throughout the poem, Rossetti supplies vivid hallucinations, which record the shifting and disoriented mental states of the speaker: he dreams of his victim wringing out her bloody hair, envisions her bloodied form presiding over the confession, and hears her mocking laughter over and over again. At one point, the speaker warns the priest of her maddening presence: "she's at your back: / Gather your robe up, Father, and keep close, / Or she'll sit down on it and send you mad" (440–42). This warning, of course, implies a cause for the speaker's guilty, hallucination-induced raving—he is rendered insane by his own crime. But hallucinations, he attests, have always formed a part of his mental history, and he thereby suggests that a preexisting madness informs his crime. When the speaker recalls his desperate walk to meet his victim "that last day / For the last time" (7–8), he is accompanied by various manifestations of his victim's past selves:

> . . . Ah! And everywhere,
> At places we both knew along the road,
> Some fresh shape of herself as once she was
> Grew present at my side; until they seemed—
> So close they gathered round me—they would all
> Be with me when I reached the spot at last,
> To plead my cause with her against herself
> So changed. (10–17)

In imagining himself flanked by versions of his victim's younger, more compliant self, who will support him when he goes to "plead [his] cause," the speaker represents conventional notions of delusional madness. The vivid and repetitive imagery of his imaginings form a kind of dreamscape, which, as J. B. Bullen has argued, "imparts to it an almost obsessional quality; the moments of hallucination and trance suggest the operation of strongly irrational forces, and the gaps, the omissions, and the strange time scheme, all work against coherence, rationality, and control" (111).

With respect to the poem's processes of characterization, such features have easily claimed the spotlight. Faas argues that the speaker's struggles to narrate his crime "actualize the process of memory" (158) and explains, "The speaker just barely realizes how forcefully certain memories throng into his consciousness, striving for utterance; but as readers we come to recognize a set of monomaniac obsessions, which escalate to the point of providing the irresistible impulse for the murder. Except for feeling rejected by one he loves and who once loved him, the speaker lacks all immediate motivation for his deed" (160). Accordingly, Faas interprets Rossetti's use of the confession in this poem as another example of a poetic case study: in suppressing "factual motivation" the poem presents "a chain of mental events, which, like the case history of a psychotic, accounts for an otherwise incomprehensible act" (160). Yet, such comparisons to psychosis or even monomaniacal impulse imply a psychological determinism that cannot fully account for the speaker's—and the poem's—obsessive return to questions of will and responsibility. Though I will later address Rossetti's measured attention to criminal intent, including what appears to be the damningly suggestive, well-developed, and immediate motive of sexual jealousy, I first want to discuss the ways in which the poem's representation of insanity extends beyond superficial signs of frenzy and delusion and thus complicates questions of etiology. While the poem's historical context and narrative detail collaborate to highlight the problems of memory and the origins of motive, they also serve the poem's entanglement of criminal responsibility and lunacy and its obscuring of murderous subjectivity.

When speculating about the causes of insanity, Victorian psychologists cited both moral traumas and physical defects. Prichard, reproducing Esquirol's asylum data, documents several moral and circumstantial factors, including "domestic grief," romantic disappointment, political upheaval, economic hardship, religious fanaticism, "reverses of fortune," "offended self-love," "disappointed ambition," and "misanthropy" (*Treatise* 178). Such instances of moral causation could, of course, implicate the will of the sufferer: "By too great indulgence and a want of moral discipline, the passions acquire greater power, and a character is formed subject to caprice and to violent emotions: a predisposition to insanity is thus laid in the temper and moral affections of the individual" ("Insanity" 848). Meanwhile, physical causes included natural constitution, age, sex, celibacy (unmarried status), passionate temperament, prior attacks, and brain disorders, and, primarily among the "lower orders," liquor and opium, blows to the head, intestinal irritations, irregularities of uterine function, and metastasis (848–49). Prichard also cites Esquirol's study of 323 committal cases between 1811 and 1812, which revealed that "domestic chagrins" accounted for 105 cases and that "disappointments in love" counted for 45 cases (850). As these situations also accounted for a great many murders, it is easy to see how attempts to establish causation disturbed the boundaries of insanity and criminality.

Such assessments of physical and moral factors suggest that the speaker's apparent madness is fully overdetermined. His personal history includes most of the moral causes listed by Prichard and completely violates Victorian standards of moral discipline. Prior to meeting and adopting the foundling girl, the speaker reveals, he spent his life "alone, / As any hiding hunted man must live" (97–98). His wandering outlaw existence, he explains, was characterized by "nights in hiding, worn and sick / And hardly fed" (57–58), and even as a young man, he states, "the cause which gave / The wounds I die of now had brought me then / Some wounds already" (95–97). His rootless life stems from political passions, which Rossetti also links to both mental and moral aberrations.

Describing himself as a "moody comrade" (252), the speaker explains how the violent intensity of revolution bred his emotional instability. It was, he confesses, "[a] game to play, a love to clasp, a hate / To wreak, all things together that a man / Needs for his blood to ripen" (261–63). The (over)ripened blood and the nationalist fixation, however, both contribute to his increasingly unbalanced sensibility, "till at times / All else seemed shadows" (263–64). At the same time, the physical stress of his mortal wounds disrupts the course and clarity of his confession: "Ah there! My wounds will snatch my sense again: / The pain comes billowing on like a full cloud / Of thunder, and the flash that break from it / Leaves my brain burning" (404–7). Thus emphasizing his lack of sense, he ascribes to himself clear symptoms of insanity.

Intimating a catalogue of causes, "A Last Confession" also entertains the possibility of hereditary insanity. The speaker traces his sacrificial lineage through his revolutionary father:

> ... Italy,
> The weeping desolate mother, long has claimed
> Her sons' strong arms to lean on, and their hands
> To lop the poisonous thicket from her path,
> Cleaving her way to light. And from her need
> Had grown the fashion of my whole poor life
> Which I was proud to yield her, as my father
> Had yielded his. (253–60)

In the context of mental science, this revolutionary legacy carries both ideological and biological implications. Though the poem was first composed in 1848–49, when natural constitution and heredity were generally understood to be potential factors, by the time "A Last Confession" had been abandoned, buried, exhumed, revised, and published in 1870, mental science had quite systematically applied Darwinian principles to established theories of moral disorder; the notions of hereditary influences of the thirties and forties succumbed to concepts of hereditary determinism later in the century. Dr. Henry Maudsley, a rising star in mental science in the 1860s, proclaimed the insane to be the "stepchildren of Nature" (*Body and Mind* 43) and determined both crime and madness to be "antisocial products of degeneracy" (*Pathology of Mind* 78).

In spite of the materialist ambitions of these late-Victorian theories, however, they nonetheless retained the language of moral imperatives and failures. For Maudsley, self-discipline was necessary not simply to assuage individual passions, but also to temper inherited traits. In extracting insanity from the "haze which metaphysics has cast around it" (*Body and Mind* 42), Maudsley highlighted the inherent biological limitations of individual minds, or rather, brains. Noting that both criminals and madmen suffer from the "tyranny of a bad organisation" (*Body and Will* 281), Maudsley classified them both as manifestations of degeneracy, abnormality, and fragmentation: "we find, when we inquire what are the broad features of this unsoundly leavened mental temperament, that they mark, first, a partial degeneration or at any rate an incomplete sanity of moral feeling, and, secondly, a corresponding impairment or incomplete development of will" (284). Eliding the two subjectivities, criminal and lunatic, "[t]he degeneracy," he explains, "whether it be into madness or into badness, will be marked by some defect of moral feeling and will" (285).[24]

While Maudsley's theories cannot be cited as influences on the original structure and language of Rossetti's poem, the discourse of criminal insanity that circulated in the 1860s just prior to the publication of Rossetti's *Poems*, in which "A Last Confession" first appeared, offers a context for thinking about the speaker's mental states and the poem's critical reception. Maudsley, despite his belief in hereditary pathologies, advised the self-regulation of the will, which he described as "the supreme function of mental organisation" and the "most determined" evolutionary "event" that distinguishes humans from other mammals. When subjected to rigorous supervision, the will, which assembles the forces of the "infinite past," "present moods," and "present acts" and constitutes "a wholesome system of feeling and discipline," provides a resource for counteracting crime and insanity (*Pathology of Mind* 37). As Reed points out, this attention to the developmental and regulatory processes of the will further complicated the relationship between personal history, criminal madness, and individual responsibility: "Maudsley offered to do what he felt metaphysicians could not do—explain the gradual formation of the concrete will by recurrence. Through repetition, 'will remembers and learns to will, exercise building up faculty and conduct character,' so that a man is shaped by his circumstances" (141).[25] Complementing Maudsley's physiological mandate, this equation accounts for brain functions and genetic propensities, but it also implicates the development of individuals as moral agents. If questions of madness and criminality extend far into one's past, operations of the will, no matter how seemingly minute or insignificant, require constant vigilance and intervention.

Of course, moral discipline had long figured in mid-Victorian regimens of self-control, from the self-help manuals of Samuel Smiles to the moral therapies of lunatic asylums. As Smith explains, the problem of moral habit was "reinforced" by physiologists, such as Maudsley, who "portrayed habits becoming built into the body's fabric" (*Trial* 82). Because long-term self-regulation could fortify an individual and, thus, allow him to retain rational control in an emotionally charged situation, mental breakdowns and behavioral transgressions raised questions about conduct and character, which, in turn, produced an expanded notion of responsibility: "Responsibility ensued, not necessarily because any particular movement was intended, but because a chosen life history led to that movement. . . . [T]he moralist's attention was not limited to the present; it illuminated the past when the possibility of immorality began" (82). Madness and badness, therefore, take on biographical and historical significance: "The insanity defence dramatised the switching between languages of moral choice and determinism, both between medical and legal discourses and within the medical discourse itself. The difficulty was exacerbated by the problem of earlier responsibility for later conduct; the boundary of crime and insanity became a question of biography" (82).

It is not surprising, then, that biographical questions of moral lassitude and transgressive conduct sustain the narrative structure of "A Last Confession" or that the formalities of confession perform a critical function in the text's slippage between confirming and denying the force of moral habit. Foucault describes confession as a "ritual of discourse" which "unfolds within a power relationship" in "the presence (or virtual presence) of a partner who is not simply the interlocutor but the authority who requires the confession, prescribes and appreciates it, and intervenes in order to judge, punish, forgive, console, and reconcile" (*History* 61–62). Hence, when the speaker repeatedly inserts the address "Father" into his confession, he reinforces the presence of this silent interlocutor, and he highlights his continued investment in this ritual with potential spiritual rewards. Throughout the monologue, the speaker indicates his hope that the confession might offer an escape from damnation, which he believes is imminent. Yet, as Christopher Nassaar has argued, "His appeals to the Father for sympathy are pathetic, since murder is a cardinal sin for which no forgiveness is possible, as the speaker knows full well" (36). The speaker's wish for salvation, amidst the apparent certainty of damnation, establishes a crucial affective tension in the poem; afflicted with the extremes of hope, despair, regret, and delusion, the speaker suggests a lifelong pattern of willful dissipation.

In *The Power of Lies* (1994) John Kucich critiques Foucault's "account of the omnipresence in Victorian culture of confession" (17), claiming that it neglects the "new spaces for lying" (18) opened up in this discourse of the self. A deceptive approach to confession, he argues, constitutes a rejection of the "institutional technologies of truth" or "a repudiation of the political structures associated with 'truth' production" (19). Along these lines, we might consider the ways in which Rossetti's poem opens up new spaces for rhetorical argument. At the very least, Kucich's more flexible understanding of confession explains why Rossetti's speaker fluctuates between confessional supplication and rhetorical opportunism. Confounded by the priest's associations with both reconciliation and punishment, the speaker oscillates between a confession of sin and an argument for absolution. He thus weaves strands of testimony and advocacy into his narrative history of delusion and frenzy. Instead of casting the speaker as a prostrated figure appealing for absolution or an unequivocal madman raving about the past, Rossetti creates a complex and murky transgressive subject, who, beset by fears of eternal punishment and emboldened by sexual jealousy, deploys alternating strategies of supplication and persuasion.[26] With some irony, at a time when priestly powers were being subverted by secular legal and medical authorities, Rossetti depicts the speaker's religious confession as an outright negotiation of the secular voluntarist/determinist distinction so important to medicolegal discourse and thus diminishes fundamental matters of spiritual interpretation.[27]

Accordingly, while Rossetti uses the confessional setting to allegorize the disciplinary authority of judicial proceedings and thereby imply the desperate circumstances of the criminal standing in judgment, he renders the ritual of religious confession incomplete and improper. Fulfilling the codes of the genre, the priest remains completely silent, and the poem ends before he can answer the speaker's inquiry about potential "hope." More importantly, in the process of confessing, the speaker breaches confessional etiquette and implies a wholesale rejection of the very authority from which he seeks protection. Although the speaker often strives to follow the scripted performance of the penitent, he just as frequently deviates from the script and challenges the proceedings. His obsession with damnation leads him to intimidate the priest: "... perhaps you do not hear; / But you must hear. If you mistake my words / And so absolve me, I am sure the blessing / Will burn my soul" (415–18). After admonishing the priest for any potential misinterpretation of his narrative, the speaker repeats the warning and boldly threatens the priest, arguing that if he absolves him because of a mistaken interpretation of his crime, then he too will suffer damnation:

> ... If you mistake my words
> And so absolve me, Father, the great sin
> Is yours, not mine: mark this: your soul shall burn
> With mine for it. (418–21)

The speaker even imagines the priest's painful cries in hell; recalling religious paintings of hell's torments, the speaker first imagines himself shrieking Latin phrases in hell, but then corrects himself: "Nay, but I know, / 'Tis you shall shriek in Latin" (423–24). Calling attention to his inadequate knowledge of Latin in this way, he subtly informs his listener of his own religious lapses and secular priorities. Envisioning the priest's hellish ravings, the speaker disrupts the confession's ritual functions, and in twice repeating the phrase, "If you mistake my words, / And so absolve me," Rossetti's speaker highlights the difficulties and consequences of interpretation which complicate criminals, lunatics, and poetry.

Rossetti exploits such difficulties in a variety of ways, but he most consistently positions the problem of interpretation as a discursive loophole that can be exploited by his self-conscious and murderous speaker. For example, when the speaker disrupts his own confession with a full-scale metacommentary on language and representation, he deliberately casts himself and his crime as epistemological problems. Early in the monologue, he insists on his own inscrutability: "Father, you cannot know of all my thoughts" (6). He goes on to obscure his crime in tautologies:

> O Father, if you knew all this
> You cannot know, then you would know too, Father,
> And only then, if God can pardon me.
> What can be told I'll tell, if you will hear. (17–20)

Later, the speaker argues that his clear thoughts of the past are obscured by the inadequacies of language: "You do not know how clearly those things stood / Within my mind, which I have spoken of, / Nor how they strove for utterance" (106–8). Announcing his frustration, he explains that the conventions of narrative and the limits of language cannot accommodate the complex circumstances of his transgression:

> You see I cannot, Father; I have tried,
> But cannot, as you see. These twenty times
> Beginning, I have come to the same point
> And stopped. Beyond, there are but broken words
> Which will not let you understand my tale. (426–30)

As we learn that this monologue marks his twentieth attempt, his "broken words," symptoms of the limits of expression, prevent judgment. Yet, as Foucault has also noted, confession is "a ritual in which the truth is corroborated by the obstacles and resistances it has had to surmount in order to be formulated" (*History* 62). Therefore, if we apply Kucich's comments on lying, we can fully articulate the interpretive dilemma that Rossetti outlines—"broken words" can signify either a corroboration of the truth or a manipulation of the ritual.

As I have been arguing throughout this chapter, the obscurity of the murderous subject engenders the sublime aesthetic that characterizes these particular criminal monologues and connects them to medicolegal debates. However, when the speaker insists on his own obscurity, he raises additional questions about mad posturing for the purposes of legal defense. As Victorians worried about the conveniences and injustices of insanity pleas, mental scientists discussed the possibility of defendants and defense counsel using ambiguous theories to their personal and professional advantage. Like Prichard, Winslow consoled readers with a reminder that willful crimes were almost always discernible by motive, premeditation, intention, and avoidance of detection. Quoting a colleague, he explains, "The moral circumstances which precede or accompany crime generally show whether they are the result of criminal intentions or derangement of the intellect; that is to say, that in a real criminal there is always some motive of personal interest by which the moral cause of his act may be known" (*Plea* 78). In "A Last Confession," the notion of epistemological impasse corresponds to Victorian discussions about impunity and responsibility, and the speaker's repeated references to verbal frustration suggest a guilty conscience and the vestiges of criminal intent.

With the many subversions of the confessional power relationship, the speaker appears to craft his words in order to shape the meaning of his transgression, and in his muddled attempts to claim his unattainable salvation he pastes together a two-pronged defensive argument, which reintroduces the problem of balancing contradictory explanations of character and conduct. On the one hand, his extraordinary biography, riddled with hallucinatory disruptions, evinces a degree of irresponsibility that would support a special verdict of "not guilty on the ground of insanity." Yet, his memories, and his insistence on his victim's sexual guilt, implicate the murder as a crime of passion, provoked by what he perceives as the inconstancy and potential harlotry of his beloved. Such details, of course, render him more criminal than lunatic. Regardless of the logical and strategic problems that these two strands of narrative argument encounter singly or together, they enfold medicolegal questions that compel readers to contemplate his confession in terms of madness and malice. In the juxtaposition of these two defensive strains, however, Rossetti generates an irony that thwarts any resolution or verdict on the precise mad-bad distinction that the poem invokes.

To a large extent, the poem's problems of interpretation emanate from the speaker's reiteration of a provocation argument, as they continue the pattern of confessional subversion and narrative digression. The speaker revels in sexual memories, creating the ethical disgust and moral unease necessary to stage the contest between madness and badness. His recollections of the sumptuous girl-object, who provokes his murderous rage, infuse his confession with a self-indulgent impertinence and, at times, threaten to desecrate the holy sacrament from which he seeks to benefit. Rossetti shocks his audience with the speaker's child-loving: describing a good-bye kiss, he recalls, "She was still / A child; and yet that kiss was on my lips / So hot all day where the smoke shuts us in" (198–200).[28] Shortly after this statement, the speaker attempts to sanctify this transgressive desire. He admits that it changed from "the father's, brother's love" (202) to a violent sexual passion: "And my heart beat with so much violence" (214). But he then compares that sexual passion to a "holy thought / Which is a prayer before one knows of it" (203–4). While his passionate excess and sexual frankness may recall Prichard's list of the symptoms and origins of insanity, such moments of metaphorical recovery also suggest self-interested verbal manipulation. When he utters, "May I find you yet / Mine when death wakes? Ah! be it even in flame, / We may have sweetness yet" (484–86), Ronnalie Howard has explained, "[h]is passion for her (even now that she has been some time dead)—more sensual, more powerful, more jealous than he admits—at last betrays him into blasphemy" ("Rossetti's 'A Last Confession'" 27). As the speaker's fleshly revelations continue to mock the pretense of professed guilt or the necessity of spiritual salvation, his earlier insistence on the priest's inability to understand sexual desire and womanly duplicity dismisses his judging authority altogether. A proper assessment of his crime, he explains, requires sexual familiarity with women: "What would you have me tell you? Father, father, / How shall I make you know? You have not known / The dreadful soul of woman" (448–50). For the speaker, this dreadfulness is rooted in inconstancy, which he understands as a problem of memory, one that "[f]orgets the old and takes the new to heart, / Forgets what man remembers, and therewith / Forgets the man" (451–53). In explaining his crime as a response to the provocation of dreadful womanhood, he sets it, in his estimation, beyond the priest's comprehension.

In addition to highlighting the priest's shortcomings on matters of interpretation, which, as the speaker argues earlier, might lead to the priest's own condemnation in hell, the speaker also continues to note that the inefficiencies of representation conspire to obscure his demonstration of provocation. Significantly, one of the reasons why the speaker must generate such a full account of the past is that his provocation defense hinges upon the degeneration of his victim's laughter from "the sweet sound / Which rose from her sweet childish heart" (48–49) into "another laugh" (48), the sound of an adult woman, who embodies a state of maturation that he likens to harlotry. According to his cause and effect narrative, when his victim laughingly dismisses his "parting gift" (25), a knife "with a hilt of horn and pearl" (5), he stabs her because her laugh resembles the "coarse empty laugh" (517) of a "brown-shouldered harlot" (513) whom he saw and heard as he passed through the marketplace en route to their meeting at Iglio. The harlot, we learn, laughed as a man "munched her neck with kisses" (518); and together the sexualized and racialized image and the distorted laugh generate his murderous disgust.

This changed laugh figures prominently throughout the poem, and the speaker is frustrated by his inability to precisely mimic the laugh for the purposes of the priest's assessment: "Father, you hear my speech and not her laugh; / But God heard that. Will God remember all?" (46–47). While the crime had no human witnesses, the speaker suggests, God's awareness of—and proper assessment of—the provocative laugh and the sinning woman might pardon him. Adding another layer to his defense, the speaker explains that the similarity between the two laughs symbolized "all she might have changed to, or might change to" (524). At the very least, his displacement of sexual transgression onto his victim establishes an attempt to exploit Catholic proscriptions against sexual sinning. Her guilty betrayal or, he intimates, her potential corruption, therefore, justify murder as a necessary form of paternalistic correction and protection.

Rossetti's own comments on the poem help to clarify these passages. In "The

Stealthy School of Criticism" (1871), Rossetti responds to Buchanan's criticism of the grotesquely depicted harlot in the marketplace, particularly the line that depicts a man "munch[ing] her neck with kisses" (519). Rossetti contextualizes the scene in the following terms:

> The first of these unspecified quotations is from the *Last Confession*, and is the description referring to the harlot's laugh, the hideous character of which, together with its real or imagined resemblance to the laugh heard soon afterwards from the lips of one long cherished as an ideal, is the immediate cause which makes the maddened hero of the poem a murderer. Assailants may say what they please; but no poet or poetic reader will blame me for making the incident recorded in these seven lines as repulsive to the reader as it was to the hearer and beholder. Without this, the chain of motive and result would remain obviously incomplete. Observe also that these are but seven lines in a poem of some five hundred, not one other of which could be classed with them. (793)

Rossetti's explanation of this offending passage mingles the language of insanity with the language of criminality. His reference to the "chain of motive and result" that produces the "maddened hero" and his comment on the "immediate cause which makes" the speaker "a murderer" reveal his interest in murder and madness as related features of mental crisis. The term "maddened" is also suggestively ambiguous; it partially describes, rather than unequivocally defining, the speaker's state of mind. Furthermore, Rossetti's use of the phrase "real or imagined" underscores his refusal to verify the perceptions of his speaker and suggest his deliberate use of the genre's dramatic irony to generate a fundamental obscurity. The poem's internal logic supports Rossetti's assertions about narrative progression, for the speaker obsessively returns to the problem of narrating cause and effect. Indeed, both the political and sexual content of the speaker's life story imply a cause and effect narrative of homicidal madness. Yet, ironically, the very fact that the speaker constructs the narrative in these terms raises the possibility of a willful criminality that is self-protective and opportunistic.

Pivoting as it does around the sexual identity of the victim, the speaker's narrative requires details of his victim's sexual development. In fact, a pattern emerges in the speaker's digressions; they typically serve to mark the girl's sexual development and his corresponding sexual desire—the relationship between her body and his will. Although he punctuates such digressions with apologies for his "foolish tales" (342) and for "speaking to [the priest] of some matters / There was no need to speak of" (104–5), her imputed sexual guilt—her teasing and pre-adolescent flirtations with the speaker, her possible affair with a

German lover, her potential future sexual promiscuity, her maturation into womanhood—structures his narrative arrangement and argument. The digressions, therefore, betray a rhetorical purpose while, at the same time, underscoring the speaker's lifelong and habitual lack of moral discipline. This pattern redirects his confessional biography to the discourse of moral habits, indicating both the "problem of earlier responsibility for later conduct" and a criminal consciousness of guilt that challenges his status as an overdetermined madman.

An awareness of the ironic effects of the text's dueling subjectivities helps to explicate the speaker's strange account of the sexual triangulation between a Cupid figurine, the speaker, and the "merry loving child" (143). Dwelling on their happier years, the speaker recalls that his first gift to her was "[a] little image of a flying Love / Made of our coloured glass-ware, in his hands / A dart of gilded metal and a torch" (145–47). Prompted by her curiosity about the figurine, the speaker provides her with "strange old tales" (151) of Venus and Cupid, and so begins her sexual education. The child, he explains, insisted that they hang the cupid on the wall above her bed, and as he held her up to hammer the nail, she "laughed and laughed / And kissed and kissed [him]" (166–67) until the cupid "slipped and all its fragments strewed the ground: / And as it fell she screamed, for in her hand / The dart had entered deeply and drawn blood" (169–171). The speaker then recollects that, as he comforted the crying child and bandaged her bleeding hand, he exclaimed, "'Oh!' / I said, the while I bandaged the small hand,— / 'That I should be the first to make you bleed, / Who love and love and love you!'" (172–75). According to the speaker's account, this erotic subtext is then continued by the sobbing child: "'not for the pain at all,' / She said, 'but for the Love, the poor good Love / You gave me'" (177–79).[29]

Because this memory records the girl's symbolic defloration—complete with *jouissance*, blood, pain, tears and mutual professions of love—it substantiates his accusations of inconstancy and sexual guilt. In his post-exhumation revisions to this passage, Rossetti substituted the memory of a Cupid icon and a secular lesson in erotic love for the original scenario, which involved a "little image of great Jesus Christ" and a religious lesson about "the wondrous things of Faith."[30] These alterations suggest the role of this passage in delineating the speaker's character—and considering old sins and new sciences. A gesture toward religious education would exhibit a level of moral clarity and rectitude that this speaker, as a portrait of murderous obscurity, cannot possess. And while the revised account is certainly tinged by the speaker's unreliability and raises the specter of monomaniacal obsession, it also marginalizes him with respect to Victorian attitudes about moral self-regulation and sexual propriety. Constituting a part of his history of self-indulgent transgression, this cupid scene extends the questions of responsibility further into his past; mad or bad, this murderer embodies guilt.

The speaker's subsequent lapsing into an Italian folk song functions almost identically, as the song resonates with the speaker's defensive testimony about his victim's sexual precocity. Remembering the song, the speaker explains that one day, as he brooded over politics, the child was "[l]eaping about the place and laughing" (271). After he "did almost chide her" (272), the girl "knelt / And putting her two hands into [his] breast / Sang [him] a song" (272–74). Both her song and her posture encode expressions of sexual desire and submission. As Bullen argues, "It is a sexually aggressive piece about a woman whose physical beauty is ignored by her male lover and who then wonders how to attract him. In the monologue it is rendered in the vernacular, creating a sharp contrast with the discourse of the narrator and stressing the 'otherness' of the girl's femininity" (114). The song, therefore, marks the speaker's preoccupation with the girl's role as a sexual temptress and reinforces his claims to provocation. Certainly, as a representation of a lyrical folk voice, the song also serves to authenticate the speaker's identity as an Italian patriot and to demonstrate Rossetti's own Italian credentials. The fatally wounded guerilla soldier lapsing into a folk song during his deathbed confession solidly confirms his national allegiance and suggests mental duress. But Rossetti also suggestively frames this song with respect to the rhetorical opportunism seen in other passages. The speaker offers the song as another example of his mental strain and confusion: "That I should sing upon this bed!—with you / To listen, and such words still left to say!" (333–34). Not completely distracted, however, the speaker manages to interrupt himself and redirect his priest-interlocutor to his central purpose. When the speaker, once again, self-consciously highlights his narrative disorder, Rossetti foregrounds the most substantial features of the confession—postponement and evasion.

With great consistency, postponement remains the narrative's fundamental structural feature as the speaker puts off an account of his terrible crime. When the speaker finally begins to narrate the murder, after twenty prior attempts and in the five-hundred-thirty-first line of the poem, his words encapsulate the contest between criminal intention and mad confusion. In murdering the woman, he expresses his will in a set of trochaic commands that demand her obedience:

"Take it," I said to her the second time,
"Take it and keep it." And then came a fire
That burnt my hand; and then the fire was blood,
And sea and sky were blood and fire, and all
The day was one red blindness; till it seemed,
Within the whirling brain's eclipse, that she
Or I or all things bled or burned to death. (531–37)

The metrics of this account of the crime imply both mental duress and terrible consequence. With the phrase "one red blindness" Rossetti disrupts the iambic pace and forcefully stresses the sustained intensity of the speaker's murderous will. Situating his violence "[w]ithin the whirling brain's eclipse," the speaker obscures his criminal agency, and he erases distinctions between himself and his victim in the unpunctuated listing and blurred vowel-sounds of "she / Or I or all things." Such renderings deny the agency that the words "take it and keep it" explicitly denote.

A tension between agency and absence is reinforced a few lines later when, describing the scene immediately after the murder, the speaker suggests a continued "eclipse" of consciousness: "And then I found her laid against my feet / And knew that I had stabbed her, and saw still / Her look in falling" (538–40). In contrast, however, he then sums up the horrible event by remembering his commands and imagining her obedience: "For she took the knife / Deep in her heart, even as I bade her then, / And fell" (540–42). Here, as throughout the poem, Rossetti refuses to resolve the questions raised by the speaker's conflicting expressions of willful intention and mental absence. Upholding the obscurity of the murderous subject, Rossetti presents a speaker who may be a criminal interested in obfuscating responsibility or a madman suffering the effects of an eclipsed consciousness.

These ambiguities are further reinforced at the end of the poem when the apparition of the murdered woman traumatizes the speaker precisely because she records her obedience to his commands: "And she keeps it, see, / Do you not see she keeps it?—there, beneath / Wet fingers and wet tresses, in her heart" (543–45). Like the self-constituting corpse in "Porphyria's Lover," her violated corpse—imagined and animated—provides an abject image of his murderous outrage. As such, this hallucination introduces another version of the text's unsettling oppositions; her bloody image suggests the material effects of his terrible conduct, and, yet, because imagined, it raises additional questions about the internal processes of the criminal mind. Even though the speaker conforms to definitions of delusional lunacy as he announces her bloody presence, the image of her hair and body saturated in blood returns readers to the brutality of his crime. Overpowering the mad imagery of the "whirling brain's eclipse," the image bespeaks commonsense definitions of terrible intent, particularly because the weapon is tied symbolically to their relationship. Significantly, then, at the end of the poem, she removes the knife that he has "bade" her to keep in her heart:

> ... For now she draws it out
> Slowly, and only smiles as yet: look, Father,
> She scarcely smiles: but I shall hear her laugh
> Soon, when she shows the crimson steel to God. (555–58)

This challenge, we may presume, has been the inspiration for the speaker's hastening confessional pace, for just prior to describing this vision, he confirms that he has "told all," and in a moment of apparent lucidity requests a prompt judgment from the priest: "tell me at once what hope / Can reach me still" (554–55).[31] And so, having stretched this unsettled and unsettling account across five hundred fifty-eight lines of verse, Rossetti leaves the speaker and his readers suspended on the brink of judgment.

In tying heavenly judgment to an examination of "the crimson steel," Rossetti also alludes to procedures of earthly judgments, as murder weapons could be introduced as evidence of intent at trial (Chadwick 389). Furthermore, the poem leaves readers with a collection of ambiguous circumstantial evidence, which includes markers of opportunity and motive. For example, prior to their meeting, his victim established that this would be their final meeting: "that last day / For the last time, she said" (7–8)—thus placing his rejection well before she laughs (like a harlot) when he presents her with the knife. The speaker purchases the knife en route to meet her, and the meeting takes place "in the first thin shade o' the hills" (39) along a stretch of beach amidst loud sea sounds. The secrecy of the meeting is justified by his fugitive status and his references to spies. Yet, he eludes these spies in the marketplace with the help of a "poor painted mountebank" (499), who costumes him in "patches and a zany's gown" (506) and incorporates him into his act. The secret meeting place, affording him protection from spies, also offers him the opportunity to commit murder. With such substantial allusions to conventional notions of evidence, Rossetti adds another layer of complexity to the poem's representation of murder.

With the speaker's fluctuations between self-control, self-indulgence, and self-betrayal, Rossetti creates a character that embodies the tyranny of *disorganization*. In employing a circular defensive rhetoric—in building the case for his victim's provocation and his mental absence—the speaker inadvertently records a disturbing history of sexual transgressions, unclaimed sins, and moral lapses. With questions of responsibility attended to but unresolved, the poem questions the interpretive authorities and the imaginary boundaries separating criminality and madness. At the same time, it implies that the speaker may suspect—and that readers may prefer—certain fundamental distinctions between the criminal and the lunatic.

In this way, "A Last Confession" resonates with the elision of the two categories articulated by late-Victorian psychologists. While the criminal, organized and responsible, and the lunatic, disorganized and irresponsible, continued to inform a troubled dichotomy, late-Victorian alienists seemed less interested than their mid-century counterparts in formulating checklists and taking inventories for differentiating the two. Revised and published in the wake of several controversial criminal insanity trials in the 1860s, about which leading mental scientists were very publicly at odds, "A Last Confession" sketches a portrait of a man who is, perhaps, both certainly guilty and undeniably insane.[32] In that sense, the presence of the will and the absence of the intellect, which characterize the speaker's account of the murder, recall J. F. Stephen's claim about the essential attribute of criminal responsibility: "guilt turns upon the wilfulness of the act and not upon the insanity of the prisoner" (*Papers* 81). A definition of a legally responsible but mentally incoherent subject was finally formalized in 1883 with the passing of the Trial of Lunatics Act, which created the special verdict "guilty but insane." "This phrase," Smith explains, "responded to the Queen's concern, following an assault upon her, that the verdict of 'not guilty on the ground of insanity' was not a deterrent," but it "upset legal minds because it found both guilt and a lack of *mens rea*" (*Trial* 18). As it attempts to reconcile the irreconcilable, this legal phrasing also signals an effort to address the epistemological conflicts between mental science and criminal justice and to alleviate the social anxieties generated by morally offensive characters and extraordinarily violent conduct. In the interests of disciplinary authority, the state reinvests in the interpretive power of criminal guilt.

Poetic Stress and Epistemological Distress

These four murder monologues, of course, are not the only poems to use murder and madness as thematic resources for poetic experimentation and political engagement. But these poems distinguish themselves by approaching murder and madness as shared problems of medical, legal, and literary discourse. In this way, they align the difficulties of reading the criminal, the lunatic, and the poem. And while each of these poems uses the theme of murder to develop multiple aesthetic projects—from deconstructing lyricism to historicizing character to scrutinizing gender—it is the theme of murder that centers their political and poetic meanings. Conflating mad excess and criminal control, and entangling theories of mental science, definitions of criminal law, and codes of dramatic poetics, they generate a particularly topical and sublimely obscure vision of the murderous subject—which frustrated readers and, often, disgusted critics.

In *Victorian Poetry*, Armstrong makes the point that "stress" and "conflict" underlie the formal complexities of Victorian poetry: "To understand what is stressful, and why, it is important to link linguistic and formal contradictions to the substantive issues at stake in the poems—issues of politics, gender and epistemology, the problem of relationship and the continual attempts to reinvest the content of self and other" (11). In these particular poems, the patterns and pulses of language, the intentions and interests of speakers, and the structures and props of dramatic scene work together to determine and distort the meanings of murders and the identities of murderers. As they present readers with diverse and inconclusive inventories of sins and symptoms, they signal their participation in a broader cultural debate about immunity and impunity. Using poetry's formal qualities to invite but frustrate the interpretation of crimes and poems, they use epistemological stress to support aesthetic innovation and establish modern content.

While the "judicious obscurity" of these sublime killers challenged the interpretive powers of both judicial and medical authorities, it also challenged cultural expectations about poetic authority and artistic achievement. The specific aesthetic effects and epistemological distress of such representations are reflected in critical responses, which suggest that while poets were willing to contemplate murders and lunatics, critics were expecting to contemplate conventionally virtuous intentions and noble actions. As poets objectified and examined the struggles of interpretation in their poems, critics bristled and blushed at their contorted forms and transgressive themes. In the ongoing dialogue between poetic texts and critical responses, an interesting pattern emerges: the tension between textual innovations and readerly expectations is repeatedly described as a tension between the sane and the insane. Revealing the subtleties and the pervasiveness of medicolegal anxieties, such articulations of literary taste and poetic madness pit the morally unregulated and criminally minded poet against the offended and baffled public.

For this reason, Buchanan's critique of Rossetti's predilection for "nothing completely sane" or a critic's claim that "[f]or a long time we were inclined to believe [Browning] really insane" (qtd. in Litzinger and Smalley 113) allows us to gauge the ethical stress of apprehending murderers and the epistemological distress of ascertaining madness. When reviewers attempt to establish and uphold the boundary between the sane and the insane, they also define the boundaries of poetic transgression. Regretting that Browning is "an artist working by incongruity," Bagehot remarks, "he has failed in fascinating men and women of sane taste. We say 'sane' because there is a most formidable and estimable *insane* taste" (61). For similar reasons, perhaps, the reviewer that categorizes Browning as "really insane" also notes his apparently willful insistence on unintelligibility and denounces the "muddiness of style" and "muddiness of matter" (Litzinger and Smalley 113) inherent in his work. Using such medical metaphors to define literary value and uphold literary tradition, critics diagnose insanity—and punish criminality—with harsh indictments of the degenerated tastes and unregulated aesthetics of modern poetry. The critic, in these cases, inherits the problem of distinguishing madness and badness.

While the related problem of murder was vexing courts, it, too, was irritating critics. Writing in 1849, and deploring the obscurity and contingency of murder in Browning's poetry, one critic simply protests that "in our eyes, murder is always murder" (qtd. in Litzinger and Smalley 126). Written at the height of medicolegal controversies, this confident, tautological quip reminds us of the political immediacy of murder poems. As the persistence of medical obscurity threatened to overwhelm legal distinctions between criminal agency and mad determinism—at a time when mental science charged itself with establishing accuracy in clinical diagnosis, balancing the ethics of state punishment, and rationalizing treatments through scientific advancement—dramatic poetry addressed the concomitant fear that emerging psychologies could, in fact, paralyze the judicial institutions and dismantle the ethical principles that comprise and sustain Victorian culture.

Attempting to manage the reception of his shady characters and their bad deeds, Browning included this now famous advertisement in *Dramatic Lyrics* in 1842: "Such Poems as the majority of this volume might also come properly enough, I suppose, under the head of 'Dramatic Pieces'; being, though often Lyric in expression, always Dramatic in principle, and so many utterances of so many imaginary persons, not mine." While his explanation formally disconnects the poet and the speaker and thus establishes a dramatic "principle" of the "imaginary," the dramatic fictions of "Porphyria's Lover," "My Last Duchess," "The Laboratory"—and, we might add, Rossetti's "A Last Confession"—forged strong links to the real problems of persons and boundaries complicating epistemologies of murder in Victorian England. As they assist poets in scrutinizing an imaginary boundary, the expressive efforts ("so many utterances") of these imagined murderers constitute pointed allusions to codes of responsibility and pleas of insanity. And, as they encourage skeptical reflections on the intertwined but competing domains of mental science, legal precedent, gender politics, and ethical commonsense, they link the cultural politics of poetry to the criminal politics of lunacy.

CHAPTER 3

"Household Law" and the Domestication of Murder

IN ROBERT BROWNING'S *The Ring and the Book* (1868–69), Guido Franceschini's defense lawyer, Arcangeli, imagines the aggravations that the Fisc, Bottini, will heap upon the charges against his client for the brutal murders of his wife and her parents. Among these projected aggravations, which constitute a "[p]arasite-growth upon mere murder's back" (VIII.1109), lies the fact that the murders were committed in the victims' home:

> Third aggravation: that our crime was done—
> Not in the public street, where safety lies,
> Not in the bye-place, caution may avoid,
> Wood, cavern, desert, spots contrived for crime,—
> But in the very house, home, nook and nest,
> O' the victims, murdered in their dwelling-place,
> *In domo ac habitatione propria,*
> Where all presumably is peace and joy. (VIII.1243–50)

Guido's "hurly-burly case" (VIII.106), therefore, confronts the problem of domestic ideology. As Arcangeli meanders through his legal analysis, Guido's offenses against domesticity contrast his own domestic obsessions, evident here in the idyllic connotations and confident stresses of "house, home, nook and nest." Betraying his preoccupation with the domestic idyll, his monologue consistently returns to the pleasures of dinner, the prideful satisfactions of fatherhood, and his preference for "home-sanctitudes" (VIII.1765), which he succinctly catalogues as "my fry, and family and friends" (VIII.1746). As these domestic desires overpower his professional and public ambition and offset Guido's violent affronts to domestic pieties, they also expose the mercenary posture of Arcangeli's legal strategies and thereby burnish his legal integrity. In building such a character, as Alexander Welsh has noted, Browning develops a "playfully absurd defense" (Welsh 209) that satirizes this particular defense lawyer while questioning the mechanisms of legal inquiry.[1]

Particularly relevant to a discussion of the poem's domestication of murder, are the ways in which Arcangeli's investments in domestic "peace and joy" complement the home's more violent tendencies. The intersection of Guido's domestic villainy and Arcangeli's homespun languor allows Browning to acknowledge the violent permissions and intimate consequences of state and symbolic laws governing marriage and family in Victorian England. With these complementary characters, Browning's epic poem isolates the same variables that underlie Mill's critique of legal permissions and domestic customs in *On the Subjection of Women*. Written in 1861 but published in 1869, Mill's text defines the home as a site of "domestic slavery" and husbands as "despots" and "tormentors": "I have no desire to exaggerate, nor does the case stand in any need of exaggeration. I have described the wife's legal position, not her actual treatment. . . . If married life were all that it might be expected to be, looking to the laws alone, society would be hell upon earth" (286). Explaining that not all despots exercise the extent of their powers and that husbandly despotism is frequently precluded or mitigated by genuine "feelings and interests," Mill writes, "The despotism of Louis XVI was not the despotism of Philippe le Bel, or of Nadir Shah, or of Caligula; but it was bad enough to justify the French Revolution, and to palliate even its horrors" (286). According to Mill, however, in order to ensure wives' rights the law should grant protections—not permissions—simply because of the ubiquity of abuse: "laws and institutions require to be adapted, not to good men, but to bad" (287).

In a perfect inversion of Mill's reformist proposition, the ease with which Arcangeli abandons "home-joys" for murder rights demonstrates exactly how laws and institutions are "adapted" to "bad" men. Tellingly, as permissions accrue, Arcangeli's "home sanctitudes" are configured as excessive and expedient fantasies, which serve to muddle rational and moral judgments and to obscure the legal definitions and patriarchal ideologies governing spousal relations and family life. In characterizing Arcangeli as a mercenary lawyer, a prideful patriarch, and a self-proclaimed homebody, Browning ridicules his sentimentalizing and mystifying ethos. Aware of his own compromised ethical and legal rigor,

Arcangeli seeks to obscure, or mitigate, it with rhetorical special effects. Having scoured "Law, Gospel and the Church" (VIII.729) for support and having "ecclesiasticized" (VIII.1742) his brief, he will "[r]egularize," "emphasize," "latinize," and "lastly Cicero-ize" (VIII.1743–44) it in order to mimic a proper defense. In his capacity as defense lawyer, Arcangeli quite adeptly exchanges the "home-joys" model for an "*[h]onoris causa*" (VIII.424) model, which establishes the "natural ground" (VIII.479) of "complete revenge" (VIII.478) for an uncompromising "household law" (VIII.483). In this way, a strategy of "[e]xplaining matters, not denying them!" (VIII.315), reveals wife-murder to be perfectly congruous with matrimonial law.

In 1851, eighteen years before the publication of *The Ring and the Book* and *On the Subjection of Women*, the sinister ethos of such "household law"—and the galling impunity of wife-murderers—inspired Mill and Harriet Taylor to submit an editorial missive to the *Morning Chronicle*. After several wife-murderers had recently enjoyed the benefits of judicial leniency, Mill and Taylor angrily deconstructed the legal and cultural logic of husbanding, which simultaneously charged husbands with protecting and excused their abusing. They explain that in cases of wife-murder or child-murder, "[t]he crime is greater; for it is a violation of more solemn obligations—it is doing the worst injury where there is the most binding duty to cherish and protect" (28 August 1851, 4). It is also "baser" because "the culprit" targets the trusting and the weak (4). Assessing the chronic cultural problem of "domestic ruffianism," they intimate that the domestic sphere is, in fact, an ideal criminal locale where "[t]he domestic tyrant can perpetrate his tyrannies with the utmost facility, and need never wait for an opportunity; a stronger motive therefore is required, when the brutality exists, to deter from its indulgence" (4). As they assert the language of criminal intent—the issue at stake in the acquittals and reduced charges that so appalled them—they argue that an abiding cultural faith in domestic privacy accommodates criminal opportunity and motive. Because criminal intent is frequently dismissed or explained away by lenient judges, they quip, "[t]he vow to protect thus confers a license to kill" (4).

Attesting to the long history and lingering problem of such domestic license, Browning's Arcangeli and Guido, the gourmand and the murderer, constitute a particularized version of Mill's and Taylor's legal critique. Both enjoying varying degrees of "license," and both beneficiaries of patriarchal permissions and practitioners of patriarchal excess, they represent the contradictions of domestic ideologies. In partnering Arcangeli, as defense counsel, and Guido, as defendant, Browning asks readers to recognize the interdependencies of their ostensibly opposing versions of domestic nostalgia and to revisit the longstanding and as yet unresolved dilemma of domestic authority. Arcangeli longs for "home-joy" with its attendant entitlements—paternalism, comfort, and indulgence—while

Guido longs for domestic tyranny with its attendant entitlements—control, dominance, and impunity. Both claim domestic ideology as the foundation for their personal identities, both secure for themselves the position of the patriarch, and both assert husbands' murderous rights with reiterations of "household law." With them, Browning exposes the seductive powers and practical misuses of domestic ideologies while giving material force to the abstractions of family law. In interrogating the domestic politics of this "hurly-burly case," he forces the intersection of another pair of ostensibly antithetical conceptual categories—criminality and domesticity. And establishing congruities between these two concepts, he encourages further reflection on legal discourses and social institutions as forces that determine and domesticate violence.

Examining dialectical relationships between poetic forms, generic codes, and cultural discourses and tracing the gendered structures of "household law," this chapter explicates Browning's inquiry into the precariousness of domestic protections, affections, and permissions and applies these analytical and contextual insights to the explication of two "minor" dramatic poems that imagine the murderous prerogatives of wives. Juxtaposing Browning's massive, canonical verse-novel with two lesser-known verse dramas about Greek houses in ruin, *Clytemnestra* (1855) by Edward Robert Bulwer Lytton (Owen Meredith) and *Medea, A Fragment in Dramatic Form, After Euripides* (1884) by Amy Levy, allows us to explore the poetics of domestic conflict and consider the gendered aspects of murderous rage. On the most fundamental level, these three texts are linked by their pointedly counterintuitive and unsentimental rendering of domestic spaces as "spots contrived for crime," and in domesticating crime, they also share a reliance on historical transposition to generate political meanings. Browning, of course, distills *The Ring and the Book* from the historical resources of the now infamous "yellow notebook," while Lytton and Levy modernize two classical murderous women, Clytemnestra and Medea, who have long embodied the traumatic threat of domestic breakdown.

As they exploit the opportunities of historical displacement for the purposes of contemporary gender debate, Browning, Lytton, and Levy all similarly scrutinize domesticity and rescript its patriarchal customs as criminal tendencies. Built upon the private and public foundations of matrimonial law, they suggest, the "house, home, nook and nest" is hostile to romance and amenable to violence. And, because the theme of murder entangles social prohibitions and individual agency, it allows these poets to simultaneously imagine the institutional and ideological mechanisms of oppression (and resistance) and scrutinize the discursive modes, generic forms, and interpretive practices of sensation and scandal. Challenging the legal melodramas of the courts and the press with epic and tragic reconfigurations of marital breakdown, these poets historicize and contextualize both acts of murder and representations of transgression as products of legal, sexual, and gender codes. Enacting and analyzing murderous scenarios, in which marriage contracts and domestic bargains are violently dissolved and broken, husbands, wives, and children detail the failures of marital commitments and the pressures of domestic confinements. With such ongoing commentaries and metacommentaries, Browning, Lytton, and Levy fully exploit the generic citation and differentiation integral to the hybrid forms of the verse novel and the verse drama in ways that highlight the semiotic shifting and semantic maneuvering that informed the vexed gender politics of marriage, domesticity, and criminality.

"Bad Bargain[s]," "Decent Couple[s]," and Adversarial Domesticity

In order to fully understand the domestication of murder in these three poems, a glimpse at the discursive arena in which they circulated is in order. Although a full rendering of the dense history of marriage and divorce in the nineteenth century lies well beyond the scope of this chapter, consideration of the political arguments, cultural anxieties, and textual practices that shaped Victorian marriage reform and domestic ideologies allows us to appreciate the incisive arguments of Browning's, Lytton's, and Levy's poetic critiques. Several recent literary and historical studies have explored the marriage reforms of nineteenth-century England, which dealt with issues of divorce, abuse, custody, and property, and examined the modes of representation—from matrimonial legislation to press coverage to feminist polemic to prose fiction—with which Victorians documented and interpreted these changes.[2] In particular, scholars have isolated the middle-class cult of domesticity as the dominant ideological model of homelife, and they have delineated its sentimentalized and pacified concepts of gender difference and its vision of a home-sanctuary illuminated by the hearth and protecting its inhabitants from public corruption.[3] In his recent study of domestic masculinities, John Tosh explains that within the paradigm of the separate spheres romance, the home was a place where "masculine and feminine were brought together in a proper relation of complementarity" (7). In this scenario, private households self-regulate through the organization of virtues and pleasures—Arcangeli's "home-sanctitudes." As it evolved into "a privileged site of subjectivity and fantasy" (4) and was increasingly "identified with childhood, innocence and roots," Tosh explains, the home, contrasting the corrupt public sphere, came to be identified "with authenticity itself" (3).

Most often, the public-private balancing act of this middle-class idyll constitutes our primary departure point for understanding Victorian domesticity, and a sense of the "authenticity," pervasiveness, and influence of this model almost always orients our studies of nineteenth-century domestic culture. In their exacting study, *The Spectacle of Intimacy* (2000), for example, Chase and Levenson navigate their "discontinuous history" (6) by counterposing privatized idylls and publicized spectacles: "broad norms and conspicuous exceptions" (12), "love and trouble" (12), "pursuit[s] of home peace" and "flights from disaster" (16). Demonstrating that "the norm needed and cultivated the disturbance" (12), the "home peace" version of domesticity centers their arguments. Yet, while this idyll—and its grim antithesis—was indisputably central to nineteenth-century cultural representation, another version of marriage and homelife also preoccupied Victorians, one that became crucial to negotiating marital breakdown and domestic violence in the courts and in the press.

This second model, codified in marriage and family law, rather explicitly denied the home its claims to authenticity and privacy and exposed these apparent privileges as mere romantic fictions that belied the fundamentally pragmatic and public functions of marriage. Marriage law mandated the systematic interference in intimate life, and, thus, virtuous and pleasant self-regulation succumbed to the coercive yokes and obstructive forces of public interests and legal contracts. As this disciplinary model prioritized state interests but privileged husbandly authority, coercion displaced cooperation and complementarity. Viewed through the lens of law, then, marriage—neither private nor authentic—was quite simply a repeat and command performance at the behest of the state.

The contest between sentimental reverence and state paternalism became most strikingly apparent during the mid-century renegotiation of marriage laws. In 1857 England's revised matrimonial and divorce laws reiterated this performative and disciplinary model of family life in several important ways. With the establishment of England's first divorce court, these laws ensured the dissemination of that model in public trials and newspaper reports when the court refused time and again to grant separations or divorces to petitioning spouses. The revised laws also enforced what we might call an adversarial model of spousal relations, which gained ideological force as the structures of both criminal law and family law, undergoing significant revisions in the second half of the nineteenth century, increasingly intersected uncomfortably (and publicly) in the home. Such interventions further challenged the collective fantasy of domestic autonomy by underscoring the fragility of domestic peace, emphasizing the persistence of bad behavior, and regulating formerly private transgressions. While the "home-joys" idyll normalized, and made appealing, a paternalistic and cooperative model of private life, the adversarial model insinuated a more inhospitable and combative model of domestic relations—one that was always subordinate to the power and the interests of the state.

The debates leading up to and the passage of the Divorce and Matrimonial Causes Act of 1857 highlighted the difficulties of revering marriage, facilitating divorce, and upholding state interests through the classed and gendered mechanisms of marriage law. To liberalize and economize divorce procedures was to invite uncertain social consequences. Well before the passage of the act, these legal and ideological quandaries informed the first report generated by the Royal Commissioners on Divorce, who in 1850 were appointed by Queen Victoria to study divorce, specifically divorce *à vinculo matrimonii* (from the bonds of marriage). In 1853 the commissioners articulated the conflicting issues at stake in the process of divorce reform. Marriage, they explain, was "strictly speaking" indissoluble by law, and, therefore, divorce required an expensive and laborious act of parliament "to provide one specially by passing a particular law in favour of those who can make out a case which will warrant its interference" (*First Report* 3). Quoting from William Blackstone's *Commentaries on the Laws of England,* the authors acknowledge unsettling tensions between reverence and regulation, contractual obligation and lawful renunciation:

> [T]he common law of England, which follows in this case the canon law of the Church, 'deems so highly, and with such mysterious reverence, of the nuptial tie,' that the causes of Divorce are purposely limited to a few extreme and specific provocations; and the preservation of that union, so long as it can be secured, is so manifestly essential to the best interests of society, that before it can be dissolved it must clearly be established by the strictest proof that the offence has been committed; that there is no contrivance by which the parties are endeavouring to escape from their solemn obligations to themselves and their children; that they cannot discharge their mutual duties by continuing any longer to cohabit with each other, and that the party complaining is free from guilt. (*First Report* 1)

In proper service to the "nuptial tie," the report goes on to explain, England's ecclesiastical courts aptly established stringent divorce requirements: "Divorce will only be granted for the extreme provocations adverted to above; secondly, that the law will not suffer it to be obtained on the sole confession of the parties themselves; and thirdly, that it will be refused, even though an offense has been committed which would otherwise justify it, if collusion, connivance, condonation, or recrimination can be pleaded and proved" (1). While by the mid-nineteenth century these rules based on "soundest wisdom" require "some little modification," the commissioners assert, "we conceive that in substance they ought to be maintained" (1). As the details of the report's historical review and subsequent recommendations make clear, in order to maintain the substance of "mysterious reverence" and disciplinary authority, the law must skillfully and prudently adjudicate guilt and innocence, contrivance and evidence, provocation and protection, duty and default.

The commissioners also established a more secular foundation for upholding deference to the nuptial yoke so that the conservative approach outlined in the report is further justified by citations from one of England's highly regarded ecclesiastical court judges, Lord Stowell, who in a 1790 ruling summarized the collective interests of marriage, the disciplinary power of indissolubility, and the unlikely roots of marital happiness:

> For though, in particular cases, the repugnance of the law to dissolve the obligations of matrimonial cohabitation may operate with great severity upon individuals; yet, it must be carefully remembered, that the general happiness of married life is secured by its indissolubility. When people understand that they *must* live together, except for a very few reasons known to law, they learn to soften by mutual accommodation that yoke which they know they cannot shake off; they become good husbands and good wives, from the necessity of remaining husbands and wives; for necessity is a powerful master in teaching the duties which it imposes. If it were once understood, that upon mutual disgust married persons might legally be separated, many couples, who now pass through the world with mutual comfort, with attention to their common offspring, and to the moral order of civil society, might at this moment have been living in a state of mutual unkindness, in a state of estrangement from their common offspring, and in a state of most licentious and unreserved immorality. In this case, as in many others, the happiness of some individuals must be sacrificed to the greater and more general good. (13)

Yet, while Stowell and the commissioners express confidence in the softening effects of "mutual accommodation" and dismiss the inevitable "severity upon individuals" as sacrifices for the "greater and more general good," the case for legal indissolubility necessarily falters in cases of adultery, which constitutes justifiable grounds "so consonant to reason and religion" (3) for divorce. As Barbara Leckie has argued, in such a context, adultery emerges as a "uniquely domestic crime" (62). The primary affront to the sanctity of marriage, an "extreme and specific" provocation, adultery forms the central issue in the reconsideration of divorce law, in the establishment of the divorce court, and in the increased availability of divorces *à vinculo matrimonii*. The various features of the report's arguments—the investment in disciplinary yokes, the punishment of adulterous transgressors, the suspicion of colluding partners—contribute to an adversarial model of domestic unhappiness, which, foregrounding matters of sexual discipline, informs the divorce court's proceedings and its scandalous publicity.

As Parliament sought to enact appropriate legislation, its members weighed the advantages and disadvantages of modernizing divorce law, and they continued to address the problems alluded to in the commissioners' report. They considered ways to ensure that divorcing couples would not be rewarded by the state and that a freshly liberalized divorce law would not threaten the social order. As both legal and ideological controls were considered, conventional models of spousal relations, including sexual double standards and separate spheres ideologies, set the priorities of legislators and organized the details of marital breakdown. After significant debate over the problem of equal grounds and equal access for husbands and wives, parliamentarians crafted a restrictive divorce act that privileged husbands' interests and that created only a single, centralized civil divorce court in London. By restricting access, they sought to maintain male and class privilege, and they hoped to deter petitioners, reduce divorces, and enforce marriages. As Gail Savage explains, these restrictive measures "served both to limit and disguise the real demand for divorce" in Victorian England ("Intended" 36).

In the end, the 1857 Divorce and Matrimonial Causes Act, the "cautious outcome of a long public brooding" (Chase and Levenson 191), established separate and unequal grounds for male and female divorce petitioners. Demonstration of a wife's adultery constituted sufficient legal ground for husbands to seek the dissolution of a marriage, but because only aggravated adultery legitimated a wife's claim, the burden of proof increased for petitioning wives, who were required to demonstrate adultery and additional offenses, such as cruelty, desertion, sodomy, incest, or bigamy.[4] This discrepancy, of course, upheld conventional male sexual freedoms and enforced female sexual constraints, and it privileged male prerogatives in sexual, property, and custodial matters. Petitioners who could not demonstrate adultery or aggravated adultery to the court's satisfaction were condemned to remain married or restricted to judicial separations—divorce *à mensa et thoro* (from bed and board)—which failed to nullify the legal bond of marriage and disallowed remarriage.

The gender inequalities written into the act further underscored, and indeed emerged from, an allegiance to an adversarial model of spousal relations. Documenting a discussion in the House of Lords in 1857, in which members considered the social risks of equalizing the grounds for divorce, Savage explains that their language "evoke[d] a vision of sexual relations fraught with conflict, each side giving as good as the other":

> Men asserted a natural superiority but not a moral one. The weakness of husbands, who might commit 'occasional and fugitive' acts of adultery with domestic servants or even collude to commit adultery so that wives could sue for divorce if the law made that possible, did not invalidate masculine authority over the family. The argument mounted by the defenders of unequal grounds portrayed women as active and dangerous combatants, ready and willing to commit adultery themselves or to revenge themselves upon adulterous husbands. ("Intended" 15)

With two opposing views of femininity—one which sees women as patient, long-suffering marriage preservers and one which sees them as potentially uncontrollable, vengeful, divorce-seeking producers of "spurious offspring" (Savage 18)—parliamentarians ultimately placed their faith in the socially stabilizing features of gender inequality. "In so doing," Savage observes, "they framed legislation which in turn provided an institutional apparatus that constrained and directed the ways in which private conflicts between husbands and wives could be publicly recognized, acted out, and resolved" (18). In this model of domesticity, the state penetrates the private sphere by establishing a husbandly proxy, and, through the mechanisms of sexual inequality, the state leverages the privileges of one spouse against the subjugation of the other. "Household law," then, founded upon readings of sexual transgression, affirms the preferences of the state and privileges the status of the husband while demanding a melodramatic legal script with a perpetrator and a victim. As such anxieties about private conflicts and public interests conspire to necessitate an adversarial model, that combative trope, in turn, provides a convenient basis for rationalizing sexual inequality and legal restrictions.

As this combative notion of marriage circulated within the discourse of divorce reform, domesticity accumulated criminal associations. Not surprisingly, given the recurrent themes of marital yokes and spousal conflicts, the newly established divorce court, requiring a practical schema for deciphering broken marriages, adopted an adversarial model similar to that operating in the criminal courts. Divorce cases, staged in the court and in the press like criminal cases in which an innocent party confronted a guilty party, demanded the conventional roles of perpetrator and victim. Tried by oral evidence, divorce cases required and recorded the testimony of opposing parties, and, thus, Victorians witnessed the voices of husbands and wives publicly cataloging intimate conflicts and abuses as well as the trivialities and minutiae of domestic life. As the testimony of witnesses, including that of household servants and observant neighbors, was introduced into evidence, the domestic imperatives of privacy, loyalty, and discretion eroded, and the dissolution of privacy aided the disciplinary functions envisioned by the state.

As Martin Wiener argues in *Reconstructing the Criminal*, when husbands and wives brought each other to court and charged one another with adulterous transgressions, divorce proceedings mimicked their criminal counterparts both in terms of format and procedure and in terms of punishment and deterrence: "[t]hough a civil institution, the divorce court was (like bankruptcy court) in tone not unlike a criminal court, punishing the guilty party not through imprisonment but through public denunciation" (73). Moreover, divorce courts, like criminal courts, had "the secondary aim of deterring, through its stigma, others from falling into guilt" and of "educating the public, through its proceedings and decisions published in the newspapers, in the rules of respectable conjugal behavior" (73). Courts of law and courts of public opinion focused on culpability, and, "if a marriage failed, someone was responsible and that person must be called to the bar of justice" (73). This paradigm secured a doctrine of marital discipline and a deference to—if not a reverence for—nuptial yokes. Within the adversarial framework, at least, marital failures appear to emanate from the actions of particular, identifiable, and legally accountable transgressing individuals, not from more systematic or diffuse institutional pressures, constraints, and inequalities.

As the divorce court and an observant public scrutinized married and family life in ways that paralleled and sometimes initiated criminal trials and legal procedures, an authentic and private idea of homelife was clearly imperiled, and, while the unhappiness of one spouse was legally sanctioned, the unhappiness of both spouses was explicitly denounced. Acknowledging that marital unhappiness was a tricky affair, the commissioners explained in their report that acts of "recrimination, connivance, and condonation" (the divorce court term for forgiving—or appearing to forgive—an adulterous offense) must be "deemed and treated as bars to the suit" (22), for they significantly undermined, even mocked, the social foundations and disciplinary functions of marriage. Flouting the binary logic of the adversarial model, mutual unhappiness, mutual disgust, mutual adultery, mutual guilt, or mutual victimization threatened the semiotics of guilt and innocence and, in the process, hinted at the possibility of broader institutional failures or social dysfunction. Therefore, the law forbade collusion, in which, for example, a husband "would 'accept' a charge of adultery in order to escape a marriage" or in which spouses "would suppress evidence of mutual guilt" (Horstman 101). Similarly, even specious evidence of condonation could erase the legal significance of otherwise culpable behaviors.

The potential judicial and social menace of colluding spouses also inspired a range of deterrent procedural measures. In the parliamentary debates preceding the 1857 Divorce Act, a fear that rampant collusion would lead to high divorce rates and social chaos was cited as a reason for restricting access to a central court in London (Savage, "Intended" 13). At the beginning of the reform process, the commissioners suggested that the court be given "large discretion" in "adjusting the rights" (*First Report* 22) of husbands and wives with respect to property and children. In procedural matters, their report recommended that a judge be charged with "examining the parties" and "ordering any witnesses" (22) and that oral testimonies, rather than the written testimonies used by the ecclesiastical courts, be used in order to prevent collusion. It also proposed the use of written depositions and signed narrative records to secure the accuracy and authenticity of divorce proceedings. A structural resistance to collusion might also be improved, the commissioners suggested, by endowing the judge with the right to call witnesses and by submitting controvertible facts to the collective common sense of a jury (22). By 1860, spousal collusion was thought to be so common that an amendment to the Divorce Act granted discretionary powers to the Attorney General, who, acting through an agent, the Queen's Proctor, could charge suspected petitioning spouses with collusion. Charged, like criminals, with collusion, petitioners' cases were suspended until they could adequately disprove the charges; likewise, if guilty, petitioning couples were subject to punitive fines.[5]

In addition to tainting the domestic idyll with such disciplinary interventions, Chase and Levenson contend, divorce reform also signified, for some opponents of reform, the "long-dreaded fall into degraded modernity" (188). Acknowledging this blighted descent, Lord Redesdale penned an urgent critique of the commissioners' initial proposal of "common legal remedy" in marriage matters. Embedded in his lament is a disdain for democratization and decentralization:

> These divorces will thus be opened to another and numerous class, but a still more numerous class will be equally excluded as at present. Once create an appetite for such license by the proposed change, and the demand to be permitted to satisfy it will become irresistible. The cry for cheap law has of late been universally attended to, and the result will too probably be that these delicate and important questions will be brought before inferior tribunals, where the number of the judges (each acting separately) will render anything like uniformity of decision upon the circumstances which are to rule in refusing applications, impossible, and must ultimately lead to extreme facility in obtaining such Divorces. ("Lord Redesdale's Opinion" 26)

Subjected to "cheap law" and "inferior tribunals," the marital yoke loses its force, and divorce becomes "irresistible." Such anxieties about compromised authority and legal remedy, of course, reveal the many classed and gendered investments in the marital yoke.

While Redesdale and his counterparts wrestled with the implications of this "license" to divorce, another significant mid-century intervention in domestic relationships, the 1853 Act for the Better Prevention and Punishment of Aggravated Assaults upon Women and Children, forced Victorians to grapple with what Mill and Taylor labeled the "license to kill." Simultaneously challenging domestic pieties and increasing state intervention in the home, this act, the first decisive criminalization of domestic abuse, allowed magistrates to inflict six-month sentences for aggravated assaults. The discussion and passage of the bill inspired public reflections on the appropriate punitive measures for these new-found offenders, and an amendment to the bill, which was eventually defeated, even introduced the possibility of corporal punishment for offending husbands (127).[6] This act also contributed to adversarial and criminal inflections of domesticity. Although the language and intent of the act challenged conventional notions of patriarchal authority and household law, wives' continued reluctance to testify against husbands and their economic dependence on husbands diminished its application and enforcement. Twenty-five years later, the Matrimonial Causes Act of 1878 provided maintenance and separation allowances for abused wives and thereby acknowledged the necessity of legal and financial protection for victims of assault. Notably, in both instances, the state preferred to grant legal protections rather than legal personhood to wives. The application of the criminal code to sort out domestic tyranny and economic inequality only deepened the associations between criminality and domesticity. Extending "the criminalization of harmful behavior" into the hitherto private domestic sphere (Wiener, *Reconstructing* 82), they reconfigured ideas about the commission of crime within Victorian homes.

As these various examples of procedural and legal changes indicate, over and over again, the politics of domesticity required that the public sphere subject the private sphere to the rigors of adversarial law. While Victorian citizens negotiated a concept of marriage that contradictorily celebrated and sanctified marriage, enforced resigned capitulation to the nuptial yoke, and privileged a model of domestic combat (whether in cases of abuse or divorce—or both), the law always preferred acquiescence to the marital yoke. In *Cruelty and Companionship* (1992), A. James Hammerton documents the law's continued privileging of institutional integrity over individual safety or autonomy, and he documents the paternalistic (and pragmatic) investments in marital preservation following the 1878 Matrimonial Causes Act:

> [L]ocal magistrates' courts increasingly took on a more paternalistic role, eager to intervene in an attempt to make the wife forgive, the husband reform and the family reunite, and thus avoid the fragile division of slender economic resources. Magistrates, together with a growing army of police court missionaries, probation officers and clerks of the court came to see themselves as marriage menders. (39)

In a more direct disciplinary mode, Judge Cresswell Cresswell, the Judge-Ordinary of the divorce court, repeatedly explained to petitioners, witnesses, and juries that a willingness to separate simply did not constitute an entitlement to separate because, as he summed up in one case, "the adjudication of quarrels between man and wife was of great social importance, and involved consequences much more enduring than were involved in the pecuniary questions generally submitted to juries" (*Times,* 18 February 1859, 9). Furthermore, the law required that only one party could be deserving of a divorce—the clearly wronged, victimized party. Similar advisories appeared in more informal and unofficial newspaper commentaries. The *Times*, reporting on the first jury trial in the newly established civil court and dutifully covering the entire "mass of circumstances" involved in the case, editorialized on the implications of granting a separation and adjudicating squabbles:

> They had made a bad bargain and they must abide by it. If man and wife knew that by getting into squabbles and making themselves unhappy they might obtain a judicial separation, that knowledge might be an encouragement to them not to attempt to curb their tempers; whereas, if they knew that if they did not curb their tempers they must continue to be miserable, they might set about it and become a decent couple. (1 December 1858, 11)

Located far below the elevated heights of the domestic romance, this pragmatic corollary necessitates abiding by a "bad bargain" and espouses a strikingly modest proposal. Recommending a double-edged course of civility and mediocrity, the inflexible law advises its unhappy subjects to "become a decent couple."

Advocating a reformist, feminist agenda, Francis Power Cobbe in "A Lesson in Matrimony," which appeared in *The Echo* in 1869, documents divorce cases not to "lament divorce itself," as Susan Hamilton argues, but to argue that "our marriages turn out so badly because they are not well made" (234); surveying the public record of marriages and divorces, Cobbe concludes, "there is something radically wrong with our present matrimonial system" (qtd. in Hamilton 232). Of course, feminist critique was not the dominant Victorian mode of analysis, but the juxtaposition of these differing critical responses reminds us that as domestic ideology and marriage law situated themselves awkwardly with respect to one another, the prerogatives of state control became more glaringly apparent. As a result, the domestic idyll was not always the predominant cultural shorthand for articulating family relations in Victorian England. While the separate spheres model and the companionate model imagined spouses enjoying and sharing their respective gender-appropriate domestic comforts, which sanctify their union and fortify the social order, the law—and it various proponents—insisted upon a bleaker picture of control, capitulation, and coercion. The default model of marital relations, it would seem, imagined disciplinary and adversarial scenes of domesticity with occupants perpetually tensed by the pressures of rectitude and restraint.

And with this bleaker picture, the newspaper press—from the *Times* to the *Divorce News and Police Reporter*—found a thoroughly marketable commodity. As divorce proceedings were transferred from the legislature to the newly established Divorce and Matrimonial Causes Court in London, the press capitalized on the publicization of the private sphere. Transformed by a more sensational agenda, Stowell's softening yoke became a "galling yoke" (*Times*, 12 March 1859, 9) under which unhappy spouses might be heard "groaning" (15 July 1859, 5). Newspapers documented the divorce court's practices, proceedings, and caseloads, thereby contributing to and profiting from what Chase and Levenson have called the "political theater of private life" (14). "Scandal was a perpetual resource," they argue, because "the Victorian investment in family life unfolds in the awareness that at any moment it can turn into the antifamily of popular sensation" (7). In the popular imagination, they explain, "the naming of private histories became one of the avocations of the age," and generates "the spectacle of intimacy" (12).

As a glance through the thorough divorce court reportage in the *Times* reveals, this spectacular intimacy included catalogues of pecuniary embarrassments, drinking habits, sexual infidelities, ill-treatment, verbal taunts, physical assaults, and obscene language (often indicated with blank spaces and dashes).[7] In trial transcripts, however, readers also glimpsed (legally irrelevant) testimony on the minute tensions, myriad belittlements, and daily squabbles of married life. Petitioners quarreled about such things as a Newfoundland dog endangering the furniture (*Times*, 1 December 1858, 11) or the inequalities of butter distribution: "he complained that she eat fresh butter herself, and only allowed to him salt butter" (25 November 1858, 8). Documenting the cumulative slights of her domestic life, Mrs. Emily Cherry, a widow who married a man with eleven children, complained of "having no room made for her in the family circle near the lamp of an evening" and of having didactic portions of the thirteenth chapter of the first of Corinthians "pointedly read at her" (16 December 1858, 8). Yet, even more striking than the courtroom litanies of the immense cruelties and intense banalities of domestic life, is the court's repeated insistence, time and time again, that long-term exposure to chronic bad behavior fails to merit legal separation or divorce.[8]

In examining the opportunistic and innovative methods for representing the tumult of mid-century family law and family life, recent textual scholarship has favored journalistic scandal, political melodrama, and sensational fiction.[9] With notable exceptions, these genres upheld clear boundaries between innocence and guilt, boundaries which accommodated polemicist tactics, such as those used by Caroline Norton, and facilitated novel plots such as those popularized by Elizabeth Braddon and Wilkie Collins.[10] Yet, such binaries, as we have seen, were also mandated by predominant legal fictions, and the law's sensationalizing bent, as Anne Humpherys explains, contributed significantly to textual representations of marital breakdown:

[B]ecause the only ground for divorce was adultery, and for women adultery

> aggravated by cruelty or worse, the details in the press reports were by necessity sensational and scandalous. Indeed, while novels that dealt with sexual infidelity and marital brutality were denounced as shocking and indecent and circulating libraries refused to handle them, the reports of divorce court proceedings were uncensored and available to every person who could read. ("Coming Apart" 224–25)

While divorce court coverage inspired "the first governmental restriction of newspaper reporting of judicial proceedings" (220), the allure of such uncensored representations, as Savage contends, created the "aura of scandal attaching to divorce, which made the subject endlessly fascinating to newspaper readers" but "in fact misrepresented the mundane reality of marital breakdown in Victorian society" ("Intended" 19). The primacy of adultery in divorce cases, Leckie explains, inspired a journalistic "epistemology of adultery" that "wr[ote] adultery as a domestic detective story" in which "the goal for the judge, jury, and reader alike is to read the signs by which adultery betrays itself, to determine the truth of this uniquely domestic crime" (62).[11] Divorce reports, "part record, part entertainment" (Humpherys, "Coming Apart" 221), and their "distortions and misrepresentation of the social realities of marital conflict," ultimately deterred petitioners and thereby "functioned to mitigate the potential threat that divorce posed to the gender and social orders" (Savage, "Intended" 37). Domestic scandal, as Hammerton argues, privileged "the darker side of conjugal life," and it inspired condemnations of "behaviour, from both sexes and in all social classes, which was inconsistent with the middle-class domestic idyll and with heightened emotional expectations of marriage" (2). Falling short of the domestic romance central to Hammerton's study of marital conflict, however, the "darker side" and the scandal-seeking public gaze increased scrutiny of domestic violence. In doing so, they also corroborated the ominous adversarial notions inscribed in the legal model, and, thus, as "a locus of conflict" (14) or a site of crime, the home even threatened to reclaim some authenticity—albeit in a profoundly sinister way.

In charting divorce's contributions to "the spectacle of intimacy," Chase and Levenson argue that, although the divorce act was "far from radical in its legal and material consequences" (185), the "specter of divorce" (185) haunted Victorians because it placed divorce "intractably within the repertoire of possibilities" (186). Furthermore, they note, "because the difficult political struggle had made family breakdown so conspicuous in the cultural reverie—in Parliament, in the press, in prose fiction—no legal act could relieve the turbulent fantasy" (186). In tracing the representational influences of the divorce court, studies in the novel have been particularly interested in the ways in which historical cases of and debates about marital violence are filtered through the generic formats and influenced by the aesthetic affiliations of narrative fiction. In *The Private Rod,*

Marlene Tromp explores how the marginal status of the sensation novel allowed it to generate radical challenges to both high literary forms and conservative legal traditions. In *Bleak Houses,* Lisa Surridge, juxtaposing newspaper stories and novel plots and highlighting "moments in which generic, legal, and social discourses were particularly and visibly unstable" (7), examines how realist fiction developed the theme of domestic violence and explored the cultural functions of the "public scrutiny of private conduct" (10) not to reject marriage but to challenge male violence and regulate marital conduct.

Reading poetry, with a similar attention to the dialectal relationships between genre and discourse as well as their counterdiscursive frictions, this chapter proposes a different reading of the moral panics and textual mediations surrounding the publicity of marriage and divorce. This reading highlights the ways in which the inaccessibility and unavailability of divorce was equally unsettling, and, along these lines, the poems under discussion here—also purveyors of "cultural reverie"—can be said to invert the "turbulent fantasy." Rather than defending an institution and critiquing conduct, these texts indict marriage. Playing with the contentious politics of martial yokes and domestic discipline, they conjure a combative and criminalized vision of spousal relations and present the home as a source of murderous motive and a site of violent opportunity. Extending the theme of misbehavior to the theme of murder, Browning, Lytton, and Levy interrogate the adversarial model of spousal relations and implicate its destructive absurdities. Accordingly, with the domestication of murder, they challenge the horrors of divorce by imagining more brutal and lethal alternatives.

In the context of marriage, murder has specific political meanings. Riveting instances of murder, unlike lesser forms of domestic violence or more salacious forms of transgression, check what Francis Power Cobbe, writing on "wife-torture" in 1878, criticized as "a certain halo of jocosity which inclines people to smile whenever they hear of a case of [an assault on a wife by her husband] (terminating anywhere short of actual murder)" (133). Murder also exaggerates—often to the point of absurdity—the contractual demands of the law when, for example, it very succinctly confronts the problem of contractual extrication and marital dissolution and challenges the fictions of marital unity and female coverture. Examining divorce novels, Humpherys has argued that divorce reform broke the stranglehold of the marriage plot in the Victorian novel and developed narrative analyses of the difficulties of extrication. The most commonly used "Caroline Norton plot," she argues, focuses on the long-suffering wife in which "a brutal and/or egregiously adulterous husband is repeatedly excused, forgiven, and often nursed by the heroic wife until finally he or she dies"; less often, the oppressed flees, and even less often, the husband reforms ("Breaking Apart" 44). Meanwhile, in the "Jane Eyre plot," a husband is "tricked into a bad marriage or his wife turns bad quickly, and then he falls in love with a good woman who should be his wife" (44). Both tropes present problems of how "to extricate the heroine or hero from the mistaken marriage" and "whether to allow her or him to make a second more fulfilling one" (44), and these novels often demonstrate an "intent to expose legal injustice" and the "denial of any remedy" (46). In the poems under discussion here, murder, with great ironic and traumatic force, offers the longed-for "remedy."

In writing marriage plots as murder plots, Browning, Lytton, and Levy, despite significant textual and historical differences, demonstrate striking consistency in their characterization of the home's murderous orientation as overdetermined. Husbands and wives, thwarted by the intrinsic features of the marriage contract or the disciplinary functions of patriarchal authority, resort to murder because the strictures of domestic arrangements preclude less drastic solutions to marital conflict. Accordingly, readers witness the civilizing edifice of a disciplined domestic economy collapse under the weight of murderous violence. This collapse exposes the folly of domestic pieties, the structure of gender oppression, and the absence of adequate legal remedy, and because these murderers offer rationally, legally, and politically informed reasons for their actions, their crimes serve a variety of specific critical purposes. The synthesis of murderous action, domestic locale, and dramatic voice allows these poets to present a somewhat unusual vision of homicidal criminality: decisive, murderous action arises from the paradoxical convergence of frustrated agency, overdetermined subjectivity, and domestic confinement. The remainder of this chapter explores the specific textual and contextual details of such criminal representations.

Divorce Rights and Wife-Murder in Robert Browning's *The Ring and the Book*

In the often-quoted final line of *The Ring and the Book,* Browning proclaims the poetic value of "Linking our England to his [Lyric Love's] Italy!" (XII.870) and thus concludes the Roman murder case with a firm nod to Victorian times. Notably, this announcement occurs just after the poet-narrator claims, "Art may tell a truth / Obliquely" (XII.855–56), and Browning's not-so-oblique linking of a Roman murder trial and "our" Victorian England accesses the disarray of Victorian domestic politics. As Browning places "this old woe . . . on the stage again" to "[a]ct itself o'er anew for men to judge" (I.824–25), he explicitly and emphatically commands his audience, "Examine it yourselves!" (I.38). Addressed to "the British Public," who, by 1868, over ten years after the establishment of the divorce court, constituted an audience learned in the political rhetoric of public scandal and marital breakdown, the poem's first book apprises readers of the legal questions defining this case of marriage and murder. Though often described as a murder poem, as Simon Petch has noted, "[m]arriage, as the locus of the competing demands of nature, trust, and contract, is the most charged legal site in Browning's poem" ("Equity and Natural Law" 110), and for this reason, marriage also focalizes the poem's questions about institutional force and violent agency.[12]

An interpretation of the doomed marriage quite simply determines the murders' status as criminal or non-criminal while their domestic locale, as Arcangeli reminds us, aggravates—or perhaps mitigates—their meaning. The "Roman murder-case" (I.121), as the notebook records, focused on the determination of criminal responsibility through a central question: "'Wherein it is disputed if, and, when, / Husbands may kill adulterous wives, yet 'scape / The customary forfeit'" (I.130–31). Starkly emphasizing the criteria of license and right, Browning asks readers to consider whether adultery or murder more forcefully affronts the marriage bond. Two interpretations of the killings—affront or necessity—yield two possible verdicts: "murder, or else / Legitimate punishment of the other crime [adultery], / Accounted murder by mistake" (I.133–35).

In analyzing Browning's epic crime poem, literary scholars have often focused on the noisy polyphony that follows this introduction. As the poem's eleven speakers, "voices we call evidence" (I.833), select and highlight divergent details of the marriage in order to interpret and reinterpret the murders, they secure the deconstruction of truth itself. The poem's stake in domestic politics, however, is most strikingly revealed in unexpected but recognizable symmetries between the monologues of Guido and Pompilia. As the monologues of husband and wife—killer and victim—rebut *and* corroborate one another, Browning problematizes the conventions of adversarial discourse so integral to marriage reforms, divorce petitions, and scandalous spectacles.

In doing so, Browning selects an outrageously unsympathetic figure, Guido, who easily courts characterization as a monstrous aberration, obsessed with power, pathetic in his aristocratic ravings, and representative of old Roman corruption. He then uses him to embed a much more topically resonant, and perhaps unexpected, critique of marriage. In their respective testimony and debate, statements and accusations, rebuttals and refutations, Guido and Pompilia reconstruct the traumatic dynamic of their marriage and homelife. As Melissa Valiska Gregory has argued, Browning "persistently portrays the dynamics of the home as deeply painful for both men and women, and focuses especially on the various forms of masculine violence occurring in the struggle for sexual dominance between husbands and wives" (494). In *The Ring and the Book,* when both Guido's and Pompilia's accounts of marriage and murder coalesce on crucial points of causality and consequence, they reveal the roots of such struggle in the violent permissions of household law and the oppressive strictures of domestic ideology. The yoke of marriage, rather than inspiring "mutual accommodation," cruelly forces violent resistance. Regardless of how skewed, unreliable, or ambiguous the facts of this murder case, the only two speakers with firsthand knowledge of the marriage and the murders cite the domestic roots of their destruction and trace their actions, transgressions, and victimization to marriage's "galling yoke."

Attentive to the advantages of explaining, not denying, Guido's first monologue elaborates a patriarchal structure of marriage. Fortifying his claims with an impenetrably circular logic, Guido's case relies heavily upon the reiteration of legal tautologies: "the law's the law: / With a wife I look to find all wifeliness, / As when I buy, timber and twig, a tree— / I buy the song 'o the nightingale inside" (V.603–6). And the law, he maintains, obliges his mastery: "The obligation I incurred was just / To practice mastery, prove my mastership:— / Pompilia's duty was—submit herself" (V.716–18). Jettisoning the embellishments of the "dusty crumblings of romance" (V.696), he discourses unapologetically on the economy of marriage. "We talk of just a marriage," he argues, "The every-day conditions and no more; / Where do these bind me to bestow one drop / Of blood shall dye my wife's true-love-knot pink?" (V.697–700). When Guido poses the rhetorical question, "Purchase and sale being thus so plain a point, / . . . . From the bride's soul what is it you expect?" (V.574–77), he responds by expressing marriage as a contract in which a husband's will subsumes all: "Why, loyalty and obedience" (V.578).

To temper, yet support, these claims, Guido disingenuously qualifies his dogmatic approach to husbanding by noting that symbolic dictates forced him to choose his particular domestic "path." He recalls that as "eldest son and heir and prop o' the house" (V.212), he was commanded to marry and forced to domesticate himself. Occupying a somewhat feminized state, he is told, "Here's your post, / By the hearth and altar" (V.213–14). When he returns from Rome to be "content at home" (V.366), Guido is led by Paulo, his priest-brother, to marry Pompilia. His marriage, therefore, complies with a triply mandated familial, class, and religious decree. Even after his condemnation, he presents himself as a hapless victim of an erring domestic ideology, noting, "I am one huge and sheer mistake,—whose fault? / Not mine at least, who did not make myself" (XI.938–39). In this sense, then, he identifies himself as an initially reluctant but nonetheless zealous enforcer of patriarchal codes. In making these arguments, Guido paradoxically invokes a powerlessness to avoid husbandly power in order to write a narrative of his domestic oppression. His murderous violence thus becomes a righteous attempt to maintain the dignity of a flagging institution.

Despite logical inconsistencies, or perhaps because of them, Guido manages to implicate a dishonored and fickle Roman society as the accomplice to his violent tyranny while noting its responsibility for his initial presence at "the hearth and altar." In this way, he traces his crimes to a restoration of an honor lost to state authority as much as to an adulteress wife. He shifts his crime, then, from a premeditated murderous frenzy to a loyal enforcement of matrimonial law. While clearly drawing upon a defensive legal rhetoric, which, as Arcangeli insists, must explain not deny, Guido exposes the ideological structures of marital tyranny. Set as they are amongst other corroborating and misogynist voices in the poem, which implicate sexual double standards and advocate legal latitude, his claims that society formed him—his brutal self—retain some credibility. Furthermore, when he articulates his violence as a physical embodiment of domestic ideology, he is able to question the condemnation of his judges:

> Father and mother shall the woman leave,
> Cleave to the husband, be it for weal or woe:
> There is the law: what sets this law aside
> In my particular case? (V.581–84)

Lacking more attractive ideological veneers, Guido's "purchase and sale" version of marriage and his proclamation of guilt seem starkly uncivilized. Yet his testimony about previous legal and church support for such uncivilized tactics, later confirmed in Pompilia's testimony, and his bewilderment at its present withdrawal, tie his brutality to a history of legal permissions. For this reason, Guido, as wife-murderer, claims his superior integrity. Citing his ideologically consistent brutality, he can claim to have always been "[m]arching in mere marital rectitude!" (V.859) while the law has lapsed. Guido can defend "the irregular deed" (V.99) because the very irregularities of the law's application and enforcement, the law's transgressions, have framed and, in fact, demanded violence.

For Guido, the failures of legal discipline in marriage matters create domestic breakdowns that can be overcome only through more unambiguous forms of control. The court's refusal to share Guido's strict interpretations of the law lead him to practice murder. His "desecrated hearth" (V.1034) results from Pompilia's alleged affair with Caponsacchi and marks murder as "the natural vengeance" (V.1070) against a "thief, poisoner and adulteress" (V.1975). His singular folly, Guido argues, was his restraint—his initial failure to give material force to the violence of the law—and he frankly surmises that if he had severed Pompilia's finger to instruct her in wifely submission, he would have received "reproaches,—but reflections too!" (V.966). Guido's particular model of a Blackstonian application of "moderate correction" appears excessive and thus grimly parodies the familiar legal precedent lurking behind the notion.[13] Yet, Guido explains, applications of verbal abuse failed because they simply continued to abstract his power in language. That he "[c]alled her a terrible nickname, and the like" (V.984), stands as the "gentle course" (V.986) which he now deems "the fool's" (V.980). Similarly, when, upon their apprehension in Castelnuovo, he forgoes the legally justifiable murders of Pompilia and Caponsacchi and instead turns the "criminals" over to legal authorities, Guido's ends are frustrated by their nonviolent approach to punishment. To Guido's dismay, for flight and apparent adultery, Pompilia is sent to a convent and Caponsacchi to Civita Vecchia.

Guido's repeated insistence on the hypocritical restraint of legal authorities allows him to indict the judges—and the state— as institutions that establish the motives and the conditions for murder. Because they tacitly acknowledge "the crime" (V.1228) of adultery but only punish it lightly, he argues, "the cure grew worse disease" (V.1947). As Guido's murderous motive and multifaceted defense becomes entangled in the politics of divorce, Browning introduces the idea of divorce as a pressure-valve required to prevent more violent ends. The ecclesiastical court refuses the divorce that could end the domestic struggle that began in a secret marriage and continued through the revelation of Pompilia's illegitimate birth, her overt resistance, her flight with Caponsacchi, her assault upon Guido with his sword, and her exile to the convent for adultery. Only at this point of refusal does Guido admit defeat: "I am irremediably beaten here" (V.1393).

However repulsive Guido's actions and explanations, the fact that the murders occur after the Church rejects his divorce petition underscores Guido's violent dissolution of the marriage as a decision that he understands as "the will / To do right" (V.1622–23). The Church's response to his petition, "'Annul a marriage? 'Tis impossible!'" (V.1813), forms Guido's defense: "Well, let me have the benefit, just so far, / Of the fact announced,—my wife then is my wife, / I have allowance for a husband's right" (V.1816–18). Amidst this muddle of state rights and husband rights, it is by the claim to "husband's right" that Guido finally forces legal abstraction to confront its sanctioning of corporeal violence. Without divorce rights, in other words, he claims murder rights.

Guido, of course, asserts Pompilia's adultery in order to legalize, under seventeenth-century Roman law, his murders as a restoration of his honor. But Guido's accusations also resonate in nineteenth-century England, where adultery informed divorce law and criminal law and thus offered another example of their gendered interdependencies. While a wife's adultery did not legalize her murder outright, it permitted a reduction in the charge from murder to manslaughter. Providing leniency not available to women who killed adulterous husbands, this permission—if not for intentional lethal force at least for extreme violent rage—tacitly approved the husband rights so vehemently articulated by Guido two hundred years earlier (Doggett 50). As Wiener has documented in his recent study of masculinity and criminality, "In the course of the Victorian era wife killing appeared to be particularly resistant to the 'civilizing offensive'" affecting masculine identity and male behavior:

> In an increasingly "civilized" society, the home seemed to have become the "last retreat" of men's violence. In recorded homicide a new, more "modern" social pattern developed of fewer total cases overall, but with a substantially higher proportion of them taking place within the family, or within intimate relations, and thus with women rather than men as typical victims. Yet the rise in the domestic proportion of homicide prosecutions was not only the result of diminution elsewhere; it also reflected the increasing readiness of the law to "invade" the home.... (*Men* 146)

These historical details suggestively contextualize Guido's predicament, for he finds himself caught precisely between a long history of consent and a recent willingness to monitor, convict, and condemn wife-killing. Such changes inspire Guido's challenge to the ruling of Innocent XII in which Guido sees a newfangled intolerance for wife-murder. He asks, "Why do things change? Wherefore is Rome un-Romed?" (XI.265), and replies, "Ah, but times change, there's quite another Pope" (XI.276). As cultural models of respectable masculinity increasingly hinged on exhibitions of personal restraint, Guido exemplifies the limitations of that project.

With such historical links, Browning confirms that Guido is ideologically adrift, and, perhaps for this reason, Guido constructs working-class men as character witnesses. In fact, he credits the influence of his "own serving-people" (V.1551) with his final violent resolve. "Not one of us," they explain to Guido, "[b]ut would have brained the man debauched our wife, / And staked the wife whose lust allured the man, / And paunched the Duke, had it been possible, / Who ruled the land, yet barred us such revenge!" (V.1557–60). This account of the murders conjures stereotypical Victorian attitudes about working-class masculinity and criminality, but because Guido's speech is unreliable and his character is unethical, his invocation of working-class support only amplifies his aristocratic arrogance while exposing his attempt to further implicate the motivations of his paid accomplices. A less desperate aristocrat might purport to lead the people, not admit to eagerly following the murderous advice of "[r]esolute youngsters" (V.1562). When Guido scapegoats his servants, he attempts to displace the origins of male violence onto an othered class. At the same time, by virtue of his eager participation, he implies the widespread appeal of husbands' violent prerogatives. The male collusion addressed in Guido's claims—and actions—recognizes the presumed marriage rights of husbands and the violent desire to preserve honor and control as a masculine, rather than an aristocratic, birthright.

As the monologue progresses, Browning broadens the historical horizon of such violent entitlements. While traveling to Rome to commit the crimes, Guido attempts to call to mind the ideological origins of the violence he is about to inflict—an intertextual approach Arcangeli enacts in his rehearsal of a defense.

He searches his mind for "some snatch / Of a legend, relic of religion, stray / Fragment of record very strong and old / Of the first conscience, the anterior right, / The God's-gift to mankind, . . . the one law, right is right" (V.1571–78). His pastiche of textual documentation and legal precedent lays the foundation for his later self-assurance: "I did / God's bidding and man's duty, so, breathe free" (V.1702–3). As "law's mere executant" (V.2003) and "defender" (V.2004), Guido tells the court that he has "Blackened again, made legible once more / Your own decree, not permanently writ, / Rightly conceived but all too faintly traced" (V.1997–99). Insofar as his role in the poem is to embody the logic of patriarchy *in extremis* and to trace its violent legal history, he speaks accurately: he writes the law of marital and domestic authority clearly, permanently, and darkly in the blood of his victims. As Guido alternately abstracts this process in the legal language of his defense and renders it concrete through his metaphors and his murders, his maneuvering helps to position the critical value of the case, for it is the scrutiny of this very process that seems to particularly interest Browning.

Speaking well after his crimes and after his trial, the condemned Guido, "the same man, another voice" (I.1285), continues to insist on the inevitable intersections of marriage and murder. He imagines Rome as a community of propertied and "manly" men who understand, condone, and claim their murderous rights:

> . . . All honest Rome approved my part;
> Whoever owned wife, sister, daughter,—nay,
> Mistress,—had any shadow of any right
> That looks like right, and, all the more resolved,
> Held it with tooth and nail,—these manly men
> Approved! (XI.39–44)

Despite his condemnation and imminent execution, Guido contends that, although the Pope condemns spousal murder, everyday men and honorable institutions continue to excuse it: "there be nods and winks / Instruct a wise man to assist himself / In certain matters nor seek aid at all" (XI.1530–32). Contemplating his death sentence, he confidently explains, "Frown law its fiercest, there's a wink somewhere" (XI.2001). In fact, Pompilia also describes her futile appeal to the Governor in exactly these terms; she arrives at his palace just in time to witness Guido and the Governor "[e]xchanging nod and wink for shrug and smile" (VII.1279). This lexicon of nods and shrugs—the nod of complicity and the shrug of consent—is fundamental to Browning's depiction of patriarchal domesticity, and with reference to it, these two monologues document the ominous everyday structure of legal permissions. Demonstrating a link between smiles and shrugs, winks and nods, and marriage and murder, Browning sketches an unsettling social portrait, and moments such as this in which murderer and victim corroborate one another's claims, suggest the institutional, rather than purely individual, origins of domestic violence.

Compromising his claims to "[m]arital rectitude," Guido's second monologue delivers disorganized affronts and blasphemies. Yet, it nonetheless complements the arguments for domestic discipline applied in his first monologue. Guido has been defeated by the Pope's belief in Pompilia's sexual innocence and his denial of Guido's murderous right. Pompilia's restoration to an ideally chaste, victimized, pacified, silenced wife and woman frustrates Guido's stance as a lawful hero who "judged, sentenced, and punished" a disobedient and adulterous wife, whom he has earlier sought to dismiss as a "hysteric querulous rebel" (V.1828). The long project of devaluing and discrediting Pompilia included his sexual assaults, which, as Pompilia recalls, Guido described as an opportunity to damn her: "'Give me the fleshly vesture I can reach / And rend and leave just fit for hell to burn!'" (VII.783–84). Accordingly, as he approaches his own death, calling attention to the abject decomposition of the dead Pompilia, he seeks a similar defilement: "What you call my wife / I call a nullity in female shape, / Vapid disgust, soon to be pungent plague . . ." (XI.1110–12). And, in a vengeful apostrophe to his dead wife, he warns, "Beware me in what other world may be!— / Pompilia, who have brought me to this pass!" (XI.2101). Presented as ravings, these claims also reveal a defensive logic. In refuting the justice of his condemnation, Guido must subvert Pompilia's authority, which relies upon a notion of her innocence and her victimization and, amongst these "voices we call evidence," becomes the interpretive crux of the case.

Before the Pope's ruling, most of the other voices in the poem presume the greater authority of the husband. Pompilia's newfound authority, Guido argues, results from the fact that "The mob's in love, I'll wager, to a man, / With my poor young good beauteous murdered wife" (XI.1823–24). Guido, anxious as ever about class hierarchies, blames the representational powers of song sheets in which Pompilia's violated, dying self outweighs his emboldened masculine authority:

> And eyes, on warrant of the story, wax
> Wanton at portraiture in white and black
> Of dead Pompilia gracing ballad-sheet,
> Which, had she died unmurdered and unsung,
> Would never turn though she paced street as bare
> As the mad penitent ladies do in France. (XI.1826–31)

Here again is the iconic imagery of victimized wife and brutalizing husband,

and in this passage, Browning suggests both the representational power of the crime ballad and the imperatives of melodramatic binaries in order to chart Guido's fall. When Guido credits the ballad with gaining a public sympathy for her plight, a political pressure to which he believes the Pope is susceptible, he cites the inversion of class and honor that continually plague him. In the public forum of working-class literature, the nobleman loses his credibility to the illegitimate daughter of a prostitute. At the same time, Browning's ballad references highlight the fact that only Pompilia's violent death authorizes her voice. The crime and her wounds speak for her in ways that she could not and compel an audience of listeners that, while living, she could not.

Because Guido's condemnation renders his campaign against her public honor and her otherworldly salvation futile, he redirects his ravings towards dismantling the abstract value of purity and sullying the revered sacrament of marriage. After deconstructing Pompilia's popular authority, Guido attacks the wifely ideal itself, which has been instrumental in his ruin:

> Why, when a man has gone and hanged himself
> Because of what he calls a wicked wife,—
> See, if the turpitude, he makes his moan,
> Be not mere excellence the fool ignores! (XI.2205–8)

His proposed union with Lucrezia Borgia, a reference which inspires his priest-interlocutors to hold up their crucifixes, extols the evils of a sinning woman, whose evil he can and will surpass:

> Oh thou Lucrezia, is it long to wait
> Yonder where all the gloom is in a glow
> With thy suspected presence?—virgin yet,
> Virtuous again in face of what's to teach—
> Sin unimagined, unimaginable,—
> I come to claim my bride,—thy Borgia's self
> Not half the burning bridegroom I shall be! (XI.2212–18)

He thus deconstructs "[m]arital rectitude" and mocks the companionate ideal that so annoys him. In proposing a marriage in hell with a mythic poisoner and sexual predator, Guido attempts to undo all of the gendered codes that he ruthlessly enforced in his marriage and then opportunistically invoked in his defense.

His relentless attempts to apply patriarchal law with rhetorical and material force culminate in this shocking scene where husband and wife vie for transgressive dominance. Espousing this model of adversarial excess before a collection of upheld crucifixes, Guido even claims "impenitence" (XI.2229) as an act of resistance and a legal loophole. Just as he manages to attain this level of performative power, however, Guido's final words mark his surrender, and they underscore the desperate dialogue with Pompilia that his monologues have consistently implied: "Abate,—Cardinal,—Christ,—Maria,—God, . . . / Pompilia, will you let them murder me?" (XI.2424–25). With Guido's wild rhetorical energy reduced to pathetic verbal exhaustion, this apostrophe to his murder victim encapsulates the poem's commentary on the state's interests, investments, and interference in domestic matters. But, in a perversion of the eternal bond of marriage (the much touted yoke), Guido's desperate inquiry also neatly condenses the intricate and unending dialogue between husband and wife—murderer and murder victim—upon which the poem builds its scrutiny of adversarial domesticity.

Toward the same end, Pompilia's monologue both contrasts and corroborates Guido's assertions. Pompilia is a murder victim whose voice is only heard and recorded because she dies over the course of days. As she hovers between a tragic life and a certain death, her remarkable status grants her an uncustomary wifely authority, which, as Guido laments, allows this "pale frail wife" (XI.1675) to "shimmer through the gloom o' the grave, / Come and confront me" (XI.1680–81) and "turn / My plausibility to nothingness!" (XI.1686–87). Pompilia herself bitterly critiques the horrific origins of her death-bed authority, noting that it lies only in the "twenty-two dagger wounds, / Five deadly" (VII.38–39) with which Guido has violently asserted his husband rights. She is "to die tonight" (VII.40), she explains, and "[f]our days ago, when I was sound and well / And like to live, no one would understand" (VII.908–9).

Fittingly, then, Pompilia tells the story of silenced womanhood. Violante, Guido, the Archbishop, the Governor, the Friar, and the Court, which exiled her to the convent, prohibit her speech at various crucial points in her life. She describes her childhood wedding as an induction into silence. Violante, acting without Pietro's knowledge, instructs her that she "must hold [her] tongue, / Such being the correct way with girl-brides" (VII.382–83). And Pompilia reminds her audience: "Remember I was barely twelve years old— / A child at marriage" (VII.734–35). Significantly, like Guido, Pompilia regards her acquiescence to the marriage as an economic exchange. She, however, barters herself: "hardly knowing what a husband meant, / I supposed this or any man would serve" (VII.410–11) to "purchase" the "praise of those I loved" (VII.408). She recalls a secret ceremony of uncertain vow-making in which Paolo required her to "[r]ead here and there, made me say that and this" (VII.446) and:

> . . . told me I was now a wife,
> Honoured indeed, since Christ thus weds the Church,
> And therefore turned he water into wine,
> To show I should obey my spouse like Christ. (VII.446–50)

Pompilia, again equating wifehood with silence, "was quiet, being a bride" (VII.471). Only as a murdered wife can Pompilia speak with frankness and anger about the violent correlations between marriage and murder: "I was the chattel that had caused a crime" (VII.520).

Throughout her monologue, Pompilia disclaims any desire to catalogue Guido's actions: "... no, I leave my husband out! / It is not to do him more hurt I speak" (VII.1134–35). Commenting on the intentions and omissions of her speech, Pompilia signals (and perhaps feminizes) the difficulties of expression, but she also highlights the purpose of her monologue—to defend her sexual self and thereby indict her murderous husband. As Gregory has argued, "Browning fills her monologue with metaphors and ellipses, blank spaces, and oblique references where the reader must imagine violence rather than (as in so much of Browning's early work) experience its painfully intimate details" (503). Marriage is a "blank" (VII.574) and rape a silence marked by ellipses:

> Remember I was barely twelve years old—
> A child at marriage: I was let alone
> For weeks, I told you, lived my child-life still
> Even at Arezzo, when I woke and found
> First ... but I need not think of that again—
> Over and ended! (VII.734–39)

Gregory considers these elliptical omissions as part of Browning's "investigation into modes of achieving lyric self-expression without forcing violence upon his audience" (504), but while Pompilia sidesteps "the traditional role of courtroom plaintiff" (504) by refusing to completely narrate the crimes against her, she also asks the reader to acknowledge the violent possibilities and permissions of marriage. In this way, her monologue indicts marriage itself as a violent and false covenant rather than detailing or isolating Guido's individual perversions and transgressions. Both Guido and Pompilia sketch narratives that forge an uneasy agreement about cause and effect by pointing to the institutional powers and ideological pressures that determine their violent ends.

While Guido idealizes household law, Pompilia idealizes romantic love. Pompilia, like Guido, erects an ideal vision of marriage against which to measure the disorder of her own experience: "Marriage on earth seems such a counterfeit" (VII.1824). Aware that her authentic ideal cannot be realized on earth, Pompilia seeks to expose the "home-joys" version of domesticity, based upon husbandly love, religious devotion, and paternal protection, as a façade masking deeper structures of patriarchal violence and state control:

> Everyone says that husbands love their wives,
> Guard them and guide them, give them happiness;

'Tis duty, law, pleasure, religion: well,
You see how much of this comes true in mine! (VII.152–55)

Marital rape, which Pompilia only reluctantly documents in her monologue, leads her to connect her own experience to that of her biological mother, the prostitute from whom Violante purchased her:

My own real mother, whom I never knew,
Who did wrong (if she needs must have done wrong)
Through being all her life, not my four years,
At the mercy of the hateful,—every beast
O' the field was wont to break that fountain-fence,
Trample the silver into mud so murk
Heaven could not find itself reflected there,—(VII.864–70)

Her angry comparison between abused wife and dehumanized prostitute, of course, echoes the arguments of nineteenth-century feminists who read the sexual economies of marriage and the legal liabilities of wifehood through metaphors of prostitution. Comparing her mother's trampled and profaned life "[a]t the mercy of the hateful" with the sexual, physical, and psychological debasement of her marriage, Pompilia cynically undercuts angelic and sacred formulations of wifehood and domesticity.[14]

As Ann Brady has argued, when Pompilia rejects wifely submission, publicizes her oppression, and flees with Caponsacchi, she violates parental, secular, and ecclesiastical authorities. Demonstrating "self-possession," "self-direction," and a "sense of sole responsibility for the preservation of self," she resists patriarchy in ways that constitute "radical behavior" and "radical judgment" (14). Yet, Pompilia's attempt to murder Guido, it is worth noting, signifies a much more significant challenge to patriarchal control. Not only does Pompilia assault Guido with his own sword at Castelnuovo, but, overcoming her habitual and enforced silence, she shouts, "Die, . . . devil, in God's name!" (VI.1546). Oddly, critics often neglect this passage, but it is here that the notion of marriage's violent core—its adversarial mandate—is most solidly confirmed. Though Pompilia later qualifies the intentions informing her actions, she nonetheless enacts and articulates an open revolt against marriage law, Guido, and the cast of collaborators that ensure her domestic imprisonment. In terms of scale, of course, her momentary act of resistance hardly compares to the systematic violence of Guido, but its symbolic functions are crucial to the poem's vision of domestic combat and its commentary on bad bargains.

In narrating her rebellion, Pompilia charts her resistance with details that reveal her intent and that powerfully implicate the ways in which the marriage engenders violence. Pressed by Guido's presence as "master" and by the guards who are taking custody of "her angel" (Caponsacchi), Pompilia recalls, "I did for once see right, do right, give tongue / The adequate protest" (VII.1591–92). Referring to her attempt to kill Guido as her single "adequate protest" and her "first / And last resistance" (VII.1622–23), she effectively argues that violence offered the only possible end to the marriage. The assertion that violence offers the only available recourse, of course, is precisely Guido's argument, and, significantly, both husband and wife describe their murderous violence as an effort to "do right." At such points where their monologues converge, Browning forges an unsettling connection between the yoke of marriage and the outbreak of violence. *The Ring and the Book*, then, becomes more than a demonstration and critique of male violence, for it offers collective testimony about the inescapable and escalating tensions of bad marriage. The flight and apprehension—and Pompilia's and Guido's accounts of the impossibility of divorce—create an unhappy vision of marriage as a prison closely guarded by legal, social, and religious codes.

Although in the aforementioned lines Pompilia boldly claims her own murder rights, in subsequent passages she exhibits a desire to situate the details of her rebellion in more acceptable terms. She authorizes her actions in a religious language of duty rather than secular language of protest, and with such discursive maneuvering, Browning exposes the contradictory ideological demands inflecting her character and her speech. All at once, this murdered child-wife must negotiate proper testimony, proper womanhood, and proper victimhood. When Pompilia confesses her actions, she also casts her violence as a service to God and positions it as the rescue of God's angel, Caponsacchi:

> I did spring up, attempt to thrust aside
> That ice-block 'twixt the sun and me, lay low
> The neutralizer of all good and truth.
> If I sinned so,—never obey voice more
> O' the Just and Terrible, who bids us—"Bear!"
> Not—"Stand by, bear to see my angels bear!"
> I am clear it was on impulse to serve God
> Not save myself,—no—nor my child unborn! (VII.1594–1601)

The strands of this explanation are complex. Pompilia displaces responsibility for her violence and denies her interests in defending herself. She differentiates between acceptance of the violence against her, which she had been instructed to "bear," and a rejection of the violence against Caponsacchi, which, she argues, marital codes do not require her to bear. She forces this distinction even further when she notes that she did not attack Guido for the sake of her unborn child, who would presumably also fall under Guido's tyrannical authority. Her violence against her husband, she attempts to argue, functions as a response to a higher authority ("serve god"), which necessarily overrides corrupt earthly systems of marital authority. The reference to an unborn child at this point also supports her claims to Guido's paternity and, thus, implicitly denies the charge of adultery with Caponsacchi. While admitting to the attack, then, Pompilia refuses to acknowledge any shirking of womanly forbearance, and, at the same time, she undermines Guido's claim to *honoris causa*. Her use of discursive pastiche and rhetorical confusion once again reflects the labyrinth of gendered and classed codes that she must negotiate—even as she dies.

As Pompilia continues, these strategies resurface when the explanations for her violence shift slightly:

> But when at last, all by myself I stood
> Obeying the clear voice which bade me rise,
> Not for my own sake but my babe unborn,
> And take the angel's hand was sent to help—
> And found the old adversary athwart the path—
> Not my hand simply struck from the angel's, but
> The very angel's self made foul i' the face
> By the fiend who struck there,—that I would not bear,
> That only I resisted! (VII.1614–22)

Differing only slightly, both explanations serve to replace self-interest with self-effacement. In this instance, she acts, "[n]ot for [her] own sake," but for the sake of the "babe unborn." This minor adjustment allows Browning to suggest the care with which Pompilia attempts to master and adhere to the codes of wifehood and womanhood while she simultaneously indicts and rejects them as factors in her demise. Even as a murdered woman, she remains wary of the perils of submitting the private circumstances of her marriage to the public record. Because criminalizing and condemning Guido, her "old adversary," requires the maintenance of her wifely purity, she confronts these impossible contradictions with a doublespeak, one that mirrors and inverts Guido's own self-interested language. Accordingly, Pompilia masks her intent and denies her own interests, in order to tame the transgression that she enacted against her "master." Her reference to an angel's support helps to secure the role of innocence and right, which can absolve her and condemn Guido.

In spite of her rhetorical maneuvers, however, her attack on Guido reinforces the often unacknowledged agreement between these two adversaries about how the institution of marriage overdetermines their violent ends. Though it is tempting to scan their monologues in an effort to ascertain the veracity of one testimony or the other, as criminal and divorce courts mandated, the striking resemblances between Guido's and Pompilia's narratives work against this interpretive approach. Browning, explicitly interested in the difficulties and contingencies of interpretation, constructs correlations that underscore causal relations between the marriage bond and its violent dissolution. As the narratives of crime mutate into tales of marriage—and back again—Browning suggests that marriage and murder form essential parts, beginning and end, of the same coercive contract.

This argument about the nature of a "bad bargain" is echoed in other monologues as well and establishes a kind of critical refrain. The voice of Half-Rome, for example, asserts that marriage is the "knot / Which nothing cuts except this kind of knife" (II.66–67). A similar connection between marriage and murder appears when Pompilia recollects Pietro's words upon discovering her secret marriage to Guido. When Guido comes to claim his bride, an astonished Pietro cries to Violante, "You have murdered us, / Me and yourself and this our child beside!" (VII.492–93). Pietro's certain application of the word "murder" suggestively encapsulates the troubling slippage between marriage and murder that Browning sustains throughout the poem. Of course, Browning does not suggest that all marriages end in murder, but the poem uses this slippage to elaborate the lingering disillusionment with marriage law and marriage reform in Victorian England. He uses extreme violence to reinscribe patriarchal permissions, and to exaggerate the adversarial model, and thereby critique the notion that marital yokes and husbandly discipline produce decent couples.

Accordingly, the problem of marital yokes, spousal antagonism, and inadequate remedy appears when Pompilia traces murder to the legal difficulties of divorce, citing Rome's rejection of Guido's divorce petition: "People indeed would fain have somehow proved / He was no husband: but he did not hear, / Or would not wait, and so has killed us all" (VII.156–58). And though here she critiques Guido's impatience and expresses confidence in an eventual legal divorce, she explicitly depicts the murder as a divorce. After asking, "I—pardon him?" (VII.1709), she explains:

> Let him make God amends,—none, none to me
> Who thank him rather that, whereas strange fate
> Mockingly styled him husband and me wife,
> Himself this way at least pronounced divorce,
> Blotted the marriage-bond: this blood of mine
> Flies forth exultingly at any door,
> Washes the parchment white, and thanks the blow. (VII.1712–18)

Pompilia's thanks for "the blow," her acceptance of Guido's irrevocable "divorce," her appreciation of the now publicly visible blot on the "marriage-bond" (which had hitherto been privatized and concealed), and her exultation in the purification of her violent death combine to register a deeply bitter and ironic anger. At the same time, they focus the poem's grim conclusions about marriage and divorce. The narrative and rhetorical logic of both accounts affirms that the radical annulment, the murders with which Guido finally "pronounced divorce," constitutes the only solution possible within the confines of Roman society. Emphasizing this cultural oppression, Pompilia's monologue ends with a full rejection of earthly marriage law and a vision of companionate marriage undertaken by angels—removed from a social context valuing "birth, power, repute so much, / Or beauty, youth so much, in lack of these!" (VII.1831–32).

If we consider the symmetries of these two monologues, we can see how the poem challenges the codes of legal melodrama and public scandal circulating in Browning's murder poem and in Victorian England. With the voices of Half-Rome, The Other Half-Rome, and Tertium Quid—and with the Pope's contemplation of the historical significance of his ruling—Browning represents the "public anxiety" (I.1141), "the vibrations in the general mind" (I.844), produced by marital violence. Placed between the "world's outcry" (I.839) and the "world's guess" (I.842), the murder case, initially introduced as a problem of "if, and, when, / Husbands may kill adulterous wives," raises more questions about institutional force and individual frailty than a narrative condemning the monstrous outrage of a violent devil, fated for execution, and lamenting the passive victimization of a virtuous saint, fated for martyrdom, can address. While responding to the noisy debates that accompany shocking crimes and failing marriages, the stories of Pompilia and Guido function as political critiques of the melodramatic mandates and legal discourses that threaten to misrepresent and misinterpret their marriage and her murder. While the voices of the public and of the law wish to uphold the binaries of martyrdom and monstrosity, or adultery and honor, Guido and Pompilia, although drawing heavily upon these polarities (because they are consistently subjected to them), develop a critique of marriage law and its entire apparatus of customs and permissions. Because Guido's murder of Pompilia and the state's execution of Guido both interrogate the power dynamics of marital yokes and bad bargains, the poem ultimately exceeds the limits of the central question posed by the "the old yellow book." The question of "if, and when" requires an analysis of the violence supporting the mechanisms of marriage, which, Pompilia argues, "has killed us all."

As the converging monologues of Pompilia and Guido serve to expose the inadequacies of popular exegesis, Browning uses the verse novel's polyphony and the epic's massive scale to interrogate the reductive processes and ideological blindspots determining its generic and discursive methodologies. As Felluga has argued, the development of the verse novel correlates to the marginalization of poetry in the Victorian literary marketplace. In developing verse analogues to the novel, he argues, "poetry could attempt to play to that market as best it could by exploring the characteristics that made the novel such a popular success (narrative sequentiality, realistic description, historical referentiality, believable characters, dramatic situations, fully realized dialogism and, above all, the domestic marriage plot)" ("Verse Novel" 171). Suggesting an interest in the literary marketplace, Browning's poetic maneuvering also suggests a stake in the cultural and political marketplace surrounding marriage and divorce, one that includes the sensation novel but also the newspaper press. Responding to the poem's unusual approach to content and context, a review in *The British Quarterly Review,* lamenting Browning's interest in "mere vulgar murders" rather than "really noble" actions, characterized the text as both a "story which would suit a contemporary sensation novelist" ("Browning's Poetry" 456) and "the newspaper in blank verse" (457). Such observations return us to the performative and intertextual experiments of poetry—and the dialectical interplay of genre and discourse—in the marketplace of Victorian verse.

Considering the development of genre with respect to historical and cultural instability, Felluga considers that genres may be "perceived as belonging to a particular regimen but also as regimented against other genres" ("Novel Poetry" 495). As *The Ring and the Book* exemplifies a poetic response to the representational practices of the novel, the newspaper, and the court in cases of marital violence and domestic cruelty, its most striking argument "against other genres" emanates from its performance of and differentiation from their codes. While demonstrating an interest in scandal, the disgressive witnesses to and participants in this domestic murder plot undermine their own interpretive authority with their idiosyncratic and self-interested asides and their allegiances to prefabricated and outmoded narrative frameworks. To understand the laws of marriage and the laws of murder in representational terms, the poem suggests, the laws of genre must be revised and reimagined. *The Ring and the Book* has a great deal to say about textual production and legal fictions, but it is worth noting that in alluding to but not reproducing the framework of novels and newspapers, Browning generates the most startling feature of the text: the likenesses of Guido's and Pompilia's dramatic monologues. With their words, set amidst the crumbling integrity of matrimonial laws and the unstable resources of public gossip, readers glean some semblance of authenticity. With this unlikely symmetry—establishing the twinned testimonies of mutual disgust—Browning centers his critique.

"High Justice" and Husband-Murder in Edward Robert Bulwer Lytton's *Clytemnestra*

Of course, when it comes to interrogating marriage law and domestic ideology, murderous wives and mothers signify much differently than murderous husbands and fathers. Guido's crimes, as well as his rhetoric of impunity, for instance, crystallize the immense cultural machinery upholding wifely subjugation. As Guido explains in his defense, he merely embodies the abstracted ideologies and legal permissions of patriarchal hegemony. At the same time, his household crimes resonate with the developing Victorian discourses condemning abusive fathers and husbands, criminalizing domestic assault, and mandating protections for legally compromised wives. Murderous wives and mothers, in marked contrast, subvert this gendered system of permissions and protections. Neither respecting masculine authority nor requiring male rescue, domestic murderesses explode ideologies of feminine passivity, wifely patience, male protection, and husbandly dominance. And, while murderous wives and mothers countered representations of domesticated femininity, companionate marriage, and romantic love, they also threatened disciplinary models of marriage that aligned state and husbandly power.

Until 1828, English law had formally recognized the dense cultural symbolism of such wifely transgressions. Wives who killed their husbands, like servants who killed their masters or mistresses and ecclesiastics who killed their superiors, were guilty of "petit treason." Quoting Blackstone's legal interpretation of such acts, Maeve Doggett explains that these social relationships "embodied 'obligations of duty, subjection and allegiance' similar to those characterizing the relation between citizen and sovereign" (50).[15] Lytton's *Clytemnestra* and Levy's *Medea* play upon this relationship between domestic and political ordering by refashioning scenarios of domestic violence in Greek drama and positing causal links between marriage and murder. These texts allowed both authors to ignore the popular Christian rhetoric underlying justifications for the naturalness of domestic patriarchy and the compensatory enjoyments of angels in the house. Expressing themselves as sexual and psychological subjects, Lytton's and Levy's wives and mothers forego the domestic comforts of everyday "trifles" (2), the daily refinement of "minor morals" (7), and the measured exercise of "moral power" (49) advocated by Sarah Stickney Ellis in *The Women of England* (1838). As both poets secularize the dynamics of household law, they reconfigure these tragic murderesses as particularly modern women who express the dissatisfactions and injustices of gender inequality in terms immediately connected to marriage and divorce laws of the Victorian period.

Modern readers are not particularly familiar with Lytton's poetry, but among Victorian readers his poems, published under the pseudonym Owen Meredith, alternately inspired admiration and elicited contempt. A protégé of the Brownings, Lytton influenced a coterie of Oxford students with his debut poetry collection, *Clytemnestra, the Earl's Return, the Artist, and Other Poems,* which Chapman and Hall published in 1855, and, as Florence Boos has documented, his early work likely influenced William Morris's approach to medievalism.[16] At the same time, many critics challenged his work as derivative amateurism or outright plagiarism. Swinburne labeled him a "pseudonymous poeticule" and parodied his work in "Last Words of a Seventh-Rate Poet" (1880) (qtd. in Mitchell 83). Despite his poetic pursuits, however modest or contested, Lytton ultimately fulfilled the demands of his novelist-father, Edward Bulwer-Lytton, and established his national reputation, not as a writer, but as a career diplomat.[17] In 1876, he became Viceroy to India, just as Queen Victoria was preparing to assume the title of Empress of India. While his biographers have acclaimed his literary work and attempted to revitalize his poetic reputation, his diplomatic stature invariably outshines his artistic achievements. Yet, although Lytton's work remains significantly marginalized in our contemporary studies of Victorian poetics, *Clytemnestra* merits attention here because it deploys an ancient and familiar spousal murder in order to represent Victorian England's anxious domestic politics and because it does so with attention to the imbrications of genre and discourse.

Signifying its own importance, *Clytemnestra* headlined Lytton's first poetry collection and thereby assumed particular responsibility in launching his poetic career. Lytton composed and published the verse drama during the especially tense arena of marriage debates between the establishment of the Royal Commission on Divorce in 1850 and the passage of the Divorce and Matrimonial Causes Act in 1857, and he appropriated details from the national conversation on marriage reform in order to establish the homicidal motives and critical perspectives of Clytemnestra. Working in tandem, the dramatic voices and the narrative logic of Lytton's *Clytemnestra* suggest that murder offers a form of recourse for legally, politically, and socially compromised wives. Poised in this symbolic position, murder affords, in Clytemnestra's terms, a "high justice" that, with the sharp reprisals of the knife, condemns the sexual double standard that privileges and ensures husbandly dominance and patriarchal power. In murdering Agamemnon—husband and king—Clytemnestra gains both the household and the state. In adapting Clytemnestra's story to Victorian times, Lytton retrieves and reorganizes portions of the Orestian saga of family breakdown in order to consider the legal and psychological dilemmas of marital unhappiness. Because *Clytemnestra* balances extensive commentary on the dejected experience of wifely oppression with the terrific outcome of a murderous rebellion, Lytton forces the abstraction of unhappiness to be read through its tangible results.

Though writing the verse drama in his early twenties, the young, unmarried Lytton undoubtedly possessed insights into such matters, for he existed in especial proximity to the political, legal, and scandalous implications of marital disintegration and discord. His parents, the novelist and MP, Edward Bulwer-Lytton and his wife, Rosina (née Wheeler), were the notorious adversaries of one of the most publicly vitriolic and endlessly scandalous society marriages of mid-nineteenth-century England.[18] Though his parents obtained a judicial separation in 1836, after nine years of marriage, they were ineligible for divorce, both before and after the Divorce Act, because they both had committed adultery. Yet, as Marilyn J. Kurata has argued, "[a]lthough English law made divorce impossible in this case because both partners possessed grounds for divorce, other laws offered means of controlling a recalcitrant wife" (45). Accordingly, on various occasions, Bulwer-Lytton used the arsenal of marital weapons available to the mid-Victorian husband: financial control, child custody, secret surveillance, forced asyluming, and physical assault.[19] Skillfully wielding publicity as her instrument of redress, Rosina retaliated with newspaper letters, allegorical novels, and public appearances in which she vilified her husband's character and disrupted his dignified political image.[20] According to most biographers, Lytton almost unwaveringly aligned himself with his father in his parents' matrimonial feuds—and even ushered his outraged mother off the stage of British scandal and onto the continent in order to salvage his father's reputation.[21] *Clytemnestra*, however, complicates this standard biographical view of his domestic allegiances and gendered sympathies. Fixing its gaze on Clytemnestra, the poem registers an attempt to depict, to understand, and to analyze the feminine subject position in the context of marital breakdown.

In a few striking ways, the Bulwer-Lytton family saga resembled the Orestian nightmare portrayed in *Clytemnestra*. It includes an outraged wife and mother, who explicitly lamented the strictures of womanhood and sought compensation with increasingly radical methods, and a pompous, controlling patriarch, whose official state duties and political self-fashioning took precedence over his private, family duties. Their family story also includes the tragically early death of the daughter and sister, Emily, whom Lytton once referred to as a "murdered girl" and whose early death inspired mutual accusations of neglect in the parents' ongoing battles (qtd. in Raymond 75).[22] In the ongoing recriminations, Emily appeared an innocent martyr to the neglect, incompetence, and selfishness of her warring parents. Furthermore, as Marie Mulvey-Roberts contends, the "Bulwers feared the murderous inclinations of one against the other" (124), and many of the family's struggles were broadcast to and witnessed by an observant and fascinated public. While *Clytemnestra* is certainly not a fully autobiographical domestic allegory, the struggles of the Bulwer-Lytton family signal the poem's historical context and Lytton's interest in the destructive forces lurking within the disharmonies and injustices of married life. Equally important are his poem's commentaries on publicity. With his representations of the chorus—alternately accusatory and placated—Lytton encompasses the broader cultural theater of marriage and divorce on the implied stage of the closet drama and thereby addresses the generic patterning of domestic romances and marital scandals.

With a text that is both safely literary and suggestively political, Lytton authorizes his work—and launches his career—with a classical crime. The literary alchemy of the ancient and the modern, especially in the context of crime, also attends to questions of authorial legitimacy and textual vulgarity that surrounded crime writing in the Victorian period. In fact, just before Lytton began to exploit the violent and criminal resources of Greek tragedy for his début volume, his father had attempted to defend his crime novels—*Paul Clifford* (1830), *Eugene Aram* (1832), and *Lucretia; Or, The Children of the Night* (1846)—against charges of glorifying criminals and wallowing in vulgarities. In his defensive essay, "A Word to the Public" (1847), Bulwer-Lytton defends his work by plotting the literary relationship between the ancient and the modern. The "delineation of crime," he explains, "in every age" has been the "the more especial and chosen thesis of the greatest masters of art quoted to us as authorities and held up to us as models" (14), and his catalogue of evidence includes the infamous murderers of several canonical favorites: Clytemnestra, Medea, Orestes, Oedipus, Phaedra, Richard, Hamlet, Othello, and Macbeth.

These dramatic texts and characters do not celebrate crime, he argues, but rather exhibit and embody tragic necessity: "Crime, in fact, is the essential material of the Tragic Drama. Take crime from tragedy, and you annihilate tragedy itself" (16). Literary crimes generate "moral terror" because they induce speculation about and confrontations with "some destroying or dangerous agency" (20). "Look a little deeper," Bulwer-Lytton confides, "and you will find that there are only two kinds of this agency—the first, supernatural, such as Fate" and "the second agency is human crime" (20). Arguing that modern novelists must be permitted to depict modern crimes rather than crimes "clad in the pomp of history" (24), he asserts, "the past cannot monopolise the sorrows and crimes of ages" (25). For, with the Greeks, fate "was the main instrument of woe and crime. . . . [b]ut, with us, guilt or woe has its source in ourselves. Our conscience is our oracle, our deeds shape our fate" (54). In Bulwer-Lytton's argument about the necessity of a modern crime literature, one might glean a corollary argument about the merits of revising ancient crimes. While Bulwer-Lytton defends the literary merits of modernity's "vulgar" crimes, his son's *Clytemnestra*, "clad in the pomp of history" and dwelling in the realms of poetry, exploits the aesthetic and moral comforts of classical crime in order to confront the modern discourses of domestic scandal and household law. Combining the ancient crime with the modern motive, Lytton invokes the "moral terror" of wifely rebellion. Moreover, the ancient Greek context also affords Lytton an opportunity to jettison Christian dogma from his analysis of spousal relations. Effectively secularizing the text, it allows Lytton to interrogate the symbolic laws of the home without having to honor—or address—Christian-based domestic pieties. A poetic comparison reveals the latitude gained by this secular bent. Penning their verses of mid-Victorian homelife at precisely the same time, Coventry Patmore enshrines an "Angel in the House" (1854) while Lytton domesticates a high tragic murderess.

In critiquing the poem, Victorian commentators—both private and public—frequently relied on the dramatic template of Aeschylus and the genre codes of Greek tragedy as their evaluative tools. Elizabeth Barrett Browning described Clytemnestra as "too ambitious because after Aeschylus, but full of promise indeed" (Harlan and Harlan, *Letters* 27). Accusations of plagiarism also surfaced as several reviewers scrutinized his Greek and Shakespearean imitations and documented his contemporary literary borrowings.[23] More interesting than the problems of generic authenticity and authorial originality, which Lytton himself addressed, is the poem's discursive collage of literary precedents and contemporary gender debates surrounding the subject of domestic conflict.[24]

While Victorian critics eagerly scrutinized the text's derivative style, its possible plagiarisms, and the impossibly lofty agenda of transposing Greek tragedy into Victorian culture (and imitating the notoriously obscure Aeschylus), their critical language also frequently revealed their preoccupation with the poem's representation of marriage. As the reviewer for *Tait's Edinburgh Magazine* noted, Lytton's *Clytemnestra* had a "curious involution of the modern and the antique about it" ("Owen Meredith's Poems" 682). In slipping between ancient and modern paradigms, Lytton demonstrates his conceptual showmanship by enlarging the scope of Clytemnestra's character and by redefining the causalities of tragedy. These alterations combine to interrogate the semiotics of fate and crime. The involutions of past and present allow readers to consider psychological and ideological explanations for crime. A curse on the house of Atreus, therefore, resembles a bad nineteenth-century marriage while crime and fate emerge paradoxically as socially determined and individually motivated entities.

Clytemnestra consists of twenty separate scenes that range from the lone soliloquies of Clytemnestra to discussions between the chorus and other main characters. In revising the story, Lytton makes significant structural changes; most important, of course, is the centering of Clytemnestra. The drama pivots around Clytemnestra's thoughts and deeds—and the always vexed relationship between these two components of crime. Accordingly, Lytton's *Clytemnestra*, unlike Aeschylus's *Agamemnon*, opens onto Clytemnestra's soliloquy rather than a watchman's exposition. Inducted into the drama via Clytemnestra's sentiments and thoughts, readers immediately encounter the murderously unhappy wife, after a night of troubled and troubling sleep, explicating the psychological perils of domesticity, articulating her adulterous desire for Aegisthus, and contemplating the immanent return of Agamemnon from war. As Clytemnestra lays out her adulterous anxieties, her murderous motive and intent present themselves for inspection when she suggests, as she apostrophizes the morning sun, that she suffers the punishment of sleepless guilt without having committed the crime:

> Wherefore to me—to me, of all mankind,
> This retribution for a deed undone?
> For many men outlive their sum of crimes,
> And eat, and drink, and lift up thankful hands,
> And take their rest securely in the dark.
> Am I not innocent—or more than these?
> There is no blot of murder on my brow,
> Nor any taint of blood upon my robe. (I.4)[25]

Clytemnestra proclaims, however, that the darker crime exists in her thoughts: "It is the thought! It is the thought! . . . and men / Judge us by acts!"(I.4). While commenting on the origins of her adulterous transgression, "one wild hour of unacquainted joy" (I.4), Clytemnestra reveals that she has just awakened from a dream in which Helen ruefully reminds Clytemnestra that her similar inconstancy started a war. "Allured by love," Helen explains, she "[fe]ll off from duty"; and a "baleful" procession of slaughtered Trojan warriors passes through Clytemnestra's mind, affirming the extensive social consequences of one woman's sexual impropriety (I.4). Here, then, Lytton introduces the troubling equations of thought and action, motive and deed, which are then interrupted by "the tread of nimble feet" (I.5) as the town awakes and gathers for Agamemnon's return.

As the first scene suggests, imagining modern social foundations for traditionally fated criminality required a fully developed psychological portrait of Clytemnestra. Writing to his father in 1853, Lytton explicitly claimed an interest in ascribing psychological complexity to this long-generalized icon. He highlights the poetic innovations and thematic limitations that underlie his interest in generating modernized circumstantial contingencies for this icon of "strongnatured passionate" womanhood, and he characterizes the text as an "experiment" and a "failure" (qtd. in Harlan 71):

> The character of Clytemnestra always seemed to me one of the great creations of fiction, and yet it is one of wh. we really know very little—for in Aesch: she is more a goddess than a human being, and stalks out & in, like the old executioners with a mask, does her deed and disappears, while in Euripides she is a mere virago—a common sort of Madam Lafarge. About a year or two ago, I began a sketch of the character in blank verse; in wh. I endeavoured to suppose wht. might be the feelings of a strong-natured passionate woman under the circumstances wh. form the plot of the drama of Aesch: But not

liking wt. I had done, threw it by & forgot all about it. Some time back, in looking over old papers I found the sketch, & set to work upon it again. It almost unconsciously, however, grew into dramatic form, and I then changed the plan, & added choruses after the manner of a Greek drama. (qtd. in Harlan 71–72)

Dwelling on the verse drama's nature as a "poetical exercise" (71), Lytton confesses something "impertinent" (71) in the work since it "brings one flat against the great Greek masters & Shakespeare too, both of whom crush one, of course" (71), and he argues that "poetry shd now be in front, & not behind, the age; the times are so quick" (71). Yet, because Lytton rewrites Clytemnestra during a national conversation about family law, amidst the renewed idealization of the separate spheres, and against the sentimentalization of the family, he imbues this verse drama with a modernizing stance. In refining Clytemnestra's voice and complicating her motivations, he dismisses the conventional portrait of this disgruntled adulteress and high-tragic murderess. As Harlan has argued, Lytton "sought to penetrate the austere silences of the Greek drama by analyzing and psychologizing" and "mak[ing] explicit and rational what in Aeschylus is symbolical and passionate" (72). In spite of his disclaimers, then, *Clytemnestra* attempts to develop a modern content.

The replacement of symbol and passion with analysis and psychology also informs the important semiotic triangle connecting Clytemnestra, the Chorus, and Agamemnon, which Lytton establishes early in the second scene and continues throughout the entirety of the poem. The chorus, exhibiting deference and bearing offerings, inquires after Clytemnestra: "But tell us wherefore, O godlike woman, / Having a lofty trouble in your eye, / You walk alone with loosened tresses?" (II.6). The observant chorus then engages Clytemnestra in conversation on the well-being of Agamemnon. The Chorus states, "But more than all I reckon that man blest, / Who, having sought Death nobly, finds it not" (II.9), and Clytemnestra replies: "Except he find it where he does not seek" (II.9). When the Chorus counters, "You speak in riddles" (II.9), Clytemnestra merely redirects, "with garlands wreathe the altars, / While I, within, the House Prepare" (I.9). In this oblique yet ominous exchange, Clytemnestra both publicizes her dissent and invokes her duty. Yet, what in public appears the overseeing of domestic preparations is, in fact, the crafting of a murderous snare.

Because Lytton yokes the exercise of household duty with the plot of murderous retribution, he forces a point about the private traumas and the public mandates of separate spheres ideology. While anticipating a reunion of brothers and a restoration of a noble household, the chorus also articulates the possibility that Agamemnon's public deeds, primarily the sacrifice of Iphigenia for the benefits of war, may have private repercussions: "My heart is fill'd with vague forebodings, / And opprest by unknown terrors / Lest, in the light of so much gladness, / Rise the shadow of ancient wrong" (II.11). Breaking down the convenient dichotomy of private and public, this vague apprehension then takes more specific form: "For the unhappy sacrifice of a daughter; working evil / In the dark heart of a woman; / Or some household treachery, / And a curse from kindred hands!" (II.12). The chorus, the vocal proponents of fate's powers and the record-keepers of family wrongs, effectively comes to represent the ever curious and scandalized public, which enforces social propriety as it attempts to cast its gaze into the home and bear witness to its intimate transgressions. As we shall see, Lytton complicates the role of the chorus throughout the drama, configuring it as an unreliable and unstable force of public opinion creating and consuming the "spectacle of intimacy."

The public's instability and appetite for spectacle, Clytemnestra explains to Aegisthus, allows her to manipulate "the arts / That guide the doubtful purpose of discourse / 'Thro many windings to the appointed goal" (VIII.49) in order to "draw [the citizenry] on to such a frame of mind / As best befits our purpose" (VIII.49). While Clytemnestra uses Iphigenia's sacrifice to position herself ethically, Lytton uses it to particularize Clytemnestra's crime as the revenge of an unloved housewife whose false consciousness slips away when her daughter's sacrifice materializes the absolute powers of the family patriarch and when her "heart" responds to the affection of Aegisthus. Priming the chorus to accept her murderous project, she questions their belief in "terrible necessity" (IX.54). Asking, "Was it a murder or a sacrifice?" (IX.55), she interrogates the "foul infanticidal lie" (IX.55). Similarly, as the chorus proffers an ethical equation that accepts "this single, individual loss" for the "universal good" (IX.55), Clytemnestra counters with a criminal accusation: "Can all men's good be helped by one man's crime?" (IX.55). As the chorus begins to acquiesce, calling the sacrifice "an evil thing" (IX.56), Clytemnestra exploits maternal politics. Agamemnon, she explains, simply "did not bring [Iphegenia] forth" (IX.57), and while he enjoyed war, "his blythe pastime on the windy plain" (IX.57), Clytemnestra "sat apart, / Silent, within the solitary house: / Rocking the little child upon [her] breast" (IX.57). Having been swayed by the arts of discourse, the chorus begins to expect retributive justice, and Clytemnestra notes with satisfaction that her "mischief works apace!" (IX.60).

The entirety of the next scene, the mid-point of the play, is given over to the chorus's narration, in great lyrical detail, of Iphigenia's sacrifice, which leads the chorus to doubt Agamemnon: "Oh, what falling off is this, / When some grand soul, that else had been sublime, / Falls unawares amiss, / And stoops its crested strength to sudden crime!" (X.63). A clear indication of Clytemnestra's political savvy and the public's impressionability, this scene also implicates Agamemnon's own bloody choices and thereby deepens—and genders—the psychological complexity of Clytemnestra's murderous rage. As Boos has argued, "Lytton's

'Clytemnestra' is not exactly a feminist rewriting of Aeschylus, but it recalibrates the scales of judgment to balance the guilt of an arrogant child-murderer against that of his vengeful wife" (37). In the end, Boos notes, Clytemnestra's actions are "understandable but not attractive" (40), an apt expression that also describes Victorian England's simultaneously queasy and riveted response to the public politics of marital breakdown.

Although we witness Clytemnestra confidently manipulating public opinion, we also see her struggling with her own internal judgments. While she maintains her performative sensibilities and strategically masks her internal revolution with outward subordination "as best befits a wife / And woman" (IV.21), she privately strengthens her resolve with countless and contradictory reflections on necessity, justice, and fate. With a nod to destiny, for example, she refuses to "shrink" from the "forecast event" which "hurls" her into the "abyss of crime" (IV.21–22):

> . . . What need
> Of argument to justify an act
> Necessity compels, and must absolve?
> I have been at play with scruples—like a girl.
> Now they are all flung by. I have talk'd with Crime
> Too long to play the prude. . . .
> Crime's easier than we dream. (IV.22)

Yet, significantly, this event has been "forecast" by none other than Clytemnestra in her opening soliloquy. In such passages, then, Lytton highlights the struggle between her self-motivated intentions and what she considers girlish scruples. Throughout the play, Clytemnestra undergoes a clear psychological struggle between the imperatives of feminine identity and her unwomanly willfulness. This gender dilemma appears as Clytemnestra laments her womanhood as inadequate to her character.

> O fate! to be a woman! You great Gods
> Why did you fashion me in this soft mould?
> Give me these lengths of silky hair? these hands
> Too delicately dimpled! and these arms
> Too white! too weak! Yet leave the man's heart in me,
> To mar your master-piece—that I should perish,
> Who else had won renown among my peers,
> A man, with men—perchance a god with you,
> Had you but better sex'd me, you blind Gods! (IX.51)

In fact, fate, as in this passage, is often construed as a gendering of, rather than a preordination of, her crimes, which are necessitated by the mismatching, or misgendering, of body and will.

Though her references to gods clearly suit Lytton's Greek context, her references to fate more frequently designate a patriarchal hegemony rather than an interventionist cosmology. For example, Clytemnestra, reflecting on men as warriors and women as war slaves—"long hair'd virgin wailing at the shrines" (IX.51)—again denounces fate's gendering properties:

> O fate, to be a woman! To be led
> Dumb, like a poor mule, at a master's will,
> And be a slave, tho' bred in palaces,
> And be a fool, tho' seated with the wise—
> A poor and pitiful fool, as I am now,
> Loving and hating my vain life away! (IX.51)

Done in by limited options, Clytemnestra curses both her hatred for her husband and her love for Aegisthus because both signify subordination and futility—a "vain life."

Furthermore, her tragic oversight, which she bemoans, has been her failure to perceive marital injustices, a kind of gendered *hamartia* that led her to believe that her own homelife would rise above that of other women. Speaking to Aegisthus, she confesses that she was "foolish" not to read other wives'—indeed, all women's—unhappiness as a warning:

> ... And tho' I saw
> All women sad—not only those I knew,
> As Helen ...
> Not only her—but all whose lives I learn'd,
> Medea, Deianeira, Ariadne,
> And many others—all weak, wrong'd, opprest,
> Or sick and sorrowful, as I am now—
> Yet in their fate I would not see my own
> Nor grant allegiance to that general law
> From which a few, I knew a very few,
> With whom it seem'd I also might be number'd,
> Had yet escaped securely:—so exempting
> From this world's desolation everywhere
> One fate—my own! (VII.36–37)

In describing "all women" as "weak, wrong'd, opprest" and "sick and sorrowful" and proclaiming the "world's desolation everywhere," Clytemnestra reveals her sense of the scale of women's oppression and the magnitude of her own folly. Her poignant regret highlights the collective oppression of women, for the home, she claims, is inevitably—fatefully—the space of solitude and alienation: "I moved about, a shadow in the house, / And felt unwedded though I was a wife" (VII.47). But she has also expressed a sense of compromise, though not "so exacting" at present, she explains to Aegisthus, she still hopes for a reformed domestic future with him.

With her explanatory and analytical soliloquies in place, Lytton uses Agamemnon's return from war to confirm the details of Clytemnestra's critique. Agamemnon appears as the incarnation of heroic masculinity, and the chorus proclaims this stature as he marches amongst the urns being carried home from war. References to his "sublime head" (XI.70) and "eminent authority" (XI.70) join admiring shouts, such as, "what an arm," "what shoulders," "what a throat," and "Look at that sword" (XI.71), to underscore his royal masculinity and "stateliness" (XI.71). Clytemnestra's majesty appears to match his: "With what grand eyes she looks up, full in his!" (XI.72). As the chorus revels in the palpable return of paternalism, patriarchy, and royalty, the public face of a noble marriage appears to them just, secure, and right.

To underscore the falseness of this collective delusion, Lytton embellishes Aeschylus's version of Agamemnon's response to Clytemnestra's welcome and thereby renders it an aggressive dismissal of her speech and an explicit degradation of the feminine. As Clytemnestra expresses the required honorifics, Agamemnon exclaims, "Enough! Enough!" (XII.74), and he then discourses on the virtues of women's silence in fully nineteenth-century formulations of domestic propriety:

> But women ever err by over-talk.
> Silence to women, as the beard to men,
> Brings honour; and plain truth is hurt, not help'd
> By many words. To each his separate sphere
> The Gods allot. To me the sounding camp,
> Steed, and the oaken spear; to you the hearth,
> Children, and household duties of the loom.
> 'Tis man's to win an honourable name;
> Woman's to keep it honourable still. (XII.74–75)

Clytemnestra's "over-talk," of course, is not an error but a posture, and as Agamemnon confines Clytemnestra to the custodial role of keeping his honor, his strict adherence to the doctrine of separate spheres, which casts the home as a place of silence and peace and the public sphere as a place of violence and war, profoundly undermines his strength and status. Given Clytemnestra's fully expressed murderous intent, Agamemnon's reference to "plain truth" charges the scene with a dramatic irony, for readers know that Clytemnestra's formal rhetoric of welcome, her "over-talk," belies an intimate contempt and a malicious plan, which she has plainly spoken in "many words" throughout the drama. Agamemnon's words thus appear both blindly complacent and arrogantly provocative.

Although Clytemnestra summons the perfunctory apology, she prefaces it with an aside that mocks the domestic entitlements of presumed impunity of husbands:

(O beast! O weakness of this womanhood!
To let these pompous male things strut in our eyes,
And in their lordship lap themselves secure,
Because the lots in life are fallen to them.
Am I less heart and head, less blood and brain,
Less force and feeling, pulse and passion—I—
Than this self-worshipper—a lie all thro'?) (XII.75)

Now relegated to parenthetical aside, in contrast to the bold declaiming that opens the play, Clytemnestra's speech nonetheless reclaims for woman the organs of agency and force. As Agamemnon takes leave of the reception in order to bathe, he inquires, "Is our house order'd?" (XII.76), and thus, Lytton furthers the dramatic irony of domestic breakdown. Clytemnestra responds that the palace is "order'd fair / Befitting state" (XII.77), including the "purple-paven, silver-sided bath, / Deep, flashing, pure" (XII.77). While the ideologies of domesticity, presumptions of womanly submission, and the privileges of husband rights define Agamemnon's perspective, the audience observes in this scene a seething confrontation between a rebel and a tyrant in which the tyrannical "self-worshipper" remains completely oblivious to his imminent and complete overthrow. Basking in his heroic return from war, he adheres to a gendered code of dominance that has shifted unbeknownst to him during his long absence.

Satisfied that his house is ordered, Agamemnon instructs Clytemnestra to attend to Cassandra, thus confirming Clytemnestra's earlier judgments about women, slaves, and war. Notably, Lytton preserves Cassandra's life so that Clytemnestra may express sympathy for their common experience as women: "Our fortunes are not so dissimilar, / Slaves both—and of one master" (XV.88). Cassandra, therefore, stands as a fellow subjugated woman rather than a competitor in a patriarchal sexual economy, and this distinction enables Lytton to clarify for his audience that Clytemnestra's crime constitutes a wholesale rejection of patriarchal authority and not a momentary (but momentous) flare-up of sexual jealousy.

In Agamemnon's attempt to assert his authority via the reiteration of separate spheres, Lytton also establishes the interpretive schema for the murder. Occurring behind the closed, locked doors of the home, the murder is overheard in the streets by the agitated public. Choric voices avow that "[s]ome hideous deed is being done within" and call to "[b]urst in the doors" (XVI.96). This scene overthrows the binary comforts espoused so forcefully by the returning war hero, and the inversion is striking. As "[t]he house is fill'd with shrieks" (XVI.95), the noises of dishonorable violence astonish the public, which, assembled to celebrate a homecoming, listens helplessly to the demise of the patriarch, the household, and the state. The sounds of outrageous crime that emerge from the palace include Agamemnon's cries, which serve to detail the crime. He identifies, in gendered terms, the killer, "Murderess! oh, oh!" (XVI.95), and the method, "Stabb'd, oh!" (XVI.97), while maintaining his characteristic boldness, "I will not die" (XVI.95). The conspirators are also overheard: Aegisthus instructs Clytemenstra, "Thrust there again!" and Clytemnestra affirms, "One blow has done it all" (XVI.98). As the astonished public grapples with the meaning of these verbal fragments, a choric voice exclaims and questions, "My heart stands still with awe! / Where will this murder end?" (XVI.98). The relationship between the chorus outside and the crime within is emphasized by the locale of the murder scene—a spatial representation of domesticity and publicity. The scandal of adultery, therefore, gives way to the monumental horror of murder, constituting the final, ironic reply to Agamemnon's arrogantly naïve question about whether or not the house is "order'd."

In the next scene, Electra, the crime's sole eyewitness, rushes from the house with Orestes in order to secure his escape and thus ensure his capacity to enact a future "high vengeance" (XVII.99). Responding to the citizenry's inquiries, she presents an account of the crime. She calls attention to Aegisthus's passivity as he "halted, half irresolute" (XVII.99), and she highlights Clytemnestra's vigorous agency:

But Clytemnestra on him flung herself,
And caught the steel, and smit him through the ribs.
He slipp'd, and reel'd. She drove the weapon thro,'
Piercing the heart!" (XVII.99)

Contemplating the meanings of this crime, the chorus further articulates the ironic reversal of the private/public opposition: "But Death, that fear'd to front him in full field, / Lurk'd by the hearth and smote him from behind" (XVII.100). Electra then exhorts the crowd to assist in protecting Orestes and assuring a future restoration of proper order, and she represents the chaos of the present, curiously, in terms of the virtual nonparticipant, Aegisthus, rather than the "devilish woman, lying long in lurk" (XVII.99) who orchestrated and executed the crime: "The house runs blood. Aegisthus, like a fiend, / Is raging loose, his weapon dripping gore" (XVII.101). As Electra and the chorus lament the fall of the state and the death of a patriarch, the transformed Aegisthus, now thirsting for power, demands Orestes and threatens Electra, who, boldly dismissing him, calls him "half a man" (XVIII.110) and, with rather comical alliteration, a "[b]lundering bloodshedder" (XVIII.111). She then threatens him with the future avenging powers of Orestes.

The shocking spectacle of the crime scene, however, disrupts Aegisthus's and Electra's mutual posturing when, the palace doors are "*thrown open*" (XIX.112) and reveal Clytemnestra standing over the body of her victim and shouting: "Argives! behold the man who was your King!" (XIX.112). This positioning of murderer and victim visually underscores Clytemnestra's murderous agency even as she verbally ascribes the deathblow to "Fate" (XIX.112). In marked contrast, her subsequent explanation uncovers a deeply personal agency:

> He who set light by woman, with blind scorn,
> And held her with the beasts we sacrifice,
> Lies, by a woman sacrificed himself.
> This is high justice which appeals to you. (XIX.113)

Clytemnestra thus expresses some satisfaction in this tit-for-tat gender equity, acquired by leveraging the effects of paternalist misogyny and domestic violence for the destruction of patriarchal ideology and its embodied authority. As the plotted crime and the expressed rage of the opening soliloquy are enacted, Clytemnestra asserts the purpose of her spectacular revolution. Implicating longstanding analogies between state power and husbandly power, she combines high treason and petit treason.

At this point, Clytemnestra's insistence on "high justice" also confronts Victorian anxieties about women's anger, the frightening antithesis of a feminine ideal of long-suffering patience, passivity, and, of course, silence. In her murderous euphoria, she unequivocally represents the possibility that the resources of patience, whether naturally formed or culturally constructed, are, in fact, finite and, in this instance, completely depleted. The representation of Clytemnestra's crime, and her public interpretation of it, appropriates the discursive trick of pitching arguments *in extremis* in order to generate an ideological and institutional critique. Nowhere is this more apparent than when, contemplating Agamemnon's military strength, Clytemnestra proclaims the superior power of her private disdain:

> O triple brass,
> Iron, and oak! the blows of blundering men

Clang idly on you: what fool's strength is yours!
For, surely, not the adamantine tunic
Of Ares, nor whole shells of blazing plates,
Nor ashen spear, nor all the cumbrous coil
Of seven bull's hides guard the strongest king
From one defenceless woman's quiet hate. (III.16–17)

The armor and weaponry of war, long-celebrated emblems of male strength and public purpose, thus prove useless when set against the quiet and long-growing hate of the domesticated woman.

Because Clytemnestra consistently interprets her actions in terms of the separate spheres dichotomy, she signals Lytton's ongoing attention to Victorian domestic ideology. Sacrificed to war, Iphigenia embodies the subordination of the private to the public and the feminine to the masculine. Aligning herself with her daughter, then, Clytemnestra again proclaims an affiliation of womanhood, and her use of the term "sacrificed" to characterize her murder of Agamemnon reconnects his husbandly oppression to his strategic killing of Iphigenia. This completion of the sacrificial cycle, Clytemnestra explains, ushers in a new political order because it answers and overthrows the laws of patriarchal dominance. Manipulating the public's desires for justice, she highlights the immediate problem of masculine authority and thereby sidelines the language of fated retribution and ancient wrongs that have defined choric speculation throughout the play.

Accordingly, christened in the blood of a fallen monarch, she imbues her ascension to power with modern and secular revolutionary sentiments. Proclaiming, in the aftermath of a murder, "Now it is time to laugh!" (XIX.115), Clytemnestra attempts to replace gravity with levity, and she seeks to dispel both the public's skepticism and its bloody memories by promising a moderate and peaceful rule:

A milder sway, if mildly you submit
To our free service and supremacy.
Nor tax, nor toll, to carry dim results
Of distant war beyond the perilous seas
But gateless justice in our halls of state,
And peace in all the borders of our land! (XIX.115–16)

As Clytemnestra articulates this bargain, a utopian state without wars or prisons in exchange for their immediate and collective submission, her efforts to insert emotional levity and political optimism into these murderous events, which the chorus has been reading as a tragic plot, is abruptly interrupted by Electra's flinging herself onto the blood-soaked body of her dead father and asserting the tragic necessity of retribution. Yet, in spite of Electra's performative invocations of tragic imperatives, Clytemnestra's rhetorical powers continue to persuade as she offers her traumatized daughter a "mother's heart" and "[s]afe silence. And permission to forget" (XIX.116)—and Electra appears to relent.

This scene reveals Lytton's interest in exposing the scaffolding of the two fundamental discourses of *Clytemnestra:* ancient Greek tragedy and contemporary marriage debates. With Clytemnestra advocating a gendered political revolution and Electra insisting on tragic determinism, Lytton stages the two discourses in a competition for interpretive power. As Clytemnestra verbally subdues her angry daughter, Lytton privileges the modern content. Electra desires the familiar comforts of patriarchy, including its obsession with adultery, which she upholds early in the play when she expresses confidence that her returning father will "destroy the base adulterer, / And efface the shameful past" (VI.26). Explaining the contrasting figures to his father, Lytton stated that Clytemnestra represents the "active" principle and Electra represents the "suffering" principle (Harlan 72). With their oppositional rhetoric, Lytton suggests that the tragic, ancient mode insistently perpetuates and obsessively redresses past suffering while the revolutionary, modern view seeks to invest in futurity—and femininity.

Questioning the causalities of individual agency and divine fate, the final scene of *Clytemnestra* continues to entertain modern and ancient explanations for the crime and its relationship to the past and the future. The chorus concludes the play with a chant that repeats the phrase, "Destiny is over all" (XX.122). But, even though Lytton includes this discourse of fate, his changes to the drama challenge its explanatory power. In the end, despite her earlier references to the dejected state of all married women, Lytton's Clytemnestra imagines a reformed union with Aegisthus. Because their partnership is quite literally built upon the violent dissolution of a combative model of marriage, the play hints at the possibility of and a desire for a companionate and equitable alternative to the more conventional model of the husband-centered family and the male-dominated state. Clytemnestra's final words express the promise of a reformed domestic contract: "Thou lovest me! O love, we have not fail'd. / Give me thy hand. So . . . Lead me to the House. / Let me lean on thee. I am very weak" (XX.121). Exhausted by crime, Clytemnestra and Aegisthus enter their "House" to continue a partnership sealed in crime. Momentarily displaced are the portended revenge of Orestes and the sulky judgments of Electra.

Yet, crucial textual details thwart this happy ending. The emphatically different perspectives and behaviors of the two transgressing lovers trouble Clytemnestra's companionate model of domesticity and monarchy.[26] Most significantly, the contingencies of the illicit romance, which have inflected Clytemnestra's crimes and motivations throughout the play, continue to resonate here. For example, Clytemnestra must prompt Aegisthus to declare his love. Just before the ending, we see Clytemnestra fretting, "But, if he cease to love me, what is gain'd?" (XX.120), and, after she queries, "Aegisthus, dost thou love me?" (XX.121), Aegisthus claims, "As my life!" (XX.121). His response inspires her final confidence in their relationship and her feminized physical weakness, which requires her to "lean" on him as they enter the palace. Clytemnestra, however, has clearly not parsed Aegisthus's line, for his language encodes a telling subtext. He has witnessed the life-taking powers of this particular wife, as she drove a knife through the ribs and into the heart of her husband, and his future safety, citizenship, and life are now hers to control. Given this context, "As my life!" signifies the nature of his compromised condition, and it also quite pointedly alludes to her earlier threat that without committing to her and her crime, Aegisthus, a "poor baffled crownless schemer," would be ruined—if not dead. Her romantic prompting and prodding at the end of the play, then, reminds readers of the private anxieties underlying her public pronouncement, which Clytemnestra, in fact, laments throughout the play. At the end of the play, with just a few words and gestures, we see the culmination of Lytton's skepticism. Doomed and overdetermined, men and women cannot overcome the pressures and limitations of an adversarial and hierarchical domesticity.

Several particular impediments become most relevant to Lytton's analysis. For instance, Lytton fully demonstrates that Clytemnestra exceeds her two male counterparts in willful purpose and psychological grit. As we have seen, Agamemnon's self-satisfied dismissal of Clytemnestra and his presumption of uncontested power leave him vulnerable in the bathtub, and Aegisthus's terrified hesitation mobilizes her murderous resources and places her in the role of supreme and singular agent. In terms of narrative logic, then, both Agamemnon and Aegisthus contribute to the making of Clytemnestra the murderer. Agamemnon's public interests establish Clytemnestra's private hurts and provoke her murderous outrage. Similarly, she frightens Aegisthus with her tenacious criminal plotting, which he had long entertained in theory but dislikes in practice. As Electra contemptuously explains, he blunders his conspiratorial duties and renders Clytemnestra solely responsible for Agamemnon's death.

Demonstrating how entrenched gender inequalities might yield disastrous results, such details also undermine crucial ideologies of masculinity. Clytemnestra out-strategizes and overpowers Agamemnon. As they live out the adversarial model of spousal relations, he relies on traditional forms of control while she opts for new methods. Likewise, Aegisthus's failed collusion undercuts notions of male agency and male rescue. Earlier in the play, examining Agamemnon's shield, Clytemnestra reads its nicks and scratches as signs of his physical prowess. Then noting, "Aegisthus' hands are smaller" (III.16), she acknowledges his conspiratorial impotence and signals her ferocious power. Even more importantly, however, both Agamemnon's and Aegisthus's actions and inactions suggest that Clytemnestra has no adequate match in marriage, love, or governance. Far from modeling a partnership of equals or investing in a companionate ideal, Lytton's verse drama marks the absence—and perhaps implies the impossibility—of spousal cooperation or domestic comfort. This conspicuous absence establishes the play's relentlessly pessimistic critique of marriage.

Details throughout the play set readers up to appreciate the spectacle of the doomed lovers at the end of the play and to read it as an exacting critique. The companionate marriage, the longed-for alternative to authoritarian models, is introduced early in the play when Clytemnestra uses it to justify her adulterous transgressing and her criminal plotting. She deploys the language of love to contest the definition of adultery as treason: "If I had loved him once—if for one hour— / Then were there treason in this falling off. / But never did I feel this wretched heart / Until it leap'd beneath Aegisthus' eyes" (III.14). For Clytemnestra, romance continues to function as both an interpretive framework and an intended goal, but she observes that Aegisthus is "wavering in nature" and "trembling ever on extremes" (XV.85) and is passive even in love: "his was never yet the loving soul / But rather that which lets itself be loved" (XV.86). She wonders if he will misinterpret her actions and intentions and "[r]emembering the crime, remember not / It was for him that [she is] criminal" (XV.87). Similarly, she adjusts her rhetoric and seeks to feminize her agency: "'Tis not for him, but for myself in him, / For that which is my softer self in him—I have done this, and this—and shall do more" (XV.86). Her anxieties about exercising her will and feminizing her self, stemming directly from the romantic idyll, complicate her project of self-liberation.

Meanwhile, Aegisthus, concerned about public opinion, portends, "all the Greeks will hate us" (VII.33), and warns, "we shall be dishonour'd" (VII.34). Failing to comprehend that Clytemnestra is motivated by her revolutionary contempt for female subjugation and her ambitious desire to reconstruct the state, he recommends that they "part now" and offers "[f]light" (VII.38) as a more prudent solution to their adulterous dilemma. Clytemnestra, however, seeks to confront and overthrow, and operating in a Macbethian mode, she mocks his lack of strength and cites her fatal error in entrusting her future to him: "This was the Atlas of the world I built!" (VII.39). Even suggesting that his lack of support constitutes "retribution" for her adultery, she proclaims, "a universe [her love] lies ruin'd here" (VII.39). Ever invested in his participation, however, she both rallies and bullies him, admonishing him to "be a man for once" (VII.39) as she explains to him that assuming power of the house is the only viable option. The public, she explains, valuing strength and hating weakness, will embrace their cause. She questions his integrity, asking, "lives there nothing of the ambitious will?" (VII.40). She recalls the "proud plots" and "dextrous policy" that characterized years of pillowtalk (VII.40), and explains that to abandon their murderous plot would be shameful: "For to conceive ill deeds yet dare not do them / This is not virtue, but a two-fold shame" (VII.41–42). As Clytemnestra's rhetoric escalates, as she seeks to recover "[her] King! [her] chosen! [her] glad careless helpmate" (VII.43), the idea of companionship and partnership begins to recede.

Increasingly exasperated as Aegisthus wavers and shrinks, she finally announces that she will commit the crime herself: "What! Shrinking still? / I'll do the deed. Do not stand off from me" (VII.44). Yet, Aegisthus's "stand[ing] off" then forms a central anxiety. When in response to Clytemnestra's assertion that he fears her, Aegisthus claims to "worship" (VII.44) her, he betrays the absence of love, romance, or equality. As a rhetorical last resort, when the language of romance has failed, she warns this "poor baffled crownless schemer" that his fate rests in her power:

Without my love
What rests for you but universal hate,
And Agamemnon's sword? Ah, no—you love me,
Must love me, better than you ever loved—
Love me, I think, as you love life itself! (VII.45–46)

Here, then, is the antecedent to the final scene in which he claims, as instructed, to love Clytemnestra "[a]s my life!"; and therein lies the adversarial core of their domestic partnership.

At the end of the play, if not throughout, readers see Clytemnestra's anxieties legitimized. Boos notes that *Clytemnestra* intimates a "rhetoric of female self-defense" (37) and revises Aeschylus's more masculine Clytemnestra by ascribing to her "acceptable 'womanly' desires for love" (38). Given that Lytton sought to imagine a markedly feminine psychology, we might assume that he resorted to or relied upon conventional tropes of feminine subjectivity. However, it is also worth noting that companionate aspirations and romantic discourse in *Clytemnestra* always succumb to or are thwarted by uncooperative gender identities and inhospitable domestic ideologies. Conventional femininity, for example, rendered Clytemnestra a "weak, passionate, unhappy woman" (VII.44), but that weakened self attracted Aegisthus, who envisions her now as a "Terrible Spirit." In seeking a masculine political power, therefore, Clytemnestra unwittingly sacrifices opportunities for love and companionship, which require a feminized identity. Clytemnestra's particular tragedy, then, stems from an ideological miscalculation about the unwanted presence of female agency in any romance plot.

Noting their frustrations with the text, Victorian reviewers somewhat obliquely acknowledged Lytton's critique of domestic romance. Describing

Clytemnestra, a critic for the *Dublin University Magazine* explains: "She is, in [Owen Meredith's] hands, neither the bold virago, indifferent to consequences, of Aeschylus, nor the depraved woman, by turns violent, sophistical and weak, that Sophocles represents her. She is a woman, haughty, proud, self-willed, yet possessed by one sentiment, her love for Aegisthus, which exhibits her a woman in her heart, and is the mainspring of all her errors and sins" ("Clytemnestra" 487). The reviewer goes on to complain that her love "but little elevates her" and that Aegisthus is a "poltroon, who loves her a little, and fears her more" (488). But the fact "that the woman who has this deep love in her heart should repine at the fate that made her woman—should despise her sex, and long after manhood—is revolting, because it is utterly outside the bounds of nature—"(488). Such observations might be reinterpreted in terms of the gender tragedy that Lytton develops in the play.

Clytemnestra's gender bending is less a "revolting" perversion of nature than a daring attack on a particular set of gender norms. Another reviewer, diagnosing the "general unhealthiness of the poems relating to love" ("Meredith's Clytemnestra" 302) and presenting them as characteristic of "the Byronic or Bulwerian kind" (302), maintains: "They never sparkle with health, or kindle with hope.... To us, these pieces wear the look of one who knows more than he ought to know; it may be a wrong impression, but it is none the less painful. Or else there is some fatality in the author's choice of subjects relating to woman" (302). It is difficult to believe that this reviewer did not know the true identity of "Owen Meredith." Regardless, the identification of Byronic and Bulwerian romantic pathologies and feminine fatalities—and certainly the claim that "he knows more than he ought to know"—correctly assert Lytton's interest in disturbing the domestic, gender, and sexual politics of Victorian England. His is indeed a "painful" view, and the profound failures of the romantic idyll that mark Lytton's version of this ancient tragedy establish the principal dramatic and political ironies of the text.

The dramatic irony that underpins this domestic failure thus fully engages the mixture of Greek paradigms and modern politics that characterizes the entire drama. As Clytemnestra insists upon performing a scene of domestic happiness, the psychological tensions of the domesticated subject, as "conflictual complexes," emerge even as the chorus sings the powers of fate: "Who shall say 'I stand!' not fall? / Destiny is over all! (XX.122). The chorus has relied on fate throughout the play as a device for explaining outrageous violence. Yet, Clytemnestra has consistently demystified fate, applying the term variously—to persuade the public, to delineate her will, and to denote gender hegemony. At the end of the play, the audience, privy to Clytemnestra's public suasions and inner reflections, senses the ironic inadequacy of the chorus's continued fate-based sensibilities. Just as the notion of fate cannot impinge upon the explanatory power of the intimate rage that Clytemnestra expresses and enacts, it also cannot resolve the unsatisfying implications of Clytemnestra's domestic bargain with Aegisthus.

In Lytton's *Clytemnestra*, then, the epistemology of gender trumps the epistemology of fate, and, because Lytton effectively accesses the Victorian contest of gendered prerogatives, individual rights, and domestic duties, the ending portrays neither triumphant love nor tragic destiny—but just another "bad bargain." Clytemnestra and Aegisthus might just become a "decent couple," but under the heavy yoke of domesticity—articulated throughout this verse drama as a psychological yoke of entrenched and internalized sexual inequalities—their partnership will never match the high drama of its origins in adulterous romance and revolutionary crime. In positing such tragic mediocrity, Lytton exploits the formal freedoms of closet drama. Dispersing high tragedy into twenty clipped scenes, Lytton elaborates the psychological traumas of marriage, the systematic processes of marital breakdown, and the risky investments of unexacting lovers. Bending gender and genre in this way, he domesticates Clytemnestra's ancient crimes for his particularly modern commentary on the ominous nature of household law.

Domestic "Compact[s]" and Child-Murder in Amy Levy's *Medea*

Composed in 1882 and published in *A Minor Poet and Other Verse* in 1884, Amy Levy's *Medea. A Fragment in Drama Form, After Euripides,* similarly scrutinizes the psychological perils of domestic bargains.[27] Compressed into two scenes, Levy's modernized *Medea* accommodates the adversarial model of domesticity by eliminating many of the voices of Euripides' original drama and leaving only Medea and Jason, and Aegeus and Nikias (as "Citizens of Corinth"), to convey a tragic plot of spousal bitterness. Levy presents Jason and Medea as hostile adversaries whose household arrangements, initially negotiated under the influence of sexual desire, romantic love, and heroic adventure, succumb to the divisive public mandates and patriarchal agendas of domestic arrangements. Highlighting the self-interested benefits of husbandly authority and the solitary suffering of wifely subordination, Levy obscures Jason's obligations to gods, fates, and Kreon and omits Medea's sympathetic audiences with nurse, tutor, and chorus. Stripping away these influences, Levy enumerates the emotional, psychological, and sexual intimacies of spousal antagonism. With pointed representations of Jason's politicized marriage-making and Medea's psychologized home-making, Levy, like Lytton and Browning, imagines the home's emotional charge, which the disciplinary mechanisms of domesticity—from placating domestic ideologies to authoritative patriarchal decrees—can never fully neutralize or contain.

In particular, beginning with Medea's dehumanizing, domestic alienation and culminating in Medea's shameful, criminal isolation, the narrative logic of Levy's verse drama provocatively aligns the psychological consequences of marriage and murder—for women. Deemed a fragment, Levy's *Medea* concludes with a fully incriminating portrait of marriage and domesticity, and, offering neither consolation nor remedy, she abandons a fugitive Medea, exhausted by "fruitless striving" and propped against a rock, "outside the city" (55).[28] "This is the end," she proclaims, "Thus go I forth / Into the deep, dense heart of the night—alone" (56). Imbued with a sense of domestic fatalism, Levy's *Medea* also dramatizes the relationship between private discord and public voyeurism as the gossipy commentators, Aegeus and Nikias, who are seen engaging in "idle talk" (38) and "conferring in whispers" (47) throughout the drama, perceive and interpret events according to facile notions of femininity, domesticity, and criminality. With their inaccurate commentaries, Levy acknowledges the troubled communications between the private actors and the public spectators of domestic upheaval while probing the gendered logic of such private-public distinctions.

When she invokes Euripides in the title of her poem, Levy signals a political and poetic interest in outrageous femininity, and she situates her text within a broader context of Victorian Medeas. As Edith Hall points out, Euripides' *Medea* enacts the only premeditated maternal child-killing, unmitigated by madness, in Greek tragedy. The infanticidal radicalism of the Euripidean Medea so affronted Britain's maternal codes that "[o]n the British stage it was not until 1907 that Euripides' *Medea* was performed, without alternation, in English translation" (Hall "Legislation" 42). Exacerbating her violent offenses, Euripides' Medea renounces feminine duty, invests in masculine-coded honor, and enjoys the impunity of a charioted escape. With her multivalent transgressions—from public speaking to murderous revenge—she fully unsettles distinctions between "private and public, friend and foe, and especially between man and woman" (Hall, "Introduction" xvii). In mid-century London, the disruptive domestic politics of the Medea plot enjoyed particularly topical resonance. As Hall explains, during the divorce controversy of 1856 and 1857, the national obsession with marital matters created a "British epidemic of *Medea* plays," and Medea was "one of the most ubiquitous heroines on the London stage" (56).

In particular, Medea frequented Victorian burlesque theatre, where, as Fiona Macintosh has recently reminded us, she was "transposed" into a travestied comic figure but nonetheless encoded "relatively radical" gender critiques ("Medea Transposed" 77). In *Medea; Or, The Best of Mothers, with a Brute of a Husband* (1856), for example, Robert Brough characterizes Medea as "a conjugal lesson, surpassing in intensity anything of similar description attempted even at this establishment, an awful warning to every single individual" while describing

Jason as "a hero of antiquity, of fabulous courage, about to marry the second time without the slightest hesitation." In the productive disjunction between satirical levity and tragic weight—with Jason embodying the remarrying kind and Medea portending marital doom—Brough invites a timely and comical lessoning on the serious politics of divorce and matrimonial law.

Writing almost thirty years after Brough, Levy complicates the "conjugal lesson" of male lassitude and female fury in order to assess the conflict of spousal interests and the precariousness of domestic bargains. Born in 1861, Levy missed the mid-century marriage debates that inspired Brough's (and Lytton's) Greek revival, but her Medea's murderous exasperation suggestively alludes to the persistence of women's inequality. Although women's legal status continued to improve over the latter half of the nineteenth century, as Atkins and Hoggett have argued, the legal gains of the Married Women's Property Acts of 1870 and 1882 coincided with the "entrenchment of housewife marriage" (106). The colliding interests of marriage contracts and domestic pressures, emerging from what Mary Poovey terms the "uneven developments" of law and ideology, inform Levy's historicized understanding of late-Victorian gender politics.[29] As Linda Hunt Beckman notes in her recent biography, at thirteen, Levy reviewed *Aurora Leigh* for *Kind Words* and published "The Ballad of Ida Grey" in the feminist journal, the *Pelican*, thereby demonstrating a "precocious attraction to women's rights" and, I would add, her historical awareness of women's struggles and feminist discourse (Beckman 18).

A poet with an equally historicized sense of literary genre, Levy enfolds this tension into her Medea plot, but, instead of developing a fully structured feminist political allegory, she sketches the psychological momentum, rather than the political motivation, of Medea's violence. In this way, the bleakness of Medea's domestic experiences and the extremity of her psychological suffering inform the outrageousness of her crimes. For example, Levy excises Euripides' "Women of Corinth" speech, in which Medea catalogues the systematic social wrongs of woman—from arranged marriage and shameful divorce to painful birth and domestic boredom. But she extracts from that famous speech a pithy summary argument and installs it as an epigraph: "Of all ensouled and minded things, women are the natural beings who struggle most."[30] With these lines, Levy prioritizes female subjectivity as the primary site of gender oppression and the most pressing issue of marriage politics. Accordingly, she traces Medea's murderous violence to the affective extremes of domestic oppression, thus avoiding more conventional formulations of Medea's crimes as vengeful defiance or political argument.

Reconstructing the domesticated subject-position of the notorious, filicidal Medea, Levy gathers the resources of dramatic poetics to indict decades of piecemeal legislation and ideological lethargy, and, in this way, Levy's psychological poetics constitutes a particularly feminist stance, one that recalls Philippa Levine's comments on "anachronistically" applying "feminism" to explicate Victorian women's discourse. Levine argues that feminism "signif[ies] a perspective far more concrete and thoughtful (if still contested and admirably plural) than an attachment to any vague notion of 'rights' or 'equality' might suggest. Its commitment to a thorough and holistic understanding of the pervasiveness and connectedness of a host of gendered subordination lends it consistency and vision" (1). Moreover, in the context of family politics, Levine explains:

> The family in Victorian England was the site of confined domestication whose grip on women was firm and frequently total. It constituted one element of the polarized ordering of the social fabric which critically defined role and standing for both women and men. The binary opposition of home and work, of private and public translated into and percolated through to a bewildering range of thought, action and material circumstance. Feminists seized upon the cruelties, the injustices and the dangers that attached to that polarization, appropriating and subverting it to their design. (10)

While sidestepping focused "rights" arguments, Levy fashions her *Medea* to highlight the polarizing effects of family politics. For example, she forcefully highlights Jason's self-interested exchange of a passionate illegitimacy for a conventional respectability, which begins in his domestication of Medea and culminates in his marital bargain with Kreon. Jason, of course, trades on Medea's expendability, and insofar as Levy articulates the kind of feminist critique that Levine traces in Victorian discourse, Medea's destruction of Jason's proposed family underscores a "holistic understanding" of women's domestic oppression in Victorian England. Striking at scions and royals, Medea bluntly exposes the methods of procuring, protecting, and publicizing family assets. With the legal and ideological features of domesticity—maternity, paternity, patrilineality, respectability, legitimacy—under scrutiny, Levy constructs a dramatic "assessment of gendered wrongs" (Levine 1) and offers a wholesale rejection of domesticity as an unregenerate form of social contracting.

Demonstrating the political ingenuity of poetic design, Levy initiates her verse drama with a soliloquy. Speaking to herself in front of her home, Medea proclaims herself "lone and weary and sad" (33). Acknowledging her status as a foreigner, but emphasizing her alienation as a wife, she catalogues the sources of her dejection. A Colchian among Corinthians, she identifies herself as "[a]lien" (34) and describes herself as "[h]ungry" (35) for love. Detailing the features of Corinth, where "marble-cold" (34) and "fair" people (34) greet her with "hatred" (35) and "hostile eyes" (35), she laments, "I, an alien here, / That well can speak the language of their lips, / The language of their souls may never learn" (34). Lacking opportunities for companionship and communication, she is misread:

"I am very meek. / They think me proud, but I am very meek, / Ready to do their bidding" (35). Occupying this emotional slum, suffering from hunger, cold, and loneliness—the very antitheses of domestic comforts—Medea observes a contrast between her present self and her former self. Now "a creature reft of life and soul" (35), she was formerly "a creature in whose veins ran blood / Redder, more rapid, than flows round most hearts" (34). Levy intertwines notions of ensoulment and embodiment by offering bodily metaphors—the hunger for love or the flow of blood—to describe Medea's domesticated state. In this way, Levy alludes to the predicaments of wifely personhood. Housebound and hated, Medea endures a kind of physical and psychological *coverture,* and suffers her own negation.

Throughout the poem, the critical observations of Aegeus and Nikias, who pronounce judgments upon Medea as wife, mother, and woman, confirm her marginalization. While Aegeus judges Medea "fair enough" (36) but "strange" (37), Nikias detests such "swart skins and purple hair" and "black, fierce eyes where the brows meet across" (37). Meanwhile, Nikias admires Jason's "gracious presence" (37), his "strange and subtle strength," his "gold-curled head," and his "smooth tones" (44). Racializing gender in this way, the stinging prejudices of Nikias and Aegeus, which pit Jason, civilized and "fair," against Medea, "strange" and "swart," affirm the social layers of Medea's subordination.[31] Their smug, objectifying voyeurism also contextualizes Medea's definition of herself as monstrous: ". . . I have poured the sap / Of all my being, my life's very life, / Before a thankless godhead; and am grown / No woman, but a monster" (41). Alluding to her bad bargain with Jason, a "thankless godhead," Medea again defines her bartered self with bodily metaphors. The deadening, almost vampiric, effects of Jason's household law, render her a bloodless or sapless thing. Playing with the civilizing pretenses of domesticity and the political meanings of Medea's ethnic otherness, Levy pits a vital barbarity against a banal civility and twists the conventions of domestic rhetoric.

Although Medea precisely detects the circumstantial origins of her alterity, she nonetheless remains subdued by persistent memories and nostalgic desires. Overhearing Jason's name spoken by Aegeus and Nikias, Medea acknowledges, "I wax white and do tremble; sudden seized / With shadowy apprehension" (36), but yields to passionate loyalties, for "woman's chiefest curse" (36), she explains, is:

> That still her constant heart clings to its love
> Through all time and all chances; while the man
> Is caught with newness; coldly calculates,
> And measures pain and pleasure, loss and gain;
> And ever grows to look with the world's eye
> Upon a woman, tho' his, body and soul. (36)

Similarly, when Medea overhears the citizens' "idle talk" describing Jason's "wise" (36) marriage alliance with Kreon (for Glaukê), she exclaims, "'Tis false, 'tis false. O Jason, they speak false!" (38). Surveying Levy's poetic oeuvre and personal life, Beckman has asserted that Levy was "obsessed by" the "theme of woman's constancy" but not necessarily "convinced of the truth of this tenet of nineteenth-century gender ideology" (95). Here, with Medea's expression of women's cursed fidelities and her disbelief at "strange rumours" (39) of Jason's betrayal, Levy establishes the sexual and material interests of heterosexual romance. When Jason, having "coldly calculate[d]" his political "loss and gain" with "the world's eye," later defines the "shadowy apprehension" with a specific decree, his callous bargains obviate romantic fidelities and domestic sentiments. In establishing her compromised status, Levy uses Medea's cloying regret to underscore the radicalism of her murderous transformation.

While Medea dramatizes the pathetic qualities of a domesticated femininity, Jason signifies the unsavory ethos of a domesticating masculinity. Neither contractually legitimate nor politically advantageous, Jason and Medea's conjugal cohabitation—a sexually but not legally consummated "marriage"—nonetheless inspires Jason to perform conventional household rituals. Jason's first words to Medea introduce his disciplinary strategies: "Your looks are wild Medea; you bring shame / Upon this house, that stand with hair unbound / Beyond the threshold. Get you in the house" (38). Preoccupied with rumors of his marriage negotiations, however, Medea remains on the threshold and struggles to activate Jason's loyalties. In addition to citing "[t]he long years passed in this Corinthian home" (39) and "[t]he great love I have borne you through the years" (39), she reminds Jason of his profound indebtedness to her:

> O strong you were; but not of such a strength
> To have escaped the doom of horrid death,
> Had not I, counting neither loss not gain,
> Shown you the way to triumph and renown. (39)

Medea's recollections incite Jason to regret and repress his former dependency. Dismissing any obligatory gratitude, he responds:

> And better had I then, a thousand times,
> Have fought with my good sword and fall'n or stood
> As the high Fates directed; than been caught
> In the close meshes of the magic web
> Wrought by your hand, dark-thoughted sorceress. (39–40)

The clash between Medea's historical memory and Jason's dismissal of her "magic web" revisits the problem of Medea's compromised subjectivity. Marking her disempowerment, Levy conspicuously downplays her magical powers in order to underscore the debilitating effects of domestication, which saps Medea of magical, psychological, and sexual force and, therefore, fortifies Jason's control.

Medea declaims her weakened state, "Lo, I who strove for strength have grown more weak / Than is the weakest" (41), and she laments the fact that her magical powers prove ineffectual—and irrelevant—in the loveless economy of the patriarchal household: "What avail / Charms, spells and potions, all my hard-won arts, / My mystic workings, seeing they cannot win / One little common spark of human love?" (41). Linking the concurrent loss of her "mystic workings" and "human love" (41), Medea registers sexual and emotional deprivation and conjures the circumstances of her careless domestic bargain ("counting neither loss nor gain") with Jason. Her now obsolete "hard-won arts" indicate an unrewarded and unacknowledged sacrifice of self, and her domestication consists of social and sexual annihilation:

> Behold me now, your work, a thing of fear—
> From natural human fellowship cut off,
> And yet a woman—sick and sore with pain;
> Hungry for love and music of men's praise,
> But walled about as with a mighty wall,
> Far from men's reach and sight, alone, alone. (41)

"[W]alled about" and "cut off" (41) from "human fellowship," "men's praise," and "love," Medea, "thing" and "woman," attributes her degraded homelife to Jason's "work." His "work," her alienation, then, does not arise as the byproduct of domestic duties but functions—quite intentionally—as the central mechanism of Jason's domestic rule. For this reason, Medea's continued speech on the home's threshold irritates Jason because it threatens the privatizing effects of his home rule. Monitored by Jason and transgressed by Medea, the threshold forms the boundary between the private and public spheres upon which Jason expects to stage his respectability and authority. Seeking to prevent an inexpedient spectacle of troubled intimacy, Jason ushers her into the home, and offsetting his self-possessed masculine poise with a reference to her compromised feminine dishevelment, he condemns her "wide-eyed, unveiled, unfilleted" (42) appearance. In this verbal skirmish, Medea's unrestrained (and notably sexualized) feminine pathos offsets Jason's disciplinary male reserve. Yet, as Nikias observes, Jason "speaks low and smooth," but "there is that within his level tones, / And in the icy drooping of his lids / (More than his words, tho' they are harsh enough) / Tells me he hates her" (40). Summing up, Nikias reads "wrath and hate and scorn" in Jason's "white cheeks" and "knitted brows" (42).

His hatred on display, Jason nonetheless attempts to defend his actions and defuse Medea's affective arguments by blurring distinctions between romantic loyalties and political advantages. He questions the sincerity of her professed love and cites her failure to embrace his public interests: "Can I deem it so, / When what does most advantage me and mine / You shrink to hear of?" (42). Seeking to temper Medea's skepticism with appeals to maternal and familial interests, he contends that his proprietary union with Glaukê constitutes an investment in Medea's and their sons' political future. Because his seemingly "hard" proposal signifies "a blessing, wrapped and cloaked about / In harsh disguisements" (43), he advises, her present submission may yield her future rule:

> And in those days Medea's sons and mine
> Shall stand at my right hand, grown great in power.
> Medea, too, if she do but control
> Her fiery spirit, may yet reign a queen
> Above this land of Corinth. I have said. (43)

Concluding his previous comments with a despotic "I have said," he likewise punctuates the announcement of his new marriage contract and the banishment of Medea and their sons:

> That I have sworn to take as wedded wife
> Glaukê, the daughter of our mighty king,
> In this, in nowise hurting you and yours.
> For you all fair provision I have made,
> So but you get beyond the city walls
> Before the night comes on. Our little ones—
> They too shall journey with you. I have said. (43)

Ironically upholding household laws at the very moment he intends to abandon them, Jason expects Medea to adhere to the private ethos of wifely sacrifice and obedience while he brokers a political marriage to secure his public influence and power. At the same time, he expects his political promises to his illegitimate and neglected family to silence opposition because framed in "I have said."

After Jason maliciously pronounces this divorce, an admiring Nikias comments, "Well said" (43), and Aegeus contends, "But none the better that 'twas false" (4). When Nikias in turn replies, "I'd sooner speak, for my part, fair than true" (44), Levy prompts readers to recognize that Jason builds his domestic autocracy upon style rather than substance. Though Nikias and Aegeus are clearly prejudicial commentators, their observations alert readers to important character details. Having emptied his words of intent, Jason appears to believe that domesticity is a fundamentally dictatorial and rhetorical endeavor. Signaling his exit and his orders with an "I have said," he simultaneously nullifies and exercises his husbandly authority. His redistribution of affections and allegiances underscores the extent to which Jason opportunistically invests in domestic authority but neglectfully shirks domestic obligations. With his insistence on disciplinary authority, his symbolically freighted decree of divorce, and his banishment of Medea and their "little ones," he unconditionally negates their conjugal union and waives away the custodial prerogatives of paternal guardianship. Divesting himself from these particular familial roles, he renders domestic sentiments and parental affections irrelevant—committing household violations most often attributed exclusively to Medea. In marked and stunning contrast, having gone from homebound to homeless, from *femme coverte* to *femme sole*, in a single decree, Medea signals her own exit not with rhetorical flourishes but with murderous actions. In a clever set of discursive inversions, Levy demonstrates that while Jason claims license to divorce, Medea claims license to kill, and, while Jason exchanges one domestic scenario for another more advantageous one, Medea rejects domesticity entirely.

In the monologue that follows Jason's bold decree, Medea metamorphoses from the downtrodden and degraded Medea to the troubling and tragic Medea of theatrical infamy. Responding to Jason's authoritative "I have said," Medea states, "As you have said, O Jason, let it be" (45) and claims not to protest a "compact never in fair justice framed" (45). But she only momentarily assumes this posture of compliance, and she immediately launches into an analysis of their sexual domestic "compact" and his political marriage plot and reveals the mocking intent of her initial "[a]s you have said":

> For you, you thought: This maid has served me well
> And yet may serve me. When I touch her palm
> The blood is set a-tingle in my veins;
> For these things I will make her body mine. (45)

While he rakishly devised a system of sexual service, Medea tells Jason, "I stood before you, clean and straight, / And looked into your eyes with eyes that spake: / Lo, utterly, for ever, I am yours" (45). Reflecting on her trampled status, Medea must retrieve her "gift"—her *self*—by "gather[ing] it up":

> And since that you, this gift I lavish laid
> Low at your feet, have lightly held and spurned—
> I in my two arms, thus, shall gather it up
> So that your feet may not encounter it
> Which is not worthy of your feet to tread! (45)

Liberated by Jason's rejection, a self-possessed Medea claims a moral integrity that dwarfs Jason's. While she elevates her love to a magnanimous gesture, a lavishly bestowed "gift," she reduces Jason to its mere unworthy recipient. Medea's earlier moments of pronounced self-abasement increase the rhetorical weight of this speech, which, beginning with a well-mannered and humble assent, concludes in exclamatory and insulting defiance.

As her monologue progresses, Medea's analytical rebuttals evolve into ominous threats, which stage the psychological transition from demoralized subordinate to murderous agent. Taking on a patronizing tone, Medea reviews Jason's domestic logic and instructs, "Yet pause a moment, Jason" and then, with even more condescension, repeats, "Ah, Jason, pause" (46). That he considered her "meek enough" and "[c]ontent with what [he] gave" (46), she explains, constitutes a gross miscalculation:

> You never knew Medea. You forget,
> because so long she bends the knee to you,
> She was not born to serfdom.
>   I have knelt
> Too long before you. I have stood too long
> Suppliant before this people. You forget
> A redder stream flows in my Colchian veins. (46)

With the retrieval of her past self—signified here, as in the opening soliloquy, by the "redder stream" in her "veins"—she finds the resources for overthrowing Jason's authority: "Now behold me free, / Ungyved by any chains of this man wrought / Nothing desiring at your hands nor his" (46). Having "[u]ngyved" herself, she transcends romantic conceits and sexual desires and enters "an awful realm / Where is nor love, nor pity, nor remorse, / Not dread, but only purpose" (47). Undistracted by domestic obligations or ethical attachments, Medea embodies only destructive "purpose." She has exchanged her sentimental haze for an angry lucidity, and she replaces a cultural fantasy of feminine compliance with a feminist fantasy of female rebellion. In contrast to Lytton's Clytemnestra, Levy's Medea threatens Jason—and the entire local system of patriarchal operations—plainly, directly, and publicly:

>   There shall be
> A horror and a horror in this land;
> Woe upon woe, red blood and biting flame;
> Most horrid death and anguish worse than death;
> Deeds that shall make the shores of Hades sound
> With murmured terror; with an awful dread

Shall move generations yet unborn:
A horror and a horror in the land. (47)

While Medea foretells the violent consequences of Jason's familial negligence, the metrics of her warning forcefully underscore the psychological momentum of her crimes. In the syncopations of "Woe upon woe, red blood and biting flame," Levy measures Medea's terrible intent. The metaphorical bloodletting of her domestication will be retributively turned back onto the wholly complicit "land."

This upsurge of verbal energy, in turn, highlights the extremes of Jason's emphasis on rhetoric over action in matters of spousal antagonism, for he categorizes her speech as a mere public raving, and, practicing his usual disciplinary methods, simply ushers Medea, once again, into the house with angry epithets and a vague warning: "Shrew, triple-linked with Hell, get you within. / Shame not my house! 'Tis your own harm you work" (47). Concluding the first scene, Jason's lines generate a pronounced incongruity. Blinded by his bargain-based understanding of domestic life and his rhetoric-based practice of spousal antagonism, Jason fails to acknowledge the emotional charge of domestic life and the psychological authenticity of Medea's "purpose." In response to her promise of "[a] horror and a horror in the land"—resonating in hell and across generations—Jason merely issues his habitual directive, "get you within," and a wholly inadequate retort, "Shame not my house!" In the contrast between Medea's exclamation of social destruction ("the land") and Jason's obsession with domestic propriety ("my house"), Levy creates a dramatic irony that attests to Jason's patriarchal folly. Attempting to enforce his husbandly authority, which, of course, he has just negated, Jason ignores the birth of murderous "purpose."

Such ironies inform the signifying power of Medea's subsequent crimes. Throughout the poem, Levy locates Medea's speeches and crimes on the threshold of the home, and, merging dramatic space and speech, she comments on the disciplinary function of separate spheres ideology. When Medea transforms the threshold of the home into a bloody scene of filicide, she literalizes both the logic and the failure of Jason's household laws. As the first scene culminates in Jason's attempts to redomesticate Medea, the second scene opens with a frenzied spectacle of their public exposure. With a "crowd of people running to and fro" (48), Nikias and Aegeus unravel a "bloody rumour" of "awful purport" (48) and mediate the details of the crime spree that bisects the text. The social aftereffects of the murder help to configure Levy's radicalized Medea plot.

In filtering the crimes through the astonished witnesses, Levy depicts the interpretive preferences and unreliable perspectives of public opinion. Nikias, who presides over the telling, ascertains that Medea has deployed her sons to murder Glaukê and Kreon and then, having used these "tender boys" as "her crime's instruments" (49), murdered them when, bewildered by events, they returned to her for solace and protection. Her crimes completed, Nikias explains, Medea deposited the bodies of these "[i]nnocent doers of most deadly deed" (50) to be discovered by Jason on "his own home's threshold" (55). Nikias, less inspired by regicide, virtually ignores the demise of Kreon and Glaukê and develops his crime narrative around the sensational scene of child-murder. Proclaiming, "I saw the deed, I, Nikias, with these eyes!" (51), he foregrounds Medea's particularly maternal violations:

> Half apprehending what thing had befallen,
> Fled forth unmarked, and all affrighted reached
> The house of Jason, where Medea stood
> Erect upon the threshold. (51)

As her sons stand "[h]iding their faces" (51) in her robe, Medea responds, "I will not have ye, for I love ye not!" (52). Nikias's credibility notwithstanding, his account—the only account—of the infanticide sharpens the edge of Levy's critique. Notably absent are the Euripidean antecedents: Medea's expressions of motherly hesitation and the fretful death cries of her protesting children. With these absences—and Medea's "I love ye not!"—Levy enforces the notion of dreadful "purpose." With her subsequent actions, also narrated by Nikias, Medea actualizes her stark rejection of maternal affection with a double murder:

> Forth from her gathered garment swiftly drew
> A thing that gleamed and glinted; in the air
> she held it poised an instant; then—O gods!
> How shall I speak it?—on the marble floor
> Was blood that streamed and spurted; blood that flow'd
> From two slain, innocent babes! (52)

As the scandal-mongering Nikias revels in the narrative and verbal tropes of crime reporting and as his interlocutor, Aegeus, seeks to absorb and assess the spectacular details of a knife "that gleamed and glinted" and of "blood that streamed and spurted," Levy addresses the semiotic processes of publicity. Nikias can fully—and enthusiastically—articulate the status of Medea's bloody victims but not the details of the murder ("How shall I speak it?"). Significantly, however, Nikias subsequently records the strange sounds of Medea's murderous fury. Above the crowd's "wail / Of lamentation" (53), he recalls, "[a] fierce long shriek, that froze the blood i' the veins, / Rang out and rose, cleaving the topmost cloud"

(53). As the transcendent shriek of the killer obscures the mournful wail of the crowd, Levy once again implicates Medea's murderous "purpose." Emanating from the adversarial endgame of domestic strife, her "purpose" disentangles her from social sympathies and domestic pieties. Paradoxically, the inarticulate shriek manages to articulate the profound alienation of the wife-turned-criminal in a way that conventional crime narratives, such as that put forth by Nikias, cannot.

In fact, throughout the public's crime reporting, Levy insists that amongst the characters of the play, the symbolic power of Medea's crimes remain obscured. Aegeus, expressing "woe" for "the state," "Kreon slain," "hapless Glaukê," and "our Jason," assigns "three times woe for her that did the deed— / Her womanhood sham'd; her children basely wrong'd" (48). Scripting her motives according to the conventions of romantic tragedies, he situates the murders within the context of spurned love: "'[t]was her love / That wrought the deed—evil, yet wrought for love" (49). Favoring melodrama, a dismissive Nikias replies, "Spare me such love" (49), and proceeds to document Medea's maternal villainy. He recalls a "summer's morn" on which she "looked into [her son's] eyes, / Not gladly, as a mother with her child, / But stirred by some strange passion; then the boy / Cried out with terror, and Medea wept" (50). As a result, Nikias "never yet could deem, / Ev'n ere the horror, that Medea held / The love of human mothers in her breast" (49). In the end, Nikias's persuasive reading prevails, and Aegeus concedes, "You judged this thing aright; / This woman was dark and evil in her soul; / Black to her fiend-heart's root; a festering plague / In our fair city's midst" (54). Espousing a "fiend heart" theory of her crimes, Nikias and Aegeus categorize her criminality as innate rather than circumstantial, and their shared misjudgments force readers to consider and question the epistemological barriers of gender politics.

The public's errant logics and mistaken conclusions, in fact, cast into relief the symbolic power of Medea's crimes. The threshold theatrics of the poem's domestic cruelties and crimes resonate fully with Victorian conceptions of the architecture of the home. While the home's interior gathered "nook and nest" associations, the home's threshold possessed signifying powers of its own. In *Family Fortunes* (1987), Davidoff and Hall reflect on the threshold indicators of private and public space in Victorian England: "Clean steps, doors, and window ledges, gleaming brass knockers, and starched white curtains dramatically demonstrated the break between private rectitude and public squalor" (382). Reversing this semiotic equation, Levy offers a picture of private squalor and public rectitude—stunningly embodied in the corpses of Jason's banished boys sprawled on "his own home's threshold." Their corpses embody the negating powers of his banishment. Thus counterposing the inauthenticity of Jason's public rectitude and the sincerity of Medea's domestic dejection, Levy indicts the material consequences of Jason's household law more than she denounces or sensationalizes Medea's crimes. In pairing Medea's violent extremism with Jason's domestic despotism, Levy complicates the equations of provocation and culpability and introduces mitigations such as those entertained by Mill, who argued, "The despotism of Louis XVI was not the despotism of Philippe le Bel, or of Nadir Shah, or of Caligula; but it was bad enough to justify the French Revolution, and to palliate even its horrors" (286). Because the children's bloody bodies saturate the home's threshold, the staging ground for Jason's despotic husbanding throughout the drama, Medea's infanticides symbolize a brutal and revolutionary comeuppance.

As Armstrong has suggested, Levy's *Medea* appears "to rationalise and justify feminine violence," to represent the "destructive impulse of the rejected," and to dramatize "the fury and anguish of the woman who is dispossessed and denied" (*Victorian Poetry* 375). One of her most interesting accomplishments in this regard is Levy's savvy ability to objectify and thus critique the maternal politics that invariably come to bear on representations of child-murder and of Medea. With her intricate alignments of domesticity and spectacle, she manages to foreground paternal politics and patriarchal policies. She accomplishes this in part because she courts readerly sympathies and skepticism when she mediates Medea's crimes through the perspective of the always crude and presumptuous Nikias. But she also insists that while Medea's crimes grotesquely renounce all ordering principles of familial sentiment and domestic rectitude, Jason's autocratic neglect and his arrogant decrees precede Medea's violent crimes in rendering such ideals illusory and defunct. Presenting domestic ideals as expedient methods for organizing and hierarchizing gendered relations, Levy links the politics of infanticide to the politics of marriage in order to launch her thoroughly feminist critique of domesticity.[32]

As Thaïs Morgan has commented, "As with divorce, so infanticide raises the question of the distribution of the power between the sexes. The child holds a special position at the intersection of the capitalist economy and the gender economy that structured Victorian society. Who produces, owns, and manages a child, and through the child, the future of society: the man or the woman?" (294). Levy emphasizes these predicaments of household management with a simple plot: Jason banishes his children, and Medea murders them. Only when Medea thus forcefully redistributes domestic power does Jason relinquish his claims to discipline and punish Medea. Nikias narrates Jason's public decree at the crime scene when it becomes apparent that Medea has escaped:

"Let no man seek this woman; blood enough
Has stained our city. Let the furies rend

Her guilty soul; nor we pollute our hands
With her accursèd body . . ." (54)

With his matrimonial and political aspirations wholly thwarted, a humbled and humiliated Jason transfers authority to the furies, and, attempts, once again, to leverage some public power via rhetorical force. Contrasting their pure citizenship with Medea's defiled criminality, he invokes stock formulae of public outrage and personal insult.

At the end of the second scene, Levy shifts locales, and we see Medea speaking from "outside the city." No well-connected sorceress escaping in a god-sanctioned chariot, this Medea lurks alone in the dark "beyond men's eyes, beyond / The city's hissing hate" (55). Defamiliarizing the classical Medea in this way, Levy substitutes somber defeat for tragic vengeance. Medea speaks of her time in Corinth as the dream of a woman who "strove and wept and yearned for love / In a fair city" and who "was blind indeed" (55). "I have fought with the Fates / And I am vanquished utterly" (55), she proclaims, and, as in *Clytemnestra,* this fated universe bespeaks the hegemony of domestic imperatives, which nurture despots and expel dissidents:

> This is the end:
> I have dash'd my heart against a rock; the blood
> Is drain'd and flows no more; and all my breast
> Is emptied of its tears.
> Thus go I forth
> Into the deep, dense heart of the night—alone. (56)

Medea is, once again, engaged in lonely soliloquy, and the social and psychological status of Levy's fugitive Medea, drained of blood and tears, precisely parallels that of the housebound Medea, who, "lone and weary and sad" (33), lamented her dejection at the opening of the play. In rendering the domesticated wife and the escaped murderer in like terms, Levy provocatively parallels the social annihilation of wives and murderers. In her evolution from housewife to killer to fugitive, Medea's status does not change.

This grim conclusion forcefully reveals the extent of Levy's feminist critique. For Levy, a renegotiation of domestic arrangements, such as that attempted by Lytton's Clytemnestra, offers no solution to the injustices of household law, which casts women as the loveless and unloved objects in a series of unequal exchanges. With the outlaw Medea lurking on the margins of the city in painful solitude, Levy continues to engage the poetics and politics of affect that inform her rereading of Euripides' Medea. While Medea's murderous rage allows Levy to render the psychological devastation of her domestication and banishment in the terrible images of terrible crimes, Medea's quiet fugitive despair represents the complete negation of the feminine. Casting Medea in such stark terms, Levy's *Medea* enacts a wholesale dismissal of Victorian domesticity and rigorously disavows any possibility for reformed alternatives.[33]

The Politics of Genre: The Murderous Scandal and the "Cool Queer Tale"

In scrutinizing marriage and murder, Browning, Lytton, and Levy each organize their poetic resources differently. While *The Ring and the Book,* versifying the found curiosity of a bookstall, deploys narrative polyphony and symmetry, *Clytemnestra* and *Medea* condense and compress the grand stage tragedies of ancient Greece. Yet, collectively their texts exhibit striking consistencies. They share a common thematic interest in dramatizing the bad bargains of married couples, the psychological effects of marital yokes, and the immense pressures of household law. Such commonalities alert us to central anxieties of marriage law and domestic ideology in Victorian England. Aligning these three different representations of domestic murder from three different decades allows us to see particularly poetic approaches to exploring the problem of marriage reform and divorce law, to plot some ideological consistencies across time and texts, and to observe how the same legal and cultural problems lingered unresolved for several decades.

On the most fundamental level, murder offers a way of interrogating the disciplinary functions of marriage law and domestic ideology—of imagining homes, to use Stallybrass and White's phrasing, as "discursive sites where social classification and psychological processes are generated as conflictual complexes" (25). In murderous scenarios, the fictions of homelife—from the legal notions of *coverture* and marital unity to the sentimental notions of separate spheres and paternal protection—lose their force. In their murder plots, Browning, Lytton, and Levy imagine spousal combat in the context of public pressures and personal frustrations. As they insist on the emotional extremes and psychological problems of the home, they contest the two most popular social models of domesticity; for, in these poems, the soothing effects of "home-sanctitudes" and the "softening effects" of disciplinary yokes are entirely absent. Instead, domesticity functions as a kind of house arrest, and, similarly, marriage, with its "galling" yokes and hierarchical imperatives, always appears, on some level, to be the primary culprit and the determining force in cases of outrageous violence: it is the "knot / Which nothing cuts except this kind of knife."

The breeding of violent offenders in the home, of course, clearly challenges stock formulations of criminality, which frequently expressed crime as a condition of modern decay and imagined criminals emerging from urban squalor. And, as each of these poems depicts the home as a symbolically resonant locale that operates as both a cause and a site of murder, their bloodied interiors and thresholds overturn the binaries of domestic purity and public corruption. While the domestic sites and scenes of crime clearly jettison ideological constructions of a domestic idyll, they even more pointedly exploit and critique the discourse of adversarial marriage and the reverence for "mutual accommodation." As murderers forcefully and authoritatively explicate their motivations and expectations, they claim their crimes as the distinct features of domestic arrangements. At the same time, however, operating within a prisonhouse of legal barriers and ideological controls, these killers depict their crimes as symbolically appropriate modes of redress or singularly available acts of resistance to an uncompromising law.

In depicting ominous links between marital unhappiness and murderous agency, these poets draw upon the performative features of poetic voice and the discursive significance of poetic genre. With respect to murder, their poems, unlike the poems discussed in previous chapters, have little interest in obscuring the origins of murderous subjectivity, in introducing the possibilities of criminal lunacy, or in diminishing the processes of premeditation. Instead, the home provides a contextualized understanding of intimate struggles between individuals and institutions, which, in turn, inflect intimate struggles between murderers and their victims. Murderers' soliloquies and murder-victim dialogues analyze murderous motive and opportunity as the particular effects of domestic ideology, matrimonial law, and gender inequality.

The focused and frank expressions of murderers and their crimes are then set against the wayward and contrived commentaries of the public. Interrogating the modes and manners of public opinion, Browning, Lytton, and Levy carefully enfold the voices of witnesses and voyeurs, who, representing the ill-informed and widely disseminated speculations of their Victorian counterparts, articulate muddled social investments in marital yokes and domestic rectitude. These poets therefore scrutinize rather than affirm the codes of legal melodrama and sensational scandal. Recalling Browning's emphatic directive, "Examine it yourselves!" (I.38), the integration of formal techniques and political content forces readers to consider the play of gender and genre in representations and misrepresentations of marriages and murders.

The particular generic characteristics, instructive agendas, and critical postures of these texts become even clearer when placed within a wider historical network of domestic murder poems. Just as these poets looked back to glimpse literary and legal precedents, we might look forward to speculate about the interconnections of literary development and cultural change. Offering a coda to this study of nineteenth-century representations of domestic crime, a speculative but suggestive discussion of Thomas Hardy's short lyric poem, "Her Second Husband Hears Her Story" (1928), casts into relief the distinct generic and political priorities of its fully public and extremely bloody Victorian counterparts. Published in the 1920s, when cultural reconsiderations of marriage, divorce, and remarriage had shifted away from the noisy outcries and anxious tones of the nineteenth century, "Her Second Husband Hears Her Story" images marriage and murder in private and lyrical tones. Hardy's claim that the poem represents "a true story" situates his text, perhaps disingenuously, as a social record rather than a social argument.[34]

The poem presents a bedtime conversation between a wife and her second husband in which the wife explains how she killed her first husband by stitching him too tightly to their bed, the very one upon which the newlyweds now sit in conversation. The second husband, incredulous and puzzled, exclaims, "I do not see how / How you could do it, seeing what might betide" (4–5). The wife replies that her crime originated in her fear of his habitual drunken abuse after "he came home one midnight, liquored deep— / Worse than I'd known— / And lay down heavily, and soundly slept" (6–8). Fearful that he might "wake up, and attempt embracing" (24), she practically employs her domestic skills to protect herself:

> Then, desperate driven, I thought of it, to keep
> Him from me when he woke. Being an adept
>
> With needle and thimble, as he snored, click-click
>   An hour I'd sewn,
> Till, had he roused, he couldn't have moved from bed,
> So tightly laced in sheet and quilt and tick
> He lay. And in the morning he was dead. (9–15)

She covers up her crime by simply removing the stitches "[e]re people came" (16), and his death "thus 'twas shown to be a stroke" (18).

The crime brings about no public upheaval, only the husband's comment that "it sounds strange—told here and now to me" (20). Her second husband does, however, attempt to interpret her actions through legal definitions of homicidal intent. He asks, "Did you intend his death by your tight lacing?" (21). The wife replies with an ambiguous "O, that I cannot own" (22). The husband's conclusion, and the last line of the poem, is simply: "Well, it's a cool queer tale!" (25). While criminal intent remains unstated, in linking domestic labor and crafty resistance, the poem wryly reimagines the exercise of household duty as a form of murderous agency. As the housewife constitutes a potential threat in an intimate disguise, the subdued conversation and lyrical inflections of the poem leave open the question of whether the wife seeks to confess a bad memory or issue a subtle warning. With this ambiguity, Hardy's "Her Second Husband Hears Her Story" illustrates an alternate take on wife-abuse and husband-murder; in this case, murder, like marriage, is very practical and very private.[35]

The quiet and private act of murder committed by an abused wife, now enjoying her second marriage, also suggests the evolution of marriage discourse and the shifting importance of publicity. Hardy's decision to write an often sensationalized crime as an unplanned sewing project highlights by contrast the aggressively public voices and political interventions of Victorian poems—in which speakers voiced extended monologues about murderous motive and denounced the domestic bargains necessitating their crimes. Attentive to such cultural changes, Hardy, no stranger to Victorian representations of violent marriages and sexual outrages, enacts an ironic inversion of domestic ideology: no longer requiring the fully legible expressions of the knife, murder becomes the silent work of "needle and thimble." And no longer demanding a public reckoning or confronting an astonished community, the murderer refuses to unequivocally "own" or refute any malicious intentions behind the "click click" that brings her snoring husband to his end. In its privatization of domestic tragedy, "Her Second Husband Hears Her Story" allows us to trace the generic contours of domestic discord from the old traditions of *honoris causa* to the revolutionary aspirations of "high justice" to the pragmatic remedy of the "cool queer tale." With this comparison in mind, we might speculate about how the dialectical relations between genre and discourse in turn signal the historical relationships between poetic form and cultural content, and how the heights of domestic romance and the depths of domestic conflict allowed poets to examine the epistemological and legal contingencies of murder and the subjectivities and identities of murderers.

⇥ Epilogue ⇤

The criminal classes are so close to us that even the policeman can see them.
They are so far away from us that only the poet can understand them.

—Oscar Wilde, "A Few Maxims for the Instruction of the Over-Educated"

A SITE OF EXPRESSIVE DIFFICULTIES and epistemological struggles, a sublime transgression and a capital offense, a modern content and a poetic enterprise, murder supplies ample evidence of Victorian poetry's "aestheticised politics" and "politicised aesthetics." With measured representations of stabbings, stranglings, smotherings, poisonings, bludgeonings, and drownings, poets used the characteristic particularity and performativity of poetic form to highlight the politics of interpretation and explore the play of genre. In commending modes of cultural and textual analysis that exchange the abstract for the particular, Gallagher and Greenblatt celebrate the allure of the "encounter with the singular, the specific, and the individual" (6). These terms, and their analytical implications, aptly describe the disruptive presence of murder poems amongst the ideologies, institutions, and disciplines informing and regulating criminal discourse.

Exchanging the abstract for the particular, murders in verse, variously mediated through the elaboration of bloody details, lyrical confessions, metrical ironies, suggestive rhymes, structural ambiguities, dramatic soliloquies, legal testimonies, discursive hybrids, and generic combinations, reveal the extent to which the formal features and generic conventions of poetry generated opportunities for cultural critique and poetic experimentation. Set within a self-consciously modern culture, which was continually and publicly reevaluating its methods of disciplining criminals and controlling crime, murder poems—as double forms, verbal technologies, and performative speech—rather mischievously administered overwhelming doses of psychological details and intimate circumstances. In doing so, they exposed and interrogated the fictions and abstractions of criminal theories, policies, and laws.

Attentive to the historicity of poetry and murder, we can look beyond intimations of "transhistorical truth"—and rethink the stability of transhistorical themes—and instead highlight "historically embedded social and psychological formations" (Gallagher and Greenblatt 7). In Stallybrass and White's formulation, this allows us to see the poetics and politics of murder as an encounter with the cultural embeddedness of "conflictual complexes." In the poetry under discussion here, "historically embedded social and psychological formations" and "conflictual complexes" are directly and explicitly considered. Going well beyond transmitting ideology in "subtle or covert" fashion, they position themselves skeptically and polemically with respect to other legal, political, and aesthetic representations of murder. According to Gallagher and Greenblatt, the "commitment to particularity" and the recovery of "dense networks of particulars" (19) in New Historicist methodology protects against the loss of intricate meanings and local details. A similar kind of historicism is encouraged by all of the poems examined here. Most explicitly rendered in the advertised "full particulars" of astonishing disclosures, a resistance to abstraction and authority extends to the intimate psychological struggles of the criminal poet, the expressive idiosyncrasies of dramatic speakers, the hybrid innovations of the verse novel, and the modern renovations of ancient tragedies.

Finding poetic materials in the unsettled and unsettling epistemologies of murder, these poems also establish the cultural engagements and cultural politics of Victorian verse. As Antony Harrison argues, "encounters with poetic texts were an unusually complex psychological and emotional event for nineteenth-century readers. This was true not only because of the anticipated formal difficulties of such texts but also because of the widespread expectations that poetic words on a page *meant* a good deal more than other writing: they embodied the voice of a being possessed of extraordinary epistemological capacities" (10). While Harrison is primarily concerned with the middle-class experience of reading poetry, his comments have particular resonance for all of the poems examined in this book, as they establish a "productive friction" (Hadley 10) between low content and high form—and often thwart the very expectations that Harrison illustrates. In linking the domains of high literature and the politics of sensational curiosity, we find, then, another manifestation of poetry's double form. Through the suggestive interplay of discourse and genre, through the semiotic operations of content and form, these texts extended the "cultural work" of poetic representation and established its modern content.

With an epigrammatic shorthand, Wilde, offering (much-needed) instruction to the "over-educated" and differentiating the scrutiny of the poet from the surveillance of the police, challenges the myopic failings of a disciplinary state and grants the poet the capacity for understanding and interpreting crime. In more subtle and less comical ways, the poems of this study both claim and challenge expressive sensibilities and interpretive power. Leveraging generic difference—for the purposes of political appropriation and contestation, generic variety and hybridity, and verbal particularity and incommensurability—poets adapt a variety of aesthetic modes (the sublime, the grotesque, the melodramatic, the tragic) and assume a variety of counterdiscursive stances as they reconsider the congruities and incongruities of crime and culture.

Historicizing murder and poetry, by examining dialectical relations between genre and discourse, we can begin to recover neglected texts, and, recognizing and acknowledging associations among major and minor, canonical and non-canonical, anonymous and notorious poets, we can reconsider lines of literary influence and retrace paths of intertextuality in ways that expand the terrain of Victorian poetry studies. While *Crime in Verse* has relied upon a relatively small set of close and contextualized readings to make its arguments, its methods and its conclusions support a broader reexamination of poetic representations of murder. Answering Armstrong's call for studies in poetic networking, we might assemble or imagine networks of murder poems. However speculative or contingent, such assemblages might highlight the occasions on which the sound effects and the staged authority of verse were publicized and rhetorically posed. We might, for example, revisit the verse editorials of daily newspapers or the singsong communiqués of "Jack the Ripper." Or, preferring more established poets, we might return to Wordsworth's *Sonnets upon the Punishment of Death* (1841), in which the intellectual precision, iambic cadences, and rhyming couplets of the sonneteer are used to insult the sloppy sentimentality and reform-minded aspirations of abolitionist parliamentarians and pamphleteers. Or, enjoying poetic scandal and humiliation, we might reconsider Sydney Dobell's *Balder* (1854), in which, suffering emotional traumas and generating textual confusion, the frustrated and "felonious" (281) speaker finds murderous motive in poetic ambition. As these brief references, and the preceding chapters, suggest there is much work to be done on the topic of crime in verse.

Notes

Introduction

1. For studies of the interdisciplinary and ideological features of criminal discourse in nineteenth century England, see Michel Foucault, *Discipline and Punish: The Birth of the Prison;* Marie-Christine Leps, *Apprehending the Criminal: The Production of Deviance in Nineteenth-Century Discourse;* Martin J. Wiener, *Reconstructing the Criminal: Culture, Law and Policy in England, 1830–1914* and *Men of Blood: Violence, Manliness and Criminal Justice in Victorian England;* and Judith Rowbotham and Kim Stevenson, *Criminal Conversations: Victorian Crimes, Social Panic, and Moral Outrage.*

2. This list cites only a few notable examples of the kinds of scholarly work that shape our notions of literary crime—the chapters of this book offer a more complete picture. While many of these studies focus exclusively on the novel, important interdisciplinary projects, such as Jan-Melissa Schramm's *Testimony and Advocacy in Victorian Law, Literature, and Theology* and Simon Joyce's *Capital Offenses: Geographies of Class and Crime in Victorian London,* also contribute substantially to our understandings of narrative representation and criminal discourse.

3. Subsequent chapters acknowledge the particularities and develop the insights of these studies of crime poetry, but I include a brief list here. Increasingly refined and focused studies of the narrative, dramatic, and lyrical dimensions of Robert Browning's murder poems extend from Robert Langbaum's *The Poetry of Experience: The Dramatic Monologue in Modern Literary Tradition* to the section entitled "Browning's Ring Around a Murder" in Alexander Welsh's *Strong Representations* to Melissa Valiksa Gregory's "Robert Browning and the Lure of the Violent Lyric Voice: Domestic Violence and the

Dramatic Monologue." Studies of Barrett Browning's treatment of gendered crimes include Margaret Reynolds's annotated edition of *Aurora Leigh;* Amanda Anderson's chapter, "Reproduced in Finer Motions: Encountering the Fallen in Barrett Browning's *Aurora Leigh*" in *Tainted Souls and Painted Faces;* Marjorie Stone's "Between Ethics and Anguish: Feminist Ethics, Feminist Aesthetics, and Representations of Infanticide in 'The Runaway Slave at Pilgrim's Point' and *Beloved*" and "Genre Subversion and Gender Inversion: *The Princess* and *Aurora Leigh*"; E. Warwick Slinn's chapter, "The Mark as Matrix: Subject(ion) and Agency in Barrett Browning's 'The Runaway Slave at Pilgrim's Point'" in *Victorian Poetry as Cultural Critique;* Elizabeth H. Battles's "Slavery Through the Eyes of a Mother: 'The Runaway Slave at Pilgrim's Point'"; Sarah Brophy's "Elizabeth Barrett Browning's 'The Runway Slave at Pilgrim's Point' and the Politics of Interpretation"; and Ann Parry's "Sexual Exploitation and Freedom: Religion, Race, and Gender in Elizabeth Barrett Browning's 'The Runaway Slave at Pilgrim's Point.'" Analyses of Oscar Wilde's ballad include Seamus Heaney's "Speranza in Reading: On 'The Ballad of Reading Gaol'"; Leonard Nathan's "The Ballads of Reading Gaol: At the Limits of the Lyric"; Karen Alkalay-Gut's "The Thing He Loves: Murder as Aesthetic Experience in 'The Ballad of Reading Gaol'"; and Regenia Gagnier's chapter, "Art for Love's Sake: 'Salome' and 'Reading Gaol'" in *Idylls of the Marketplace.*

Chapter 1

1. Crime ballads were part of a much larger broadside trade, which comprised many genres and covered numerous topics. Execution ballads in particular contributed significantly to the cultural experience of capital punishment and flourished until just after public executions ended in 1868. Rather than repeating basic information about broadsides and ballads, this chapter builds upon existing histories in order to focus on devising and applying new critical strategies. For histories of the broadside trade, see Hindley's *History of the Catnach Press* and *Life and Times of James Catnach;* Shepard's *History of Street Literature, John Pitts, Ballad Printer,* and *The Broadside Ballad;* and Hepburn's recent study, *A Book of Scattered Leaves.* For a discussion Irish street ballads, see Georges Denis Zimmerman's *Songs of Irish Rebellion.*

2. Woodcuts were not fabricated to depict specific crimes or executions, but, rather, were used repeatedly and often incongruously. Prose reports contained information gleaned from trial coverage and public discussion. The separate authorship of the ballad, its visibility on the page, its audibility in the streets, and its inconsistencies in the use of woodcut images and journalistic prose make the case for individual ballads as independent texts, and, accordingly, this chapter focuses on the verse forms of the broadside trade. The specific publication year of a ballad is not always indicated. Whenever possible, I have dated ballads from newspaper coverage of crimes, trials, and executions.

3. While ballad historians typically describe them as working-class "hacks" making little more than a shilling per song, in 1861 the *National Review* extolled their gothic everyman qualities: "That self-denying mind, indifferent to worldly fame, which characterised the architects of our cathedrals and abbeys, would seem to have descended on our ballad-writers" ("Street Ballads" 409). In response to the statement, "Oh, anybody writes them," the author notes, "we walk about the streets with a new sense of wonder, peering

into the faces of those of our fellow-lieges who do not carry about with them the external evidence of overflowing exchequers, and saying to ourselves, 'That man may be a writer of ballads'" (410).

Many publishers, with the exceptions of the notorious James Catnach and John Pitts, have fallen into obscurity as well. Hindley, Shepard, and Hepburn discuss ballad publishers and writers in their histories. See also Hughes's "Foreword" in *Curiosities of Street Literature;* Mayhew's *London Labour and the London Poor;* Vincent's *Literacy and Popular Culture in England;* Gretton's *Murders and Moralities;* James's *Print and the People;* and Vicinus's *Broadsides of the Industrial North.* For details about John Morgan, a known Victorian ballad writer, and for a full discussion of class, audience, and authorship, see Hepburn's *A Book of Scattered Leaves.*

4. As cheap ephemera, broadsheets were discarded by consumers and were rarely collected by libraries. For years, contemporary scholars have had to labor to read a full selection, but that problem is now being remedied as libraries make their broadside collections available online. While anthologies, such as Hindley's, have made these texts available, they have also fostered a habit of generalizing about thousands of texts by reading a very small proportion of the originals. Because printers produced hundreds and hundreds of crime ballads, including multiple songs for each crime and each execution, conjectures that they are uniform and undifferentiated are inaccurate. My analysis selects a relative few of the many hundreds that I have examined in order to focus on instances in which the ballads play with genre codes in the most aesthetically striking and politically resonant ways. These examples of generic play and political critique, however, are by no means rare, and they demonstrate that the generic codes of the street ballad produced and inspired poetic tinkering and innovation, political innuendo and analysis, and ethical interrogation and dissent.

5. Several contemporary studies have reviewed the methodologies of Mayhew. In addition to Joyce's commentary in *Capital Offenses,* see Anne Humpherys's *Travels in the Poor Man's Country: The Work of Henry Mayhew;* Gertrude Himmelfarb's *The Idea of Poverty;* and Deborah Epstein Nord's "The Social Explorer as Anthropologist." For a concise discussion of "criminal conversations" and the "rhetoric of reassurance" across a range of texts, including Mayhew's, see David Taylor's "Beyond the Bounds of Respectable Society" in Rowbotham and Stevenson's *Criminal Conversations.*

6. David Philips identifies this writer as Archibald Alison, "Sheriff of Lanarkshire, High Tory and arch-opponent of trade-unions" (82).

7. Charles Smith's account of the ballad trade explains the devalued labor of the ballad writer: "The established honorarium for a new song is a shilling, though eighteen pence is sometimes given for something 'particular spicy.' This miserable payment is defended by the publisher on the ground that, whatever he pays for a song, he cannot make it his own. 'If I print a new song,' says he, 'on Wednesday, my neighbor is selling it on Thursday. How can I afford to pay for property which is at another man's use as it is at mine?'" (254). The *National Review* reports that ballad writers could not support themselves in the trade (unless they sang and sold copies of their texts after printing) because "the price of an original ballad, in these buying-cheap days, has been screwed down by publishers to somewhere about a shilling sterling" ("Street Ballads" 409). The author of "The Poetry of Seven Dials" reports: "If one of the patterers writes a Ballad on a taking subject, he hastens at once to Seven Dials, where, if accepted, his reward is 'a glass of rum,

a slice of cake, and five dozen copies,'—which, if the accident or murder be a very awful one, are struck off for him while he waits" (404). Vincent explains that ballad writers were "remunerated at a level well below that of the average factory worker. It was a trade founded in pennies" (200).

8. Because of their "come all ye" introductions ("attend all you feeling parents dear," "you kindest fathers, tender mothers," "you feeling Christians," "good people") and pat conclusions ("hanging is too good for such a villain," "she her desserts will get," or "the blood of the murdered will not cry in vain"), Gatrell describes crime ballads as "objective correlatives" of "acquiescence, approval, identification with the law" (156). Reflections on generic regularity highlight a lack of political currency in textual codes that have not changed in "some two hundred years" (169). For similar reasons, Neuburg critiques their "muted" politics ("Literature of the Streets" 197), Cooper sees their "thread[s] of didactic quality" as collectively "confirm[ing] the lesson of the gallows" (26), and Kalikoff reads them as "moral fable[s]" that reassure audiences that "criminals are always subdued by society" (14–15). Casting crime ballads as working-class failures and novels as middle-class achievements, Grossman dismisses them as a "ritualized and unindividualized" whole, "indoctrinating docility" and "inculcat[ing]" only one 'right' response to the punishment of vastly different people and crimes" (29). Kalikoff grants a historical dynamism to street balladry, but, relying on Hindley's anthologized selection and understanding ballads as simple melodramas, her study, like the others mentioned here, does not account for the sheer variety of street ballads or the case-specific details of particular crimes and trials.

9. For another example of self-referential and self-parodying ballad humor, see "Trial and Execution of Betty the Cook, Who was Tried by the Servants in the Kitchen, and Executed in the Scullery, for Lying Too Long in Bed in the Morning."

10. Hindley notes that spells of good behavior sometimes required the publication of fictional "cocks" in order to sustain business: "the patterer must live; and lest the increase of public virtue should condemn him to starvation, the 'Seven Dials Press' stepped forward to his aid, and considerately supplied him with—'cocks'" (Hindley, *Life* 361). For a discussion of "cocks," see Hepburn's *Book of Scattered Leaves*.

11. This line features Hamlet's reference to the power of the play to uncover the truth about his uncle's crime and his father's murder. Its suggestion that truth can be found through the *representation* of crime resonates with the analytical aesthetic of these "astonishing disclosures."

12. An excerpt from this *Times* report is also cited in Wiener's *Men of Blood* (140–41).

13. See also Margaret Arnot's "The Murder of Thomas Sandles: Meanings of a Mid-Nineteenth-Century Infanticide" and Cath Quinn's "Images and Impulses: Representations of Puerperal Insanity and Infanticide in late Victorian England." For discussions of legal and medicolegal developments, see Roger Smith's *Trial by Medicine*, Nigel Walker's *Crime and Insanity in England*, and J. P. Eigen's *Witnessing Insanity: Madness and Mad-Doctors in the English Court*.

14. As Jill L. Matus has argued, wet-nursing inspired particular moral judgments about sexual fallenness, innate criminality, and social contagion. Paraphrasing C. H. F. Routh's alarmist discussion of wet-nursing in *The Lancet* in 1859, Matus summarizes the biological questions underlying his theories: "If blood was the medium through which the

inheritance of criminality or insanity was passed, was not milk a vital and essential fluid like blood?" (161).

15. At Brough's trial, Dr. Forbes Winslow testified that she exhibited the signs of a "structurally disorganized" brain and experienced a case of "transient insanity" during which she killed her children ("Recent Trials" 616). Her prior good mothering and her medical history were cited as evidence of a temporary insanity. Two other psychologists concurred at trial. After the case sparked controversy, Winslow explained:

> In discussing the merits of this case, much stress has been laid upon the alleged immoral character of Mrs. Brough. It has been asserted that she was a depraved woman; that she was detected in an act of gross infidelity; and fearing the consequences of her vice, she, from a feeling of revenge, deliberately and premeditatively sacrificed the lives of her children, and then attempted her own! We do not deny that she was an adulteress; but if we are to form our judgment of her moral character from the evidence adduced at the trial, she is certainly not the horribly depraved woman represented by those who have severely animadverted upon her escape from the extreme penalty of the law. (622)

He went on to dismiss claims that moral lassitude made her responsible for her own mental breakdown: "we dismiss altogether the argument of Mrs. Brough's legal accountability, based upon the presumption that her insanity was self-created, and the result of an habitual indulgence of a criminal passion" (625). After her death in Bethlem in 1862, an autopsy "revealed blood clots in her brain, which Dr. Hood correlated with a partial paralysis evident before the crime" (Smith, *Trial* 57).

16. By the mid-1850s, psychological readings of women's violence were not out of keeping with general sentiment. Smith explains, "Femaleness was a major element in medico-legal decisions. Female criminal lunatics came nearest to enabling medical discourse to describe legally exculpatory conditions. This reflected a shared assumption that woman was closer to nature than man; medical discourse was therefore more appropriate to women's lives" (*Trial* 160). However, this ballad significantly rejects melodramatic polarities and strict notions of individual responsibility in a case where these definitions were hotly debated. It avoids, for example, the sensationalizing of the adulterous affair, unlike the *Times*, which highlighted the "circumstances" that surrounded the crime as having "no parallel in the history of crime" (*Times*, 10 August 1854, 11).

17. Emma Pitt's case also raised questions about adequate charges and appropriate punishments. As Marland explains, "the severity of the penalty for infanticide, death by hanging, compared with the mildness of the punishment for concealment was picked out as a particular failing of the law" (170). For a discussion of concealment and murder, long-contested in English law, see Mark Jackson, *New-Born Child Murder: Women, Illegitimacy and the Courts in Eighteenth-Century England*, and Peter C. Hoffer and N. E. H. Hull's *Murdering Mothers: Infanticide in England and New England 1558–1803*.

18. Newspaper reports of the case used multiple spellings, including Duggan, Duggin, and Duggen.

19. In the nine years between 1826 and 1835, England saw 514 executions, with multiple executions fairly common (Gatrell 617). In marked contrast, in the thirty-one years between 1837 and 1868, 347 murderers were hanged in public (594).

20. For examples of broadside ballads accommodating multiple hangings, see "A Copy of Verses on those Under Sentence of Death" printed on the broadside "Sentences of the Prisoners at the Old Bailey Sessions, September 12" (1824), and "The Sorrowful Lamentation and Last Farewell to the World of Eight Unhappy People, Who Are to Die at the Old Bailey, on Tuesday the First."

21. This was the case until the Criminal Evidence Act passed in 1898 and granted defendants the right to testify under oath on their behalf even while retaining counsel. For a summary of debates surrounding the passage of the Prisoner's Counsel Act, see Cairns's *Advocacy and the Making of the Criminal Trial, 1800–1865*. See also Emsley's *Crime and Society in England, 1750–1900*.

22. Because ballad authors are unknown and because the illusion of criminal authorship is crucial for the meaning of these texts, I refer to the fictive authors, the featured criminal poets, as the speakers throughout the chapter.

23. The effect of anonymous authorship has particular significance in the first-person ballads since it upholds the marketing illusion that these expressive verse autobiographies emanated from the desperate minds of condemned criminals. These reality effects have not been treated explicitly in ballad criticism, and, in fact, authorial anonymity contributed to their obscurity in contemporary scholarship. In the absence of specific authorship, ballad scholars have sometimes drawn on publisher's politics and histories, particularly those of James Catnach and John Pitts, for interpretation. Other critics stress rhetorical forms and generic conventions to determine meaning. Both approaches offer interpretive control over a voluminous, authorless body of work and help to sort out the discursive layers of state condemnation and execution, criminal autobiography and confession, ballad conventions and literary tragedy, as well as individual cases and public opinion. These approaches tend to ignore, however, the details of individual ballads that reveal the political features of ballad poetics.

24. A legal loophole created by the 1840 Insane Prisoner's Act enabled Townley's belated reprieve, and Parliament later amended the act in response to public controversy over the questions of judicial discrimination raised by Wright's execution and Townley's institutionalization. For histories of the Townley case as an application of the insanity plea, see Smith's *Trial by Medicine* and Walker's *Crime and Insanity in England*. For Victorian medical commentaries on the case, see Maudsley and Robertson's *Insanity and Crime: A Medico-Legal Commentary on the Case of George Victor Townley*; "The Sequel of the Townley Case" in the *Journal of Mental Science*; and "Insanity and Crime" in the *Social Science Review*. For a brief discussion of Townley in the context of dramatic poets, see Faas's *Retreat into the Mind*.

25. This cause-and-effect scenario is explicitly rendered in "A Copy of Verses on F. B. Courvoisier, who was Executed for the Murder of Lord William Russell," printed in Bristol. The ballad states that Lord Russell "caught him in the act of plunder / . . . which made him plan the horrid deed." Yet, this particular ballad positions the problem with respect to more conservative moral advice: "Let Honesty then guide your actions / And in your stations be content."

26. For a discussion of the combined effects of the criminal's speech, the ethics of counsel, and the rise of adversarialism in the Courvoisier case, see Cairns's *Advocacy and the Making of the Adversarial Criminal Trial, 1800–1865*.

27. Armstrong's list of poetic networks and pairings is inspired by existing studies,

some of which are published in the same two-volume special issue of *Victorian Poetry* in which her comments appear. This issue, entitled "Whither Poetry?" and edited by Linda Hughes, stages a dialogue between two "generations" of Victorian poetry scholars and offers selections of innovative new work in the field and commentaries on the evolving methodologies and priorities of Victorian poetry studies.

28. Browning's vision of the condemned prisoner in his cell, the tortured psychology of condemnation, and the legal appeals in Guido's final monologue are coincident with the popular vision of the condemned criminal presented over and over again in execution ballads. Guido pastes together various legal and religious defenses to challenge his death sentence—rather than to deny his crimes. Among these is a claim of madness and a request for asylum: "Sirs, my first true word, all truth and no lie, / Is—save me notwithstanding! Life is all! / I was just stark mad,—let the madman live / Pressed by as many chains as you please pile!" (XI.2418–21).

29. More concerned with establishing the poem's affinities with Speranza's Irish nationalist ballad, "Trial of the Brothers Sheares," Heaney does not elaborate these parallels. He argues that Speranza's (Lady Wilde's) political ballad, "The Trial of the Brothers Sheares in '98," which appeared in a volume dedicated to Oscar Wilde and his brother, established an important antecedent for Wilde's own political ballad. Heaney seeks to "draw attention to these parallels and foreshadowings and coincidences of style and behaviour between mother and son" and notes, "by recalling it, the provenance of the ballad is illuminated even if its stylistic faults are not extenuated" (101). Because the ballad represents the kind of work "not usually discussed within the academy" (101) and a text in which "Wilde the aesthete was stripped of his dandy's clothes to become Wilde the convict" (102), Heaney argues, "the poem does give credence to the idea of poetry as a mode of redress" (102).

Chapter 2

1. In January 1843, Daniel M'Naghten, a Scottish laborer, whose name is spelled variously in historical documents and press coverage, shot Edward Drummond, Prime Minister Robert Peel's private secretary, whom he mistook for the Tory Prime Minister himself. Drummond died several days later.

2. At trial, M'Naghten's attorney, Alexander Cockburn, launched an insanity defense. Applying recent medical theories not yet formally recognized in jurisprudence, including notions of partial insanity, he included the testimony of Dr. Forbes Winslow, who had just published *The Plea of Insanity in Criminal Cases* and who, controversially, provided diagnostic testimony about M'Naghten without ever having interviewed him. The jurors, instructed by the presiding judge to determine whether, at the time of his crime, M'Naghten had been "capable of distinguishing between right and wrong" and had been "sensible that [his act] was a violation of the law of God or of man," shocked the public with an acquittal on the ground of insanity (Walker 95). M'Naghten was committed to Bethlem Hospital and later Broadmoor, where he died in 1865. M'Naghten's trial is recorded in William C. Townsend's *Modern State Trials*. For analysis of the trial and its judicial significance, see Nigel Walker's *Crime and Insanity in England;* Roger Smith's *Trial by Medicine;* Jane Campbell Moriarty's *The Role of Mental Illness in Criminal Trials;* and Donald West and Alexander Walk's *Daniel McNaughton: His Trial and the Aftermath*.

3. Upon being apprehended, M'Naghten stated, "The Tories in my native city [Glasgow] have compelled me to do this," and he explained that these Tories had been following him, that they had accused him of crimes of which he was innocent, and that they "wish[ed] to murder [him]" (Walker 91).

4. After the M'Naghten verdict, the House of Lords responded to the apparent lapse in the application of criminal law with an extensive investigation into the legal test of insanity. The Lords devised a series of questions pertaining to the language of insanity and responsibility, the role of medical evidence at trial, and the proper instruction of juries. They called upon the English judges to address each question, and their responses became the "M'Naghten Rules," a set of guidelines for English courts to consider and adjudicate insanity. "In effect," Smith argues, the rules "restated the 'right-wrong test': a man was not responsible for his criminal deed if, at the time of committing it, he was unable to know that the deed was wrong" (*Trial* 15). In discussing mental science and juridical authority, Walker cites the influence of Isaac Ray's *Treatise on the Medical Jurisprudence of Insanity* (1838). An American doctor, Ray could "make all his points by attacking English judges and counsel without the tact that was needed where his own courts were concerned" (Walker 89). The text criticizes legal notions of criminal responsibility, and because Alexander Cockburn used this text in his defense of Daniel M'Naghten, it influenced criminal cases and statutes.

5. Walker documents the increased recognition of insanity in murder trials, a trend that reflects the increased application of mental science theories and the increased use of defense counsel resulting from the 1836 Prisoner's Counsel Act. Walker's glimpse at the gradual but steady increase in insanity acquittals also underscores the exaggerated nature of public anxiety on the subject. Of persons indicted for murder between 1834 and 1843, 2 percent were found unfit to plead, and 7.5 percent were acquitted as insane. Between 1844 and 1853, 4.7 percent were found unfit, and 7.5 percent were acquitted as insane. Between 1854 and 1863, 5.7 percent were found unfit, and 10.1 percent were acquitted as insane. Between 1864 and 1873, 5.8 percent were found unfit, and 9.6 were acquitted as insane (Walker 86).

6. Rodensky offers a useful examination of the Victorian discourse of criminal responsibility. Problematizing the "straightforwardness" that characterized J. F. Stephen's assertion that "[t]he general rule is, that people are responsible for their actions," she explores "the necessary fractures in Victorian ideas and ideals about criminal responsibility" across a multigeneric expanse of legal discourse comprising "legal opinions, statutes, treatises, histories, [and] articles" (3).

7. The Criminal Lunatics Act (1800) established the idea of criminal lunacy by introducing the special verdict of "not guilty on the ground of insanity." The Criminal Lunatics Amendment Act (1816) provided for the transfer and custody of insane persons charged with crimes, and the Insane Prisoner's Act (1840) further addressed the logistics of asylum transfers and certification procedures. This act was amended by The Insane Prisoners Amendment Act (1864) after George Victor Townley avoided a capital sentence because the 1840 act allowed prisoners to be certified between the trial and the sentencing. The Lunatics Care and Treatment Act (1845) and the Lunatic Asylums Act (1845) established the Commissioners of Lunacy and mandated county asylums. The Criminal Lunatics Asylum Act (1860), responding to demands that the criminally insane be separated from other lunatics, resulted in the construction of Broadmoor. The Trial of Lunatics Act

(1883), responding to pressure from the queen, revised the exculpatory language of the special verdict to a more deterrent-minded "guilty but insane." The Criminal Lunatics Act (1884) addressed issues of mercy and the Home Secretary's powers to appoint doctors and certify insanity.

8. Smith points out that because the "[t]reatment of the insane . . . became a potent symbol for society's ability to regulate its affairs" (*Trial* 5), asylum reform resonated with a Victorian faith in institutionally driven social progress and corresponded to England's national sensibility. W. F. Bynum explains that "[b]y the 1850s, when the asylum movement was in full swing . . . , British psychiatrists could look upon the combination of moral therapy and non-restraint as genuinely indigenous, humane, and therapeutically sound. They also saw it was peculiarly adapted to Britain, with its well developed tradition of individual liberty and toleration. . . . Thus, although moral therapy was generally linked to medical therapy in the total therapeutic programme, and although the non-restraint system was not rigidly observed in many asylums, these two themes were the most visible ones around which the nascent psychiatric profession emerged in early Victorian Britain" (229).

In his 1833 entry in *Cyclopaedia of Practical Medicine,* Prichard cites Esquirol's assessment of madness and civilization: "In barbarous nations, among whom the mind is uncultivated. . . . [m]adness is comparatively rare (850). In contrast, Esquirol observes, the "changes . . . which have taken place during the last thirty years in our moral sentiments and habits, have produced more instances of madness in France than all our political calamities. We have exchanged our ancient customs and fixed habits, our old and established sentiments and opinions, for speculative theories and dangerous innovations" (850). In 1843, John Barlow proclaimed, "The cases of insanity, we are told, have nearly tripled within the last twenty years!—a fearful increase even after allowing to the utmost for a larger population!" (49).

In the second half of the century, anxieties about civilization evolved into more explicit narratives of regression and degeneration. By the late Victorian period, Veida Skultans argues, insanity "is no longer seen as a problem to be grappled with by individual will-power, but it has become a major social problem which threatens the health of the nation rather than mere individual autonomy. The insane are thought to constitute a reservoir of bad heredity" (*English Madness* 133). Writing in 1870, Dr. Henry Maudsley explained, "I should take up a long time if I were to enumerate the various brute-like characteristics that are at times witnessed among the insane; enough to say that some very strong facts and arguments in support of Mr. Darwin's views might be drawn from the field of morbid psychology. We may, without much difficulty, trace savagery in civilization, as we can trace animalism in savagery; and in the degeneration of insanity, in the *unkinding,* so to say, of human kind, there are exhibited marks denoting the elementary instincts of its composition" (*Body and Mind* 51).

9. The role of history, of course, has been central to definitions of the genre—from Robert Langbaum's contest between sympathy and judgment, to Herbert Tucker's historicized individual via the "art of disclosure," to Isobel Armstrong's statement that "psychological states are rooted in history" (*Victorian Poetry* 146). Placing "the genius of the dramatic monologue" in "the effect created by the tension between sympathy and moral judgment" (85), Langbaum highlights its ability to create a psychologized, historicized, and relativist judgment: "We adopt a man's point of view and the point of view of his

age in order to judge him—which makes the judgment relative, limited in applicability to the particular conditions of the case" (107). Tucker links history to character formation: "[s]ubjectivity [is] ironically demystified by the historical contextualization that is the generic privilege of the dramatic monologue and ... one of its indispensable props in the construction of character" ("Dramatic Monologue" 22). With a focused application of Armstrong's insights into the epistemological mischief of a "double form" exploring "utterance both as subject and as object," this chapter adds another facet to discussions of history and dramatic poetics. In these murder poems, the mystification of subjectivity caused by medicolegal debates further complicates the interpretive irony, relativism, or authority of history.

10. Explorations of psychology were frequently associated with modernity. Armstrong notes that "[n]early all the commonest evaluative words in criticism at this time carry a psychological, human/social or moral reference," and the repeated use of terms such as "human," "sympathy," "the sympathies," "the affections," and "feelings" reinforced this psychological poetics (*Scrutinies* 6).

11. Skultan's *Madness and Morals: Ideas on Insanity in the Nineteenth Century* and *English Madness: Ideas on Insanity, 1580–1890* provide an overview of nineteenth-century mental science. Rylance's *Victorian Psychology and British Culture 1850–1880* offers a "taxonomy" of nineteenth-century mental science theories. Scull's *Museums of Madness* and *The Most Solitary of Afflictions* cover asylum practices. Hunter and MacAlpine's *Three Hundred Years of Psychiatry, 1535–1860* and Bourne Taylor and Shuttleworth's *Embodied Selves: An Anthology of Psychological Texts, 1830–1890* anthologize excerpted mental science documents. Smith's *Trial by Medicine* and Walker's *Crime and Insanity in England* provide succinct histories of the medicolegal context.

12. Prichard did not originate the theories reported in his treatise, nor was he a mental scientist by training or profession. He collected continental research from the first decades of the nineteenth century and presented and popularized its conclusions in Victorian England.

13. In an effort to establish linguistic parallelism with monomania, Prichard suggests the words "Parapathia" or "Pathomania" to describe moral insanity (*Treatise* 10). Esquirol's discussion of *folie raisonnante* sparked debates about ideas of madness marked by delusion and frenzy and madness marked by reason and irresistible impulse. Though "moral insanity" had been used early in the century, Prichard publicized these new definitions of madness in his *Treatise on Insanity,* which by all accounts became the standard text on madness until John Charles Bucknill and Daniel H. Tuke published their *Manual of Psychological Medicine* (1858).

14. Writers consistently warned about the misapplications and inconsistencies of insanity pleas in criminal and civil courts. In the *Juryman's Guide,* Sir George Stephen cited the misjudgments inherent in criminal lunacy: "Men of science declare that monomania is consistent with sanity in all other points, and a jury acquits; we may be in error, but in our view such monomania amounts only to this, that a long-cherished feeling of malignity, or of criminal desire, has at length burst the bounds of common sense—as all criminality of desire, if not resisted in its incipient stages, invariably does,—and having obtained liberty to range, plunges its self-immolated victim into an abyss, as the herd of swine were precipitated into the sea by the legion of devils, when these same devils were once let loose to take their course" (141). He explains that, although monomania manifests itself

in many crimes and transgressions, "it is in murder only, because it is now almost the only capital crime, that juries give credence to it" (141). He continues: "Nor is monomania, if such it may be called, peculiar to crime. There are very few men of active minds who are totally exempt from the habitual indulgence of some whim or fancy, which strengthens as life advances, and the gratification of which, at last, becomes essential to comfort, if not to happiness. Some select benevolent pursuits, as schools, visiting societies, or repositories. Some late distinguished men carried anti-slavery enthusiasm to monomaniacal pitch; we ourselves confess to a failing that way.... The essential difference between such cases and the monomania of criminal courts, is, that legitimate passion may in the one be indulged to the extent of folly, but takes a direction in which it cannot fall into crime; in the other it becomes criminal, because its direction is originally wrong: in both cases it is still passion, and not often abstractedly wrong" (142). Dr. Forbes Winslow critiqued the wholesale dismissal of responsibility in cases of partial insanity:

> I am not prepared to give an unqualified assent to the dogma, that in every case of mental derangement,—without any reference to its degree or character,—ought the person to be screened from the penalty awarded by the laws for criminal offences. I am ready to admit, that if insanity be clearly established to exist, a *primâ facie* case is made out in favour of the prisoner; but that because a person may be proved to be strange and wayward in his character; to fancy himself a beggar when he may have the wealth of Croesus, or to be ill when he is in the buoyancy of health—to believe that such a person ought, of necessity, to be exonerated from all responsibility, is a doctrine as unphilosophical and untenable as it is opposed to the safety and well being of society. ("Criminal Insanity" 42)

15. By the 1870s, "Maudsley argues for the existence of insanity even where it 'has so much the look of vice or crime that many persons regard it as an unfounded medical intervention'" (qtd. in Skultans, *Madness* 7).

16. See Faas and Mason for detailed discussions of "Porphyria's Lover," its antecedent texts, and theories of moral insanity. An excerpt in *Blackwood's* entitled "Extracts from Gosschen's Diary" (1818) was written by John Wilson, but *Blackwood's* marketed the piece as an excerpt from the memoir of a German priest who records a condemned murderer's confession of his murder of his mistress therein. Directly inspired by "Gosschen's Diary," Brian Procter's "Marcian Colonna" (1820) is a poem about a man who murders his mistress. Procter exploits the aesthetic of the murdered woman's body and the topic of the murderer's calm but mad resolve, but he also retains more conventional elements of frenzy and mania. As Mason explains, "In both these sources not only is the murderer a lunatic, but his madness is described and discussed at some length" (257). Faas notes that though neither text "directly mentions or discusses 'moral insanity,'" they each, like "Porphryia's Lover," portray a murderer who "glories in his crime and justifies it with great show of pseudo-logic and persuasiveness" (56). Mason concludes that "Browning could not have failed to entertain the idea that Porphyria's murderer is a lunatic, as this is the essential character of his model in the two sources" (257). The "suggestive similarities between certain prominent innovations in the psychiatric theory of the day and the notion of mind suggested by 'Porphyria'" (258) and Browning's association with Procter and Procter's position as a Metropolitan Commissioner in Lunacy in the 1830s also underpin

his case for Browning's interest in insanity. In *The Life of Robert Browning* (1910), Griffin and Minchin locate the composition of "Porphyria" in St. Petersburg in 1834. Though this composition date precludes the direct influence of Prichard's *Treatise,* it affords a possible historical connection to Prichard's article on "Insanity" in the *Cyclopaedia of Practical Medicine* (1833) as well as earlier, continental discussions of moral insanity in the first decades of the century.

17. "Porphyria" was first published with "Johannes Agricola" in the *Monthly Repository* in January 1836. In *Dramatic Lyrics,* published in 1842, the two poems appeared under the heading "Madhouse Cells." In 1849, still featured with its companion poem in "Madhouse Cells," it was retitled "Porphyria's Lover." In 1863, "Porphyria's Lover" appeared independent of a companion poem or a madhouse cell in *Dramatic Romances.* Although the committal of his homicidal lover to a madhouse in 1842 would have situated the text rather explicitly within the context of diagnostic controversy and asylum reform, the heading seems an incongruous afterthought. Placing the figure in a "madhouse cell" renders the dramatic setting impossible and the representation of madness conventional. As Mason argues, "[O]nly if Porphyria's lover is grossly hallucinated can his utterance be consistent with such an environment. Moreover, if I am right about his particular species of lunacy, then hallucination is exactly the wrong sort of symptom for him to exhibit; it would shatter the delicate and startling portrayal of rational lunacy..." (265).

18. In *Browning's Hatreds,* Karlin discusses the poem as a study in "aristocratic *hauteur*" and "sexual hatred." Exploring the poetics of domestic violence and the theme of "violent heterosexuality" (507), Melissa Valiska Gregory discusses the politics of identification and judgment that allow Browning to "engage the disquieting and outlandish (for the period) subject of domestic conflict in the first place" (494).

19. Ralph Rader has argued that the couplets, reflecting the Duke's "deliberate calculation" (136) in acknowledging the murder, operate "to give a sense of submerged pattern running, like the Duke's hidden purpose, through the whole" (139). Loy D. Martin has suggested that whether they signify an author's presence or a character's motive, "we are observing a doubleness or bifurcation of the text" (112), which ultimately suggests "an ontological division between what language *is* as an artificial and malleable aesthetic medium and what it *says* as a constant medium of human communication" (112–13). Extrapolating from this, Martin writes that Browning thereby establishes the "alienation between poetry and discourse" (113) and differentiates poetic skill in language from that of "unspecialized language consumers" (113), such as Renaissance dukes or Victorian poetry readers.

20. In his infamous attack on Rossetti, Robert Buchanan discusses "A Last Confession," noting that it is "in the minutest trick and form of thought, suggestive of Mr. Browning" ("Fleshly School" 342). In differentiating himself from Browning, Rossetti claimed the figure of the Italian patriot as the seed of inspiration. In a letter to Franz Hüffer in 1873, Rossetti responds to Hüffer's comparison of the two poets: "May I ask you to cut out the last paragraph in this page about Browning? The first nucleus of the *Confession* was the *very* earliest thing in the whole book, and was the simple and genuine result of my having passed my whole boyhood among people just like the speaker in the poem" (Doughty and Wahl, Vol. 3, 1233). He goes on to express his literary rights to the subject:

> Browning by travel and cultivation, imported much the same sort of thing into English poetry on a much larger scale; but this subject, if any, was my absolute

birth-right, and the poem was conceived and in a manner begun long before 1848 (the date afterwards put to it, as characteristic of patriotic struggles,) and at a time when Byron and Shelley were about the limits of my modern English poetic studies. (1233)

In a letter to Swinburne, he claims that "A Last Confession" is "maybe the best of all my doings" and the "outcome of the Italian part of me" (Doughty and Wahl, Vol. 2, 762–63). Though his letter clearly represents an argument for his own literary authority both as an Italian and as a reader of transgressive poetry, it also reflects Rossetti's poetic use of Italianness, which allows him to merge an aesthetic ideology of passionate excess with a desperate and violent political situation.

21. Jerome McGann has described the poem as a "politically disillusioned commentary on the situation in Europe, and especially Italy, after 1848" (*Collected Poetry* 383), but the poem's psychological interests in murderous subjectivity also help to explain the unheroic figure of the Italian patriot. If we emphasize Italian politics, the speaker's crime becomes a more generic crime of passion, a literary convenience for depicting more pressing political ideals. The stabbing, then, as disabling secret and narrative climax, signifies a tragic violence with which "A Last Confession" performs "operatic" gestures (Bullen 112). To be sure, Rossetti reinforces this convention when he claims the poem as a study of the "deadliest of all passion-woven complexities," the explication of "terrible Love turned to Hate," and a representation of "the savage penalty exacted for a lost ideal" ("Stealthy School" 793). Moreover, the speaker's violent political, sexual, and religious transgressions clearly synthesize the sensual and affective interests of Pre-Raphaelitism and Rossetti's own Art Catholic aesthetic. Victorian psychology, however, armed with moral theories of madness, undermined the mythologizing power of criminal passion. Its ideological force shrank under scientific scrutiny, giving it a flatness unsuitable for the sophisticated character development afforded by dramatic monologues.

22. Despite the fact that the poem exemplifies what he sees as the annoying traits of the collection, the "protracted hankering after a person of the other sex; it seems meat, drink, thought, sinew, religion for the fleshly school" (343), Buchanan grants an exception to "A Last Confession," finding it less offensive than others because in it "[fleshliness] is fiercely held in check by the exigencies of a powerful situation and the strength of a dramatic speaker" (339). More generally, poetry of the transgressive limit alarmed critics like Matthew Arnold, George Henry Lewes, and Walter Bagehot because they saw in it the taste of the "scattered, headless" (66) middle class in modern art. Buchanan's indictments somewhat echo Bagehot's claim that "grotesque" art "takes the [character] type, so to say, *in difficulties*. It gives a representation of it in its minimum development, amid the circumstances least favorable to it, just while it is struggling with obstacles, just where it is encumbered with incongruities. It deals, to use the language of science, not with normal types but with abnormal specimens" (Bagehot 56). Bagehot's invoking of the scientific language of "normal types" and "abnormal specimens" is also marked by the discourse of insanity. When Bagehot deploys the term "grotesque" to disapprove of a poetics of "ugly reality" (63), an art of "abnormal specimens," or a portrayal of a "distorted and imperfect image" that might appeal to "the *half* educated" (66) quality of readers, the popular fascination with high-profile criminal insanity trials is, perhaps, implicated in the condemnation.

23. In acknowledging Browning's influence, critics have typically cited "Porphyria's Lover" and "My Last Duchess" as the poem's literary antecedents, but in its fascination with manic excess, "A Last Confession" is more closely aligned with "The Laboratory." Though often neglected in contemporary scholarship, "The Laboratory" inspired Rossetti's first watercolor, which he completed in 1849. Its composition thus overlaps with the years given by William Michael Rossetti for the original drafting of "A Last Confession."

24. Maudsley was notorious for such elisions. His concern with improper leavening intertwines history, will, and responsibility, but Maudsley also decentered the will: "When we reflect how much time and what a multitude of divers experiences have gone to the formation of character, what a complex product it is, and what an inconceivably intricate inter-working of intimate energies, active and inhibitive, any display of it in feeling and will means, it must appear a gross absurdity for any one to aspire to estimate and appraise all the component motives of a particular act of will" (*Body and Will* 29). He explains: "What the metaphysician has done is plain enough: he has converted into an entity the general term which embraces the multitude of particular volitions, themselves varying infinitely in power and quality, and has then referred them all to it as cause. So he talks habitually as if will had always the same nature, whereas these is no such thing. . . . A general will is not an entity, it is no more than a notion. No wonder that there is neither common end nor end to philosophical disquisitions concerning a notion of which each person is free to have his own notion" (17).

25. Maudsley writes: "Moreover, the particular will-faculty of the particular purposive act must be built up gradually by culture and practice; it may be a late acquisition which is unstable and easily lost, or it may be so grounded in the nature that it is merged and disappears in automatism. Therefore . . . the particular wills of particular acts may be impaired or abolished while the several wills of other acts are unimpaired, or . . . the single wills of single acts may survive amidst the general wreckage, like columns, broken or entire, of a ruined temple which still stand upright in its ruins; so giving rise to the manifold and diverse disintegrations of will which, despite the postulate of its metaphysical unity, are met with in the concrete" (*Pathology of Mind* 142). The idea of a character in ruins offers an apt metaphor for the speaker depicted in "A Last Confession."

26. Applying Langbaum's template of sympathy and judgment, Ronnalie Howard argues, "Internally the movement of the poem is determined by the narrator's strategy, his desire in the face of death to lessen the magnitude of his crime, to secure relief from the torments of his conscience, to obtain pardon, or at least sympathy, from the priest" ("Rossetti's 'A Last Confession'" 23). In a later publication she argues that sympathy for the murderer ultimately overtakes judgment because "the real villain is the Austrian occupation," which creates an "unstable world in which passionate natures become accustomed to living with violence, in which love and hate become intertwined" (*Dark Glass* 100). He is ultimately, then, a "victim of his times" (100). Though the speaker clearly develops a narrative strategy, as Howard argues, Rossetti neither resolves the matter through circumstance, lunacy, or religious principles nor asks readers to operate primarily within the context of sympathy and judgment. In fact, the text often thwarts both operations by forcefully contrasting his expressive mode and his rhetorical manner.

27. In 1848, an article reprinted in the *Journal of Psychological Medicine and Mental Pathology* advised priests that knowledge of physiology might "aid them at the confessional": "To administer advice and consolation, he should be aware of the failings of his

patient, and how much is due to temperament and constitution. In fact, the good priest should have a tolerable acquaintance with physiology, in order to be most useful in his vocation" ("Moral Theology" 559).

28. Continuing his narrative, the speaker recalls the day when, at fourteen, she "asked [him] / If she was not a woman" (223) and when he observed her "breasts half-globed / Like folded lilies deepset in the stream" (225–26). Rossetti must have carefully considered the implications of her liminal status and the boundary of womanhood. In the draft stages of the poem, this passage occurs when the girl is thirteen years old; Rossetti changed it to fourteen for its publication in *Poems*. The speaker's account of his victim's sexual attributes is jarring because she occupies the margin between girl and woman, and at times his sexual responses take place when she is unambiguously still a child. His sexual desire thus fully transgresses Catholic and Victorian codes of sexual morality and thereby establishes him as man of habitual moral laxity—with all of its implications for guilt and responsibility. While Rossetti provides ample material for a critique of gendered violence (the entire mad-criminal scenario centers upon this fleshy core), an analysis of feminine othering and victimization within the poem remains unfinished, supplanted by an interest in his masculine subject's inscrutable complexities. Rossetti's fleshly aesthetic functions in the context of criminal insanity, as the conspicuous sexual dynamics of the crime feed theories of criminal motive and monomaniacal obsession. While Rossetti uses the speaker's misogynist arguments to develop the poetics of obscurity, the eroticization of the girl-woman takes on a life of its own and, therefore, becomes one example of his larger poetic and artistic project of aestheticizing the feminine and radicalizing Victorian sensual and erotic representation. For an analysis of the dynamics of violence and desire, see Bullen's *The Pre-Raphaelite Body*, which includes a discussion of the poem's psychosexual dynamics and its place in Rossetti's Pre-Raphaelite aesthetics.

29. A modified version of this recollection forms the speaker's wish to reunite with his victim again in hell: "Ah! be it even in flame, / We may have sweetness yet, if you but say / As once in childish sorrow: 'Not my pain, / My pain was nothing: oh your poor poor love, / Your broken love!'" (485–89).

30. See "'A Last Confession' (fair copy manuscript with corrections, Fitzwilliam Museum)," Rossetti Archive.

31. Rossetti removed the words "if God / Can Pardon me" from these lines, leaving only "what hope / Can reach me still" to allude to the question of divine judgment that informs the language of the confession. This revision further undercuts confessional religiosity and divine justice. The fragmented nature of the proceeding functions similarly. No priestly words pronounce judgment, and no dialogic reconciliation occurs because, at the end of his confession—and, most likely, his life—the speaker is lost in a hallucination of his victim's revenge. His final words, then, conjure secular understandings of criminality, madness, and passion.

32. See Smith's *Trial by Medicine* for discussion of some of these controversial trials. Faas argues that the poem can be most readily connected to the case of George Victor Townley. Considering the physicians consulted in the Townley case, Faas wonders "how Dr. Hitchman and Dr. Winslow would have adjudicated the mental state of Rossetti's protagonist in 'A Last Confession'" and asks, "Was the speaker's obsessive behavior sufficient for certifying him as morally insane or as incapable of distinguishing right from wrong at the time of the deed?" (167). Responding to his own query, he writes, "As in the Townley

case, the learned doctors probably would have disagreed. . . ." (167). Rossetti's drafting of the poem predates the Townley case and is clearly not directly inspired by it. However, Rossetti courts the kinds of diagnostic obscurities inherent in most theories and cases of criminal lunacy, and for Victorians reading *Poems* in 1870, the poem's indeterminacy would no doubt be recognized in these terms.

Chapter 3

1. Welsh situates his discussion of Arcangeli within his larger study of the "erosion" of "strong representations" by "stor[ies] of experience" (200). The representation of Arcangeli as a "mercenary defender of a moral monster," who works for "bread and butter" and "thank[s] God for it" (208), helps Browning to "demol[ish] the pretense of lawyers to give a true account of what has happened" by revealing that the "professional managers of evidence" are "strictly rhetoricians" (208).

2. In addition to the 1857 Divorce Act, several other important pieces of legislation publicized and altered the practices of domesticity. These include: the Act for the Better Prevention of Aggravated Assaults Upon Women and Children of 1853; the Married Women's Property Acts of 1870 and 1882; the Infant Custody Acts of 1873 and 1886; and the Matrimonial Causes Act of 1878. For histories of marriage law, see A. James Hammerton's *Cruelty and Companionship*; Joan Perkin's *Women and Marriage in Nineteenth-Century England*; Mary Lyndon Shanley's *Feminism, Marriage and the Law in Victorian England*; Allen Horstman's *Victorian Divorce*; Maeve Doggett's *Marriage, Wife-Beating and the Law in Victorian England*; and John Gillis's *For Better or For Worse*. Lawrence Stone's *Broken Lives: Separation and Divorce in England, 1660–1857* and *Family, Sex, and Marriage in England, 1500–1800* cover pre-Victorian developments in matrimonial law. For a useful discussion of the complex intersections of common law, statute law, and case law and the mid-century political context of marriage debates, see Mary Poovey's *Uneven Developments*.

3. In particular, I have in mind Poovey's *Uneven Developments*, Chase and Levenson's *The Spectacle of Intimacy*, Marlene Tromp's *The Private Rod*, Barbara Leckie's *Culture and Adultery*, John Tosh's *A Man's Place*, Kristine Otteson Garrigan's *Victorian Scandals*, and Lisa Surridge's *Bleak Houses*.

4. Insanity did not constitute grounds for divorce.

5. The male disadvantages and vulnerabilities introduced by such stringent requirements did not go unacknowledged in parliamentary debate. Anxieties about the extent to which the state should outrank the husband surfaced amidst the conversation. One member hypothesized "a case in which, under the influence of intoxication, or any other equally palliating circumstances, a man might once in his life be seduced into a house of ill-fame. Twenty years after, his wife, totally ignorant of the fact, might commit adultery; and on his seeking redress would, by the aid of spies and informers, who were always called into requisition in such proceedings, rake up the hitherto forgotten fact, and defeat his petition" (qtd. in Chase and Levenson 187–88).

6. Harriet Taylor and John Stuart Mill, among others, favored a proposed amendment to the 1853 bill which mandated the punishment of flogging for offending husbands. See Doggett's *Marriage, Wife-Beating, and the Law in Victorian England*.

7. The *Times*, Anne Humpherys explains, "reported the largest number of divorce cases and gave the fullest transcripts with the least comment," and the "whole trial was reported over a series of weeks or months from the first hearing to the judge's summing up and judgment, whereas the weeklies and later the tabloids felt under no obligation to report the trial in its entirety" ("Coming Apart" 221).

8. The repeat appearances of petitioning couples over months and years underscored both the desperation of miserable couples and the unyielding power of the divorce court. See, for example, the *Times* reporting on *Curtis v. Curtis* and *Marchmont v. Marchmont* in 1858.

9. Narrative fiction and print journalism have garnered the most critical attention in recent years. Critics have thoroughly teased out the political complexities of these genres and sometimes charted the links between the two. For analysis of melodramatic methods and Caroline Norton's work, see Poovey's *Uneven Developments* and Hadley's *Melodramatic Tactics*. Juxtaposing press reports with fictional works, Leckie's *Culture and Adultery*, Chase and Levenson's *Spectacle of Intimacy*, and Lisa Surridge's *Bleak Houses* chart interesting discursive connections between publicity and textuality.

10. For discussion of narrative fiction and marriage reform, see Trodd's *Domestic Crime in the Victorian Novel*, Tromp's *The Private Rod*, and Surridge's *Bleak Houses*.

11. Discussing the representational relationships between divorce court reportage and developments in the Victorian novel, Leckie highlights the "[d]evices of surveillance and suspicion" (91) in divorce trials and press coverage: "When the crime is a domestic crime buttressed by a legally endorsed gender discrepancy and a powerful ideology relating to marriage and women's sexuality, relating 'exactly what happened' is complicated by what arises like a leitmotif in the transcription of these cases: suspicion" (91).

12. The term "criminal" is applied to each character in the poem, and the poem enumerates many crimes inextricably linked to the laws of marriage rights, birthrights, and property rights. While I focus on murder, detailed accounts of the civil and criminal intricacies of divorce, annulment, reproduction, prostitution, adultery, rape, assault, inheritance, property, dowry, and so on, offer numerous variations on domestic transgression and terror. The stability of marriage and the security of domesticity are completely dismantled in this poem, and as Mary Ellis Gibson argues, even "the fate of Pompilia's child remains obscure" (89) and, thus, "*The Ring and the Book* proposes no reknitting of domesticity, no ending that relieves its readers of the burden of its story" (89).

13. In *Commentaries on the Law of England*, Blackstone articulated an argument for husbands' disciplinary authority: "For, as [the husband] is to answer for [his wife's] misbehaviour, the law thought it reasonable to intrust him with this power of restraining her, by domestic chastisement, in the same moderation that a man is allowed to correct his apprentices or children; for whom the master or parent is also liable in some cases to answer" (qtd. in Doggett 34). As Doggett explains, this "doctrine of reasonable chastisement" (34) was "seized upon and endlessly reproduced" (38) throughout the nineteenth century.

14. In a discussion of the Caroline Norton case, the history of feminist criticism on the poem, and debates over the woman question, Susan Brown examines Pompilia as "speaking subject" and "cultural object" (30). Arguing that her presumed innocence ignores some of her "rhetorical agency," Brown also encourages a skeptical reading of Pompilia's monologue. Ann Brady situates Pompilia's agency within the poem's critique of "sexual cynicism" (125).

15. Blackstone explained: "A wife killing her husband is petit treason; but a husband killing his wife is only murder; because of the obedience which in relation of law is due from the wife to the husband" (qtd. in Doggett 50). As Doggett explains, punishments differed as well: "Until the end of the eighteenth century, the punishment for women guilty of petit treason differed from that imposed upon murderers; it also differed from that imposed upon male petit traitors. Whilst wife-murderers and male petit traitors were hung, female petit traitors were sentenced to burning alive. In practice, many women were garroted or strangled before the flames reached them, but this was not invariably the case" (50).

16. While in Italy, Lytton became acquainted with the Brownings via a letter of introduction from the well-known literary critic and advisor John Forster, who functioned as a surrogate father and a literary agent. See Harlan and Harlan's *Letters from Owen Meredith (Robert, First Earl of Lytton) to Robert and Elizabeth Barrett Browning*. For a description of Lytton's popularity with young poets, see Harlan's *Owen Meredith*. Raymond's *Victorian Viceroy* briefly addresses Lytton's popularity in the United States.

17. In referencing the two writers as Lytton (the younger) and Bulwer-Lytton (the elder), I follow biographers' usage in naming father, Edward George Earle Lytton Bulwer-Lytton, and son, Edward Robert Bulwer Lytton. Lytton's father pressed him into diplomacy and frequently discouraged his poetic endeavors, using a variety of reasons, including, at one point, the problem of their names. Writing to his son in 1854, Bulwer-Lytton explained, "I don't think, whatever your merit, the world would allow two of the same name to have both a permanent reputation in literature" (qtd. in Harlan 62). When Chapman and Hall agreed to publish the *Clytemnestra* collection in 1855, Lytton's father only conditionally consented to the venture, requiring that Lytton adopt a pseudonym and that he cease to write verse "for *two* years following the date of this publication" (qtd. in Harlan 67).

18. When Lytton himself wrote a biography of his father, *The Life, Letters, and Literary Remains of Edward Bulwer, Lord Lytton,* he stopped in 1831 (the year of his birth)—thus avoiding the problems of representing his life, his parents' feud, his mother's institutionalization, and his sister's death.

19. For discussions of Bulwer-Lytton's husbanding tactics, see Marie Mulvey-Roberts's "Fame, Notoriety and Madness: Edward Bulwer-Lytton Paying the Price of Greatness"; Marilyn J. Kurata's "Wrongful Confinement: The Betrayal of Women by Men, Medicine, and Law"; and Mitchell's *Bulwer Lytton*.

20. According to Mitchell, Rosina Wheeler and Edward Bulwer met at a bluestocking gathering, and Harlan explains that Rosina always "bore the stamp of the Regency" (3). Rosina's "mother was apparently well-versed in Wollstonecraft and assertive in declaiming the wrongs against women, and her father refused to support his family either financially or emotionally" (Mitchell 25). An uncompromising Regency bohemian, Rosina failed to embrace the mid-century feminine ideal and publicly deplored the "passivity" of English women (Mitchell 57). In the ongoing marital combat between the warring spouses, Rosina, deprived of legal opportunities, sought redress in the manipulation of public opinion: "Exposure is the only thing that complex monster dreads," she explained, "and consequently the only check I have on him" (qtd. in Mitchell 44). Rosina published *Cheveley; or, The Man of Honor,* which caricatured her husband's wrongs, and she sent angry and obscene letters to his personal friends and political colleagues. In 1858, shortly after

Bulwer-Lytton had taken up the position of Secretary of State for the Colonies, Rosina again asserted her powers of publicity: at an "uncontested election at Hertford, while Bulwer was addressing his constituents, Rosina appeared on the platform and, addressing the assembled crowd, began a violent denunciation of him" (Harlan 87). Responding to this public incident, Bulwer-Lytton committed her to an asylum. After three weeks of public outcry and press coverage, Rosina was released, and Bulwer-Lytton was forced to resign his position (Harlan 87–88).

21. In 1858, Lytton chaperoned his mother abroad after the asylum scandal. Constantly beset by the lobbying tactics of both mother and father, Lytton departed his mother after five months and never saw her again (Harlan 88). She died in 1882.

22. The circumstances and causes of Emily's death remain obscure—in part because of the strikingly different accounts of her feuding parents. The "murdered girl" comment appears in Raymond's *Victorian Viceroy*: "The memory of that murdered girl makes it sometimes all but impossible for me to forgive the man who systematically hastened and finally extinguished her existence" (76). See also Mitchell's *Bulwer Lytton*.

23. In reviewing the volume, the *National Review* contended that "the more you read the less you admire him" ("The Poetry of Owen Meredith" 175) and that he demonstrated a "spurious poetic art, which invents decorative artifices to hide the emptiness of its form" (202). *Dublin University Magazine* noted the ever-present "danger of degenerating into mere imitation" ("Clytemnestra" 486) and explained that he "plagiarises" from Aeschylus and at times becomes "Tennysonian" (486). The *Eclectic Review* accused the poet of "free paraphrase of Shakespeare and Browning, variegated by touches, tones, and tints of Keats and Tennyson" ("Meredith's Clytemnestra" 300), labeled him a "mocking-bird" (301), and listed correspondences between lines from Owen Meredith's poems and those of other poets.

24. Writing to his father in 1853, Lytton confessed, "Since I sent off the MS I have discovered in one or two of the poems some quite unconscious plagiarisms wh. I will alter, but I know that most of them are altogether in the colour of other writers. The imitation, however, is more in *form* than in *thought*, I hope you will think. I believe language to be the last thing—the forging of an armoury of oneself" (qtd. in Harlan 60).

25. Textual citations refer to scene number and page number.

26. Commenting on the divorce press and subsequent developments in Victorian marriage, Humpherys argues that while such press coverage progressively "naturalized" divorce ("Coming Apart" 228), it contributed to the social devaluation of marriage as an arrangement for reproduction and legitimate offspring and aided the consolidation of a companionate vision of marital relationships. As Shanley has argued, marriage transmutes into a "locus for companionship and mutual support" and thus "could not be properly understood solely as an institution for sexual or reproductive bonding" ("One Must Ride Behind" 369). Significantly, in each of these poems, characters allude to an ideal companionate model to situate their murderous resolve and to frame their desperate actions. But even the companionate model fails to salvage the relationships in question. The conditions for companionate unions, it seems, are simply not yet in place. In the case of *Clytemnestra*, the portended failure of Clytemnestra and Aegisthus might also suggest negative Victorian attitudes toward remarriage.

27. For textual history and composition dates, see Lynda Hunt Beckman's *Amy Levy: Her Life and Letters*.

28. Citations refer to page numbers in *A Minor Poet and Other Verse* (1884).

29. Although she focuses on "unevenness within the construction and deployment of mid-Victorian representations of gender, and representations of women in particular" (4), Poovey's sense of the "two guises" of ideology—"apparent coherence and authenticity" and "internal instability and artificiality" (3)—aptly characterizes the quandary and the opportunity that Levy confronts in her *Medea*. For it is the unevenness, Poovey argues, that finally "allowed for the emergence ... of a genuinely—although incompletely articulated—oppositional voice" (4).

30. I am indebted to Stuart Warner for this translation.

31. For discussions of Levy's interest in ethnic and racial identities, see Linda Hunt Beckman's *Amy Levy;* Cynthia Scheinberg's "Canonizing the Jew: Amy Levy's Challenge to Victorian Poetic Identity" and "Recasting 'sympathy and judgment': Amy Levy, Women Poets, and the Victorian Dramatic Monologue"; and Josephine McDonagh's *Child Murder and British Culture.*

32. For discussions of common cultural scripts of infanticide, see Josephine McDonagh's *Child Murder and British Culture;* Margaret Arnot's "The Murder of Thomas Sandles: Meanings of a Mid-Nineteenth-Century Infanticide"; Hilary Marland's "Getting Away with Murder?: Puerperal Insanity, Infanticide, and the Defence Plea"; Cath Quinn's "Images and Impulses: Representations of Puerperal Insanity and Infanticide in late Victorian England"; Christine Krueger's "Literary Defenses and Medical Prosecutions: Representing Infanticide in Nineteenth-Century Britain"; and Ann R. Higgenbotham's "'Sin of the Age': Infanticide and Illegitimacy in Victorian London."

33. In *Child Murder and British Culture,* Josephine McDonagh categorizes Levy's *Medea* with other late-Victorian "new Medeas" dating from the late 1860s, which "represented [her] unambiguously as the killer of her children" (164). She reveals "the new ways in which child murder had figured in evolutionary discourse, as the heroic act of the queen bee, or the primal mechanism for social adaptation, that allowed Medea to be reinterpreted" as both "a champion of women's emancipation" and "a force of social progress" (165). McDonagh contends that Levy "saw child murder as the product of a barbarous and atavistic society" and thus it is "an act forced upon [Medea] by a degenerate and backward-looking society" (170). While these evolutionary metaphors and this evolutionary determinism usefully define the radicalism of Levy's Medea and the pessimism of Levy's critique, they tend to obscure the verse drama's interest in the questions of agency surrounding marriage contracting and child-killing.

34. In his handbook of Hardy's poetry, J. O. Bailey cites Edmund Blunden's *Thomas Hardy,* which records Hardy's claim that "it was a true story" (588). Bailey then offers his own vague corroboration: "I was assured by elderly people in Dorset that the event might well have occurred in some remote village" (588).

35. Perhaps, this ambiguity reflects Hardy's deliberate vagueness about his views on marital and domestic politics that received so much attention after *Tess* and *Jude the Obscure.* Speaking in 1895 of *Jude the Obscure,* Hardy wrote, "I feel that a bad marriage is one of the direst things on earth, & one of the cruellest things, but beyond that my opinions on the subject are vague enough" (*Letters* ii.98).

❧ Works Cited ☙

Alkalay-Gut, Karen. "The Thing He Loves: Murder as Aesthetic Experience in 'The Ballad of Reading Gaol.'" *Victorian Poetry* 35:3 (1997): 349–66.
Altick, Richard D. *Victorian Studies in Scarlet*. New York: Norton, 1970.
Anderson, Amanda. *Tainted Souls and Painted Faces: The Rhetoric of Fallenness in Victorian Culture*. Ithaca: Cornell University Press, 1993.
Armstrong, Isobel. *Victorian Scrutinies: Reviews of Poetry 1830–1870*. London: Althone Press, 1972.
———. "Browning and Victorian Poetry of Sexual Love." In *Robert Browning: Writers and Their Background*, ed. Isobel Armstrong. Athens: Ohio University Press, 1974.
———. *Victorian Poetry: Poetry, Poetics, and Politics*. London: Routledge, 1993.
———. "The Victorian Poetry Party." *Victorian Poetry* 42:1 (Spring 2004): 9–27.
Arnot, Margaret L. "The Murder of Thomas Sandles: Meanings of a Mid-Nineteenth-Century Infanticide." In *Infanticide: Historical Perspectives on Child Murder and Concealment, 1550–2000*, ed. Mark Jackson. Burlington: Ashgate, 2002.
Ashton, John. *Modern Street Ballads*. London: Chatto and Windus Piccadilly, 1888.
Babcock, Barbara, ed. *The Reversible World: Symbolic Inversion in Art and Society*. Ithaca: Cornell University Press, 1978.
Bagehot, Walter. "Wordsworth, Tennyson, and Browning: or, Pure, Ornate, and Grotesque Art in English Poetry." *National Review* 19 (November 1864): 27–66.
"Barbarous Murder of a Child by a Schoolmistress." In *Curiosities of Street Literature*, Charles Hindley. London: Reeves and Turner, 1871. 219.
Baring-Gould, Sabine. "Broadside Ballads." In *Strange Survivals: Some Chapters in the History of Man*. London: Methuen and Co., 1892. 180–219.
Barlow, John. *On Man's Power over Himself to Control or Prevent Insanity*. London: William Pickering, 1843.

Barrett Browning, Elizabeth. *Aurora Leigh.* Ed. Margaret Reynolds. New York: Norton, 1996.

Barthes, Roland. "The Death of the Author." In *Image—Music—Text,* trans. Stephen Heath. New York: Hill and Wang. 142–48.

Battles, Elizabeth H. "Slavery Through the Eyes of a Mother: 'The Runaway Slave at Pilgrim's Point.'" *Studies in Browning and His Circle: A Journal of Criticism, History, and Bibliography* 19 (1991): 93–100.

Beckman, Linda Hunt. *Amy Levy: Her Life and Letters.* Athens: Ohio University Press, 2000.

Black, Joel. *The Aesthetics of Murder: A Study in Romantic Literature and Contemporary Culture.* Baltimore: Johns Hopkins University Press, 1991.

Boos, Florence S. "William Morris, Robert Bulwer-Lytton, and the Arthurian Poetry of the 1850s." *Arthuriana* 6.3 (Fall 1996): 31–53.

Bourne Taylor, Jenny and Sally Shuttleworth. *Embodied Selves: An Anthology of Psychological Texts: 1830–1890.* Oxford: Clarendon, 1998.

Brady, Ann P. *Pompilia: A Feminist Reading of Robert Browning's "The Ring and the Book."* Athens: Ohio University Press, 1988.

Brooks, Peter. *The Melodramatic Imagination.* New Haven: Yale University Press, 1976.

Brophy, Sarah. "Elizabeth Barrett Browning's 'The Runway Slave at Pilgrim's Point' and the Politics of Interpretation." *Victorian Poetry* 36:3 (Fall 1998): 273–88.

Brough, Robert. *Medea; Or, The Best of Mothers, With a Brute of a Husband.* London: Thomas Hailes Lacy, 1856.

Brown, Susan. "Pompilia: The Woman (in) Question." *Victorian Poetry* 34.1 (Spring 1996): 15–37.

Browning, Robert. *The Poems of Robert Browning.* Ed. John Woolford and Daniel Karlin. New York: Longman, 1991.

———. *The Ring and the Book.* Ed. Richard Altick. London: Penguin, 1990.

"Browning's Poetry." *The British Quarterly Review* 32 (1 March 1869): 435–59.

Buchanan, Robert [Thomas Maitland]. "The Fleshly School of Poetry: Mr. D. G. Rossetti." *Contemporary Review* XVIII (October 1871): 334–50.

Bucknill, John Charles and Daniel H. Tuke. *A Manual of Psychological Medicine: Containing the History, Nosology, Description, Statistics, Diagnosis, Pathology, and Treatment of Insanity, With an Appendix of Cases.* London: J. Churchill, 1858.

Bullen, J. B. *The Pre-Raphaelite Body: Fear and Desire in Painting, Poetry, and Criticism.* Oxford: Clarendon Press, 1998.

Bulwer-Lytton, Edward. "A Word to the Public." In *Lucretia, Or, The Children of the Night.* 2nd ed. London: Saunders and Otley, 1847.

Burke, Edmund. *A Philosophical Enquiry into the Origin of Our Ideas of the Sublime and Beautiful and Other Pre-Revolutionary Writings.* London: Penguin, 1998.

Bynum, W. F. "Themes in British Psychiatry, J. C. Prichard (1786–1848) to Henry Maudsley (1835–1918)." In *Nature Animated: Historical Case Studies in Greek Medicine, Nineteenth-Century and Recent Biology, Psychiatry, and Psychoanalysis,* Vol. II, ed. Michael Ruse. Boston: D. Reidel Publishing Co, 1983. 225–42.

Cairns, David. *Advocacy and the Making of the Adversarial Criminal Trial 1800–1865.* Oxford: Clarendon, 1998.

Campbell, Thomas. "On A Late Acquittal." *Times* [London] (8 March 1843): 5.

Carpenter, William Benjamin. *Principles of Mental Physiology, With Their Applications to the Training and Discipline of the Mind, and the Study of its Morbid Conditions.* London: Henry S. King, 1874.
"Causes of the Increase of Crime." *Blackwood's Edinburgh Magazine* 56 (July 1844): 1–13.
Chadwick, Roger. *Bureaucratic Mercy: The Home Office and the Treatment of Capital Cases in Victorian Britain.* New York: Garland, 1992.
Chase, Karen and Michael Levenson. *The Spectacle of Intimacy: A Public Life for the Victorian Family.* Princeton: Princeton University Press, 2000.
Child, Francis J. "Ballad Poetry." In *Johnson's New Universal Cyclopaedia,* Vol. 1. New York: A. J. Johnson, 1875–80. 365–68.
Christ, Carol. "Browning's Corpses." *Victorian Poetry* 33 (1995): 391–401.
———. "Introduction." In *A Companion to Victorian Poetry,* ed. Richard Cronin, Alison Chapman, and Antony Harrison. Oxford: Blackwell, 2002.
"Clytemnestra, and Other Poems." *Dublin University Magazine* 46 (1855): 484–495.
Cobbe, Francis Power. "Wife-Torture in England." In *Criminals, Idiots, Women, and Minors: Victorian Writing By Women on Women,* ed. Susan Hamilton. Petersborough, Ontario:Broadview, 1995. 132–70.
Colley, Ann C. *Tennyson and Madness.* Athens: The University of Georgia Press, 1986.
"Complaints Against the New Police." Madden Broadsides. Cambridge University Library. 12.49.
Conolly, John. *An Inquiry Concerning the Indicators of Insanity, With Suggestions for the Better Protection and Care of the Insane.* 1830. London: Dawsons of Pall Mall, 1964.
Cooper, David D. *The Lesson of the Scaffold: The Public Execution Controversy in Victorian England.* Athens: Ohio University Press, 1974.
"A Copy of Verses on F. B. Courvoisier, who was Executed for the Murder of Lord William Russell." *A Collection of Broadsides Printed at Bristol.* British Library 74/1880. c.12.
"Copy of Verses on the Murder of Two Children, By Their Mother, On Battersea Bridge." British Library. 1888c.3.
"Criminal Insanity." *Journal of Psychological Medicine and Mental Pathology,* ed. Forbes Winslow. 1 (1848). London: John Churchill. 38–48.
"Cruel and Inhuman Murder of a Little Boy by his Father." Hindley, *Curiosities.* 224.
Davidoff, Lenore and Catherine Hall. *Family Fortunes: Men and Women of the English Middle Class, 1780–1850.* Chicago: University of Chicago Press, 1987.
De Quincey, Thomas. "On Murder Considered as One of the Fine Arts." In *Selected Writings of Thomas de Quincey,* ed. Philip Van Doren Stern. New York: Random House, 1937.
DeVane, William Clyde. *A Browning Handbook.* New York: Appleton-Century-Crofts Inc, 1955.
Dobell, Sydney. *The Poetical Works of Sydney Dobell.* Vol. 2. London: Smith, Elder, and Co., 1875.
Doggett, Maeve. *Marriage, Wife-Beating, and the Law in Victorian England.* Columbia: University of South Carolina Press, 1993.
Doughty, O. and J. R. Wahl, eds. *The Letters of Dante Gabriel Rossetti.* Vols. 2 and 3. Oxford: Clarendon, 1965.
"Dreadful Murder at Eriswell." Baring-Gould Broadsides. British Library. 1.1.151.

Dymond, Alfred, H. *The Law on Its Trial: Or Personal Reflections Of The Death Penalty And Its Opponents.* London: Alfred W. Bennett, 1865.

Eigen, Joel Peter. *Witnessing Insanity: Madness and Mad-Doctors in the English Court.* New Haven: Yale University Press, 1995.

Ellis, Sarah Stickney. *The Women of England: Their Social Duties, and Domestic Habits.* London: Fisher and Son, 1838.

Emsley, Clive. *Crime and Society in England, 1750–1900.* New York: Longman, 1987.

"The Esher Tragedy." Hindley, *Curiosities.* 199.

"Execution of F. Hinson." Hindley, *Curiosities.* 236.

"Execution of Five Pirates, for Murder" Hindley, *Curiosities.* 217.

Faas, Ekbert. *Retreat into the Mind: Victorian Poetry and the Rise of Psychiatry.* Princeton: Princeton University Press, 1988.

Felluga, Dino Franco. "Verse Novel." In *A Companion to Victorian Poetry*, ed. Richard Cronin, Alison Chapman, and Antony Harrison. Oxford: Blackwell, 2002. 171–86.

———. "Novel Poetry: Transgressing the Law of Genre." *Victorian Poetry* 41:4 (Winter 2003): 490–99.

First Report of the Commissioners on the Law of Divorce 1850. Irish University Press Series of British Parliamentary Papers: Marriage and Divorce. Vol. I. Shannon: Irish University Press, 1969.

Foucault, Michel, ed. *"I, Pierre Riviére, having slaughtered my mother, my sister, and my brother . . .": A Case of Parricide in the 19th Century.* Trans. Frank Jellinek. Lincoln: University of Nebraska Press, 1975.

Foucault, Michel. "What Is An Author?" In *Language, Counter-memory, Practice: Selected Essays and Interviews.* Ed. Donald F. Bouchard. Trans. Donald F. Bouchard and Sherry Simon. Ithaca, NY: Cornell University Press, 1977. 113–38.

———. *Discipline and Punish: The Birth of the Prison.* Trans. Alan Sheridan. New York: Vintage, 1979.

———. *Madness and Civilization: A History of Insanity in the Age of Reason.* Vintage, 1988.

———. *The History of Sexuality. Volume 1: An Introduction.* Trans. Robert Hurley. New York: Vintage, 1990.

Gagnier, Regenia A. *Idylls of the Marketplace: Oscar Wilde and the Victorian Public.* Stanford: Stanford University Press, 1986.

Gallagher, Catherine and Stephen Greenblatt. *Practicing New Historicism.* Chicago: University of Chicago Press, 2000.

Gatrell, V. A. C. *The Hanging Tree: Execution and the People 1770–1868.* Oxford: Oxford University Press, 1994.

Gibson, Mary Ellis. "The Criminal Body in Victorian Britain: The Case of *The Ring and the Book.*" *Browning Institute Studies* 18 (1990): 73–93.

Gillis, John R. *For Better, For Worse: British Marriages, 1600 to the Present.* Oxford: Oxford University Press, 1985.

Gregory, Melissa Valiska. "Robert Browning and the Lure of the Violent Lyric Voice: Domestic Violence and the Dramatic Monologue." *Victorian Poetry* 38:4 (2000): 491–510.

Gretton, Thomas. *Murders and Moralities: English Catchpenny Prints 1800–1860.* London: British Museum Publications, 1980.

Griffin, W. Hall and H. C. Minchin. *The Life of Robert Browning.* London: Methuen, 1910.
Grossman, Jonathan. *The Art of Alibi: English Law Courts and the Novel.* Baltimore: Johns Hopkins University Press, 2002.
Hadley, Elaine. *Melodramatic Tactics: Theatricalized Dissent in the English Marketplace.* Stanford: Stanford University Press, 1995.
Hall, Edith. "Introduction." *Medea.* Oxford: Oxford University Press, 1998.
———. "Medea and British Legislation Before the First World War." *Greece and Rome* xlvi:1 (April 1999): 42–77.
Hamilton, Susan. "The Practice of Everyday Feminism: Frances Power Cobbe, Divorce, and the London *Echo,* 1868–1875." *Victorian Periodicals Review* 35:3 (Fall 2002): 227–42.
Hammerton, A. James. *Cruelty and Companionship: Conflict in Nineteenth-Century Married Life.* London: Routledge, 1992.
Hardy, Thomas. *The Complete Poems.* Ed. James Gibson. New York: Macmillan, 1976.
———. *The Collected Letters of Thomas Hardy.* Ed. Richard Little Purdy and Michael Millgate. Vol. 2. New York: Clarendon, 1978.
Harlan, Aurelia Brooks. *Owen Meredith: A Critical Biography of Robert, First Earl of Lytton.* New York: Columbia University Press, 1946.
Harlan, Aurelia Brooks and J. Lee Harlan, Jr., eds. *Letters from Owen Meredith (Robert, First Earl of Lytton) to Robert and Elizabeth Barrett Browning.* Waco: Baylor University Press, 1936.
Harrison, Antony. *Victorian Poets and the Politics of Culture: Discourse and Ideology.* Charlottesville: University Press of Virginia, 1998.
Heaney, Seamus. "Speranza in Reading: On 'The Ballad of Reading Gaol.'" In *The Redress of Poetry.* New York: Farrar, Strauss and Giroux, 1995. 83–102.
Hepburn, James G. *A Book of Scattered Leaves: Poetry of Poverty in Broadside Ballads of Nineteenth-Century England: Study and Anthology.* Vols. 1 and 2. Lewisburg, PA: Bucknell University Press, 2001–2.
Higgenbotham, Ann R. "'Sin of the Age': Infanticide and Illegitimacy in Victorian London." In *Victorian Scandals: Representations of Gender and Class,* ed. Kristine Ottesen Garrigan. Athens: Ohio University Press, 1992.
Himmelfarb, Gertrude. *The Idea of Poverty: England in the Early Industrial Age.* New York: Knopf, 1984.
Hindley, Charles. *Curiosities of Street Literature.* London: Reeves and Turner, 1871.
———. *The Life and Times of James Catnach (Late of Seven Dials), Ballad Monger.* 1878. London: Redwood, 1970.
———. *History of the Catnach Press.* 1887. Detroit: Singing Tree, 1969.
Hoffer, Peter C. and N. E. H. Hull. *Murdering Mothers: Infanticide in England and New England 1558–1803.* New York: New York University Press, 1981.
"Homicidal Insanity." *Journal of Psychological Medicine and Mental Pathology,* ed. Forbes Winslow. 1 (1848). London: John Churchill. 330–34.
"Homicidal Mania and Moral Insanity." *Saturday Review* 15 (1863): 370–72.
Horstman, Allen. *Victorian Divorce.* London and Sydney: Croom Helm, 1985.
Howard, Ronnalie Roper. "Rossetti's 'A Last Confession': A Dramatic Monologue." *Victorian Poetry* 5:1 (Spring 1967): 21–29.

———. *The Dark Glass: Vision and Technique in the Poetry of Dante Gabriel Rossetti.* Athens: Ohio University Press, 1972.
Humpherys, Anne. *Travels in the Poor Man's Country: The Work of Henry Mayhew.* Athens: University of Georgia Press, 1977.
———. "Breaking Apart: The Early Victorian Divorce Novel." In *Victorian Women Writers and the Woman Question.* Cambridge: Cambridge University Press, 1999. 42–59.
———. "Coming Apart: The Divorce Court and the Press." In *Nineteenth-Century Media and the Construction of Identities,* ed. Laurel Brake, Bill Bell, and David Finkelstein. Hampshire and New York: Palgrave, 2000.
Hunter, Richard and Ida MacAlpine. *Three Hundred Years of Psychiatry: 1535–1860.* London: Oxford University Press, 1963.
"The Increase of Crime." *Blackwood's Edinburgh Magazine* 55 (May 1844): 533–45.
Jackson, Mark. *New-Born Child Murder: Women, Illegitimacy and the Courts in Eighteenth-Century England.* Manchester: Manchester University Press, 1996.
———, ed. *Infanticide: Historical Perspectives on Child Murder and Concealment, 1550–2000.* Burlington: Ashgate, 2002.
James, Louis. *Print and the People 1819–1951.* London: Allen Lane, 1976.
"John Bull, Can You Wonder At Crime." Baring-Gould Broadsides. British Library. 1.1.52.
Joyce, Simon. *Capital Offenses: Geographies of Class and Crime in Victorian London.* Charlottesville: University Press of Virginia, 2003.
Kalikoff, Beth. *Murder and Moral Decay in Victorian Popular Literature.* Ann Arbor: University of Michigan Research, 1986.
Karlin, Daniel. *Browning's Hatreds.* Oxford: Clarendon, 1993.
Kintner, Elvan, ed. *The Letters of Robert Browning and Elizabeth Barrett Browning 1845–1846.* Vol. I. January 1845–March 1846. Cambridge, MA: Belknap, 1969.
Knelman, Judith. *Twisting in the Wind: The Murderess and the English Press.* Toronto: University of Toronto Press, 1998.
Kristeva, Julia. *The Powers of Horror: An Essay on Abjection.* Trans. Leon Roudiez. New York: Columbia University Press, 1982.
Krueger, Christine L. "Literary Defenses and Medical Prosecutions: Representing Infanticide in Nineteenth-Century Britain." *Victorian Studies* 40:2 (1997): 271–94.
Kucich, John. *The Power of Lies: Transgression in Victorian Fiction.* Ithaca: Cornell University Press, 1994.
Kurata, Marilyn J. "Wrongful Confinement: The Betrayal of Women by Men, Medicine, and Law." In *Victorian Scandals: Representations of Gender and Class,* ed. Kristine Ottesen Garrigan. Athens: Ohio University Press, 1992. 43–68.
"Lamentation & Execution of James Longhurst." Hindley, *Curiosities.* 213.
"Lamentation of H. Lingley." Hindley, *Curiosities.* 222.
"Lamentation of J. Mapp." Hindley, *Curiosities.* 221.
"Lamentation in Newgate of the Policeman Who Boned the Mutton." Madden Broadsides. Cambridge University Library. 12.56.
"Lamentation of Samuel Wright." Harvard Law Library. Trial and Execution Broadside 205.
Langbaum, Robert. *The Poetry of Experience: The Dramatic Monologue in Modern Literary Tradition.* London: Chatto and Windus, 1957.

"Last Moments and Confession of Wm. Sheward." Hindley, *Curiosities*. 230.

Leckie, Barbara. *Culture and Adultery: The Novel, the Newspaper, and the Law, 1857–1914*. Philadelphia: University Pennsylvania Press, 1999.

Leps, Marie-Christine. *Apprehending the Criminal: The Production of Deviance in Nineteenth-Century Discourse*. Durham: Duke University Press, 1992.

Levine, Philippa. *Feminist Lives in Victorian England: Private Roles and Public Commitment*. Oxford: Blackwell, 1990.

Levy, Amy. *A Minor Poet and Other Verse*. London: T. Fisher Unwin, 1884.

"Life, Trial, Character, Confession, and Execution of Stephen Forward." Hindley, *Curiosities*. 216.

"Life, Trial, Sentence, and Execution of Catherine Wilson, for the Murder of Mrs. Soames." Harvard Law Library. Trial and Execution Broadside 233.

"Life, Trial, Sentence, and Execution of S. Adams for the Murder of his Sister-in-Law, Martha Page." British Library. 1888c.3.

"The Literature of the Streets" *Edinburgh Review* 165 (January 1887): 40–65.

"Literature of the Streets." *J. and R. M. Wood's Typographic Advertiser* 1:10 (1 March 1863): 73.

Litzenger, Boyd and Donald Smalley. *Browning: The Critical Heritage*. New York: Barnes and Noble, 1970.

Lytton, Edward Robert Bulwer. (Owen Meredith). *Clytemnestra*. London: Chapman, 1855.

Macintosh, Fiona. "Medea Transposed: Burlesque and Gender on the Mid-Victorian Stage." In *Medea in Performance: 1500–2000*. Oxford: Legenda: European Humanities Research Center, 2000. 75–99.

Marland, Hilary. "Getting Away with Murder?: Puerperal Insanity, Infanticide, and the Defence Plea." In *Infanticide: Historical Perspectives on Child Murder and Concealment, 1550–2000*, ed. Mark Jackson. Burlington: Ashgate, 2002. 168–92.

Martin, Loy D. *Browning's Dramatic Monologues and the Post-Romantic Subject*. Baltimore: Johns Hopkins University Press, 1985.

Mason, Michael. "Browning and the Dramatic Monologue." In *Robert Browning, Writers and Their Background*, ed. Isobel Armstrong. Athens: Ohio University Press, 1975. 231–66.

Matus, Jill L. *Unstable Bodies: Victorian Representations of Sexuality and Maternity*. Manchester: Manchester University Press, 1995.

Maudsley, H. and C. A. L. Robertson. *Insanity and Crime: A Medico-Legal Commentary on the Case of George Victor Townley*. London: Churchill, 1864.

Maudsley, Henry. *Body and Mind: An Inquiry into their Connection and Mutual Influence, Specially in Reference to Mental Disorder*. 1871. New York: Appleton and Co., 1890.

———. *Body and Will: Being an Essay Concerning Will in its Metaphysical, Physiological, and Pathological Aspects*. New York: D. Appleton and Company, 1884.

———. *Responsibility in Mental Disease*. London : K. Paul, Trench, Truebner, 1892.

———. *Pathology of Mind: A Study of Its Distempers, Deformities, and Disorders*. London: Julian Friedmann, 1979.

Mayhew, Henry, ed. *London Labour and the London Poor*. Vol. 1. 1861. New York: Dover, 1968.

Maynard, John. *Browning's Youth*. Cambridge: Harvard University Press, 1977.
McConville, Séan. *English Local Prisons 1860–1900: Next Only to Death*. London: Routledge, 1995.
McDonagh, Josephine. *Child Murder and British Culture 1720–1900*. Cambridge: Cambridge University Press, 2003.
McGann, Jerome, ed. *The Complete Writings and Pictures of Dante Gabriel Rossetti: A Hypermedia Research Archive*. Online. http://www.rossettiarchive.org.
"Meredith's Clytemnestra." *The Eclectic Review* 102 (September 1855): 296–302.
"Miles Weatherhill, the Young Weaver, and his Sweetheart, Sarah Bell." Hindley, *Curiosities*. 214.
Mill, John Stuart. *On The Subjection of Women*. *Essays on Equality, Law, and Education by John Stuart Mill*. Ed. John M. Robson. Toronto: University of Toronto Press, 1984. 259–82.
Miller, D. A. *The Novel and the Police*. Berkeley: University of California Press, 1988.
Mitchell, Leslie. *Bulwer Lytton: The Rise and Fall of a Victorian Man of Letters*. London–New York: Hambledon and London, 2003.
"Moral Theology; or, The Priest and The Physician." *The Journal of Psychological Medicine and Mental Pathology* 1 (1848): 557–71.
Morgan, Thaïs. "Afterword: Victorian Scandals, Victorian Strategies." *Victorian Scandals: Representations of Gender and Class*, ed. Kristine Ottesen Garrigan. Athens: Ohio University Press, 1992. 289–319.
Moriarty, Jane. *The Role of Mental Illness in Criminal Trials*. Vol. 1 of *History of Mental Illness in Criminal Cases: The English Tradition*. London: Routledge, 2001.
Mulvey-Roberts, Marie. "Fame, Notoriety, and Madness: Edward Bulwer-Lytton Paying the Price of Greatness." *Critical Survey* 13:2 (2001): 115–34.
"Murder of a Wife at Ashburnham, Near Hastings." Hindley, *Curiosities*. 226.
Nassaar, Christopher S. "The Silent Priest: Rossetti's 'A Last Confession' Revisited." *Journal of Pre-Raphaelite Studies* 6 (Spring 1997): 33–37.
Nathan, Leonard. "The Ballads of Reading Gaol: At the Limits of the Lyric." In *Critical Essays on Oscar Wilde*, ed. Regenia Gagnier. New York: G. K. Hall, 1991. 213–22.
Neuburg, Victor. "The Literature of the Streets." In *The Victorian City: Images and Realities*, ed. H. J. Dyos and Michael Wolff. London: Routledge, 1973. 191–210.
Nord, Deborah Epstein. "The Social Explorer as Anthropologist: Victorian Travellers Among the Urban Poor." In *Visions of the Modern City: Essays in History, Art, and Literature*, ed. William Sharpe and Leonard Wallock. New York: Columbia University Press, 1983. 118–30.
O'Connell, Sheila. *The Popular Print in England 1550–1850*. London: British Museum, 1999.
"On the Plea of Monomania in Criminal Cases." *Journal of Psychological Medicine and Mental Pathology* 1 (1848): 483–85.
"Owen Meredith's Poems." *Tait's Edinburgh Magazine* NS 22 (1855): 677–82.
Parry, Ann. "Sexual Exploitation and Freedom: Religion, Race, and Gender in Elizabeth Barrett Browning's 'The Runaway Slave at Pilgrim's Point.'" *Studies in Browning and His Circle: A Journal of Criticism, History, and Bibliography* 16 (1988): 114–26.
"Particulars of the Life, Trial, Confession, and Execution of Courvoisier." Harvard Law Library. Dying Speeches 271.

Paul, Charles Kegan. *Memories.* London: Kegan Paul, Trench, Trubner, and Co., 1899.
Perkin, Joan. *Women and Marriage in Nineteenth-Century England.* London: Routledge, 1989.
Petch, Simon. "Equity and Natural Law in *The Ring and the Book.*" *Victorian Poetry* 35:1 (Spring 1997): 105–11.
Philips, David. "Three 'Moral Entrepreneurs' and the Creation of a 'Criminal Class' in England, c. 1790s–1840s." *Crime, Histoire & Sociétés/Crime, History & Societies* 7:1 (2003): 79–108.
"The Plea of Insanity in Criminal Cases." *Journal of Psychological Medicine and Mental Pathology* 7:26 (1854): 184–200.
"The Poetry of Owen Meredith." *National Review* 17 (1863): 174–203.
"The Poetry of Seven Dials." *The Quarterly Review* 122 (1867): 382–406.
Poovey, Mary. *Uneven Developments: The Ideological Work of Gender in Victorian England.* Chicago: University of Chicago Press, 1988.
Prichard, James Cowles. "Insanity." *Cyclopaedia of Practical Medicine,* Vol. 2, ed. J. Forbes, A. Tweedie, and J. Conolly. London: Sherwood, Gilbert, and Piper, 1833. 824–75.
———. *A Treatise on Insanity and Other Disorders Affecting the Mind.* London: Sherwood, Gilbert, and Piper, 1835.
———. *On the Different Forms of Insanity, in Relation to Jurisprudence.* London: Hippolyte Bailliere Publisher, 1842.
Quinn, Cath. "Images and Impulses: Representations of Puerperal Insanity and Infanticide in late Victorian England." In *Infanticide: Historical Perspectives on Child Murder and Concealment, 1550–2000,* ed. Mark Jackson. Burlington: Ashgate, 2002.
Quinton, R. F. *Crime and Criminals, 1876–1910.* London: Longmans, Green, 1910.
Rader, Ralph W. "The Dramatic Monologue and Related Lyric Forms." *Critical Inquiry* 3:1 (1976): 131–51.
Radzinowicz, Leon. *A History of English Criminal Law and Its Administration from 1750.* Vol. 1. New York: Macmillan, 1957.
Raymond, E. Neill. *Victorian Viceroy: The Life of Robert, the First Earl of Lytton.* London: Regency Press, 1980.
Redesdale, Lord. "Lord Redesdale's Opinion; and Statement of his Reasons for not Entirely Concurring in the Preceding Report." *Irish University Press Series of British Parliamentary Papers: Marriage and Divorce.* Vol. I. Shannon: Irish University Press, 1969. 23–26.
Reed, John R. *The Victorian Will.* Athens: Ohio University Press, 1989.
Report of the Capital Punishment Commission. Parliamentary Papers. Volume 21: 1866.
Reynolds, Margaret. *Aurora Leigh: Authoritative Text, Backgrounds, Contexts, and Criticism.* New York: W. W. Norton, 1996.
Rodensky, Lisa. *The Crime in Mind: Criminal Responsibility and the Victorian Novel.* New York: Oxford University Press, 2003.
Rose, Lionel. *The Massacre of the Innocents: Infanticide in Britain 1800–1939.* London: Routledge, 1986.
Rossetti, Dante Gabriel. "The Stealthy School of Criticism." *The Athenaeum* No. 2303 (Dec. 16 1871): 792–94.
———. *Collected Poetry and Prose.* Ed. Jerome McGann. New Haven: Yale University Press, 2003.

Rowbotham, Judith and Kim Stevenson. *Criminal Conversations: Victorian Crimes, Social Panic, and Moral Outrage.* Columbus: The Ohio State University Press, 2005.

Rylance, Rick. *Victorian Psychology and British Culture 1850–1880.* Oxford: Oxford University Press, 2000.

Rylands, Gordon L. *Crime: Its Causes and Remedy.* London: T Fisher Unwin, 1889.

Savage, Gail. "The Operation of the 1857 Divorce Act, 1860–1910: A Research Note." *Journal of Social History* 16 (1983): 103–10.

———. "'Intended Only for the Husband': Gender, Class, and the Provision for Divorce in England, 1858–1868." In *Victorian Scandals: Representations of Gender and Class,* ed. Kristine Ottesen Garrigan. Athens: Ohio University Press, 1992. 11–42.

Scheinberg, Cynthia. "Canonizing the Jew: Amy Levy's Challenge to Victorian Poetic Identity." *Victorian Studies* 39 (1996): 173–200.

———. "Recasting 'Sympathy and Judgment': Amy Levy, Women Poets, and the Victorian Dramatic Monologue." *Victorian Poetry* 35 (1997): 173–79.

Schramm, Jan-Melissa. *Testimony and Advocacy in Victorian Law, Literature, and Theology.* Cambridge: Cambridge University Press, 2000.

Scull, Andrew. *Museums of Madness: The Social Organization of Insanity in Nineteenth-Century England.* New York: St. Martin's Press, 1979.

———. *The Most Solitary of Afflictions.* New Haven: Yale University Press, 1993.

"Sentences of the Prisoners at the Old Bailey Sessions, September 12." 1824. St. Bride Printing Library. S710.

Shanley, Mary Lyndon. "'One Must Ride Behind': Married Women's Rights and the Divorce Act of 1857." *Victorian Studies* 25:3 (1982): 355–76.

———. *Feminism, Marriage, and the Law in Victorian England, 1850–1895.* Princeton: Princeton University Press, 1989.

Shepard, Leslie. *John Pitts, Ballad Printer of Seven Dials, London, 1765–1844.* London: Private Libraries Association, 1969.

———. *The History of Street Literature.* Detroit: Singing Tree Press, 1973.

———. *The Broadside Ballad: A Study in Origins and Meaning.* Hatsboro: Legacy Books, 1978.

"Shocking Murder of a Wife and Six Children." Hindley, *Curiosities.* 234.

Shuttleworth, Sally. *Charlotte Brontë and Victorian Psychology.* Cambridge: Cambridge University Press, 1996.

Skultans, Veida, ed. *Madness and Morals: Ideas on Insanity in the Nineteenth Century.* London: Routledge and Kegan Paul, 1975.

Skultans, Veida. *English Madness: Ideas on Insanity, 1580–1890.* London: Routledge and Kegan Paul, 1979.

Slinn, E. Warwick. "The Dramatic Monologue." In *A Companion to Victorian Poetry.* Oxford: Blackwell, 2002.

———. *Victorian Poetry as Cultural Critique: The Politics of Performative Language.* Charlottesville: University Press of Virginia, 2003.

Smith, Charles Manby. *The Little World of London; or, Pictures in Little of London Life.* London: Arthur Hall, 1857.

Smith, Roger. "The Boundary Between Insanity and Criminal Responsibility in Nineteenth-Century England." In *Madhouses, Mad-Doctors, and Madmen: The Social His-*

tory of Psychiatry in the Victorian Era, ed. Andrew Scull. Philadelphia: University of Pennsylvania Press, 1981. 363–84.

———. *Trial by Medicine: Insanity and Responsibility in Victorian Trials.* Edinburgh: Edinburgh University Press, 1981.

"The Sorrowful Lamentation and Last Farewell to the World of Eight Unhappy People, Who Are to Die at the Old Bailey, on Tuesday the First." St. Bride Printing Library. S737.

Stallybrass, Peter and Allon White. *The Politics and Poetics of Transgression.* Ithaca: Cornell University Press, 1986.

Stephen, George. *The Juryman's Guide.* London: C. Knight, 1845.

Stephen, James Fitzjames. "On the Policy of Maintaining the Limits at Present Imposed by Law on the Criminal Responsibility of Madmen." Papers Read Before the Juridical Society: 1855–1858. Vol 1. London: V. and R. Stevens and G. S. Norton, 1858.

———. *A General View of the Criminal Law of England.* London: Macmillan, 1863.

———. *A History of the Criminal Law of England.* London: Macmillan, 1883.

Stewart, Garrett. *Death Sentences: Styles of Dying in British Fiction.* Cambridge: Harvard University Press, 1984.

Stone, Lawrence. *The Family, Sex, and Marriage in England, 1500–1800.* New York: Harper and Row, 1979.

———. *Broken Lives: Separation and Divorce in England, 1660–1857.* Oxford: Oxford University Press, 1993.

Stone, Marjorie. "Genre Subversion and Gender Inversion: *The Princess* and *Aurora Leigh.*" *Victorian Poetry* 25:2 (1987 Summer): 101–27.

———. "Between Ethics and Anguish: Feminist Ethics, Feminist Aesthetics, and Representations of Infanticide in 'The Runaway Slave at Pilgrim's Point' and *Beloved.*" In *Between Ethics and Aesthetics: Crossing the Boundaries,* ed. Dorota Glowacka and Stephen Boos. Albany: State University of New York Press, 2002. 131–58.

———. "Elizabeth Barrett Browning and the Garrisonians: 'The Runaway Slave at Pilgrim's Point,' the Boston Female Anti-Slavery Society, and Abolitionist Discourse in the *Liberty Bell.* In *Victorian Women Poets,* ed. Alison Chapman. Woodbridge, England: Brewer, 2003. 33–55.

"Street Ballads." *The National Review* 13:26 (October 1861): 397–419.

Surridge, Lisa. *Bleak Houses: Marital Violence in Victorian Fiction.* Athens: Ohio University Press, 2005.

Symons, Jelinger C. *Tactics for the Times: As Regards the Condition and Treatment of The Dangerous Classes.* London: John Ollivier, Pall Mall, 1849.

Taylor, David. "Beyond the Bounds of Respectable Society: The 'Dangerous Classes' in Victorian and Edwardian England." In *Criminal Conversations: Victorian Crimes, Social Panic and Moral Outrage,* ed. Judith Rowbotham and Kim Stevenson. Columbus: The Ohio State University Press, 2005. 3–22.

———. *Crime, Policing and Punishment in England, 1750–1914.* New York: St. Martin's, 1998.

Thackeray, William Makepeace. "Going to See a Man Hanged." *Fraser's Magazine* 22 (August 1840): 150–58.

Thomas, Ronald R. *Detective Fiction and the Rise of Forensic Science.* Cambridge: Cambridge University Press, 1999.

Tosh, John. *A Man's Place: Masculinity and the Middle-Class Home in Victorian England.* New Haven: Yale University Press, 1997.

Townsend, William C. *Modern State Trials,* Vols. 1 and 2. London: Longman, Brown, Green and Longmans, 1850.

"The Treatment of Crime." *Journal of Mental Science* 47 (1901): 354–55.

"Trial and Execution of Betty the Cook." St. Bride Printing Library. S 395.

"Trial, Sentence, Confession, and Execution of F. B. Courvoisier." Hindley, *Curiosities.* 193.

Trodd, Anthea. *Domestic Crime in the Novel.* New York: St. Martin's, 1989.

Tromp, Marlene. *The Private Rod: Marital Violence, Sensation, and the Law in Victorian Britain.* Charlottesville: University Press of Virginia, 2000.

Tucker Herbert F. *Browning's Beginning: The Art of Disclosure.* Minneapolis: University of Minnesota Press, 1980.

———. "Dramatic Monologue and the Overhearing of Lyric." In *Critical Essays on Robert Browning,* ed. Mary Ellis Gibson. New York: G. K. Hall and Co, 1992. 21–36.

———. "From Monomania to Monologue: 'St. Simeon Stylites' and the Rise of the Victorian Dramatic Monologue." *Victorian Poetry* 22: 121–37.

Tuke, D. Hack. "The Plea of Insanity in Relation to the Penalty of Death; Or, the Report of the Capital Punishment Commission Psychologically Reviewed. *The Social Science Review* NS 5:28 (April 2 1866).

———. *Prichard and Symonds: In Especial Relation to Mental Science with Chapters on Moral Insanity.* London: J and A Churchill. 1891.

"Verses on Daniel Good." Hindley, *Curiosities.* 195.

Vicinus, Martha. *The Industrial Muse: A Study of Nineteenth Century British Working-Class Literature.* New York: Harper, 1974.

———. *Broadsides of the Industrial North.* Frank Graham: Newcastle upon Tyne, 1975.

Vincent, David. *Literacy and Popular Culture: England 1750–1914.* Cambridge: Cambridge University Press, 1993.

Walker, Nigel. *Crime and Insanity in England,* Vol. 1. Edinburgh: Edinburgh University Press, 1968.

Walkowitz. Judith. *City of Dreadful Delight: Narratives of Sexual Danger in Late-Victorian London.* Chicago: University of Chicago Press, 1992.

Welsh, Alexander. *Strong Representations: Narrative and Circumstantial Evidence.* Baltimore: Johns Hopkins University Press, 1992.

West, Donald and Alexander Walk. *Daniel McNaughton: His Trial and the Aftermath.* Ashford, Kent: Headley, 1977.

Wiener, Martin J. *Reconstructing the Criminal: Culture, Law and Policy in England, 1830–1914.* Cambridge: Cambridge University Press, 1990.

———. *Men of Blood: Violence, Manliness and Criminal Justice in Victorian England.* Cambridge: Cambridge University Press, 2004.

Wilde, Oscar. *The Letters of Oscar Wilde.* Ed. Rupert Hart-Davis. New York: Harcourt Brace, 1962.

———. "Pen, Pencil and Poison." In *The Complete Works of Oscar Wilde: Stories, Plays, Poems, and Essays,* ed. J. B. Foreman. New York: Harper and Row, 1989.

Williams, Carolyn. "'Genre' and 'Discourse' in Victorian Cultural Studies." *Victorian Literature and Culture* 27:2 (1999): 517–20.

Winslow, Forbes. *The Plea of Insanity, in Criminal Cases.* London: H. Renshaw, 1843.
———. "Recent Trials in Lunacy." *The Journal of Psychological Medicine* 7 (1854): 572–625.
Woolford, John and Daniel Karlin, eds. *The Poems of Robert Browning.* New York: Longman, 1991.
Zimmerman, Georges Denis. *Songs of Irish Rebellion: Irish Political Street Ballads and Rebel Songs, 1780–1900.* 1966. Dublin: Four Courts Press, 2002.

INDEX

Page numbers in italics refer to the illustrations.

abjection, 30, 33, 48, 59, 64, 76, 101, 107, 127, 162
Act for the Better Prevention and Punishment of Aggravated Assaults upon Women and Children (1853), 178–79, 258n2, 258n6
Adams, S., 44
adultery, 71–72, 87–88, 137, 174, 175, 177, 181–82, 203, 247n16, 258n5; in *Clytemnestra,* 206, 213, 216, 218, 221; in *The Ring and the Book,* 185, 187, 188, 191, 197, 259n12
Aeschylus. See *Agamemnon*
Agamemnon (Aeschylus), 205, 206, 209, 220, 261n23
Alison, Archibald, 245n6
Alkalay-Gut, Karen, 244n3 (intro.)
Altick, Richard, 43, 95
Anderson, Amanda, 244n3 (intro.)
"Angel in the House" (Patmore), 205
anthropology, criminal, 11, 15, 34
Armstrong, Isobel, 13–16, 18, 25, 103–4, 108, 116, 126, 136, 164, 242, 248–49n27, 251–52n9, 252n10

Arnold, Matthew, 255n22
Arnot, Margaret, 246n13, 262n32
Art Catholicism, 147, 255n21
Ashton, John, 40
Asquith, Henry Herbert, 106
Aurora Leigh (Barrett Browning), 3, 15–16, 223, 244n3 (intro.)

Babcock, Barbara, 47
Bagehot, Walter, 165, 255n22
Bailey, J. O., 262n35
Balder (Dobell), 242
ballad: folk, 40–41; literary, 104; lyrical, 104; political, 43, 104, 249n29. *See also* ballad, crime
ballad, crime, 1, 5–6, 29–108; as "astonishing disclosures" of details, 23, 29, 30, 53–60, 62–77, 241, 246n11; as authorless texts, 80, 248nn22–23; and the broadside print industry, 6, 39–41, 54, 78, 79, 103, 244nn1–2, 244–45n3, 245n4; as challenge to class-based ideologies of crime and punishment, 6, 22–23, 29–30, 34,

39, 42, 43, 44, 46–48, 50–53, 56, 60, 92–95, 97–98, 102, 104; classed ethnographies of, 40, 43, 244–45n3; construction of audience by, 52–53, 103; dialogues between murderers and victims in, 58, 62–63; evocations of history in, 52–53, 58, 68, 73; evolution of, 6, 22, 33, 39; generic codes of, 6, 33, 245n3, 246n8, 248n23; and growth of popular literacy, 29; and hierarchies of poetic value, 4, 6, 21, 22–23, 30, 33–34, 39–42, 103–4, 108; influence on Wilde of, 104–8; introductions and conclusions of, 246n8; invoked by Browning, 104, 191–92, 249n28; irony and irreverence in, 44, 46–48, 50–52, 76, 81, 246n9; on the metropolitan police, 50–51; moralistic readings of and Christian discourse in, 43–44, 46–48, 43, 246n8; on multiple executions, 78–79, 248n20; overlooked in critical study, 3–4, 22, 29–30, 33, 103; as reflections of legal system, 6, 30, 33, 39, 46, 57, 78–80, 86–90, 92–95; shock and pathos in last lamentations of, 6, 22, 23–24, 29, 30, 47, 53, 77–90, 92–98, 100–102; signifying power of bodies in, 59–60, 74, 76; as song, 6, 29, 39–40, 54, 78, 98; suppressed by police, 39; wages for writers of, 244–45n3, 245–47n7; waning of, 40; woodcut images in, 29, 30, 244n2
"Ballad of Ida Grey, The" (Levy), 223
"Ballad of Reading Gaol, The" (Wilde), 3, 104–8, 244n3 (intro.), 249n29
"Barbarous Murder of a Child by a Schoolmistress," 73–75
Baring-Gould, Sabine, 41
Barlow, John, 122, 251n8
Barrett Browning, Elizabeth, 142, 205, 244n3 (intro.), 260n16. See also *Aurora Leigh;* "Runaway Slave at Pilgrim's Point, The"
Barthes, Roland, 80
Battles, Elizabeth H., 244n3 (intro.)

Beckman, Linda Hunt, 223, 226, 261n27, 262n31
Bell, Sarah, 46
Bethlem Hospital, 71, 247n15, 249n2
Black, Joel, 53–54
Blackstone, William, 173, 187, 201, 249n13, 268n15
Blackwood's, 36–37
Blunden, Edmund, 262n34
Boos, Florence, 201, 208–9, 219
Bourne Taylor, Jenny, 252n11
Braddon, Elizabeth, 181
Brady, Ann, 195, 259n14
British Quarterly Review, The, 200
Britten, George, 80
Broadmoor Hospital, 249n2, 250n7
Brontë, Charlotte. See *Jane Eyre*
Brooks, Peter, 56
Brophy, Sarah, 244n3 (intro.)
Brough, Mary Ann, 71–73, 74, 247nn15–16
Brough, Robert. See *Medea; Or, The Best of Mothers, with a Brute of a Husband*
Broussais, M., 127
Brown, Martin, 81
Brown, Susan, 259n14
Browning, Robert, 243n3; and Lytton, 260n16, 261n23; modulation of voices by, 19, 25, 128–29, 132, 133, 139, 141–43, 145–46, 185; and poetics of indeterminacy and interpretation of medicolegal debates, 116, 124–47, 253–54n16; and Rossetti, 254–55n20, 256n23; and textual networks, 104. See also *titles of individual works*
Buchanan, Robert (Thomas Maitland), 148, 159, 165, 254n20, 255n22
Bucknill, John Charles, 252n13
Bullen, J. B., 150, 161
Bulwer-Lytton, Edward George Earle Lytton, 202–3, 206, 220, 260nn17–19, 260–61n20, 261n22, 261n24. See also *titles of individual works*
Bulwer-Lytton, Emily, 203, 260n18, 261n22
Bulwer-Lytton, Rosina (née Wheeler),

202–3, 260n18, 260–61n20, 261nn21–22. *See also Cheveley; or, The Man of Honor*
Burke, Edmund. *See Philosophical Enquiry into the Origin of Our Ideas of the Sublime and Beautiful, A*
Bynum, W. F., 251n8
Byron, George Gordon, Lord, 220, 255n20

Cairns, David, 97, 248n21, 248n26
Campbell, Thomas. *See* "On a Late Acquittal"
capitalism, 35, 37, 48, 56
capital punishment. *See* execution
Carpenter, William, 122
Catnach, James, 54, 59, 245n3, 248n23
Chadwick, Roger, 163
Chartism, 35, 104
Chase, Karen, 172, 175, 178, 181, 182, 258n3, 259n9
Cherry, Emily, 181
Cheveley; or, The Man of Honor (R. Bulwer-Lytton), 260n20
Child, Francis J., 40
child-murder, 3, 7, 58, 65–76, 169, 209, 222, 232, 234, 246n13, 247n15, 247n17, 262nn32–33
Christ, Carol T., 127, 128, 132
Clark, Eliza, 68–71, 74
class, social, 1–6, 15, 244–45n3; and dramatic monologues' treatment of class privilege, 115, 124, 126, 134, 135, 137, 140, 144, 146; and imbalanced application of criminal insanity theories, 92–95, 120, 248n24; and middle-class reading and writing, 2, 16, 18, 140, 241, 246n8, 255n22; and middle-class gendered spheres, 26, 171; and power in *The Ring and the Book*, 185, 186, 189, 191, 197; and restrictions on access to divorce, 175, 178; and silencing of the lower classes, 38–40, 50, 76, 92, 102, 105, 106; and Victorian discourse of dangerous/criminal classes, 34–42,

46–47, 50–51, 56, 60, 75, 95–98, 100, 107–8, 189, 246–47n14; and Wilde's analysis of otherness and motive, 9–11; and working-class challenges to authority, 6, 19, 22–23, 30, 34, 39, 42, 43, 44, 46–48, 50–53, 60, 92–95, 97–98, 102, 104
closet drama. *See* drama, closet
Clytemnestra (Lytton), 25–27, 170–71, 183–84, 200–221, 223, 236; and domestic politics, 7, 25–27, 201–21, 235, 236, 261n26; and Christian dogma, 201, 204; genres and competing discourses in, 25, 27, 170–71, 202, 205, 207, 216, 219–21, 237; at head of Lytton's first poetry collection, 201, 202, 260n17; imitation/plagiarism in, 205, 261nn23–24; and Lytton's family history, 202–3; modern content of, 7, 27, 170, 201, 204–7, 215–16, 220; recentering of Clytemnestra figure in, 205; role of chorus in, 207–8, 213–14, 215, 220; Victorian criticism of, 205, 219–20, 261n23
Cobbe, Francis Power, 180, 183
Cockburn, Alexander, 249n2, 250n4
Cohen, Ralph, 108
Colley, Ann, 118
Collins, Wilkie, 181
"Complaints Against the New Police," 50
Connolly, Dr. John, 123
Cooper, David D., 246n8
"Copy of Verses on F. B. Courvoisier, who was Executed for the Murder of Lord William Russell," 44, 96–98, 248n25
"Copy of Verses on the Murder of Two Children, By Their Mother, On Battersea Bridge," 68–71, 74–75
Courvoisier, Francis B., 44, 45, 46, 95–98, 248nn25–26
Cresswell, Sir Cresswell, 179
crime: and culture, 7–11, 16, 42, 242; evolving discourses of, 1, 4, 243n1; as metaphor for modernity, 11, 15–16, 204, 237; and poetic genres,

1–7, 20–22, 28, 103–5, 108, 164–65, 240–41, 243–44n3; social foundations of motive for, 10–11, 35, 48, 75–76; and Victorian discourse of criminal classes, 34–42, 46–47, 50–51, 56, 60, 75, 95–98, 100, 107–8, 189, 246–47n14; Victorian obsession with, 15, 52–53, 95
Criminal Evidence Act (1898), 248n21
Criminal Lunatics Act (1800), 250n7
Criminal Lunatics Act (1884), 251n7
Criminal Lunatics Amendment Act (1816), 250n7
Criminal Lunatics Asylum Act (1860), 250n7
"Cruel and Inhuman Murder of a Little Boy by his Father," 65–67, 74–75
Curtis v. Curtis, 259n8

Daily Chronicle, 106
Darwinism, 15, 152
Davidoff, Lenore, 233
Davis, Robert Con, 17
Death, Maria, 87–90
death penalty. *See* execution
de Quincey, Thomas. *See* "On Murder Considered as One of the Fine Arts"
Derby Gaol, 92
Derrida, Jacques, 20, 146
Dickens, Charles, 79, 95
divorce, 7, 19, 26, 171, 172–83, 188, 198–99, 201, 223, 228–29, 236, 238, 258nn4–5, 259n7, 259n12, 261n26
Divorce and Matrimonial Causes Act (1857) (or Divorce Act), 172–73, 175, 178, 202, 203, 258n2
Divorce and Matrimonial Causes Court (or divorce court), 26, 172, 174, 175–81, 184, 259n8
Divorce News and Police Reporter, 180
Dobell, Sydney. *See Balder*
Doggett, Maeve, 188, 201, 258n6, 259n13, 268n15
Dollimore, Jonathan, 56
drama, closet, 7, 25, 27, 203, 221
drama, verse, 1, 7, 19, 170, 171, 207

Dramatic Lyrics (Browning), 166, 254n17
dramatic monologue, 1, 3, 6–7; criticism of transgressive aesthetics and badness of, 148, 159, 164–66, 255n22; and history, 250–51n9; and intertwining of psychological theories and dramatic poetry generally, 115–16, 165–66, 251–52n9; irony and indeterminacy in, 6, 116, 124, 128–29, 131, 132, 159, 160; murderous subjectivity and theories of homicidal lunacy in, 6, 19, 24–25, 114–16, 124–66; performative hybridity of, 114, 130, 148; and the sublime, 6, 25, 116, 117, 132, 140, 146, 149, 156, 165
Dramatic Romances and Lyrics (Browning), 142, 254n17
"Dreadful Murder at Eriswell," 46
Drummond, Edward, 110, 249n1
Dublin University Magazine, 220, 261n23
Duggan, Emma, 75–76, 247n18
Duggan, Walter James, 75–76, 247n18
Dymond, Alfred, 90, 92

Eagleton, Terry, 16
Echo, The, 180
Eclectic Review, 261n23
Eigen, J. P., 246n13
Ellis, Sarah Stickney, 201
Emsley, Clive, 248n21
"Esher Tragedy, The," 71–73, 74–75, 247n16
Esquirol, J. E. D., 117, 118, 120, 151, 251n8, 252n13
Eugene Aram (Bulwer-Lytton), 204
Euripides, 206. See also *Medea*
"Execution of F. Hinson," 87–90
"Execution of Five Pirates, The," 47
"Execution of John Gleeson Wilson," 30, 31, 52, 57
executions, 11, 244n1; and class conflict, 5, 6, 23, 78, 92–98; decrease in, 78–79, 247n19; and destabilizing of

center and transgressive margin, 12, 47, 67; irresolvable moral dilemma of, 47; in last lamentation ballads, 6, 22, 23–24, 29, 47, 77–90, 92–98, 100–102; movements for abolition and parliamentary reconsideration of, 37–38, 44, 65, 78, 90, 92–95, 98, 110, 112, 242; multiple, 78–79, 247n19, 248n20; as ritual of exclusion, 9; and scaffold site/practices, 5, 12, 13, 21, 65, 67, 78, 85, 87, 95, 98, 100–102, 107; as silencing mechanism, 77–78, 79, 86–87, 95, 102, 105
"Extracts from Gosschen's Diary" (Wilson), 125, 253n16

Faas, Ekbert, 116, 125, 148, 150, 248n24, 253n16, 257n32
Felluga, Dino, 20, 108, 199–200
Field, Michael, 104
Forster, John, 260n16
Forward, Stephen, 52
Foucault, Michel, 12, 16, 51–52, 77, 78, 80–81, 154, 156, 243n1

Gagnier, Regenia, 108, 244n3 (intro.)
Gallagher, Catherine, 19, 20, 240, 241
Garrigan, Kristine Otteson, 258n3
Gatrell, V. A. C., 94, 246n8
gender, 1, 3, 5, 60, 64–65, 89–90, 115, 164, 259n13; and debating domesticity and marriage in *The Ring and the Book,* 25–27, 170–71, 183–201, 236–37, 259n14; and femininity in the Catherine Wilson case, 98, 100–101; and general readings of women's violence, 247n16; and improvements in women's legal equality, 223; and inequality in grounds for divorce, 175–76, 178, 181–82; and male privilege in "My Last Duchess," 25, 140, 146; and murderous wives/mothers in Lytton and Levy, 25–27, 170–71, 183–84, 200–237, 262n29, 262n33; and poisoning as feminine crime, 144–46;

and power in "Porphyria's Lover," 25, 124, 126, 146
Gibson, Mary Ellen, 259n12
Gillis, John, 258n2
Gladstone, William, 11
Gladstone Report (1895), 106
"Going to See a Man Hanged" (Thackeray), 44, 65
Good, Daniel, 60, *61,* 62–65
Greek tragedy, 21, 27, 201, 204, 205, 207, 216, 220, 222, 236, 241
Green, Maria, 90, 93
Greenacre, James, 52
Greenblatt, Stephen, 19, 20, 240, 241
Gregory, Melissa Valiska, 185, 194, 243–44n3, 254n18
Greville, Charles, 95
Griffin, W. Hall, 254n16
Grossman, Jonathan, 2, 246n8
grotesque, 11, 55, 59, 62, 76, 82, 84, 105, 114, 132, 143, 148, 158, 159, 234, 242, 255n22

Habitual Criminals Act (1869), 37
Hadley, Elaine, 56–57, 241, 259n9
Hall, Catherine, 233
Hall, Edith, 222
Hamilton, Susan, 180
Hamlet (Shakespeare), 59, 246n11
Hammerton, A. James, 179, 182, 258n2
Hardy, Thomas. *See* "Her Second Husband Hears Her Story"; *Jude the Obscure; Tess of the d'Urbervilles*
Harlan, Aurelia Brooks, 207, 260n16, 261n21
Harlan, J. Lee, Jr., 260n16
Harrison, Antony, 13, 16–17, 18, 25, 33, 115, 241
Hazlitt, W. Carew, 8
Heaney, Seamus, 104, 244n3 (intro.), 249n29
Heinrichsen, Mrs., 57
Hepburn, James G., 244n1, 245n3, 246n10
"Her Second Husband Hears Her Story" (Hardy), 238–39, 262nn34–35

Higgenbotham, Ann R., 262n32
Himmelfarb, Gertrude, 245n5
Hindley, Charles, 50, 54, 244n1, 245nn3–4, 246n10
Hinson, Frederick, 87–90
Hitchman, Dr. John, 257n32
Hoffer, Peter C., 247n17
Hood, Dr. Charles, 247n15
Hood's Magazine, 140
Horstman, Allen, 177, 258n2
Howard, Ronnalie, 157–58, 256n26
Hüffer, Franz, 254n20
Hughes, Linda, 249n27
Hull, N. E. H., 247n17
Humpherys, Anne, 181–82, 183, 245n5, 259n7, 261n26
Hunt, Alan, 16, 17, 33
Hunter, Richard, 252n11

"I'm One of the New Police," 50
Infant Custody Acts (1873 and 1886), 258n2
infanticide. *See* child-murder
Insane Prisoner's Act (1840), 248n24, 250n7
Insane Prisoner's Amendment Act (1864), 250n7
insanity, criminal. *See* psychology
Ireland, 104, 244n1, 249n29
Italy, 147, 161, 184, 254–55n20, 255n21, 260n16

Jackson, Mark, 247n17
Jack the Ripper, 76, 242
Jane Eyre (Brontë), 183–84
Jefferys, John Richard, 65–67, 74
Jerrold, Douglas, 43
"Johannes Agricola in Meditation," 125, 254n17
"John Bull, Can You Wonder at Crime?," 48, *49*
Jones, Jane, 60, 62–64
Journal of Mental Science, 248n24
Journal of Psychological Medicine and Mental Pathology, 120, 256–57n27
Joyce, Simon, 35, 243n2, 245n5

Jude the Obscure (Hardy), 262n35

Kalikoff, Beth, 246n8
Karlin, Daniel, 126, 131, 254n18
Keats, John, 261n23
Kind Words, 223
Knelman, Judith, 98
Kristeva, Julia, 127
Krueger, Christine, 67, 262n32
Kucich, John, 57, 154, 156
Kurata, Marilyn J., 203, 260n19

"Laboratory, The" (Browning), 6, 24–25, 114, 133, 140–47, 164–66, 256n23
Lamb, Charles, 8
"Lamentation & Execution of James Longhurst," 84–87
"Lamentation of H. Lingley," 52
"Lamentation of J. Mapp," 52–53
"Lamentation in Newgate of the Police-Man, Who Boned the Mutton," 50–51
"Lamentation of Samuel Wright," 90, *91,* 92–95
Lancet, The, 246n14
Landon, Letitia Elizabeth, 104
Langbaum, Robert, 243n3, 250–51n9, 256n26
"Last Confession, A" (Rossetti), 257nn29–30; and Browning, 254–55n20, 256n23; confessional mode of, 147–49, 150, 152, 154–58, 160, 161, 163, 256n26, 257n31; conventional notions of evidence in, 163; and determinism, 150, 152, 153, 154; feminine othering and female sexuality in, 257n28; fractured speech and verbal complications in, 6, 19, 114, 116, 149, 155–58, 161–62; narrative expanse and circularity in, 114, 149, 157, 159–60; questions of interpretation, homicidal lunacy, and poetic indeterminacy in, 6, 24–25, 114, 117, 124, 147–66, 255n21, 256n26, 257n28, 257n31, 257–58n32; and politics, 147, 148, 151, 161, 255n21; and Rossetti's

literary authority, 254–55n20; and the sublime, 6, 116, 117
"Last Moments and Confession of Wm. Sheward, The" 30, 32, 81–84, 86–87
law, 1, 2, 4, 5, 6, 15; artifice of the, 24; Browning's critique of, 7, 25–27, 168–71, 187–88, 190, 199–200, 236, 258n1, 259n12; and difficulty for jurors in assessing the criminally insane, 111–12; and the Game Laws, 46; on infanticide and concealment, 67, 73, 247n17; on marriage and divorce, 7, 19, 26–27, 89–90, 167–84, 199, 201, 223, 236, 237, 258n2, 258nn4–5; and mental competence, 119; reflected in crime ballads, 6, 30, 33, 39, 46, 57, 78–80, 86–90, 92–95; replacement of personal testimony with defense counsel in, 79, 248n21, 250n5. *See also* psychology; trials, courtroom
Leckie, Barbara, 174, 182, 258n3, 259n9, 259n11
Lee, Vernon, 9
Leps, Marie-Christine, 38–39, 78
Levenson, Michael, 172, 175, 178, 181, 182, 258n3, 259n9
Levine, Philippa, 223–24
Levy, Amy: historical awareness of women's struggles of, 223, 226. *See also* "Battle of Ida Grey, The"; *Medea*; *Minor Poet and Other Verse, A*
Lewes, George Henry, 255n22
Liberals, 37
"Life, Trial, Character, Confession, and Execution of Stephen Forward," 52
"Life, Trial, Confession, and Execution of Martin Brown," 81
"Life, Trial, Sentence, and Execution of Catherine Williams, for the Murder of Mrs. Soames," 98, *99*, 100–102
"Life, Trial, Sentence, and Execution of S. Adams for the Murder of His Sister-in-Law, Martha Page, The," 44
Lingley, H., 52
literacy, 30, 140

"Liverpool Tragedies, The," 52, 57–60
Longhurst, James, 84–87
Lucretia; Or The Children of the Night (E. Bulwer-Lytton), 204
Lunatic Asylums Act (1845), 250n7
Lunatics Care and Treatment Act (1845), 250n7
Lytton, Edward Robert Bulwer (Owen Meredith): and Browning, 260n16, 261n23; discouraged by father, 260n17; literary career of, 260n16; poetry of, 201–2, 261n23; as witness to parents' scandalous marriage, 202–3, 260n18, 261n21. *See also Clytemnestra*

MacAlpine, Ida, 252n11
Macintosh, Fiona, 222
Mapp, J., 52
Marchmont v. Marchmont, 259n8
"Marcian Colonna" (Procter), 125, 253–54n16
Marland, Hillary, 69, 247n17, 262n32
marriage: adversarial model of, 7, 19, 26, 172, 174–77, 179, 180, 183, 185–86, 192, 195–98, 216–17, 221, 236–37; companionate model of, 180, 192, 199, 201, 216–19, 261n26; and culture of domestic scandal, 7, 26–27, 170, 174, 176, 180–82, 184, 199–200, 237; and domestic violence and spousal murder, 2, 5, 7, 25–27, 68, 69, 81, 87–90, 134–40, 167–71, 176, 178, 181–221, 238–39, 254n18, 258n6, 268n15; evolution in discourse of, 238–39; and ideologies of patriarchal domesticity, 7, 19, 26–27, 89–90, 167–72, 176, 179, 180, 184, 186, 194, 195, 201, 211–12, 214–15, 221–31, 234–37; and laws on marriage and divorce, 7, 19, 26–27, 89–90, 164–84, 199, 201, 223, 236, 237, 258n2, 258nn4–5; Victorian feminist critique of, 171, 180
Married Women's Property Acts (1870 and 1882), 223, 258n2

Martin, Loy D., 254n19
Martin, Sir Samuel, 37–38, 78
Marxism, 15, 16
Mason, Michael, 125, 253–54n16, 254n17
Matrimonial Causes Act (1878), 179, 258n2
Matus, Jill L., 246–47n14
Maudsley, Dr. Henry, 124, 152, 153, 248n24, 251n8, 253n15, 256n24
Mayhew, Henry, 34, 54, 55, 78, 245n5
McConville, Seán, 106
McDonagh, Josephine, 67, 262nn31–33
Medea (Euripides), 221, 222, 223, 232, 235
Medea (Levy), 7, 25–27, 170–71, 183–84, 201, 221–37, 261n27, 262n29; bodily metaphors in, 225; domestic authority and alienation in, 221–31, 234, 235–36, 262n29, 262n33; irony in, 231; and Medea versions in England, 222–23, 262n33; public sphere in, 221, 222, 226, 227, 228, 231–35, 237; thresholds in, 226–27, 231–34
Medea; Or, The Best of Mothers, with a Brute of a Husband (Brough), 222–23
medicine. *See* psychology
melodrama, 27, 30, 55–57, 59, 66, 71–72, 170, 176, 181, 192, 199, 233, 237, 242, 246n8, 247n16
Metropolitan Police Act (1829), 50
"Miles Weatherhill, the Young Weaver, and his Sweetheart, Sarah Bell," 44, 46
Mill, J. S., 13, 108, 169, 258n6. *See also On the Subjection of Women*
Miller, D. A., 2
Minchin, H. C., 254n16
Minor Poet and Other Verse, A (Levy), 221
Mitchell, Leslie, 260n20, 261n21
M'Naghten, Daniel, 109–11, 249nn1–2, 250nn3–4
M'Naghten Rules, 110, 141, 250n4
modernity, 7, 11, 13–16, 27, 112, 165, 170, 178, 237, 240–41, 252n10; and *Clytemnestra*, 7, 27, 170, 201, 204–7, 215–16, 220
Monthly Repository, 254n17
Morgan, John, 245n3
Morgan, Thaïs, 234
Moriarty, Jane Campbell, 249n2
Morning Chronicle, 169
Morris, William, 201
Mulvey-Roberts, Marie, 203, 260n19
murder: as aesthetic representation or performance, 1, 5, 8–9, 11, 41–41, 139–40, 143–44, 240; associated with the lower classes, 36–37; and criminal insanity defenses, 109–12; as narrative event, 21; and power relations between murderer and victim, 4, 12, 15, 52, 53, 145–46; as scrutiny of culture, 11–13, 51; shifting and historically contextualized understandings of, 1, 4, 5, 6, 7, 24–25, 110, 115, 240–42. *See also* crime; violence
"Murder of A Wife at Ashburnham, Near Hastings," 46–47
"My Last Duchess" (Browning), 3, 4, 24–25, 114, 133–40, 141, 142, 146–47, 164–66

Nassar, Christopher, 154
Nathan, Leonard, 244n3 (intro.)
National Review, The, 39, 43, 244n3 (ch. 1), 245n7, 261n23
Neuberg, Victor, 246n8
Newgate Prison, 10
"New Policeman, and the Somers Town Butcher, The," 50
newspapers, 2, 4, 5, 7, 21, 26, 41–42, 66, 75, 95, 106, 172, 176, 180–82, 200, 259n7, 259n9, 259n11, 261n26. *See also Times*
Nord, Deborah Epstein, 245n5
Norton, Caroline, 181, 183, 259n9, 259n14
novel, 243n2, 246n8; detective, 2, 21; Newgate, 2; moving away from marriage plots in, 183–84; success of, 199–200; and surveillance, 113, 115,

259n11. *See also* novel, verse; sensation fiction
novel, verse, 1, 3, 7, 170; as analogue to the novel, 199–200; generic hybridity and intertextuality of, 19, 104, 171, 241

Old Bailey, 98, 100
"On a Late Acquittal" (Campbell), 109–10
"On Murder Considered as One of the Fine Arts" (de Quincey), 5, 41–42, 57
On the Subjection of Women (Mill), 168, 169, 234

Page, Martha, 44
Parry, Ann, 244n3 (intro.)
"Particulars of the Life, Trial, Confession, and Execution of Courvoisier," 44, *45,* 96–98
pastoral, 40–41
Patmore, Coventry. *See* "Angel in the House"
Paul, Charles Kegan, 104
Paul Clifford (Bulwer-Lytton), 204
Peel, Sir Robert, 50, 110, 249n1
Pelican, 223
"Pen, Pencil and Poison" (Wilde), 7–11, 16
performance/performativity, 5, 10, 18, 19, 21–22, 24, 34, 48, 50, 78, 80, 86, 102, 103, 107, 108, 114, 147, 193, 237
Petch, Simon, 185
Philips, David, 36, 245n6
Philosophical Enquiry into the Origin of Our Ideas of the Sublime and Beautiful, A (Burke), 55, 116, 132–33
Picture of Dorian Gray, The (Wilde), 42
Pinel, Philippe, 127
Pitt, Emma, 73–74, 247n17
Pitts, John, 245n3, 248n23
Poems (Rossetti), 148, 153, 257n28, 258n32
poisoning, 8, 11, 75, 98, 141–46, 240
police force, 2, 34, 35, 37–39, 50–51
Poovey, Mary, 223, 258nn2–3, 262n29

"Porphyria's Lover" (Browning), 3, 6, 24–25, 114, 124–33, 141, 146–47, 162, 164–66, 253–54n16, 254nn17–19
poverty, 10, 23, 35, 37, 39–41, 48, 50–51, 75–76, 94
Pre-Raphaelitism, 147, 255n21
press. *See* newspapers
Prichard, J. C., 113, 117–21, 123, 127–29, 131, 134–35, 137, 140, 141, 145, 151, 156, 157, 251n8, 252nn12–13
Prisoners' Counsel Act (1836), 79, 248n21, 250n5
Prisons Act (1898), 106
Prisons Board, 106
prison reform, 3, 37, 106–8
Procter, Brian. *See* "Marcian Colonna"
prostitution, 17, 48, 106, 192, 195, 259n12
psychology, 11, 44, 240–41, 252nn11–12; and arguments for homicidal lunacy, 6, 19, 21, 24–25, 68–69, 92, 109–24, 127–28, 133–35, 140, 141, 149, 151–53, 156, 163–66, 248n24, 249n2, 250nn4–5, 250–51n7, 251n8, 252n13, 252–53n14, 253n15; and the asylum system, 110, 112, 123, 125, 153, 250–51n7, 251n8, 252n11, 254n17; and insanity defenses for infanticide, 67, 69, 70, 71, 246n13, 247n15; and modernity, 252n10; of murderous subjectivity in Lytton's *Clytemnestra,* 26, 201, 202, 205–7, 209, 217, 219; of murderous subjectivity in Levy's *Medea,* 221–22, 223, 230–31, 235; reflected in dramatic monologues, 6, 19, 24–25, 114–16, 124–66, 251–52n9, 253–54n16, 254n17, 256n26, 257n28, 257n31, 257–58n32; Victorian citizens' awareness of developments in, 112–13, 124
Purvis, Trevor, 16, 17, 33

Quarterly Review, 40, 78
Quinn, Cath, 246n13, 262n32
Quinton, R. F., 106

race/ethnicity, 3, 35, 38, 225, 262n31
Rader, Ralph D., 254n19
Radzinowicz, Leon, 36, 39
Ray, Isaac, 250n4
Raymond, E. Neill, 260n16, 261n23
realism, 2
Redesdale, Lord (Algernon Freeman-Mitford), 178
Reed, John R., 122, 153
Retreat at York, 123
Reynolds, Margaret, 244n3 (intro.)
Reynold's Magazine, 108
Ring and the Book, The (Browning), 3, 25–27, 167–71, 183–201; adversarial yoke of marriage in, 7, 25–27, 184–86, 192, 195–98, 236, 259n12; and the crime ballad, 104, 191–92, 249n28; generic hybridity and intertextuality of, 25, 104, 199–200; and the novel, 199–200; Pompilia and silenced womanhood in, 193–95, 259n14; questioning of the law in, 7, 25–27, 168–71, 187–88, 190, 199–200, 236, 258n1, 259n12; review of, 200; seventeenth-century murder trial transcribed in, 7, 27; unreliable narrators and polyphony in, 22, 185, 189, 193–94, 197–200, 236
Robertson, C. A. L., 248n24
Robinson, A. Mary F., 9
Rodensky, Lisa, 2, 113, 250n6
Rose, Lionel, 67
Ross, Robert, 107
Rossetti, Dante Gabriel, 143, 254–55n20, 256n23. *See also* "Last Confession, A"; *Poems* (Rossetti); "Stealthy School of Criticism, The"
Rossetti, William Michael, 256n23
Routh, C. H. F., 246n14
Rowbotham, Judith, 243n1
Royal Commission on Capital Punishment, 37–38, 78, 90
Royal Commissioners on Divorce, 173–74, 177–78, 202
"Runaway Slave at Pilgrim's Point, The" (Barrett Browning), 3

Rush, James Bloomfield, 52
Russell, Lord William, 46, 95–97, 248n25
Rylance, Rick, 252n11

Saussure, Ferdinand de, 16
Savage, Gail, 175–77, 182
Sax, Jane, 84–87
Scheinberg, Cynthia, 262n31
Schliefer, Ronald, 17
Schramm, Jan-Melissa, 79, 243n2
Scull, Andrew, 252n11
sensation fiction, 2, 104, 181–83, 200
Seven Dials district, 39, 65
Shakespeare, William, 205, 207, 261n23. *See also Hamlet*
Shanley, Mary Lyndon, 258n2, 261n26
Shelley, Percy Bysshe, 255n20
Shepard, Leslie, 244n1, 245n3
Sheward, William, 30, *32,* 81–84, 86–87
"Shocking Murder of A Wife and Six Children," 75–76
Shuttleworth, Sally, 113, 252n11
Skultans, Veida, 122, 251n8, 252n11
Slinn, E. Warwick, 13, 17–18, 21, 34, 107, 114, 147, 244n3 (intro.)
Smiles, Samuel, 153
Smith, Dr. Andrew, 34
Smith, Charles Manby, 39, 245n7
Smith, Roger, 71–72, 115, 117, 119, 153, 246n13, 247n16, 248n24, 250n4, 251n8
Smithers, Leonard, 108
Soames, Maria, 98
socialism, 35
Society for the Abolition of Capital Punishment, 98
Sonnets upon the Punishment of Death (Wordsworth), 242
Sophocles, 220
Speranza (Lady Wilde). *See* "Trial of the Brothers Sheares in '98"
Stallybrass, Peter, 11–13, 47, 115, 236, 241
"Stealthy School of Criticism, The" (Rossetti), 158–59, 255n21

Stephen, Sir George, 111–12, 134, 135, 252–53n14
Stephen, James Fitzjames, 87, 120, 121, 130, 164, 250n6
Stevenson, Kim, 243n1
Stewart, Garrett, 58
St. George's-in-the-Field's Criminal Lunatic Asylum, 92
Stone, Marjorie, 244n3 (intro.)
Stowell, Lord (William Scott), 174, 181
subjectivity, 2, 5, 6, 12, 17, 60, 80, 98, 113–16, 132, 148, 151, 152, 160, 171, 184, 219, 223, 227, 237, 252n9. *See also* will
sublime, 6, 23, 25, 55, 56, 105, 116, 117, 132, 140, 146, 149, 156, 165, 240, 242
Surridge, Lisa, 2, 183, 258n3, 259nn9–10
Swinburne, Algernon Charles, 8, 104, 202, 255n20
Symonds, John Addington, 9
Symons, Jelinger C., 36

Tait's Edinburgh Magazine, 205
Taylor, David, 36, 245n5
Taylor, Harriet, 169, 258n6
Tennyson, Alfred, Lord, 11, 104, 116, 142, 261n23
Tess of the d'Urbervilles (Hardy), 262n35
Thackeray, William Makepeace, 95. *See also* "Going to See a Man Hanged"
Thomas, Ronald R., 2
Thurtell, James, 104
Times (London), 60, 62, 64–66, 68, 73, 75, 83, 84, 85, 87–88, 90, 92, 98, 100, 109, 111, 112, 179–81, 247n16, 259nn7–8
Tories, 37, 110, 249n1, 250n3
Tosh, John, 171, 258n3
Townley, George Victor, 92–94, 120, 248n24, 250n7, 257–58n32
Townsend, William, 249n2
transportation, 10
"Trial of the Brothers Sheares in '98" (Speranza [Lady Wilde]), 249n29
"Trial and Execution of Betty the Cook," 246n9

Trial of Lunatics Act (1883), 164, 250–51n7
"Trial, Sentence, Confession, and Execution of F. B. Courvoisier for the Murder of Lord Wm. Russell," 46
"Trial and Sentence of George Britten," 80
trials, courtroom, 2, 4, 5, 6, 7, 11, 21, 22, 24, 26, 65, 66, 67, 79, 83, 85–86, 110, 112, 113, 119, 172, 174, 176–77, 180, 249n2, 255n22, 257n32, 259n7, 259n11
Trodd, Anthea, 259n10
Tromp, Marlene, 2, 183, 258n3, 259n10
Tucker, Herbert F., 137, 139, 146, 251–52n9
Tuke, Daniel Hack, 118, 252n13
Tuke, Samuel, 123
Turner, Reginald, 108

Vagrancy Act (1824), 37
Van Dieman's Land, 10
verse drama. *See* drama, verse
verse novel. *See* novel, verse
"Verses on Daniel Good," 60, *61*, 62–65
Vicinus, Martha, 54–55
Victoria, Queen, 164, 173, 202, 251n7
Vincent, David, 29, 246n7
violence, 5; ballads' detailing of, 23, 54–56, 58–60, 62–77, 241; and disorder, 60; indecipherability of, 58; marital/domestic, 2, 5, 7, 25–27, 68, 69, 81, 87–90, 134–40, 167–71, 176, 178, 181–221, 238–39, 254n18, 258n6, 260n15; maternal, 67–75, 200–201, 221–22, 232, 234, 247n15, 247n17, 262nn32–33; sexual, 3, 25, 62–65, 84, 115, 124, 126–27, 130, 131–32, 147, 148, 150, 154, 157–61, 194, 257n28; and working-class masculinity, 60, 62, 126, 189

Wainewright, Thomas Griffiths, 8–11
Walk, Alexander, 249n2
Walker, Nigel, 246n13, 248n24, 249n2, 250nn4–5

Walkowitz, Judith, 76
Weare, William, 104
Weatherhill, Miles, 44, 46
Welsh, Alexander, 168, 243n3, 258n1
West, Donald, 249n2
White, Allon, 11–13, 47, 115, 236, 241
Wiener, Martin J., 37, 60, 88, 89, 106, 176, 179, 243n1, 246n12
Wilde, Oscar, 104, 241; experience as prisoner of, 3, 106–8, 249n29. *See also* "Ballad of Reading Gaol, The"; "Pen, Pencil and Poison"; *Picture of Dorian Gray, The*
will, 121–22, 128–29, 134, 138–39, 150, 153, 159, 161–62, 164, 210, 256n24
Williams, Carolyn, 20, 103

Wilson, Catherine, 98, *99*, 100–102
Wilson, John. *See* "Extracts from Gosschen's Diary"
Wilson, John Gleeson, 30, *31*, 52, 57–58
Winslow, Dr. Forbes, 112, 123, 156, 247n15, 249n2, 253n14, 257–58n32
Wollstonecraft, Mary, 260n20
Wooldridge, Charles Thomas, 105
Wordsworth, William, 8. See also *Sonnets upon the Punishment of Death*
"Word to the Public, A" (Bulwer-Lytton), 204
Wright, Samuel, 90, *91*, 92–95

Zimmerman, Georges Denis, 244n1